O
Ju
Il
Di

O

ed

Compile

Literacy

OXFORD
UNIVERSITY PRESS

4 979770 000

BM   423

OXFORD
UNIVERSITY PRESS

Great Clarendon Street, Oxford OX2 6DP

Oxford University Press is a department of the University of Oxford.
It furthers the University's objective of excellence in research, scholarship,
and education by publishing worldwide in

Oxford   New York

Auckland   Cape Town   Dar es Salaam   Hong Kong   Karachi
Kuala Lumpur   Madrid   Melbourne   Mexico City   Nairobi
New Delhi   Shanghai   Taipei   Toronto

With offices in

Argentina   Austria   Brazil   Chile   Czech Republic   France   Greece
Guatemala   Hungary   Italy   Japan   Poland   Portugal   Singapore
South Korea   Switzerland   Thailand   Turkey   Ukraine   Vietnam

Oxford is a registered trade mark of Oxford University Press
in the UK and in certain other countries

British Library Cataloguing in Publication Data

Data available

ISBN 978-0-19-911521 1 (hardback)
ISBN 978-0-19-911522 8 (paperback)

1 3 5 7 9 10 8 6 4 2

Printed in Singapore by KHL Printing Co. Pte Ltd.

Illustrations by Peter Dennis, Photos are from Alamy Images, Corel, Ingram Publishing/Hemera, photodisc,
istockphoto p184, and Classet. Every care has been taken to acknowledge copyright, in the event of an
error, we apologise and will, if informed, endeavour to make any corrections in any future editions.

Contents

Introduction

This new edition of the *Oxford Junior Illustrated Dictionary* has been specially written for primary school children aged 7 and above. In the UK, it fulfils the Primary National Strategy requirements for KS2 YR2-YR4 and the Scottish guidelines P3, 4, and 5.

Definitions have been written in natural, everyday English and all definitions of verbs and adjectives are written as full sentences to make them easy to understand.

Special attention has been given to example sentences in order to help children understand difficult words and provide them with context. Example sentences from the best children's books including *Harry Potter and the Chamber of Secrets* by J.K. Rowling, *The Scarecrow and his Servant* by Philip Pullman, *Fantastic Mr Fox* by Roald Dahl, and *The Lion, the Witch and the Wardrobe* by C.S. Lewis show how language can be used effectively. To help find words in the dictionary easily, the alphabet has been split into four differently coloured sections or quartiles, a-f, g-m, n-s, and t-z. This makes it easier to look up words quickly. To help with spelling, all regular and irregular inflected forms of words are given. There is a special tinted feature box on word families to help children understand the links between related words. For example, the entry for **excite** includes words **excited**, **excitedly**, **exciting**, and **excitement** and are all given example sentences to show how they are used.

The indispensable Word Explorer guide explores the basic tools needed for reading and writing. It focuses on phonics, spelling, punctuation, grammar, vocabulary building, and word origins.

The *Oxford Junior Illustrated Dictionary* is an excellent companion volume to the *Oxford Junior Illustrated Thesaurus*, which enables and encourages children to be creative and imaginative in their writing.

The publisher and editors are indebted to all the advisors, consultants, and teachers who were involved in planning and compiling this dictionary. Special thanks go to Susan Rennie for her helpful advice on the Word Explorer section.

How to use this dictionary

Headwords
Headwords are the words in the dictionary that you look up. They are in alphabetical order and are printed in colour so that you can find them easily.

Word class
The word class tells you what type of word the headword is, for example, whether it is a noun, a verb, an adjective, or an adverb.

Other forms
All the different forms of a word are written here so that you can see how to spell them.

angry adjective **angrier, angriest**
If you are angry, you are annoyed or cross. *'Shut up – you!' said Peter, who was still very angry with Edmund.*—C. S. Lewis, The Lion, the Witch and the Wardrobe

Word family
Words that belong to the same word family are included in these tinted boxes. They give you extra information about words that belong to the same family and show you how they are used.

> 🏠 **WORD FAMILY**
> • **angrily** 'You fool!' he said angrily.

arch noun (*plural* **arches**)
a curved part of a bridge or building

Example sentences
The example sentences, many from the best children's books, show how the word is used. This will help you to understand what the word means.

Illustrations and photographs
The illustrations and photographs are specially selected to add extra information to the definition.

Definitions
The definition tells you what the word means. If a word has more than one meaning, the different definitions are clearly numbered.

architect noun (*plural* **architects**)
(*say* **ar**-kee-tect)
a person who draws plans for new buildings

area noun (*plural* **areas**)
1 An area is a piece of land. *There's a play area behind the library.*
2 When you measure the area of something, you measure how big it is.

Pronunciation
Some words are difficult to pronounce so we show you how you should say the word. Remember that this is not the way to spell a word.

abandon verb **abandons, abandoning, abandoned**
If you abandon someone, you go away and leave them and never go back to them.

abbreviation noun (*plural* **abbreviations**)
a short way of writing a word *Dr is an abbreviation for doctor.*

ability noun (*plural* **abilities**)
If you have the ability to do something, you can do it.

able adjective
1 If you are able to do something, you can do it. *Are you able to speak any other languages?*
2 Someone who is very able is very good at doing something.

abolish verb **abolishes, abolishing, abolished**
If you abolish something, you end it so that it does not happen or exist any more. *The school council voted to abolish the school uniform.*

about preposition
1 on the subject of *I like reading books about animals.*
2 more or less, but not exactly *There are about 25 children in my class.*

above adverb & preposition
1 higher than *In a plane, you often fly above the clouds.*
2 more than *The film is only for children above the age of 12.*

abroad adverb
When you go abroad, you go to another country.

absent adjective
Someone who is absent is not in a place. *Why were you absent from school yesterday?*

absolutely adverb
completely *You must keep absolutely still.*

absorb verb **absorbs, absorbing, absorbed**
(*in science*) To absorb water means to soak it up.

> **WORD FAMILY**
> • **absorbent** We poured water on the two types of paper to see which was more absorbent.

accent noun (*plural* **accents**)
Your accent is the way you speak, which shows where you come from.

accept verb **accepts, accepting, accepted**
If you accept something, you take it after someone has offered it to you. *My aunt offered me a drink, and I accepted politely.*

access verb **accesses, accessing, accessed**
(*in ICT*) When you access information on a computer, you find it and use it.

accident noun (*plural* **accidents**)
1 When there is an accident, something bad happens and someone gets hurt. *There's been an accident on the motorway.*
2 If something that you did was an accident, you did not do it deliberately.

> **WORD FAMILY**
> • **accidentally** I accidentally knocked a glass of water over my books.

accompany verb **accompanies, accompanying, accompanied**
1 If you accompany someone, you go with them.
So you'll be off on the ship to England in July. Your mother will accompany you.—Michael Morpurgo, The Butterfly Lion
2 If you accompany someone on a musical instrument, you play the instrument while they sing or dance.

account noun (*plural* **accounts**)
1 If you give an account of something that happened, you describe what happened. *We had to write an account of our trip to Turkey.*
2 If you have a bank account, you keep money in a bank and can take it out when you need it.

a
b
c
d
e
f
g
h
i
j
k
l
m
n
o
p
q
r
s
t
u
v
w
x
y
z

1

a
b
c
d
e
f
g
h
i
j
k
l
m
n
o
p
q
r
s
t
u
v
w
x
y
z

accurate adjective
Something that is accurate is exactly right or correct. *He managed to give the police an accurate description of the thief.*

> **WORD FAMILY**
> • **accurately** Make sure you measure everything accurately.

accuse verb **accuses, accusing, accused**
If you accuse someone of doing something wrong, you say that they did it.
Ralph accused me of stealing his sweets.

ache verb **aches, aching, ached** (*rhymes with* bake)
If a part of your body aches, it hurts.
I feel sick, and my head aches!

achieve verb **achieves, achieving, achieved**
If you achieve something, you manage to do it after trying very hard.

> **WORD FAMILY**
> • **achievement** You should be proud of your achievements.

acid noun (*plural* **acids**)
(*in science*) An acid is a chemical. There are many different kinds of acid. Lemons contain a type of acid which makes them taste sour. Some acids are very strong and can burn your clothes and skin.

acid rain noun
Acid rain is rain that is polluted with gases from cars and factory chimneys. Acid rain can harm plants and animals.

acrobat noun
(*plural* **acrobats**) someone who entertains people by doing exciting jumping and balancing tricks

across preposition
1 from one side to the other *We walked across the road.*
2 on the other side of something *The park is across the river.*

act verb **acts, acting, acted**
1 When you act, you do something. *We knew that we were in danger and we had to act quickly.*
2 When you act, you take part in a play. *Do you like acting?*

action noun (*plural* **actions**)
1 When there is a lot of action, a lot of exciting things are happening. *I like films with a lot of action.*
2 An action is something that you do. *Your action saved the animals' lives.*

active adjective
If you are active, you are busy doing things.

activity noun (*plural* **activities**)
1 When there is a lot of activity, people are busy doing things all around you.
2 An activity is something enjoyable that you do for fun. *What are your favourite activities outside school?*

actor noun (*plural* **actors**)
a person who acts in a play or film

actress noun (*plural* **actresses**)
a woman who acts in a play or film

actually adverb
really *I thought it was a wolf, but actually it was a dog.*

add verb **adds, adding, added**
1 (*in mathematics*) When you add numbers together, you count them together to make a bigger number.
2 When you add something, you put it with other things or mix it in with other things. *I added some more sugar to the mixture.*

> **WORD FAMILY**
> • When you add numbers together, you do **addition**.

address noun (*plural* **addresses**)
1 Your address is where you live. *Please write down your name and address.*
2 Someone's email address is the set of letters or numbers that you use to send them an email.

address book noun (*plural* **address books**)
1 a book in which you write people's names and addresses
2 a place on a computer where you store people's email addresses

2

adjective noun (*plural* **adjectives**)
(*in grammar*) An adjective is a word that tells you what someone or something is like. Words like *tall*, *big*, and *dirty* are all adjectives.

admire verb **admires, admiring, admired**
1 If you admire someone, you like them and think that they are very good. *Which famous person do you admire the most?*
2 When you admire something, you look at it and think that it is nice.
And that was that. We had finished. We stood back and admired our machine.—Jeremy Strong, The Hundred-Mile-An-Hour Dog

admit verb **admits, admitting, admitted**
If you admit that you did something wrong, you tell people that you did it.

adore verb **adores, adoring, adored**
If you adore something, you like it a lot. *I adore ice cream!*

adult noun (*plural* **adults**)
someone who is grown up

advantage noun (*plural* **advantages**)
something that helps you to do better than other people. *The other team had an advantage because they were older than us.*

adventure noun (*plural* **adventures**)
something exciting that happens to you

WORD FAMILY
• **adventurous** Adventurous people enjoy doing new and exciting things.

adverb noun (*plural* **adverbs**)
(*in grammar*) An adverb is a word that tells you how someone does something. *Slowly, carefully,* and *quickly* are all adverbs.

advertise verb **advertises, advertising, advertised**
To advertise something means to tell people about it so that they will want to buy it.

WORD FAMILY
• An **advertisement** or **advert** is a picture or short film that shows you something and tries to persuade you to buy it.

advice noun
If you give someone advice, you tell them what they should do.

advise verb **advises, advising, advised**
If you advise someone to do something, you tell them they should do it. *Suri's dad advised us to stay away from the river.*

aeroplane noun (*plural* **aeroplanes**)
a large machine that can travel through the air and carry passengers or goods

affect verb **affects, affecting, affected**
To affect something means to make it different in some way. *Will the rain affect our plans?*

affection noun
Affection is the feeling you have when you like someone.

affix noun (*plural* **affixes**)
(*in grammar*) An affix is a set of letters that are added to the beginning or end of a word to change its meaning. Prefixes and suffixes are both types of affix.

afford verb **affords, affording, afforded**
If you can afford something, you have enough money to pay for it.

afraid adjective
If you are afraid, you are frightened. *Mildred was afraid of the dark.* — Jill Murphy, The Worst Witch

after preposition
1 later than *We got home after lunch.*
2 following someone, or trying to catch them *The dog ran after me.*

afternoon noun (*plural* **afternoons**)
The afternoon is the time from the middle of the day until the evening.

afterwards adverb
later

again adverb
once more *Try again!*

against preposition
1 next to something and touching it *He leant against the wall.*
2 on the opposite side to someone in a game or battle *We've got a match against Luton on Saturday.*

age noun
Your age is how old you are.

aggressive adjective
An aggressive animal is likely to attack people. An aggressive person often argues and fights with other people.

ago adverb
Ago means in the past. *I first started dancing three years ago.*

agree verb **agrees, agreeing, agreed**
If you agree with someone, you have the same ideas as them and you think that they are right. *Amina says this book is boring, but I don't agree with her.*

> **WORD FAMILY**
> • **agreement** Molly nodded her head in agreement.

ahead adverb
in front of someone else *I went on ahead to open the gate.*

aid noun
1 When you come to someone's aid, you help them.
2 Aid is food, clothes, and blankets that are sent to people who need them.

aim verb **aims, aiming, aimed**
1 If you aim at something, you point a gun or other weapon at it. *Aim at the centre of the target.*
2 When you aim something, you try to throw it or kick it in a particular direction. *He aimed the ball into the far corner of the net.*

air noun
Air is the gas all around us, which we breathe. *Sometimes the air in big cities is quite polluted.*

aircraft noun (*plural* **aircraft**)
an aeroplane or a helicopter

air force noun (*plural* **air forces**)
an army that fights in the air, in aeroplanes

airport noun (*plural* **airports**)
a place where planes take off and land and passengers can get on and off

alarm noun (*plural* **alarms**)
a loud sound that warns people of danger

album noun (*plural* **albums**)
1 a book to put things like photographs or stamps in
2 a CD with several pieces of music on it

algebra noun
mathematics in which letters are used to represent numbers, for example $x + 1 = 4$

alien noun (*plural* **aliens**)
In stories, an alien is a person or creature from another planet.

align verb **aligns, aligning, aligned**
(*in ICT*) When you align text on the computer, you arrange it so that the lines all begin or end in a straight line, one beneath the other.

alike adjective
Things that are alike are similar in some way. *Although Sara and I are not sisters, everyone says we look alike.*

alive adjective
Something that is alive is living.

alkali noun (*plural* **alkalis**) (*say* **al**-ka-lye)
(*in science*) An alkali is a chemical that is the opposite of an acid. Alkalis cancel out the effects of acids.

all adjective & pronoun
1 everyone or everything *Are you all listening?*
2 the whole of something *Have you eaten all the chips?*

Allah noun
the Muslim name for God

allergic adjective
If you are allergic to something, it makes you ill, for example it makes you sneeze or

a b c d e f g h i j k l m n o p q r s t u v w x y z

gives you a rash. *I'm allergic to nuts.*

> **WORD FAMILY**
> • If you are allergic to something, you have an **allergy**.

alligator noun (*plural* **alligators**)
An alligator is an animal that looks like a crocodile. Alligators are reptiles and live in parts of North and South America and China.

alliteration noun
the use of words that begin with the same sound to create a special effect in writing, for example *five fat fishes*

allow verb **allows, allowing, allowed**
If you allow someone to do something, you let them do it and do not try to stop them. *We're not allowed to play football in the playground.*

all right adjective
1 If you are all right, you are safe and well, and not hurt. *Are you all right?*
2 If something is all right, it is quite good but not very good.

almost adverb
very nearly *We're almost home.*

alone adjective
If you are alone, there is no one with you. *It was a strange feeling, being alone in that big house.*

along adverb & preposition
from one end to the other *He ran along the top of the wall.*

alphabet noun
all the letters that we use in writing, arranged in a particular order from A to Z.

> **WORD FAMILY**
> • **alphabetical** Dictionaries list words in alphabetical order.

already adverb
before now *When we got to the station, the train had already left.*

also adverb
as well *I love football and also tennis.*

alter verb **alters, altering, altered**
To alter something means to change it.

alternative noun (*plural* **alternatives**)
An alternative is something that you can choose instead of something else. *We discussed the alternatives for our new school uniform.*

although conjunction
even though *We kept on running, although we were tired.*

altogether adverb
including all the people or things *If Mark has three apples and Raj has four, how many do they have altogether?*

aluminium noun
a type of light, silver-coloured metal

always adverb
at all times, or every time *Joshua is always late!*

amaze verb **amazes, amazing, amazed**
If something amazes you, it makes you feel very surprised.
The speed with which Babe learned amazed him. —Dick King-Smith, The Sheep-Pig

> **WORD FAMILY**
> • **amazed** Max looked amazed to see me.
> • **amazing** It was a most amazing sight.
> • **amazement** 'What?' she exclaimed in amazement.

ambition noun (*plural* **ambitions**)
something that you want to do very much *Her ambition is to be a doctor.*

ambulance noun (*plural* **ambulances**)
a van in which people who are ill or injured are taken to hospital

among preposition
1 in the middle of *Somewhere among all these books was the one I was looking for.*
2 between *Share the sweets among you.*

a
b
c
d
e
f
g
h
i
j
k
l
m
n
o
p
q
r
s
t
u
v
w
x
y
z

5

amount noun (*plural* **amounts**)
An amount of something is a quantity of it. *We'll never be able to save up such a large amount of money!*

amphibian noun (*plural* **amphibians**)
An amphibian is an animal that lives some of its life in water, and some on land. Frogs and toads are amphibians.

amuse verb **amuses, amusing, amused**
1 If something amuses you, you find it funny and it makes you laugh.
2 To amuse yourself means to find things to do. *We played games to amuse ourselves.*

> **WORD FAMILY**
> • **amused** I tried telling some jokes, but my aunt didn't look amused.
> • **amusing** It was a very amusing film.

analogue adjective
An analogue clock or watch has hands and a dial to show the time.

anchor noun (*plural* **anchors**)
An anchor is a heavy metal hook joined to a ship by a chain. It is dropped into the sea, where it digs into the bottom to keep the ship still.

ancient adjective (*say* **ane**-shunt)
Something that is ancient is very old.

and conjunction
a word that you use to join two words or phrases together *We saw lions and tigers at the zoo.*

angel noun (*plural* **angels**)
a messenger sent by God

anger noun
a strong feeling that you get when you are not pleased *The old man's voice was full of anger.*

angle noun (*plural* **angles**)
the corner where two lines meet

angry adjective **angrier, angriest**
If you are angry, you are annoyed or cross. *'Shut up – you!' said Peter, who was still very angry with Edmund.*—C. S. Lewis, The Lion, the Witch and the Wardrobe

> **WORD FAMILY**
> • **angrily** 'You fool!' he said angrily.

animal noun (*plural* **animals**)
An animal is anything that lives and can move about. Birds, fish, snakes, wasps, and elephants are all animals.

ankle noun (*plural* **ankles**)
Your ankle is the thin part of your leg where it is joined to your foot.

anniversary noun (*plural* **anniversaries**)
a day when you remember something special that happened on the same day in the past

announce verb **announces, announcing, announced**
When you announce something, you tell everyone about it. *Tomorrow we will announce the winner of the competition.*

annoy verb **annoys, annoying, annoyed**
If something annoys you, it makes you angry.

> **WORD FAMILY**
> • **annoyed** My dad looked really annoyed.
> • **annoying** Sometimes little sisters can be very annoying!

annual adjective
An annual event happens once every year. *We have an annual school outing in June.*

annual noun (*plural* **annuals**)
a book with cartoons, stories, and jokes in that comes out once a year

another adjective & pronoun
one more *Can I have another biscuit, please?*

answer noun (*plural* **answers**)
something you say or write to someone who has asked you a question *I don't know the answer to that question.*

answer verb **answers, answering, answered**
When you answer someone, you say something to them after they have asked you a question. *Can anyone answer this question?*

answerphone noun (*plural* **answerphones**)
a machine that answers your telephone and records messages when you are out

ant noun (*plural* **ants**)
Ants are tiny insects that live in large groups.

antelope noun (*plural* **antelopes**)
a wild animal that looks like a deer and lives in Africa and parts of Asia

anthology noun (*plural* **anthologies**)
a collection of poems or stories in a book

anticlockwise adverb
If something moves anticlockwise, it moves round in a circle in the opposite direction to the hands of a clock.

antique noun (*plural* **antiques**)
something that is very old and worth a lot of money

antiseptic noun (*plural* **antiseptics**)
An antiseptic is a chemical that kills germs. You often put an antiseptic on a cut to keep it clean.

antonym noun (*plural* **antonyms**)
a word that means the opposite to another word *Cold is an antonym of hot.*

anxious adjective
If you are anxious, you feel worried.

> **WORD FAMILY**
> • **anxiously** She looked around anxiously.

any adjective & pronoun
1 some *Have you got any orange juice?*
2 no special one *Take any book you want.*

anybody, anyone pronoun
any person *I didn't meet anybody on my way home.*

anything pronoun
any thing *I can't see anything in the dark.*

anywhere adverb
in any place *I can't find my book anywhere.*

apart adverb
If you keep things apart, you keep them away from each other. *We have to keep the ducks and hens apart.*

ape noun (*plural* **apes**)
An ape is an animal like a large monkey with long arms and no tail. Gorillas and chimpanzees are types of ape.

apex noun (*plural* **apexes**)
the highest point of something

apologize verb **apologizes, apologizing, apologized**
When you apologize, you say that you are sorry.
'Sorry,' Geena apologized. 'That's all I can remember.'—Narinder Dhami, Bindi Babes

> **WORD FAMILY**
> • **apology** I think I owe you an apology.

apostrophe noun (*plural* **apostrophes**) (*say* a-**poss**-trof-ee)
a mark like this ' that you use in writing

apparatus noun
the special equipment that you use to do something *What apparatus will we need to do this experiment?*

appear verb **appears, appearing, appeared**
1 When something appears, it comes into view and you can see it.
2 to seem *This key appears to be the wrong size.*

appearance noun
1 Your appearance is what you look like. *You shouldn't worry so much about your appearance.*
2 when something appears *The audience cheered after the appearance of the band on the stage.*

appendix noun
1 (*plural* **appendices**) Your appendix is a small tube inside your body.
2 (*plural* **appendices**) an extra section at the end of a book

appetite noun (*plural* **appetites**)
If you have an appetite, you feel hungry. *I'm not hungry. I've lost my appetite.*

applaud verb **applauds, applauding, applauded**
When people applaud, they clap to show that they are pleased. *The audience applauded politely.*

> **WORD FAMILY**
> • **Applause** is clapping.

apple noun (*plural* **apples**)
a round, crisp, juicy fruit

appointment noun (*plural* **appointments**)
If you have an appointment with someone, you have arranged to go and see them.

appreciate verb **appreciates, appreciating, appreciated** (*say* a-**pree**-shee-ate)
If you appreciate something, you feel glad because you have it. *You don't seem to appreciate all your toys.*

approach verb **approaches, approaching, approached**
To approach means to get nearer to something or someone.
I saw the London train approaching in the far distance.—Jacqueline Wilson, Best Friends

appropriate adjective
Something that is appropriate is suitable. *Bring warm clothes and appropriate shoes for the walk.*

approve verb **approves, approving, approved**
If you approve of something, you think that it is good or suitable.

approximate adjective
An approximate amount is almost correct, but not exact. *The approximate time of arrival is two o'clock.*

> **WORD FAMILY**
> • **approximately** The wall is approximately two metres high.

April noun
the fourth month of the year

apron noun (*plural* **aprons**)
something that you wear over your clothes to keep them clean when you are cooking or painting

aquarium noun (*plural* **aquariums**)
a large glass tank for keeping fish and other sea animals in

arch noun (*plural* **arches**)
a curved part of a bridge or building

architect noun (*plural* **architects**)
(*say* **ar**-kee-tect)
a person who draws plans for new buildings

area noun (*plural* **areas**)
1 An area is a piece of land. *There's a play area behind the library.*
2 When you measure the area of something, you measure how big it is.

argue verb **argues, arguing, argued**
When people argue, they talk in an angry way to each other because they do not agree with each other. *We always argue about who should tidy our room.*

> **WORD FAMILY**
> • **argument** I don't want to have a big argument with you.

arithmetic noun
When you do arithmetic, you do sums with numbers.

arm noun (*plural* **arms**)
1 Your arms are the long parts of your body that are joined to your shoulders. Your hands are on the ends of your arms.
2 Arms are weapons.

armour noun
metal clothes that soldiers and knights wore in battles long ago

army noun (*plural* **armies**)
a large group of people who are trained to fight on land in war

around adverb & preposition
all round *We spent the afternoon wandering around town.*

arrange verb **arranges, arranging, arranged**
1 When you arrange things, you put them somewhere neatly so that they look nice or are in the right position. *She arranged the books into two neat piles.*
2 If you arrange something, you make plans so that it will happen. *We arranged to meet at two o'clock.*

arrest verb **arrests, arresting, arrested**
When the police arrest someone, they take them prisoner.

arrive verb **arrives, arriving, arrived**
When you arrive somewhere, you get there at the end of a journey.

> **WORD FAMILY**
> • **arrival** A loud horn announced the arrival of the ship.

arrow noun (*plural* **arrows**)
a stick with a pointed end, which you shoot from a bow

art noun
drawing and painting

artery noun (*plural* **arteries**)
a tube inside your body that carries blood away from your heart to other parts of your body

article noun (*plural* **articles**)
1 a thing or an object *There are a lot of very valuable articles in the museum.*
2 a piece of writing in a newspaper or magazine
3 (*in grammar*) The words *a*, *an*, and *the* are articles.

artificial adjective (*say* ar-tee-**fish**-al)
Something that is artificial is not real, but has been made by people or machines. *She was wearing a coat made of artificial fur.*

artist noun (*plural* **artists**)
someone who draws or paints pictures

as conjunction
1 when *I fell over as I was coming downstairs.*
2 because *As it's cold, I think you should put a coat on.*

ashamed adjective
If you feel ashamed, you feel sorry and guilty because you have done something bad.

aside adverb
If you move aside, you move to one side. *Stand aside and let me past!*

ask verb **asks, asking, asked**
1 If you ask someone a question, you say it to them so that they will tell you the answer.
2 If you ask for something, you say that you want it.

asleep adjective
When you are asleep, you are sleeping.

assembly noun (*plural* **assemblies**)
the time when the whole school meets together

assistant noun (*plural* **assistants**)
1 someone whose job is to help an important person
2 someone who serves customers in a shop

asthma noun (*say* **ass**-ma)
Someone who has asthma sometimes finds it difficult to breathe.

a
b
c
d
e
f
g
h
i
j
k
l
m
n
o
p
q
r
s
t
u
v
w
x
y
z

astonish verb **astonishes, astonishing, astonished**
If something astonishes you, it surprises you a lot.

> **WORD FAMILY**
> • **astonished** I was astonished to see so many people there.
> • **astonishment** Her eyes opened wide with astonishment.

astronaut noun (*plural* **astronauts**)
someone who travels in space

at preposition
1 in a place *Tom is at home.*
2 when it is a particular time *I'll meet you at two o'clock.*

ate verb *see* **eat**

athlete noun (*plural* **athletes**)
someone who does athletics

athletics noun
sports in which people run, jump, and throw things

atlas noun (*plural* **atlases**)
a book of maps

atmosphere noun (*say* **at**-moss-fere)
the air around the Earth

atom noun (*plural* **atoms**)
(*in science*) one of the very tiny parts that everything is made up of

attach verb **attaches, attaching, attached**
If you attach things together, you join or fasten them together. *I attached the lamp to my bike.*

attachment noun (*plural* **attachments**)
a file that you send to someone with an email

attack verb **attacks, attacking, attacked**
To attack someone means to fight them and hurt them.

attempt verb **attempts, attempting, attempted**
When you attempt to do something, you try to do it.
During the first few days after the orphans' arrival at Count Olaf's, Violet, Klaus, and Sunny attempted to make themselves feel at home, but it was really no use. —Lemony Snicket, The Bad Beginning

attend verb **attends, attending, attended**
If you attend school, you go to school. If you attend an event, you go to watch it.

attention noun
1 When you pay attention, you listen carefully to what someone is saying, or watch what they are doing.
2 When soldiers stand to attention, they stand with their feet together and their arms by their sides.

attic noun (*plural* **attics**)
a room inside the roof of a house

attitude noun (*plural* **attitudes**)
Your attitude to something is what you think about it. *In sport, you must have a positive attitude if you want to win.*

attract verb **attracts, attracting, attracted**
1 If something attracts you, you feel interested in it. *A sudden noise attracted my attention.*

a b c d e f g h i j k l m n o p q r s t u v w x y z

2 To attract something means to make it come nearer. *A magnet will attract some types of metal but not others.*

> **WORD FAMILY**
> • **attraction** The force of attraction pulls metal objects towards a magnet.

attractive adjective
An attractive thing is pleasant to look at. An attractive person is beautiful or handsome.

audience noun (*plural* **audiences**)
all the people who have come to a place to see or hear something

August noun
the eighth month of the year

aunt, aunty noun (*plural* **aunts, aunties**)
Your aunt is the sister of your mother or father, or your uncle's wife.

author noun (*plural* **authors**)
someone who writes books or stories

autobiography noun (*plural* **autobiographies**)
(*say* or-toe-by-**og**-ra-fee)
a book that tells the story of the writer's own life

autograph noun (*plural* **autographs**)
(*say* **or**-toe-graf)
When a famous person gives you their autograph, they write their name down for you to keep.

automatic adjective
Something that is automatic works on its own, without a person controlling it. *We walked through the automatic doors into the airport.*

autumn noun
the time of the year when leaves fall off the trees and it gets colder

auxiliary verb noun (*plural* **auxiliary verbs**)
(*in grammar*) An auxiliary verb is a verb that is used with another verb to change its meaning slightly. *Be, have,* and *do* are auxiliary verbs. For example, in the sentence '*We are going home*', *are* is the auxiliary verb and *going* is the main verb.

available adjective
If something is available, it is there for you to use or buy. *Do you have tennis rackets available for hire?*

avalanche noun (*plural* **avalanches**)
a large amount of snow or rock that slides suddenly down a mountain

avenue noun (*plural* **avenues**)
a wide road in a town or city

average adjective
ordinary or usual *What's the average height in your class?*

avoid verb **avoids, avoiding, avoided**
If you avoid something, you keep away from it. *Rachel didn't speak to me today. I think she's avoiding me.*

awake adjective
When you are awake, you are not sleeping.

award noun (*plural* **awards**)
a prize *The girls were presented with an award for their bravery.*

aware adjective
If you are aware of something, you know about it. *I was aware of somebody watching me.*

away adverb
1 not here *Ali is away today.*
2 to another place *Put your books away now.*

awful adjective
Something that is awful is horrible or very bad. *Your coat's in an awful mess.*—Dick King-Smith, The Sheep-Pig

awkward adjective
1 Something that is awkward is difficult to do or difficult to use. *The bags were big and awkward to carry.*
2 If you feel awkward, you feel embarrassed.

axe noun (*plural* **axes**)
a sharp tool for chopping wood

a
b
c
d
e
f
g
h
i
j
k
l
m
n
o
p
q
r
s
t
u
v
w
x
y
z

Bb

baby noun (*plural* **babies**)
a very young child

back noun (*plural* **backs**)
1 Your back is the part of your body that is behind you, between your neck and your bottom.
2 An animal's back is the long part of its body between its head and its tail.
3 The back of something is the part opposite the front. *We sat in the back of the car.*

back adverb
If you go back to a place, you go there again. *He ran back home.*

background noun
The background in a picture is everything that you can see behind the main thing in the picture.

backpack noun (*plural* **backpacks**)
a bag that you carry on your back

backwards adverb
1 towards the place that is behind you
She fell over backwards.
2 in the opposite way to usual
Can you count backwards?

bad adjective **worse, worst**
1 Something that is bad is nasty or horrible. *We couldn't go out because of the bad weather.*
2 A bad person does things that are against the law.

badge noun (*plural* **badges**)
a small thing that you pin or sew on to your clothes, to show which school or club you belong to

badger noun (*plural* **badgers**)
A badger is an animal that digs holes in the ground. It has a white face with black stripes on it.

badly adverb
1 If you do something badly, you do not do it very well. *I knew I had behaved badly, and I was sorry.*
2 If you are badly hurt or upset, you are hurt or upset a lot.

badminton noun
a game in which people use a racket to hit a very light shuttlecock over a high net

bag noun (*plural* **bags**)
something that you use for carrying things in

Baisakhi noun (*say* **by**-sa-ki)
a Sikh festival which takes place in April

bake verb **bakes, baking, baked**
When you bake food, you cook it in an oven. *My aunt had baked a cake for us.*

baker noun (*plural* **bakers**)
someone whose job is to make or sell bread and cakes

balance noun (*plural* **balances**)
1 A balance is a pair of scales that you use for weighing things.
2 If you have good balance, you can hold your body steady and not fall over.
3 If a piece of writing has balance, it puts forward both sides of an argument, not just one side of it.

balance verb **balances, balancing, balanced**
1 When you balance, you hold your body steady and do not fall over. *Can you balance on a tightrope?*
2 If you balance something, you put it somewhere carefully so that it does not fall. *He balanced a coin on the end of his finger.*

balcony noun (*plural* **balconies**)
1 a small platform outside an upstairs window of a building, where people can stand or sit
2 the seats upstairs in a cinema or theatre

bald adjective
Someone who is bald has no hair on their head.

ball noun (*plural* **balls**)
1 a round object that you hit, kick, or throw in games *Try to catch the ball when I throw it to you.*
2 a big party where people wear very smart clothes and dance with each other

ballet noun (*plural* **ballets**)
(*say* **bal**-ay)
a type of dancing in which people dance on the very tips of their toes

balloon noun (*plural* **balloons**)
1 a small, colourful rubber bag that you can fill with air and use for playing with or to decorate a room for a party
2 A hot air balloon is a very big bag that is filled with hot air or gas so that it floats in the sky. People can stand in a basket underneath the balloon.

ban verb **bans, banning, banned**
If you ban something, you say that people are not allowed to do it. *They have banned skateboarding in the playground.*

banana noun (*plural* **bananas**)
a long yellow fruit that grows in hot countries

band noun (*plural* **bands**)
1 a group of people who do something together *They were attacked by a band of robbers.*
2 a group of people who play music together
3 a thin strip of material *We had to wear name bands round our wrists.*

bandage noun (*plural* **bandages**)
a strip of material that you wrap round part of your body if you have hurt it

bang noun (*plural* **bangs**)
a sudden very loud noise

bang verb **bangs, banging, banged**
1 When you bang something, you hit it hard. *He banged on the window.*
2 When something bangs, it makes a sudden loud noise. *The door banged shut.*

banish verb **banishes, banishing, banished**
To banish someone means to send them away from a place as a punishment.

bank noun (*plural* **banks**)
1 A bank is a place where people can keep their money safely. Banks also lend money to people.
2 the ground near the edge of a river or lake *We walked along the bank of the river.*

banner noun (*plural* **banners**)
a long, thin flag with words written on it
They hung up a banner with 'Welcome Home' written on it.

baptize verb **baptizes, baptizing, baptized**
When someone is baptized, they are accepted as a Christian in a special ceremony.

bar noun (*plural* **bars**)
1 a long piece of wood or metal *There were bars on the windows to stop people from escaping.*
2 a block of chocolate or soap
3 a place that serves food and drinks at a counter *Is there a coffee bar at the museum?*

barbecue noun (*plural* **barbecues**)
1 a party where people sit outside and cook food over a fire
2 a metal frame that you put food on to cook it over a fire outside

barber noun (*plural* **barbers**)
a hairdresser for men and boys

bar chart noun (*plural* **bar charts**)
a graph that uses bars of different lengths to show different amounts of things

bare adjective **barer, barest**
1 If a part of your body is bare, it has nothing covering it.
2 If something is bare, it has nothing on it or in it. *The walls of her bedroom were bare.*

bargain noun (*plural* **bargains**)
something that you buy very cheaply, for much less than its usual price

barge noun (*plural* **barges**)
A barge is a long boat with a flat bottom. Barges are used on canals.

barge verb **barges, barging, barged**
If you barge into someone, you bump into them by accident.

bark noun
the hard covering round the trunk and branches of a tree

bark verb **barks, barking, barked**
When a dog barks, it makes a loud, rough sound.

barley noun
Barley is a plant that farmers grow. Its seed is used for making food and beer.

a
b
c
d
e
f
g
h
i
j
k
l
m
n
o
p
q
r
s
t
u
v
w
x
y
z

bar mitzvah noun (*plural* **bar mitzvahs**)
a celebration for a Jewish boy when he reaches the age of 13

barn noun (*plural* **barns**)
a large building on a farm, where a farmer keeps animals, hay, or grain

barrel noun (*plural* **barrels**)
1 a round, wooden container that beer, wine, or water is kept in
2 The barrel of a gun is the tube that the bullet comes out of.

barrier noun (*plural* **barriers**)
a fence or wall that stops you getting past a place

base noun (*plural* **bases**)
1 The base of an object is the part at the bottom, which it stands on.
2 Someone's base is the main place where they live or work.

baseball noun
a game in which two teams hit a ball with a long bat and run round a square in order to score points

basic adjective
Basic things are simple but very important. *You need to learn the basic skills first.*

basin noun (*plural* **basins**)
a large bowl

basket noun (*plural* **baskets**)
A basket is a container that you carry things in. A basket is made of thin strips of straw, plastic, or metal that are twisted or woven together.

basketball noun
a game in which two teams try to score points by bouncing a ball and throwing it into a high net

bat noun (*plural* **bats**)
1 a small animal with wings that flies and hunts for food at night and hangs upside down during the day
2 a piece of wood that you use for hitting a ball in a game

bat verb **bats, batting, batted**
When you bat in a game, you try to hit the ball with a bat.

bath noun (*plural* **baths**) (*rhymes with* path)
a large container which you can fill with water to sit in and wash yourself all over

bathe verb **bathes, bathing, bathed** (*rhymes with* save)
1 When you bathe, you go swimming in the sea or a river. *We bathed in the river.*
2 If you bathe a part of your body, you wash it gently because it hurts. *Mum gave me a cuddle and bathed my cuts.*

bathroom noun (*plural* **bathrooms**)
a room with a bath, washbasin, and toilet

baton noun (*plural* **batons**)
1 a stick that a conductor of an orchestra uses to show the musicians how fast to play
2 a stick that a runner in a relay race passes to the next person in the team

battery noun (*plural* **batteries**)
A battery is an object that contains a store of electricity. You put batteries inside torches and radios to make them work.

battle noun (*plural* **battles**)
a big fight between two groups of people

bawl verb **bawls, bawling, bawled**
When you bawl, you shout or cry very loudly.

bay noun (*plural* **bays**)
a place on the coast where the land bends inwards and sea fills the space *The ship took shelter in the bay.*

beach noun (*plural* **beaches**)
an area of sand or pebbles by the edge of the sea

bead noun (*plural* **beads**)
A bead is a small piece of wood, glass, or plastic with a hole through the middle. You thread beads on a string to make a necklace.

beak noun (*plural* **beaks**)
A bird's beak is its mouth, which is hard and pointed.

beaker noun (*plural* **beakers**)
a tall cup

beam noun (*plural* **beams**)
1 A wooden beam is a long strong piece of wood that supports the floor or roof of a building.
2 A beam of light is a ray of light that shines onto something.

bean noun (*plural* **beans**)
Beans are the seeds of some plants which you can eat. Sometimes you eat just the seeds, and sometimes you eat the seeds and the pod that they grow in.

bear noun (*plural* **bears**)
a large wild animal with thick fur and sharp teeth and claws

bear verb **bears, bearing, bore, borne**
1 If something will bear your weight, it will support your weight and so you can stand on it safely.
2 If you cannot bear something, you hate it.

beard noun (*plural* **beards**)
hair growing on a man's chin *He had white hair and a long, grey beard.*

beast noun (*plural* **beasts**)
1 a big, fierce animal
2 a horrible person

beat verb **beats, beating, beaten**
1 To beat someone means to hit them hard a lot of times. *It's cruel to beat animals.*
2 If you beat someone, you win a game against them. *Anita always beats me at tennis.*
3 When you beat a mixture, you stir it hard. *Dad beat some eggs to make an omelette.*

beat noun
the regular rhythm in a piece of music *I like dancing to music with a strong beat.*

beautiful adjective
1 Something that is beautiful is very nice to look at, hear, or smell. *What beautiful flowers!*
2 Someone who is beautiful has a lovely face. *He longed to marry the beautiful princess.*

> **WORD FAMILY**
> • **beautifully** She arranged the flowers beautifully.
> • **beauty** The prince was astonished by her beauty.

became verb *see* **become**

because conjunction
for the reason that *My dad was angry because I was late.*

become verb **becomes, becoming, became, become**
to start to be *She became quite upset when we told her about the kitten.*

bed noun (*plural* **beds**)
1 a piece of furniture that you sleep on
2 a piece of ground that you grow flowers or vegetables in *Please don't walk on the flower beds.*
3 the bottom of the sea or a river *The old ship is now resting on the sea bed.*

bedroom noun (*plural* **bedrooms**)
a room where you sleep

bee noun (*plural* **bees**)
A bee is an insect that can fly and sting you. Bees use nectar from flowers to make honey.

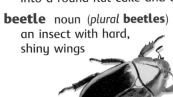

beef noun
meat from a cow

beefburger noun (*plural* **beefburgers**)
a piece of minced beef that has been made into a round flat cake and cooked

beetle noun (*plural* **beetles**)
an insect with hard, shiny wings

a b c d e f g h i j k l m n o p q r s t u v w x y z

15

before adverb, conjunction, & preposition
1 earlier than *We usually have maths before lunch.*
2 already *Have you been here before?*
3 in front of *The girl vanished before my eyes.*

beg verb **begs, begging, begged**
If you beg someone to do something, you ask them very strongly to do it.
'Oh Gran, please please please come with us,' Ruby begged.—Jacqueline Wilson, Double Act

began verb *see* **begin**

begin verb **begins, beginning, began, begun**
To begin means to start.

> **WORD FAMILY**
> • A **beginner** is someone who is just starting to learn how to do something. The **beginning** of something is when it starts.

begun verb *see* **begin**

behave verb **behaves, behaving, behaved**
1 The way you behave is the way you speak and do things. *He was behaving very strangely.*
2 If you behave yourself, you are polite and do not do anything that is rude or naughty.

> **WORD FAMILY**
> • **behaviour** How can you explain his strange behaviour?

behind adverb & preposition
at the back of *I hid behind the wall.*

believe verb **believes, believing, believed**
If you believe something, you feel sure that it is true. *I don't believe you – I think you're lying!*

> **WORD FAMILY**
> • Your **beliefs** are the things that you believe are true.

bell noun (*plural* **bells**)
a metal object that rings when something hits it

bellow verb **bellows, bellowing, bellowed**
If you bellow, you shout very loudly.

belong verb **belongs, belonging, belonged**
1 If something belongs to you, it is yours. *Does this purse belong to you?*
2 If something belongs in a place, it goes there.

below preposition
1 underneath *Can you swim below the surface of the water?*
2 less than *The temperature was below freezing last night.*

belt noun (*plural* **belts**)
a band of leather or other material that you wear round your waist

bench noun (*plural* **benches**)
a long wooden or stone seat for more than one person

bend verb **bends, bending, bent**
1 When you bend something, you make it curved and not straight.
2 When you bend down, you lean forward so that your head is nearer to the ground.

bend noun (*plural* **bends**)
a part of a road or river that curves round

beneath preposition
underneath *The ship disappeared beneath the waves.*

bent verb *see* **bend** verb

berry noun (*plural* **berries**)
a small round fruit with seeds in it *You can eat some types of berries, but others are poisonous.*

beside preposition
at the side of *Dan was standing beside me.*

best adjective
The best person or thing is the one that is better than any other. *Who's the best swimmer in your class?*

bet verb **bets, betting, bet**
When you bet with someone, you agree that they will pay you money if you are right about something, but you will pay them money if you are wrong.

better adjective
1 If one thing is better than another, it is more interesting, more useful, or more exciting.
2 If you are better than someone else, you are able to do something more quickly or more successfully.
3 When you are better, you are well again after an illness.

between preposition
1 in the middle of two people or things *I sat between Mum and Dad.*
2 among *Share the money between you.*

beware verb
If you tell someone to beware, you are warning them to be careful.

biased adjective (*say* **bi**-ast)
1 If someone is biased, they unfairly help one person or team more than another. *The referee was biased!*
2 If a piece of writing is biased, it gives only one side of an argument.

Bible noun (*plural* **Bibles**)
the holy book of the Christian religion

> **WORD FAMILY**
> • A **biblical** story or character is one that is in the Bible.

bibliography noun (*plural* **bibliographies**)
a list of books, for example books by one particular author or books about one particular subject

bicycle noun (*plural* **bicycles**)
something with two wheels, which you sit on and ride along by pushing pedals round with your feet

big adjective **bigger, biggest**
Something that is big is large and not small.

bike noun (*plural* **bikes**)
a bicycle

bilingual adjective
Someone who is bilingual can speak two languages equally well.

bill noun (*plural* **bills**)
1 a piece of paper that tells you how much money you owe someone
2 a bird's beak

billion noun (*plural* **billions**)
1,000,000,000; one thousand million

billow verb **billows, billowing, billowed**
If a sail or piece of material billows, it moves in the wind and fills with air.
His black cloak billowed out as he swung round to greet us all, revealing a scarlet lining with pockets bulging with presents.—Berlie Doherty, The Nutcracker

bin noun (*plural* **bins**)
a container for putting rubbish in

bind verb **binds, binding, bound**
If you bind things together, you tie them together tightly.

binoculars noun
two tubes that you hold to your eyes like a pair of glasses and look through to make things that are far away seem bigger and nearer

biodegradable adjective (*say* bye-oh-dee-**grade**-a-bul)
Things that are biodegradable will rot away naturally after you have used them.

biography noun (*plural* **biographies**)
a book that tells the true story of a person's life

biology noun
the study of animals and plants

bird noun (*plural* **birds**)
any animal with feathers, wings, and a beak

birth noun
The birth of a baby is when it leaves its mother's body and is born.

birthday noun (*plural* **birthdays**)
the day each year when you remember and celebrate the day you were born

a
b
c
d
e
f
g
h
i
j
k
l
m
n
o
p
q
r
s
t
u
v
w
x
y
z

biscuit noun (*plural* **biscuits**)
a kind of small, crisp cake

bit noun (*plural* **bits**)
a small amount of something *Would you like a bit of chocolate?*

bit verb *see* **bite** verb

bite verb **bites, biting, bit, bitten**
When you bite something, you use your teeth to cut it. *Dogs don't like me – they always try to bite me!*

bitter adjective
If something tastes bitter, it has a nasty sour taste.

black adjective
1 Something that is black is the colour of the sky on a very dark night.
2 Someone who is black has a skin that is naturally dark in colour.

blackbird noun (*plural* **blackbirds**)
A blackbird is a type of bird. The male is black with an orange beak, but the female is brown.

blackboard noun (*plural* **blackboards**)
a smooth, dark board that you can write on with chalk

blade noun (*plural* **blades**)
1 The blade of a knife or sword is the long, sharp part of it.
2 A blade of grass is one piece of grass.

blame verb **blames, blaming, blamed**
When you blame someone, you say that it is their fault that something bad has happened. *Everyone blamed me for the broken window, but it wasn't my fault!*

blank adjective
A blank piece of paper has nothing written or drawn on it.

blanket noun (*plural* **blankets**)
a thick warm cover that you put on a bed

blank verse noun
poetry in which the lines use patterns of rhythm but do not rhyme with each other

blast noun (*plural* **blasts**)
a sudden rush of wind or air *I felt a blast of cold air as I opened the door.*

blaze noun (*plural* **blazes**)
a large, strong fire

blaze verb **blazes, blazing, blazed**
When a fire is blazing, it is burning brightly.

blazer noun (*plural* **blazers**)
a type of jacket, especially one that children wear to school as part of their school uniform

bleach verb **bleaches, bleaching, bleached**
To bleach something means to make it white, or lighter in colour. *The sun always bleaches my hair in the summer.*

bleat verb **bleats, bleating, bleated**
When a sheep bleats, it makes a long sound.

bleed verb **bleeds, bleeding, bled**
If a part of your body is bleeding, blood is coming out of it.

bleep verb **bleeps, bleeping, bleeped**
If a machine bleeps, it makes a short, high sound.

blend verb **blends, blending, blended**
When you blend things, you mix them together.

blew verb *see* **blow** verb

blind adjective
Someone who is blind cannot see.

blind noun (*plural* **blinds**)
a piece of material that you pull down to cover a window

blink verb **blinks, blinking, blinked**
When you blink, you close your eyes and then open them again quickly.

blister noun (*plural* **blisters**)
A blister is a sore place on your skin that is caused by something rubbing against it. A blister looks like a small lump and has liquid inside it.

blizzard noun (*plural* **blizzards**)
a storm with a lot of snow and wind

block noun (*plural* **blocks**)
1 a thick piece of stone or wood
2 a tall building with lots of flats or offices inside *We live in a block of flats near the city centre.*

block verb **blocks, blocking, blocked**
If something is blocking a road or pipe, it is in the way and nothing can get past it. *Some parked cars were blocking the road.*

block graph noun (*plural* **block graphs**)
a graph that uses stacks of blocks to show different amounts of things

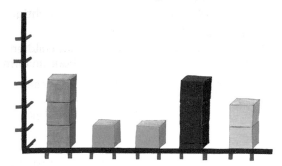

blog noun (*plural* **blogs**)
a website on which someone writes regularly about their own life or opinions

blond, blonde adjective
Someone who is blond has fair or light-coloured hair.

> **WORD FAMILY**
> • Usually we use the spelling **blond** for boys and men, and the spelling **blonde** for women and girls.

blood noun
the red liquid that is pumped round inside your body

blossom noun (*plural* **blossoms**)
the flowers on a tree

blot noun (*plural* **blots**)
a spot of ink that has been spilt on something

blouse noun (*plural* **blouses**)
a shirt that a woman or girl wears

blow noun (*plural* **blows**)
If you receive a blow, someone hits you hard.

blow verb **blows, blowing, blew, blown**
1 When you blow, you make air come out of your mouth.
2 When the wind blows, it moves along.

blue adjective
Something that is blue is the colour of the sky on a fine day.

bluff verb **bluffs, bluffing, bluffed**
When you bluff, you pretend that you are going to do something when really you are not. *He said he was going to tell the teacher, but I knew he was only bluffing.*

blunt adjective **blunter, bluntest**
Something that is blunt is not sharp. *This knife is too blunt to cut anything.*

blur noun (*plural* **blurs**)
If something is a blur, you cannot see it clearly.

blurb noun
a short piece of writing about a book, which tells you what the book is about and why it is good

blush verb **blushes, blushing, blushed**
When you blush, your face goes red because you feel shy or guilty.

board noun (*plural* **boards**)
a flat piece of wood

board verb **boards, boarding, boarded**
When you board an aeroplane, bus, ship, or train, you get onto it.

boarding school noun (*plural* **boarding schools**)
a school where children live during the term

boast verb **boasts, boasting, boasted**
If you boast, you talk about how clever you are or how well you can do things. *He's always boasting about how good he is at football.*

boat noun (*plural* **boats**)
something that floats on water and can carry people and goods over water

body noun (*plural* **bodies**)
1 Your body is every part of you that you can see and touch.
2 A body is a dead person. *The police found a man's body in the river.*

bog noun (plural **bogs**)
a piece of soft, wet ground

boil verb **boils, boiling, boiled**
1 When water boils, it bubbles and gives off steam because it is very hot. *Is the water boiling yet?*
2 When you boil something, you cook it in boiling water. *Boil the pasta for about six minutes.*

boisterous adjective
Someone who is boisterous is noisy and full of energy.
For heaven's sake, Gemma, why can't you stop being so rough and silly and boisterous?—Jacqueline Wilson, Best Friends

bold adjective **bolder, boldest**
1 Someone who is bold is brave and not afraid.
2 Bold writing is dark and easy to see.

bolt noun (plural **bolts**)
1 a piece of metal that you slide across to lock a door
2 A bolt is a thick metal pin that looks like a screw with a blunt end. You screw a bolt into a nut to fasten something.

bolt verb **bolts, bolting, bolted**
1 When you bolt a door or window, you lock it with a bolt. *Remember to bolt the back door.*
2 If you bolt, you run away suddenly. *There was a sudden crash of thunder which made all the horses bolt.*
3 If you bolt food, you eat it very quickly.

bomb noun (plural **bombs**)
a weapon that explodes and hurts people or damages things

bone noun (plural **bones**)
Your bones are the hard white parts inside your body. Your skeleton is made of bones.

bonfire noun (plural **bonfires**)
a large fire that you make outside, especially to burn rubbish

bongo noun (plural **bongos**)
a type of drum that you play with your hands

bonnet noun (plural **bonnets**)
the part of a car that covers the engine

book noun (plural **books**)
a set of pages that are joined together inside a cover

> **WORD FAMILY**
> • A **bookcase** is a piece of furniture that you keep books on. A **bookmark** is a strip of paper or cloth that you keep inside a book to mark a place.

book verb **books, booking, booked**
When you book something, you arrange for it to be reserved for you. *Dad has booked seats for the cinema tonight.*

boom verb **booms, booming, boomed**
When something booms, it makes a long, loud, deep sound. *The thunder boomed overhead.*

boomerang noun (plural **boomerangs**)
a curved stick that comes back to the person who throws it

boot noun (plural **boots**)
1 a type of shoe that also covers your ankle and part of your leg
2 the part of a car that you carry luggage in

border noun (plural **borders**)
1 the place where two countries meet *You need a passport to cross the border.*
2 a narrow strip along the edge of something *On the table was a white tablecloth with a blue border.*

bore verb **bores, boring, bored**
1 If something bores you, you find it dull and not interesting. *These silly games bore me to death!*
2 If you bore a hole in something, you make a hole.
3 *see* **bear** verb

> **WORD FAMILY**
> • **bored** I'm bored!
> • **boredom** I nearly fell asleep with boredom.
> • **boring** This is boring!

born adjective
When a baby is born, it comes out of its mothers body and starts to live.

borne verb *see* **bear** verb

borrow verb **borrows, borrowing, borrowed**
When you borrow something, you take it and use it for a while and then give it back. *Can I borrow your pen?*

boss noun (*plural* **bosses**)
the person who is in charge

both adjective & pronoun
the two of them *Hold the camera in both hands.*

bother verb **bothers, bothering, bothered**
1 If something bothers you, it worries you or annoys you. *Is the loud music bothering you?*
2 If you do not bother to do something, you do not do it because it would take too much effort. *Joe never bothers to answer his text messages.*

bottle noun (*plural* **bottles**)
a tall glass or plastic container that you keep liquids in

bottom noun (*plural* **bottoms**)
The bottom of something is the lowest part of it. *The others waited for us at the bottom of the hill.*

bough noun (*plural* **boughs**) (*rhymes with* now)
a large branch of a tree

bought verb *see* **buy**

boulder noun (*plural* **boulders**) (*say* **bole**-der)
a large rock

bounce verb **bounces, bouncing, bounced**
When something bounces, it springs back into the air when it hits something hard.

bound verb **bounds, bounding, bounded**
When you bound, you run and jump.
Babe bounded up the hill.—Dick King-Smith, The Sheep-Pig

bound adjective
If something is bound to happen, it will definitely happen. *We've got the best team, so we're bound to win.*

bound verb *see* **bind**

boundary noun (*plural* **boundaries**)
a line that marks the edge of a piece of land

bow noun (*plural* **bows**) (*rhymes with* go)
1 a knot with large loops *She tied the ribbon into a bow.*
2 a weapon that you use for shooting arrows *The men were armed with bows and arrows.*

bow verb **bows, bowing, bowed** (*rhymes with* cow)
When you bow, you bend forwards to show respect to someone or to thank people for clapping.

bowl verb **bowls, bowling, bowled**
When you bowl in a game of cricket or rounders, you throw the ball for someone else to hit.

bowling noun
a game in which you roll a heavy ball towards a set of tall sticks and try to knock them over

box noun (*plural* **boxes**)
a container with straight sides, made of cardboard or plastic

box verb **boxes, boxing, boxed**
When people box, they fight by hitting each other with their fists.

> **WORD FAMILY**
> • Someone who boxes as a sport is a **boxer**.

boy noun (*plural* **boys**)
a male child

boyfriend noun (*plural* **boyfriends**)
A girl's boyfriend is the boy she is going out with.

brace noun (*plural* **braces**)
a piece of wire that you wear across your teeth to straighten them

bracelet noun (*plural* **bracelets**)
a piece of jewellery that you wear round your wrist

bracket noun (*plural* **brackets**)
Brackets are marks like these ( ) that you use in writing.

braille noun
Braille is a way of writing that uses a pattern of raised dots on paper. Blind people can read braille by touching the dots with their fingers.

brain noun (*plural* **brains**)
Your brain is the part inside your head that controls your body and allows you to think and remember things.

brainy adjective
brainier, brainiest
Someone who is brainy is very clever.
Ali is the brainy one in our family.

brake noun (*plural* **brakes**)
the part of a car or bicycle that makes it slow down and stop

branch noun (*plural* **branches**)
1 a part that grows out from the trunk of a tree
2 (*in ICT*) a series of answers to questions in a branching database, which leads you to identify one particular thing

branching database noun (*plural* **branching databases**)
(*in ICT*) A branching database is a computer database which stores information about things, for example different types of animals or plants. You can use the database to identify something by answering a series of questions about it.

brass noun
Brass is a yellow metal. Brass is used for making some musical instruments such as trumpets and trombones.

brave adjective **braver, bravest**
Someone who is brave is willing to do dangerous things. *I knew I had to be brave and try to rescue my friends.*

> **WORD FAMILY**
> • **bravely** The soldiers fought very bravely.
> • **bravery** He was given a medal as a reward for his bravery.

bread noun
a food that is made from flour and water, and baked in the oven

breadth noun
The breadth of something is how wide it is. *We measured the length and breadth of the field.*

break verb **breaks, breaking, broke, broken**
1 If you break something, you smash it into several pieces.
2 If you break something, you damage it so that it no longer works. *Someone's broken my MP3 player.*
3 If you break a law or a promise, you do something that goes against it. *You should never break a promise.*
4 If something breaks down, it stops working. *Our bus broke down on the motorway.*

break noun (*plural* **breaks**)
1 a gap in something *We managed to escape through a break in the hedge.*
2 a short rest *We'll have a short break before we continue.*

breakfast noun (*plural* **breakfasts**)
the first meal of the day, which you eat in the morning

breast noun (*plural* **breasts**)
1 A woman's breasts are the parts on the front of her body that can produce milk to feed a baby.
2 The breast on a chicken or other bird is its chest.

breath noun (*plural* **breaths**)
the air that you take into your body and then blow out again *I took a deep breath and dived into the water.*

breathe verb **breathes, breathing, breathed**
When you breathe, you take air into your lungs through your nose or mouth and then blow it out again.

breed noun (*plural* **breeds**)
a particular type of animal *Poodles are my favourite breed of dog.*

breeze noun (*plural* **breezes**)
a gentle wind
They woke next day to brilliant sunshine and a light, refreshing breeze.—J. K. Rowling, Harry Potter and the Chamber of Secrets

bribe noun (*plural* **bribes**)
something that you offer to someone to persuade them to do something

brick noun (*plural* **bricks**)
A brick is a small block made from baked clay. People use bricks for building houses.

bride noun (*plural* **brides**)
a woman who is getting married

a b c d e f g h i j k l m n o p q r s t u v w x y z

bridegroom noun (plural **bridegrooms**)
a man who is getting married

bridesmaid noun (plural **bridesmaids**)
a girl or woman who walks behind the bride
at her wedding

bridge noun (plural **bridges**)
something that is built over a river, railway,
or road so that people can go across it

brief adjective **briefer, briefest**
Something that is brief is short and does
not last very long. *We only had time for
a brief visit.*

> **WORD FAMILY**
> • **briefly** I looked at the letter briefly, then put
> it in my pocket.

briefcase noun (plural **briefcases**)
a small case that you carry books and
papers in

bright adjective **brighter, brightest**
1 A bright light shines with a lot of light.
2 A bright colour is strong and not dull. *Grace
was wearing a bright red T-shirt.*
3 A bright day is sunny. *It was a lovely bright,
sunny day.*
4 Someone who is bright is clever and learns
things quickly.

> **WORD FAMILY**
> • **brightly** The sun was shining brightly.

brilliant adjective
1 Someone who is brilliant is very clever, or
very good at something. *Adam's a brilliant
footballer.*
2 Something that is brilliant is very good. *We
saw a brilliant film yesterday.*

brim noun (plural **brims**)
1 the edge round the top of a container *Her cup
was filled to the brim.*
2 the part of a hat that sticks out round the
bottom edge

bring verb **brings, bringing, brought**
1 If you bring something with you, you carry it
with you. *Don't forget to bring your swimming
costume.*
2 If you bring someone with you, they come
with you. *Can I bring a friend with me?*

brisk adjective **brisker, briskest**
A brisk way of walking is quick and lively.
We set off at a brisk pace.

brittle adjective
Something that is brittle is hard and dry and
will break easily. *We found some dry, brittle
twigs to make a fire.*

broad adjective **broader, broadest**
Something that is broad is wide. *At the
bottom of the field was a broad river.*

broadband noun
a system for connecting computers to the
Internet and sending information very quickly

broadcast verb **broadcasts, broadcasting,
broadcast**
To broadcast something means to send it
out as a television or radio programme.
The match will be broadcast live on television.

broccoli noun
a dark green vegetable

brochure noun (plural **brochures**)
(say **broh**-shoor)
a small book that gives you information
about something

broke, broken verb *see* **break** verb

bronze noun
a hard, brown,
shiny metal

brooch noun
(plural **brooches**)
(say broach)
a piece of
jewellery that
you pin to your
clothes

broom noun
(plural **brooms**)
a brush with a long handle that you use for
sweeping floors

brother noun (plural **brothers**)
Your brother is a boy who has the same
parents as you.

brought verb *see* **bring**

brow noun (plural **brows**) (rhymes with now)
1 Your brow is your forehead. *Oscar stood up
and wiped the sweat from his brow.*
2 The brow of a hill is the top of it.

brown adjective
1 Something that is brown is the colour
of soil.

2 Brown bread is made with the whole wheat grain, not just the white part.

browse verb **browses, browsing, browsed**
1 When you browse in a shop, you look around to see if there is anything you like.
2 (*in ICT*) When you browse on a computer, you look for information on the Internet.

bruise noun (*plural* **bruises**) (*say* brooze)
a dark mark on your skin that you get when you have been hit

brush noun (*plural* **brushes**)
A brush is an object with short, stiff hairs on the end of a handle. You use a brush for cleaning things, and you also use a brush for painting.

brush verb **brushes, brushing, brushed**
When you brush something, you clean it using a brush.

bubble noun (*plural* **bubbles**)
Bubbles are small balls of air or gas inside a liquid, for example like the ones you find in fizzy drinks.

bubble verb **bubbles, bubbling, bubbled**
When a liquid bubbles, it makes bubbles. *The toffee bubbled and sizzled on the stove.—Catherine Storr, Clever Polly*

bucket noun (*plural* **buckets**)
a container with a handle that you use for carrying water

buckle noun (*plural* **buckles**)
the part of a belt that you use to fasten the two ends together

bud noun (*plural* **buds**)
a small lump on a plant that will later open into a flower or leaf

Buddhist noun (*plural* **Buddhists**)
someone who follows the Buddhist religion and follows the teachings of the Buddha

WORD FAMILY
• The religion that Buddhists follow is **Buddhism**.

buffet noun (*plural* **buffets**) (*say* **boof**-ay)
1 a meal where a lot of different cold foods are put onto a table and you help yourself to the food that you want
2 a place where you can buy drinks and snacks on a train

bug noun (*plural* **bugs**)
1 an insect
2 a germ that gets into your body and makes you ill *I don't feel well. I think I've got a stomach bug.*
3 a problem in a computer program that makes it go wrong

build verb **builds, building, built**
When you build something, you make it by joining or fixing different parts together. *It took nearly three years to build this bridge.*

WORD FAMILY
• A **builder** is someone who builds houses and other buildings.

building noun (*plural* **buildings**)
a structure like a house, school, shop, or church

built verb *see* **build**

bulb noun (*plural* **bulbs**)
1 the part of an electric lamp that gives out light
2 A bulb is a part of a plant that grows under the ground and looks like an onion. Daffodils and tulips grow from bulbs.

bulge verb **bulges, bulging, bulged**
If something bulges, it sticks out because it is so full. *His pockets were bulging with sweets.*

bull noun (*plural* **bulls**)
a male cow, elephant, or whale

bulldozer noun (*plural* **bulldozers**)
a heavy machine that moves earth and makes land flat

bullet noun (*plural* **bullets**)
a small piece of metal that is fired from a gun

a b c d e f g h i j k l m n o p q r s t u v w x y z

bullet point noun (*plural* **bullet points**)
When you use bullet points, you write something as a series of short points, one under the other, with a large dot before each one.

bully verb **bullies, bullying, bullied**
To bully someone means to hurt them or be unkind to them.

bully noun (*plural* **bullies**)
someone who hurts other people or is unkind to them

bump verb **bumps, bumping, bumped**
If you bump something, you knock it or hit it. *I bumped my head on the shelf.*

bump noun (*plural* **bumps**)
1 the noise that something makes when it falls to the ground *The book fell to the ground with a bump.*
2 a small lump on your skin that you get when you have knocked it

bumper noun (*plural* **bumpers**)
A bumper is a bar along the front or back of a car. The bumper protects the car if it hits something.

bun noun (*plural* **buns**)
1 a small, round cake
2 a round piece of bread that you eat a burger in

bunch noun (*plural* **bunches**)
a group of things that are tied together *What a lovely bunch of flowers!*

bundle noun (*plural* **bundles**)
a group of things that are tied together *She was carrying a bundle of old clothes.*

bungalow noun (*plural* **bungalows**)
a house without any upstairs rooms

bungee jumping noun
the sport of jumping off a high place attached to a very long piece of elastic, which stops you just before you hit the ground

bungle verb **bungles, bungling, bungled**
If you bungle something, you do it very badly.

bunk noun (*plural* **bunks**)
a bed that has another bed above or below it *Can I sleep in the top bunk?*

buoy noun (*plural* **buoys**) (*say* **boy**)
an object that floats in the sea to warn ships about danger

burger noun (*plural* **burgers**)
a piece of minced meat that has been made into a round, flat cake and cooked

burglar noun (*plural* **burglars**)
someone who goes into a building and steals things

burial noun (*plural* **burials**)
When there is a burial, a dead person is buried.

burn verb **burns, burning, burned or burnt**
1 When something burns, it catches fire. *Paper burns easily.*
2 If you burn something, you damage it or destroy it using fire or heat. *We burnt all our rubbish on a bonfire.*
3 If you burn yourself, you hurt your skin with fire or heat. *Be careful you don't burn in the hot sun.*

burrow noun (*plural* **burrows**)
a hole in the ground that an animal lives in

burst verb **bursts, bursting, burst**
if something bursts, it suddenly breaks open *Don't blow the balloons up too much or they'll burst.*

bury verb **buries, burying, buried** (*rhymes with* merry)
1 When you bury something, you put it in a hole in the ground and cover it over.
2 When a dead person is buried, their body is put into the ground.

bus noun (*plural* **buses**)
something that a lot of people can travel in on a road

bush noun (*plural* **bushes**)
a plant that looks like a small tree

bushy adjective
Bushy hair is very thick.
Joseph Hannibal is a bear of a man with a bushy black beard and twitchy eyebrows that meet in the middle so he always looks angry.—Michael Morpurgo, The Wreck of the Zanzibar

business noun (*plural* **businesses**) (*say* **bizz**-niss)
1 When people do business, they buy and sell things.
2 a shop or company that makes or sells things *My uncle runs his own business making sports equipment.*

a
b
c
d
e
f
g
h
i
j
k
l
m
n
o
p
q
r
s
t
u
v
w
x
y
z

busy adjective **busier, busiest**
1 If you are busy, you have a lot of things to do.
2 A busy place has a lot of people and traffic in it.

but conjunction
however *We wanted to play tennis, but we couldn't because it was raining.*

butcher noun (*plural* **butchers**)
someone who cuts up meat and sells it in a shop

butter noun
Butter is a yellow food that is made from milk. You spread butter on bread.

butterfly noun (*plural* **butterflies**)
an insect with large colourful wings

button noun (*plural* **buttons**)
1 a small round thing that you use to fasten clothes by pushing it through a small hole in the clothes
2 a part of a machine that you press to switch it on or off

buy verb **buys, buying, bought**
When you buy something, you get it by giving someone money for it.

buzz verb **buzzes, buzzing, buzzed**
When something buzzes, it makes a sound like a bee.

buzzer noun (*plural* **buzzers**)
A buzzer is something that makes a buzzing sound, for example when you press it or when you connect it to an electric circuit.

by preposition
1 near *You can leave your shoes by the front door.*
2 travelling in *We're going by train.*

byte noun (*plural* **bytes**)
(*in ICT*) You measure a computer's memory by saying how many bytes it has.

> 🏠 **WORD FAMILY**
> • A **megabyte** is one million **bytes**.
> A **gigabyte** is one thousand million bytes.

Cc

cab noun (*plural* **cabs**)
1 a taxi
2 the part at the front of a lorry, bus, or train where the driver sits

cabbage noun (*plural* **cabbages**)
a round, green vegetable with a lot of leaves that are wrapped tightly round each other

cabin noun (*plural* **cabins**)
1 a room for passengers in a ship or aeroplane
2 a small hut *They lived in a log cabin in the woods.*

cable noun (*plural* **cables**)
1 strong, thick wire or rope
2 A cable is a bundle of wires that are held together in a plastic covering. They carry electricity or television signals.

cactus noun (*plural* **cacti**)
A cactus is a plant with a thick green stem that has no leaves but is covered in prickles. Cacti grow in hot, dry places and do not need much water.

cafe noun (*plural* **cafes**)
(*say* kaff-ay)
a place where you can buy a drink or food and sit down to eat or drink it

cage noun
(*plural* **cages**)
a box or small room with bars across it for keeping animals or birds in

cake noun (*plural* **cakes**)
a sweet food that you make with flour, fat, eggs, and sugar and bake in the oven

calcium noun (*say* **kal**-see-um)
Calcium is found in some foods and is used by your body to make bones and teeth.

calculate verb **calculates, calculating, calculated**
When you calculate an amount, you do a sum and work out how many or how much it is. *If one ice cream costs 80p, can you calculate how much six ice creams will cost?*

> 🏠 **WORD FAMILY**
> • When you calculate something, you do a **calculation**.

calculator noun (*plural* **calculators**)
a machine that you use to do sums

calendar noun (*plural* **calendars**)
A calendar is a list of all the days, weeks, and months in a year. You can write on a calendar things that you are going to do each day.

calf noun (*plural* **calves**)
1 a young cow, elephant, or whale
2 Your calf is the back part of your leg between your knee and your ankle.

call verb **calls, calling, called**
1 When you call to someone, you speak loudly so that they can hear you. *'Look out!' he called.*
2 When you call someone, you tell them to come to you. *Mum called us in for tea.*
3 When you call someone a name, you give them that name. *We decided to call the puppy Patch.*
4 When you call someone, you telephone them. *I'll call you later.*

calligram noun (*plural* **calligrams**)
A calligram is a poem in which the way the letters are printed shows the meaning of the words. For example, the word grow might be printed getting bigger, to show the idea of growing.

calm adjective **calmer, calmest**
1 If the sea or the weather is calm, it is still and not stormy. *It was a lovely calm day.*
2 If you are calm, you are quiet and not noisy or excited. *He told everyone to stay calm and not panic.*

> 🏠 **WORD FAMILY**
> • **calmly** He walked calmly out of the room.

camcorder noun (*plural* **camcorders**)
a camera that you use for taking video pictures

came verb *see* **come**

camel noun (*plural* **camels**)
A camel is a big animal with one or two humps on its back. Camels are used to carry people and goods in deserts, because they can travel for a long time without eating or drinking.

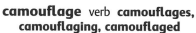

camera noun (*plural* **cameras**)
a machine that you use for taking photographs

camouflage verb **camouflages, camouflaging, camouflaged**
If something is camouflaged, it is hidden because it looks very like the things around it.

camp noun (*plural* **camps**)
a place where people stay for a short time in tents or small huts

camp verb **camps, camping, camped**
When you camp, you sleep in a tent.

can noun (*plural* **cans**)
a tin with food or drink in

can verb **could**
If you can do something, you are able to do it. *Can you swim?*

canal noun (*plural* **canals**)
a river that people have made for boats to travel on

cancel verb **cancels, cancelling, cancelled**
When you cancel something that was arranged, you say that it will not happen. *The chess club was cancelled this week because the teacher was ill.*

candle noun (*plural* **candles**)
A candle is a stick of wax with string through the centre. You light the string and it burns slowly to give you light.

cane noun (*plural* **canes**)
a long, thin stick made of wood or bamboo

canine noun (*plural* **canines**)
Your canines are the pointed teeth at the front of your mouth.

a b **c** d e f g h i j k l m n o p q r s t u v w x y z

cannot verb
can not *I cannot understand what you are saying.*

canoe noun (*plural* **canoes**) (*say* ka-**noo**)
a light, narrow boat that you move by using a paddle

can't verb
can not *I can't read your writing.*

canvas noun
a type of strong cloth that is used for making tents and sails

cap noun (*plural* **caps**)
1 a soft hat with a stiff part that sticks out at the front, over your eyes
2 a lid for a bottle or other container *Please put the cap back on the toothpaste.*

capable adjective
If you are capable of doing something, you can do it. *You're capable of better work than this.*

capacity noun (*plural* **capacities**)
The capacity of a container is the amount that it can hold.

capital noun (*plural* **capitals**)
A country's capital is its most important city. *London is the capital of England.*

capital letter noun (*plural* **capital letters**)
Capital letters are the big letters you put at the beginning of names and sentences. A, B, C, D, and so on are capital letters.

captain noun (*plural* **captains**)
1 The captain of a ship or aeroplane is the person in charge of it.
2 The captain of a team is the person in charge of it, who tells the others what to do.

caption noun (*plural* **captions**)
words that are printed next to a picture and tell you what the picture is about

capture verb **captures, capturing, captured**
To capture someone means to catch them. *My grandfather was captured by enemy soldiers during the war.*

car noun (*plural* **cars**)
something that you can drive along in on roads

caravan noun (*plural* **caravans**)
a small house on wheels that can be pulled by a car from place to place

card noun (*plural* **cards**)
1 Card is thick, stiff paper.
2 A card is a piece of card with a picture and a message on it. You send cards to people at special times like their birthday or Christmas.
3 Cards are small pieces of card with numbers or pictures on them, that you use to play games. *Do you like playing cards?*

cardboard noun
very thick, strong paper

cardigan noun (*plural* **cardigans**)
a knitted jumper that has buttons down the front

care noun (*plural* **cares**)
1 If you take care when you are doing something, you do it carefully. *You should take more care with your schoolwork.*
2 If you take care of someone, you look after them.

care verb **cares, caring, cared**
1 If you care about something, it is important to you. *I don't care where I sit.*
2 If you care for someone, you look after them.

careful adjective
If you are careful, you make sure that you do things safely and well so that you do not have an accident.

> **WORD FAMILY**
> • **carefully** He picked the eggs up carefully.

careless adjective
If you are careless, you are not careful and so you make mistakes or have an accident.

caretaker noun (*plural* **caretakers**)
someone whose job is to look after a building

a b c d e f g h i j k l m n o p q r s t u v w x y z

cargo noun (*plural* **cargoes**)
the goods that are taken in a ship or aeroplane from one place to another

caring adjective
A caring person cares about other people and tries not to upset them.

carnival noun (*plural* **carnivals**)
A carnival is a large party that takes place in the streets. People dress up in fancy dress and there is music and dancing.

carnivore noun (*plural* **carnivores**)
an animal that eats meat

WORD FAMILY
• **carnivorous** Lions are carnivorous animals.

carpenter noun (*plural* **carpenters**)
someone whose job is to make things out of wood

carpet noun (*plural* **carpets**)
a thick, soft material that is put on a floor to cover it

carriage noun (*plural* **carriages**)
1 The carriages on a train are the parts where people sit.
2 something that is pulled by horses for people to travel in

carried verb *see* **carry**

carrot noun (*plural* **carrots**)
a long, thin, orange vegetable

carry verb **carries, carrying, carried**
1 When you carry something, you hold it in your hands or arms and take it somewhere.
2 If you carry on doing something, you keep doing it. *I called to Rosie, but she carried on walking and didn't answer me.*

cart noun (*plural* **carts**)
A cart is a wooden vehicle that you can put things in to take them somewhere. Some carts are pulled by horses, and others are pushed along by people.

carton noun (*plural* **cartons**)
a small plastic or cardboard box in which food or drink is sold

cartoon noun (*plural* **cartoons**)
1 a funny drawing that makes people laugh
2 a film that has drawings instead of real people

cartwheel noun (*plural* **cartwheels**)
When you do a cartwheel, you put your hands on the ground and swing your legs into the air in a circle.

carve verb **carves, carving, carved**
1 When you carve something, you make it by cutting wood or stone into the right shape.
2 When you carve meat, you cut slices from it.

case noun (*plural* **cases**)
1 a box for keeping things in
2 a suitcase

cash noun
money

cast verb **casts, casting, cast**
1 To cast something means to throw it. *He cast the coins into the water.*
2 To cast a spell on someone means to say a spell that will affect them.

castle noun (*plural* **castles**)
a large, strong building with thick, stone walls

casual adjective
Casual clothes are clothes that you wear when you are relaxing.

WORD FAMILY
• **casually** He was casually dressed in jeans and a T-shirt.

cat noun (*plural* **cats**)
A cat is a furry animal that people often keep as a pet. Lions, tigers, and leopards are large, wild cats.

catalogue noun (*plural* **catalogues**)
a list of all the things that you can buy from a place, sometimes with pictures of the things

catch verb **catches, catching, caught**
1 If you catch something that is moving through the air, you get hold of it. *Try to catch the ball.*
2 To catch someone means to find them and take them prisoner. *The police finally caught the bank robbers.*
3 If you catch an illness, you get it.
4 When you catch a bus or train, you get on it.

caterpillar noun (*plural* **caterpillars**)
a small animal that looks like a worm and will turn into a butterfly or moth

cathedral noun (*plural* **cathedrals**)
a big, important church

cattle noun
cows and bulls

caught verb *see* **catch**

cause noun (*plural* **causes**)
The cause of something is the thing that makes it happen. *We don't know the cause of the explosion yet.*

cause verb **causes, causing, caused**
To cause something to happen means to make it happen. *The wind caused the door to slam.*

cautionary tale noun (*plural* **cautionary tales**)
a story that gives you a warning about something, for example one that warns you not to be selfish

cautious adjective (*say* **kor**-shuss)
If you are cautious, you are very careful not to do anything that might be dangerous.

> **WORD FAMILY**
> • **cautiously** 'Is there anyone there?' she called cautiously.

cave noun (*plural* **caves**)
a big hole in the rock under the ground or inside a mountain

CD noun (*plural* **CDs**)
A CD is a round, flat disc on which music or computer information can be stored. CD is short for **compact disc**.

CD-ROM noun (*plural* **CD-ROMs**)
A CD-ROM is a round, flat disc on which computer information is stored. CD-ROM is short for **compact disc read-only memory**.

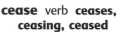

cease verb **ceases, ceasing, ceased**
If something ceases, it stops happening. *The moment the snow ceased Pinocchio set off for school with his brand new spelling book under his arm.*—James Riordan, retelling of Pinocchio

ceiling noun (*plural* **ceilings**) (*say* **see**-ling)
the part of a room above your head

celebrate verb **celebrates, celebrating, celebrated**
When you celebrate, you do something special because it is an important day. *Hindus and Sikhs celebrate Diwali in October or November.*

> **WORD FAMILY**
> • **celebration** Everyone joined in the celebration.

celebrity noun (*plural* **celebrities**)
a famous person

cell noun (*plural* **cells**)
1 a small room in which a prisoner is kept in a prison
2 (*in science*) Cells are the tiny parts that all living things are made of.

cellar noun (*plural* **cellars**)
a room underneath a building

cello noun (*plural* **cellos**) (c- in this word sounds like ch-)
A cello is a musical instrument like a big violin. You sit down and hold it between your knees to play it.

Celsius adjective (*say* **sell**-see-us)
We can measure temperature in degrees Celsius. Water boils at 100 degrees Celsius.

cement noun
the substance that builders use to hold bricks together

cemetery noun (*plural* **cemeteries**)
a place where dead people are buried

a b c d e f g h i j k l m n o p q r s t u v w x y z

centigrade adjective
We can measure temperature in degrees centigrade. Water boils at 100 degrees centigrade.

centimetre noun (plural **centimetres**)
We can measure length in centimetres. There are 100 centimetres in one metre.

centre noun (plural **centres**)
1 The centre of something is the part in the middle of it. *There was a large table in the centre of the room.*
2 a place where you go to do certain things *Have you been to the new sports centre yet?*

centre verb **centres, centring, centred**
(*in ICT*) When you centre a word or picture on a computer, you move it to the middle of the screen.

century noun (plural **centuries**)
a hundred years

cereal noun (plural **cereals**)
1 Cereals are plants such as wheat and corn that are grown by farmers for their seeds.
2 A breakfast cereal is a food that you eat at breakfast. Cereals are often made from wheat, oats, or rice, and you eat them with milk.

ceremony noun (plural **ceremonies**)
A ceremony is an event at which something important is announced to people. There is usually a ceremony when people get married, or when someone has died.

certain adjective
If you are certain about something, you are sure that it is true. *Are you certain it was Jessica that you saw?*

> **WORD FAMILY**
> • **certainly** I'm certainly not going to do your work for you!

certificate noun (plural **certificates**)
a piece of paper that says you have achieved something

chain noun (plural **chains**)
a metal rope that is made of a line of metal rings fastened together

chair noun (plural **chairs**)
a seat for one person to sit on

chalk noun (plural **chalks**)
1 a type of soft white rock *We could see the white chalk cliffs in the distance.*
2 a white or coloured stick that you use for writing on a blackboard

challenge verb **challenges, challenging, challenged**
If you challenge someone to a race or competition, you ask them to take part in it.

champion noun (plural **champions**)
the person who has won a game or competition and shown that they are the best *Anita is now the 100 metres champion in our school.*

chance noun (plural **chances**)
1 A chance to do something is a time when it is possible for you to do it. *This is our last chance to escape.*
2 When something happens by chance, it just happens, with no one planning or organizing it.

change verb **changes, changing, changed**
1 When you change something, you make it different. *If you don't like your first design, you can always change it.*
2 When something changes, it becomes different. *Caterpillars change into butterflies or moths.*
3 When you change something, you get rid of it, and get a different one instead. *I'm going to take these trousers back to the shop to change them.*

change noun
1 Change is the money you get back when you give too much money to pay for something *The shopkeeper gave me my change.*
2 (plural **changes**) When there is a change, something becomes different.

channel noun (plural **channels**)
1 a narrow area of sea *It doesn't take long to cross the English Channel.*
2 a television station *Which channel is the football on?*

a b **c** d e f g h i j k l m n o p q r s t u v w x y z

chaos noun (*say* **kay**-oss)
When there is chaos, everything is very confused and no one knows what is happening.

chapter noun (*plural* **chapters**)
one part of a book *I read three chapters of my book last night.*

character noun (*plural* **characters**)
1 a person in a story *Who is your favourite character in the book?*
2 Your character is the sort of person you are. *The twins look the same, but they have very different characters.*

charge noun (*plural* **charges**)
A charge is the amount of money that you have to pay for something.
in charge If you are in charge of something, you have the job of organizing it or looking after it.

charge verb **charges, charging, charged**
1 If you charge money for something, you ask for money.
2 If you charge at someone, you rush at them suddenly. *I was worried the bull might charge at us.*

charity noun (*plural* **charities**)
an organization that raises money and uses it to help people who are poor or need help

charm noun (*plural* **charms**)
1 If someone has charm, they are pleasant and polite and so people like them.
2 a magic spell
3 a small ornament that you wear to bring good luck

charming adjective
1 Something that is charming is pretty and lovely.
2 Someone who is charming is pleasant and polite.

chart noun (*plural* **charts**)
1 a big map
2 a sheet of paper that has rows of numbers or dates on it
the charts a list of the pop songs that are most popular each week

charter noun (*plural* **charters**)
a document that explains what rights people have

chase verb **chases, chasing, chased**
To chase someone means to run after them and try to catch them.

chat verb **chats, chatting, chatted**
When people chat, they talk in a friendly way.

chatroom noun (*plural* **chatrooms**)
a place on the Internet where people can have a conversation by sending messages to each other

chatter verb **chatters, chattering, chattered**
1 If you chatter, you talk a lot about things that are not very important.
2 When your teeth chatter, they bang together because you are cold.
He stood there so long that his teeth would have been chattering with cold if they had not been chattering with fear.—C. S. Lewis, The Lion, the Witch and the Wardrobe

cheap adjective **cheaper, cheapest**
Something that is cheap does not cost very much money.

> **WORD FAMILY**
> • **cheaply** They're selling everything really cheaply in the sale.

cheat verb **cheats, cheating, cheated**
If you cheat in a game or test, you break the rules so that you can do well.

cheat noun (*plural* **cheats**)
someone who cheats in a game or test

check verb **checks, checking, checked**
If you check something, you look at it carefully to make sure that it is right. *Remember to check your spellings.*

checkout noun (*plural* **checkouts**)
the place in a shop where you pay for things

cheek noun (*plural* **cheeks**)
1 Your cheeks are the sides of your face.
2 Cheek is talking or behaving in a rude way towards someone.

cheeky adjective **cheekier, cheekiest**
If you are cheeky, you are rude to someone and do not show that you respect them.

cheer verb **cheers, cheering, cheered**
When you cheer, you shout to show that you are pleased.
Everyone started cheering again, as we slowly climbed to safety.—Narinder Dhami, Bindi Babes

cheerful adjective
If you are cheerful, you are happy.
I get to feel so fed up sometimes, and then Tracey comes in and she's always happy and cheerful and chatty.—Michael Morpurgo, Cool!

> **WORD FAMILY**
> • **cheerfully** He whistled cheerfully as he worked.

cheese noun (*plural* **cheeses**)
a type of food that is made from milk and has a strong, salty taste

chef noun (*plural* **chefs**) (*say* shef)
someone who cooks the food in a hotel or restaurant

chemical noun (*plural* **chemicals**)
A chemical is a substance that is found in nature or made in a science laboratory. Some chemicals are dangerous and can harm you.

chemist noun (*plural* **chemists**)
someone who makes or sells medicines

chemistry noun
the subject in which you study the substances that things are made of and how these substances behave, for example when they are mixed together

cheque noun (*plural* **cheques**)
a special piece of paper that a person can sign and use instead of money

cherry noun (*plural* **cherries**)
a small round red fruit with a stone in the middle

chess noun
a game in which two people move special pieces across a black and white board

chest noun (*plural* **chests**)
1 a big, strong box
2 Your chest is the front part of your body between your neck and your waist.

chew verb **chews, chewing, chewed**
When you chew food, you keep biting on it in your mouth before you swallow it.

chick noun (*plural* **chicks**)
a baby bird

chicken noun (*plural* **chickens**)
a bird that is kept on farms for its meat and eggs

chickenpox noun
an illness that gives you red itchy spots on your body

chief noun (*plural* **chiefs**)
a leader who is in charge of other people

child noun (*plural* **children**)
1 a young boy or girl
2 Someone's child is their son or daughter.

childhood noun (*plural* **childhoods**)
the time when you are a child

childish adjective
Someone who is childish behaves in a silly way, like a young child.

childminder noun (*plural* **childminders**)
a person who looks after children during the day while their parents are at work

chilli noun (*plural* **chillis**)
a small red or green pepper that has a very hot taste and is added to food to give it a strong, hot flavour

chilly adjective **chillier, chilliest**
If you are chilly, you are slightly cold. If the weather is chilly, it is quite cold.

chime verb **chimes, chiming, chimed**
When a clock or bell chimes, it makes a ringing sound.

chimney noun (*plural* **chimneys**)
a tall pipe that takes smoke away from a fire inside a building

a b c d e f g h i j k l m n o p q r s t u v w x y z

chimpanzee noun (*plural* **chimpanzees**)
A chimpanzee is an African ape. Chimpanzees look like large monkeys and have long arms and no tail.

chin noun (*plural* **chins**)
Your chin is the part at the bottom of your face, under your mouth.

chip noun (*plural* **chips**)
1 Chips are small pieces of fried potato.
2 If there is a chip in something, a small piece of it has broken off.
3 A computer chip is the small electronic part inside it that makes it work.

chip verb **chips, chipping, chipped**
If you chip something, you break a small piece off it. *The plates were old and chipped.*

chocolate noun (*plural* **chocolates**)
a sweet food that is made from cocoa and sugar

choice noun (*plural* **choices**)
1 When you make a choice, you choose something. *There were lots of bikes to choose from, and I think I made a good choice.*
2 If there is a choice, there are several different things to choose from. *There's a choice of vanilla, chocolate, or strawberry ice cream.*

choir noun (*plural* **choirs**) (*say* **kwire**)
a group of people who sing together

choke verb **chokes, choking, choked**
When you choke, you cannot breathe properly. *The room was full of smoke, which made me choke.*

choose verb **chooses, choosing, chose, chosen**
When you choose something, you decide that it is the one you want.

chop verb **chops, chopping, chopped**
When you chop something, you cut it with a knife or axe.

chop noun (*plural* **chops**)
a thick slice of pork or lamb with a bone still attached to it

chopsticks noun
a pair of thin sticks that you hold in one hand and use to eat food

chore noun (*plural* **chores**)
Chores are small jobs that you need to do every day around the house.

chorus noun (*plural* **choruses**) (ch- in this word sounds like k-)
The chorus is the part of a song or poem that you repeat after each verse.

chorus verb **choruses, chorusing, chorused** (ch- in this word sounds like k-)
To chorus a word means to all say it at the same time.
'Yes, Miss Hardbroom,' chorused the girls miserably.—Jill Murphy, The Worst Witch

chose, chosen verb *see* **choose**

Christian noun (*plural* **Christians**)
(**ch-** in this word sounds like **k-**)
someone who follows the Christian religion and believes in Jesus Christ

> **WORD FAMILY**
> • The religion that Christians follow is **Christianity**.

Christmas noun (*plural* **Christmases**)
(**ch-** in this word sounds like **k-**)
December 25th, when Christians celebrate the birth of Jesus Christ

chronological adjective (ch- in this word sounds like k-)
Chronological writing describes events in the same order as the events happened.

chrysalis noun (*plural* **chrysalises**)
(*say* **kriss**-a-liss)
the hard cover that a caterpillar makes round itself before it changes into a butterfly or moth

chuckle verb **chuckles, chuckling, chuckled**
When you chuckle, you laugh quietly to yourself.

chug verb **chugs, chugging, chugged**
When a train or lorry chugs along, it moves along slowly.

chunk noun (*plural* **chunks**)
A chunk of something is a large piece or lump of it.

church noun (*plural* **churches**)
a building where Christians pray and worship

cinema noun (*plural* **cinemas**)
a place where people go to watch films

cinquain noun (*plural* **cinquains**)
a poem with five lines, in which each line has a fixed number of syllables

circle noun (*plural* **circles**)
a round shape like a ring or a wheel

> **WORD FAMILY**
> • Something that is round like a circle is **circular**.

circle verb **circles, circling, circled**
To circle means to go round in a circle.
Birds circled around above us.

circuit noun (*plural* **circuits**) (*say* sir-**kit**)
A circuit is a path that electricity flows around. If there is a break in a circuit, the electricity cannot flow.

circumference noun (*plural* **circumferences**)
The circumference of a circle is how much it measures round its edge.

circumstances noun
The circumstances of an event are the things that are happening around it and might affect it. *The police need to know the circumstances surrounding the accident.*

circus noun (*plural* **circuses**)
a show in which clowns, acrobats, and sometimes animals perform in a large tent

citizen noun (*plural* **citizens**)
a person who lives in a town, city, or country

citizenship noun
the rights and responsibilities of being a citizen of a country *At school we have lessons in citizenship.*

cockerel noun (*plural* **cities**)
a big town

civilization noun (*plural* **civilizations**)
the way of life of a particular group of people *We're doing a project on the ancient Greek civilization.*

claim verb **claims, claiming, claimed**
  1 When you claim something, you say that you want it because it is yours.
  2 If you claim that something is true, you say that it is true.

clamber verb **clambers, clambering, clambered**
When you clamber over things, you climb over them.
We had to clamber down a steep hillside.—Jostein Gaarder, The Frog Castle

clang verb **clangs, clanging, clanged**
When something clangs, it makes a loud, ringing sound.

clash verb **clashes, clashing, clashed**
When things clash, they make a loud sound like the sound of two metal objects banging together.

clasp verb **clasps, clasping, clasped**
If you clasp something, you hold it tightly.

class noun (*plural* **classes**)
a group of children who learn things together

classify verb **classifies, classifying, classified**
When you classify things, you arrange them into different groups depending on what they are like.

classroom noun (*plural* **classrooms**)
a room where children have lessons

clatter verb **clatters, clattering, clattered**
When things clatter, they make a loud rattling or banging noise.

clause noun (*plural* **clauses**)
(*in grammar*) a group of words that contains a verb and makes up one part of a sentence

claw noun (*plural* **claws**)
An animal's claws are its sharp nails.
Crabs have huge, sharp claws.

a
b
c
d
e
f
g
h
i
j
k
l
m
n
o
p
q
r
s
t
u
v
w
x
y
z

coach noun
Clay is a type of sticky mud that becomes very hard when it dries out. Clay is used for making pots and pottery.

clean adjective **cleaner, cleanest**
Something that is clean has no dirt on it. *I changed into some clean clothes.*

clean verb **cleans, cleaning, cleaned**
To clean something means to take the dirt off it so that it is clean.

clear adjective **clearer, clearest**
1 If water or glass is clear, it is not dirty and you can see through it.
2 If a picture or sound is clear, you can see it or hear it easily. *Please speak in a nice, clear voice.*
3 If something is clear, you can understand it. *All this mess has to be tidied up. Is that clear?*
4 If a place is clear, there is nothing blocking it or getting in the way. *The road is clear now.*

> **WORD FAMILY**
> • **clearly** I could see his face quite clearly.

clear verb **clears, clearing, cleared**
To clear a place means to get rid of things that are in the way. *I helped clear the table after dinner.*

clench verb **clenches, clenching, clenched**
When you clench your teeth or fists, you close them tightly.

clever adjective **cleverer, cleverest**
Someone who is clever learns things quickly and easily.

> **WORD FAMILY**
> • **cleverly** The machine had been designed very cleverly.

click verb **clicks, clicking, clicked**
1 When something clicks, it makes a short sound like the sound a light switch makes.
2 (*in ICT*) When you click on something on a computer, you move the mark on the screen so that it is on that thing and then you press the button on the mouse.

cliff noun (*plural* **cliffs**)
a steep hill made of rock next to the sea

climate noun (*plural* **climates**)
The climate that a place has is the sort of weather that it has. *India has a very hot climate.*

climb verb **climbs, climbing, climbed**
1 To climb means to go upwards. *She climbed the stairs slowly.*
2 When you climb, you use your hands and feet to move over things. *They climbed over the rocks.*

cling verb **clings, clinging, clung**
When you cling to something, you hold on to it very tightly.

clinic noun (*plural* **clinics**)
a place where you can go to see a doctor or nurse

clip noun (*plural* **clips**)
a fastener that you use for keeping things in place *You need a paper clip to keep all those pieces of paper together.*

clip verb **clips, clipping, clipped**
To clip something means to cut it with scissors or shears.

clip art noun
pictures that you can copy from a CD-ROM or the Internet and use on your computer

cloak noun (*plural* **cloaks**)
a piece of clothing that you wrap around your shoulders and fasten round your neck

cloakroom noun (*plural* **cloakrooms**)
the room where you can hang your coat

clock noun (*plural* **clocks**)
a machine that shows you the time

clockwise adverb
If something moves clockwise, it moves round in a circle in the same direction as the hands of a clock. *Turn the handle clockwise.*

clockwork adjective
A clockwork toy is worked by a spring which you have to wind up.

close adjective **closer, closest** (*rhymes with* dose)
1 If you are close to something, you are near it. *Don't get too close to the fire.*
2 If you take a close look at something, or keep a close watch on something, you do it very carefully.

close verb **closes, closing, closed** (*rhymes with* doze)
1 To close something means to shut it. *Please can you close the door when you go out?*

2 When a shop closes, it is no longer open and people cannot go there. *The shop closes at half past five.*

closed adjective
If something is closed, it is not open.

cloth noun
material for making things like clothes and curtains

clothes, clothing noun
the things that you wear to cover your body

cloud noun (*plural* **clouds**)
Clouds are the large grey or white things that sometimes float high in the sky. Clouds are made of drops of water that often fall as rain.

> **WORD FAMILY**
> • **cloudy** It was a dull cloudy day.

clown noun (*plural* **clowns**)
someone in a circus who wears funny clothes and make-up and does silly things to make people laugh

club noun (*plural* **clubs**)
1 a group of people who get together because they are interested in doing the same thing
We've got a chess club at school.
2 a thick stick that is used as a weapon

clue noun (*plural* **clues**)
something that helps you to find the answer to a puzzle

clump noun (*plural* **clumps**)
A clump of trees or bushes is a group of them growing close together.

clumsy adjective **clumsier, clumsiest**
If you are clumsy, you are not careful and so are likely to knock things over or drop things.

clung verb *see* **cling**

clutch verb **clutches, clutching, clutched**
When you clutch something, you hold on to it very tightly.
I staggered to my bedroom and lay on my bed, clutching my tummy.—Jacqueline Wilson, Best Friends

clutter noun
a lot of things in an untidy mess

> **WORD FAMILY**
> • **cluttered** The house was cluttered with junk.

coach noun (*plural* **coaches**)
1 a bus that takes people on long journeys
2 The coaches on a train are the carriages where people sit.
3 someone who trains people in a sport

coal noun
Coal is a type of hard, black rock that people burn on fires. Coal is found under the ground.

coarse adjective **coarser, coarsest**
Something that is coarse is rough or hard.
His clothes were made of coarse cloth.

coast noun (*plural* **coasts**)
the land that is right next to the sea
We went to the coast last Sunday.

coat noun (*plural* **coats**)
1 a piece of clothing with sleeves that you wear on top of other clothes to keep warm
2 An animal's coat is the hair or fur that covers its body.
3 A coat of paint is a layer of paint.

cobra noun (*plural* **cobras**)
A cobra is a poisonous snake. A cobra can lift the front part of its body off the ground and spread the skin on its neck so that it looks like a hood.

a
b
c
d
e
f
g
h
i
j
k
l
m
n
o
p
q
r
s
t
u
v
w
x
y
z

cobweb noun (*plural* **cobwebs**)
a thin, sticky net that a spider spins to trap insects

cockerel noun (*plural* **cockerels**)
a male chicken

cocoa noun
Cocoa is a brown powder that tastes of chocolate. It is used for making hot chocolate drinks and also for making chocolate cakes and biscuits.

coconut noun (*plural* **coconuts**)
A coconut is a big, round, hard nut that grows on palm trees. It is brown and hairy on the outside and it has sweet, white flesh inside that you can eat.

cocoon noun (*plural* **cocoons**)
a covering that some insects spin from silky threads to protect themselves while they are changing into their adult form

cod noun (*plural* **cod**)
a sea fish that you can eat

code noun (*plural* **codes**)
a set of signs or letters that you use for sending messages secretly

coffee noun (*plural* **coffees**)
a hot drink that is made by adding hot water to roasted coffee beans that have been ground into a powder

coil verb **coils, coiling, coiled**
To coil something means to wind it round and round in the shape of a lot of circles. *The snake was coiled round a branch.*

coin noun (*plural* **coins**)
a piece of metal money

cold adjective **colder, coldest**
1 Something that is cold is not hot. *The sea was really cold!*
2 Someone who is cold is not friendly.

cold noun (*plural* **colds**)
an illness that makes you sneeze and gives you a runny nose

collage noun (*plural* **collages**) (*say* **coll**-arj)
a picture that you make by gluing small pieces of paper and material

collapse verb **collapses, collapsing, collapsed**
1 If something collapses, it falls down. *Several buildings collapsed after the earthquake.*
2 If someone collapses, they fall over because they are ill.

collar noun (*plural* **collars**)
1 The collar on a piece of clothing is the part that goes round your neck.
2 a thin band of leather or material that goes round an animal's neck

collect verb **collects, collecting, collected**
1 If you collect things, you get them and keep them together.
I've been collecting books for years, and I'm very proud of my collection.—Lemony Snicket, The Bad Beginning
2 When you collect someone, you go to a place and get them. *Mum collected us from school as usual.*

WORD FAMILY
• A set of things that someone has collected is a **collection**.

collective noun noun (*plural* **collective nouns**)
(*in grammar*) A collective noun is a noun that

a b c d e f g h i j k l m n o p q r s t u v w x y z

is the name of a group of things, people, or animals. *Flock* and *herd* are collective nouns.

college noun (*plural* **colleges**)
a place where you can go to study after you have left school

colloquial adjective
Colloquial language is language that you use when you are speaking or writing to your friends and family.

colon noun (*plural* **colons**)
a mark like this : that you use in writing

colossal adjective
Something that is colossal is extremely big. *Well, James, have you ever in your life seen such a marvellous colossal Centipede as me?*—Roald Dahl, James and the Giant Peach

colour noun (*plural* **colours**)
Red, green, blue, and yellow are different colours.

> **WORD FAMILY**
> • Something that has a lot of bright colours is **colourful**.

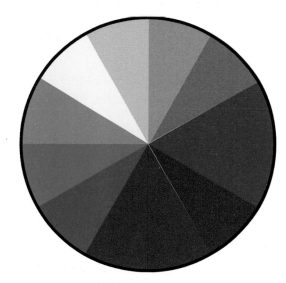

column noun (*plural* **columns**)
1 a thick stone post that supports or decorates a building
2 a line of numbers or words one below the other

comb noun (*plural* **combs**)
A comb is a strip of plastic or metal with a row of thin teeth along it. You use a comb to make your hair neat and tidy.

combine verb **combines, combining, combined**
When you combine things, you join or mix them together.

> **WORD FAMILY**
> • A **combination** is a set of things that have been joined or mixed together

combine harvester noun (*plural* **combine harvesters**)
a machine that cuts down corn and separates the seeds from the stalks

come verb **comes, coming, came, come**
1 To come to a place means to move towards it. *Do you want to come to my house after school?*
2 When something comes, it arrives in a place. *Has the letter come yet?*

comedian noun (*plural* **comedians**)
someone who entertains people by making them laugh

comedy noun (*plural* **comedies**)
a play, film, or TV programme that is funny and makes you laugh

comet noun (*plural* **comets**)
an object that moves around the sun and looks like a bright star with a tail

comfort verb **comforts, comforting, comforted**
When you comfort someone, you are kind to them and try to make them feel better when they are hurt or upset.

comfortable adjective
1 If something is comfortable, it is pleasant to use or to wear and does not hurt you at all. *The bed was large and very comfortable.*
2 If you are comfortable, you are relaxed and are not in any pain.

> **WORD FAMILY**
> • **comfortably** Is everyone sitting comfortably?

comic adjective
Something that is comic is funny and makes you laugh.

comic noun (*plural* **comics**)
1 a magazine for children that has stories told in pictures
2 a person who does funny things to make people laugh

a
b
c
d
e
f
g
h
i
j
k
l
m
n
o
p
q
r
s
t
u
v
w
x
y
z

comma noun (*plural* **commas**)
a mark like this , that you use in writing

command verb **commands, commanding, commanded**
If you command someone to do something, you tell them to do it.
'Get out of here immediately!' she commanded.—Jostein Gaarder, The Frog Castle

comment noun (*plural* **comments**)
something that you say about a person or thing *You shouldn't make rude comments about someone's appearance.*

commentary noun (*plural* **commentaries**)
a description of something that is happening, for example a race or game

commit verb **commits, committing, committed**
To commit a crime means to do it. *We are determined to find out who committed this terrible crime.*

committee noun (*plural* **committees**)
a group of people who meet to talk about things and decide what to do

common adjective **commoner, commonest**
Something that is common is normal and ordinary.

common noun noun (*plural* **common nouns**)
(*in grammar*) A common noun is a noun that is the name of a thing. For example, *hat*, *dog*, and *teacher* are all common nouns.

common sense noun
If you have common sense, you are usually sensible and make the right decisions about what to do and how to behave.

commotion noun
When there is a commotion, a lot of people are making a noise and moving about all at once.

communicate verb **communicates, communicating, communicated**
When people communicate, they talk or write to each other.

> **WORD FAMILY**
> • **Communication** happens when people talk or write to each other.

community noun (*plural* **communities**)
all the people who live in a place

compact disc noun (*plural* **compact discs**)
a CD

companion noun (*plural* **companions**)
a friend who is with you

company noun (*plural* **companies**)
1 A company is a group of people who make and sell things, or do things together.
2 If you have company, you are not alone.

comparative adjective
(*in grammar*) The comparative form of an adjective is the part that means 'more', for example *bigger* is the comparative form of *big*.

compare verb **compares, comparing, compared**
When you compare things, you try to see how they are the same and how they are different.

compass noun
(*plural* **compasses**)
1 an instrument with a needle that always points north
2 A compass is an instrument that you use for drawing circles. It is also called a **pair of compasses**.

compatible adjective
Things that are compatible will work well together.

competition noun (*plural* **competitions**)
a game or race that people take part in and try to win

complain verb **complains, complaining, complained**
If you complain, you say that you are not happy about something or do not like something. *'You didn't wait for me,' she complained.*

> **WORD FAMILY**
> • **complaint** I want to make a complaint.

complete adjective
1 Something that is complete has all its parts and has nothing missing. *Is the jigsaw complete, or are there some bits missing?*

a b c d e f g h i j k l m n o p q r s t u v w x y z

2 If something is complete, it is finished. *After three days the work was complete.*

3 Complete means in every way. *Winning the game was a complete surprise.*

> 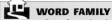 **WORD FAMILY**
> • **completely** The building was completely destroyed.

complicated adjective
Something that is complicated is difficult to understand or do.
No one had ever explained to us exactly who all our relations were because it was far too complicated.—Narinder Dhami, Bindi Babes

compliment noun (*plural* **compliments**)
If someone gives you a compliment, they say something nice about you.

composer noun (*plural* **composers**)
someone who writes music

> 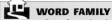 **WORD FAMILY**
> • To **compose** music means to write it.

compound noun (*plural* **compounds**)
(*in grammar*) a word that is made up of two words joined together. *Bedroom* and *blackboard* are compounds.

comprehension noun (*plural* **comprehensions**)
an exercise in which you read or listen to a text and then answer questions to check that you have understood it

compulsory adjective
If something is compulsory, you have to do it.

computer noun (*plural* **computers**)
A computer is a machine which can store information and do calculations. You can also play games on computers.

concave adjective
Something that is concave curves inwards in the shape of a bowl.

concave

conceal verb **conceals, concealing, concealed**
(*say* kon-**seel**)
To conceal something means to hide it.

concentrate verb **concentrates, concentrating, concentrated**
When you concentrate, you think hard about the thing you are doing. *I'm trying to concentrate on my work!*

concern verb **concerns, concerning, concerned**
If something concerns you, it is important to you and you should be interested in it. If something does not concern you, it is nothing to do with you.

concerned adjective
If you are concerned about something, you are worried about it.

concert noun (*plural* **concerts**)
a show in which people play music for other people to listen to *We're giving a concert at the end of this term.*

conclude verb **concludes, concluding, concluded**
If you conclude that something is true, you decide that it is true after you have thought about everything carefully.

> 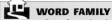 **WORD FAMILY**
> • **conclusion** I came to the conclusion that Indira must have been lying to me.

concrete noun
a mixture of cement and sand used for making buildings and paths

condition noun (*plural* **conditions**)
1 The condition something is in is how new or clean it is, and how well it works. If it is in good condition, it looks new and works properly. If it is in bad condition, it is old or dirty, or does not work properly.
2 The conditions in which a plant or animal lives are everything in the world around it, for example how hot or cold it is, or how much rain there is. *Very few plants will grown in these dry conditions.*
3 A condition is something you must do before you can do or have something else. *You can go to the fair on condition that you're home by eight o'clock.*

conduct verb **conducts, conducting, conducted**
1 When you conduct music, you stand in front of the musicians and control the way they play.
2 (*in science*) If something conducts electricity or heat, it allows it to pass through easily.

conductor noun (*plural* **conductors**)
1 someone who stands in front of an orchestra and controls the way the musicians play
2 something that conducts electricity or heat

cone noun (*plural* **cones**)
1 a shape that is round at one end and goes in to a point at the other end
2 a hard, brown fruit that grows on pine trees and fir trees

confectionery noun
sweets and chocolates

confess verb **confesses, confessing, confessed**
If you confess, you admit that you have done something wrong.

> **WORD FAMILY**
> • **confession** The prisoner made a full confession.

confident adjective
If you are confident, you are not nervous or afraid.
Patty took a deep breath. She felt confident that her machine would work, but she could not be absolutely sure.—Alexander McCall Smith, The Banana Machine

> **WORD FAMILY**
> • **confidence** You should have more confidence in yourself.

conflict noun (*plural* **conflicts**)
an argument or a fight

confuse verb **confuses, confusing, confused**
1 If something confuses you, you cannot understand it.
2 If you confuse things, you get them muddled up in your mind.

> **WORD FAMILY**
> • **confused** I felt confused and upset.
> • **confusing** The map was rather confusing.
> • **confusion** If we try to change our plans now, it will only lead to confusion.

congratulate verb **congratulates, congratulating, congratulated**
If you congratulate someone, you tell them that you are pleased that something special has happened to them.
We all congratulated Salim on winning the race.

> **WORD FAMILY**
> • **congratulations** Congratulations! You've won!

conjunction noun (*plural* **conjunctions**)
(*in grammar*) a word that you use to join two parts of a sentence together. *And* and *but* are conjunctions.

conjuror noun (*plural* **conjurors**)
someone who entertains people by doing tricks that look like magic

connect verb **connects, connecting, connected**
To connect things means to join them together. *You need to connect the printer to your computer.*

> **WORD FAMILY**
> • **connection** Has your computer got an internet connection?

connective noun (*plural* **connectives**)
(*in grammar*) a word or phrase that you use to join different sentences or parts of sentences. *However*, *and*, and *meanwhile* are connectives.

conquer verb **conquers, conquering, conquered**
To conquer people means to beat them in a battle or war.

conscience noun (*say* **kon**-shuns)
Your conscience is the feeling inside you that tells you what is right and wrong. *I had a guilty conscience about being so mean to Sara.*

conscious adjective (*say* **kon**-shuss)
When you are conscious, you are awake and able to understand what is happening around you. *He slowly became conscious again after the operation.*

consequence noun (*plural* **consequences**)
something that happens as a result of something else

conservation noun
taking good care of the world's air, water, plants, and animals *Using less paper will help with conservation of the rainforest.*

consider verb **considers, considering, considered**
When you consider something, you think about it carefully.

considerate adjective
If you are considerate, you think about other people and are kind and thoughtful in the way you behave.

consonant noun (plural **consonants**)
Consonants are all the letters of the alphabet except a, e, i, o, and u, which are vowels.

constant adjective
Something that is constant goes on all the time.

> **WORD FAMILY**
> • **constantly** He moans constantly!

constellation noun (plural **constellations**)
a group of stars

construct verb **constructs, constructing, constructed**
To construct something means to build it.

consume verb **consumes, consuming, consumed**
1 to eat or drink something All the food was quickly consumed.
2 to use something We must reduce the amount of energy that we consume.

contain verb **contains, containing, contained**
To contain something means to have it inside. His next present also contained sweets – a large box of Chocolate Frogs from Hermione.—J. K. Rowling, Harry Potter and the Philosopher's Stone

container noun (plural **containers**)
A container is anything that you can put other things into. Buckets, cups, bags, boxes, and jars are all containers.

contents noun
The contents of something are the things that are inside it.

contest noun (plural **contests**)
a competition

continent noun (plural **continents**)
A continent is one of the seven very large areas of land in the world. Asia, Europe, and Africa are all continents.

continue verb **continues, continuing, continued**
If you continue doing something, you go on doing it. Miss Hardcastle opened the window and then continued talking.

continuous adjective
Something that is continuous goes on happening and never stops. The factory machines made a continuous humming noise.

> **WORD FAMILY**
> • **continuously** My aunt talked continuously for two hours!

contract verb **contracts, contracting, contracted** (say kon-**tract**)
When a muscle contracts, it becomes shorter and tighter.

contraction noun (plural **contractions**)
A contraction is a short form of one or more words. Haven't is a contraction of have not.

contradict verb **contradicts, contradicting, contradicted**
If you contradict someone, you say that what they have said is wrong.

contribute verb **contributes, contributing, contributed**
If you contribute money, you give it to help pay for something.

> **WORD FAMILY**
> • **contribution** Would you like to make a contribution to our school fund?

a
b
c
d
e
f
g
h
i
j
k
l
m
n
o
p
q
r
s
t
u
v
w
x
y
z

control noun (*plural* **controls**)
The controls are the switches and buttons that you use to make a machine work.

control verb **controls, controlling, controlled**
When you control something, you make it do what you want it to do. *You use these levers to control the model aeroplane in the air.*

convenient adjective
If something is convenient, you can reach it and use it easily.

conversation noun (*plural* **conversations**)
When people have a conversation, they talk to each other.

convex adjective
Something that is convex curves outwards in the shape of a ball.

convex

convince verb **convinces, convincing, convinced**
If you convince someone about something, you make them believe it.

cook verb **cooks, cooking, cooked**
When you cook food, you prepare it and heat it so that it is ready to eat.

WORD FAMILY
• A **cooker** is a machine on which you cook food. **Cookery** is preparing food.

cook noun (*plural* **cooks**)
someone whose job is to cook

cool adjective **cooler, coolest**
Something that is cool is slightly cold. *I'd love a cool drink.*

coordinates noun
two numbers or letters which tell you exactly where a point is on a grid or map

cope verb **copes, coping, coped**
If you can cope with something, you can manage to do it.

copper noun
a shiny brown metal

copy verb **copies, copying, copied**
1 When you copy something, you write it down or draw it in the same way as it has already been written or drawn. *She copied the poem in her best writing.*
2 (*in ICT*) When you copy something from one file to another file on a computer, you move it to the second file but do not delete it from the first file.
3 When you copy someone, you do exactly the same as them.

copy noun (*plural* **copies**)
something that is made to look exactly like something else

coral noun
a type of rock that is made in the sea from the bodies of tiny creatures

cord noun (*plural* **cords**)
a thin rope

core noun (*plural* **cores**)
The core of an apple or pear is the hard part in the middle of it.

cork noun (*plural* **corks**)
something that is pushed into the top of a bottle of wine to close it

corn noun
the seeds of plants such as wheat, which we use as food

a b c d e f g h i j k l m n o p q r s t u v w x y z

corner noun (*plural* **corners**)
1 the place where two edges meet *He was sitting by himself in the corner of the room.*
2 the place where two streets meet

correct adjective
Something that is correct is right and has no mistakes. *All my answers were correct.*

> 🏠 **WORD FAMILY**
> • **correctly** You answered all the questions correctly.

correct verb **corrects, correcting, corrected**
When you correct something, you find the mistakes in it and put them right.

> 🏠 **WORD FAMILY**
> • **correction** I had to make a few corrections to my work.

corridor noun (*plural* **corridors**)
a passage in a building with rooms leading off it

cost verb **costs, costing, cost**
The amount that something costs is the amount you have to pay to buy it. *How much did your new bike cost?*

costume noun (*plural* **costumes**)
clothes that you wear for acting in a play

cosy adjective **cosier, cosiest**
A cosy place is warm and comfortable.

cot noun (*plural* **cots**)
a bed with sides for a baby

cottage noun (*plural* **cottages**)
a small house in the country

cotton noun
1 thread that you use for sewing
2 a type of cloth that is used for making clothes

cough verb **coughs, coughing, coughed** (*rhymes with* off)
When you cough, you make a rough sound in your throat and push air out through your mouth.

could verb *see* **can** verb

council noun (*plural* **councils**)
a group of people who are chosen to discuss things and make decisions for everyone
Do you want to be on the school council?

councillor noun (*plural* **councillors**)
someone who is a member of a council

count verb **counts, counting, counted**
1 When you count things, you use numbers to say how many there are. *I counted the books.*
2 When you count, you say numbers in order. *Can you count to 1000?*

counter noun (*plural* **counters**)
1 the table where you pay for things in a shop
2 a small, round piece of plastic that you use for playing some games

country noun (*plural* **countries**)
1 A country is a land with its own people and laws. England, Australia, and China are all countries.
2 The country is land that is not in a town. *Do you live in the town or in the country?*

couple noun (*plural* **couples**)
1 two people who are married or going out with each other
2 A couple of things means two of them.

couplet noun (*plural* **couplets**)
two lines in a poem which are next to each other and rhyme with each other or have the same rhythm

coupon noun (*plural* **coupons**)
a special piece of paper which you can use to pay for something

courage noun
the feeling you have when you are not afraid, and you dare to do something difficult or dangerous *Somehow I found the courage to carry on fighting.*

> 🏠 **WORD FAMILY**
> • **courageous** That was a very courageous thing to do.

course noun (*plural* **courses**)
1 The course of an aeroplane or a ship is the direction it travels in.
2 a set of lessons
3 a piece of ground where people play golf or run races

a b c d e f g h i j k l m n o p q r s t u v w x y z

court noun (*plural* **courts**)

   1 a piece of ground that is marked out so that people can play a game such as netball or tennis

   2 a building where people decide whether someone is guilty of committing a crime

   3 The court of a king or queen is the place where they live and rule the country.

cousin noun (*plural* **cousins**)

   Your cousin is a child of your aunt or uncle.

cover verb **covers, covering, covered**

   When you cover something, you put something else over it. *She covered him with a blanket.*

cover noun (*plural* **covers**)

   a piece of material which goes over or round something

cow noun (*plural* **cows**)

   a large animal that is kept on farms for its milk and meat

coward noun (*plural* **cowards**)

   someone who is afraid when they ought to be brave

cowboy noun (*plural* **cowboys**)

   a man who looks after the cattle on large farms in America

crab noun (*plural* **crabs**)

   A crab is an animal with a hard shell on its back, which lives in the sea. Crabs have ten legs and large, powerful claws for catching food.

crack noun (*plural* **cracks**)

   1 a thin line on something where it has nearly broken *There's a crack in this mirror.*

   2 a sudden loud noise *We heard a crack of thunder.*

crack verb **cracks, cracking, cracked**

   1 When you crack something, you break it so that it has lines on it but does not break into pieces. *Be careful not to crack the glass.*

   2 When something cracks, it makes a sharp noise like the noise a dry twig makes when you break it.

cradle noun (*plural* **cradles**)

   a bed with sides for a young baby

crafty adjective **craftier, craftiest**

   Someone who is crafty is clever and very good at getting what they want.

cramp noun

   If you get cramp, you get a pain because one of your muscles has suddenly become stiff and tight.

crane noun (*plural* **cranes**)

   a large machine for lifting heavy things

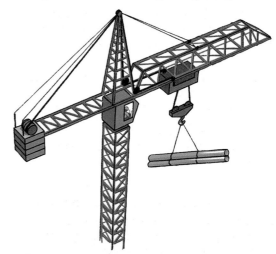

crash noun (*plural* **crashes**)

   1 an accident in which a car, lorry, train, or plane hits something

   2 the noise of something falling or crashing *I heard a loud crash as the tree fell.*

crash verb **crashes, crashing, crashed**

   1 If something crashes, it bumps into something else and makes a loud noise.

   2 (*in ICT*) If a computer crashes, it stops working suddenly.

a b c d e f g h i j k l m n o p q r s t u v w x y z

crate noun (*plural* **crates**)
a large box

crawl verb **crawls, crawling, crawled**
1 When you crawl, you move along on your hands and knees. *We crawled through the tunnel.*
2 When a car or train crawls along, it moves very slowly.

crayon noun (*plural* **crayons**)
a coloured pencil

crazy adjective **crazier, craziest**
Someone who is crazy does very silly or strange things. Something that is crazy is very silly or strange.

creak verb **creaks, creaking, creaked**
If something creaks, it makes a rough, squeaking noise.
The house creaks in the wind, like a ship at sea.—Michael Morpurgo, The Wreck of the Zanzibar

cream noun
Cream is a thick white liquid that is taken from milk. You eat cream with fruit and other sweet foods.

crease verb **creases, creasing, creased**
When you crease something, you make untidy lines in it by pressing on it. *Don't sit on my jacket—you'll crease it.*

create verb **creates, creating, created** (*say* kree-**ate**)
When you create something new, you make it.

> **WORD FAMILY**
> • **creation** We read some stories about the creation of the world.

creature noun (*plural* **creatures**)
any animal *Bats are fascinating creatures.*

creep verb **creeps, creeping, crept**
1 When you creep, you move along with your body very close to the ground.
Mr Fox crept up the dark tunnel to the mouth of his hole.—Roald Dahl, Fantastic Mr Fox
2 When you creep, you walk very quietly and secretly. *We crept away and nobody saw us.*

creep noun (*plural* **creeps**)
1 a nasty person
2 If something gives you the creeps, it frightens you.

> **WORD FAMILY**
> • **creepy** The old house was very creepy.

crept verb *see* **creep** verb

crescent noun (*plural* **crescents**)
a curved shape, like the shape of a new moon

crew noun (*plural* **crews**)
a group of people who work together on a boat or aeroplane

cricket noun
1 a game in which two teams hit a ball with a bat and try to score runs by running between two wickets
2 an insect that makes a shrill chirping sound

cried verb *see* **cry**

crime noun (*plural* **crimes**)
something bad that a person does, which is against the law

criminal noun (*plural* **criminals**)
someone who has done something bad that is against the law

crisp adjective **crisper, crispest**
1 Food that is crisp is dry and breaks easily.
I would love a nice, crisp piece of toast.
2 Fruit that is crisp is firm and fresh.

crisp noun (*plural* **crisps**)
Crisps are thin, crisp slices of fried potato that you eat as a snack.

criticize verb **criticizes, criticizing, criticized** (*say* **krit**-iss-ize)
If you criticize someone, you say that they have done something wrong.

> **WORD FAMILY**
> • **criticism** I have one small criticism of your idea.

croak verb **croaks, croaking, croaked**
When a frog croaks, it makes a loud, rough sound.

crocodile noun (*plural* **crocodiles**)
A crocodile is a large animal that lives in rivers in some hot countries. Crocodiles are reptiles, and have short legs, a long body, and sharp teeth.

a b c d e f g h i j k l m n o p q r s t u v w x y z

a
b
c
d
e
f
g
h
i
j
k
l
m
n
o
p
q
r
s
t
u
v
w
x
y
z

crook noun (*plural* **crooks**)
1 someone who steals things
2 a shepherd's stick with a curved top

crooked adjective
Something that is crooked is not straight.

crop noun (*plural* **crops**)
a type of plant which farmers grow as food

cross adjective **crosser, crossest**
If you are cross, you are angry or in a bad temper.

> **WORD FAMILY**
> • **crossly** 'Leave me alone,' she said crossly.

cross noun (*plural* **crosses**)
a mark like x or +

cross verb **crosses, crossing, crossed**
1 When you cross a road or a river, you go across it. *How are we going to cross the river with no boat?*
2 When you cross your arms or legs, you put one over the other.
3 When you cross out writing, you draw a line through it.

crossing noun (*plural* **crossings**)
a place where you can cross the road safely

crossword noun (*plural* **crosswords**)
a puzzle in which you answer clues and write down words which cross over each other in a square

crouch verb **crouches, crouching, crouched**
When you crouch, you bend down so that you are very close to the ground.
By the time we reached the house Streaker was crouching down on the front doorstep.—Jeremy Strong, The Hundred-Mile-An-Hour Dog

crow noun (*plural* **crows**)
a big, black bird

crowd noun (*plural* **crowds**)
a large number of people *There were crowds of people in the streets.*

> **WORD FAMILY**
> • **crowded** The fair was very crowded.

crown noun (*plural* **crowns**)
a special hat made of silver or gold which a king or queen wears

cruel adjective **crueller, cruellest**
If you are cruel to someone, you hurt them or are very unkind to them.

> **WORD FAMILY**
> • **cruelty** I hate cruelty to animals.

crumb noun (*plural* **crumbs**)
Crumbs are very small pieces of bread or cake.

crumble verb **crumbles, crumbling, crumbled**
When something crumbles, it breaks into a lot of small pieces. *The old buildings were beginning to crumble.*

crumple verb **crumples, crumpling, crumpled**
When you crumple something, you make it very creased. *My clothes were all crumpled in the bottom of my bag.*

crunch verb **crunches, crunching, crunched**
When you crunch food, you eat it by breaking it noisily with your teeth.

crush verb **crushes, crushing, crushed**
When you crush something, you squash it by pressing it hard. *Mind you don't crush the flowers.*

crust noun (*plural* **crusts**)
The hard part around the outside of bread.

cry verb **cries, crying, cried**
1 When you cry, tears come out of your eyes.
2 When you cry, you shout something. *'Look out!' she cried.*

crystal noun (*plural* **crystals**)
1 Crystal is a type of mineral that is found in rock. It is hard and clear like glass.
2 a small, hard, shiny piece of something *Crystals of ice had formed on the window.*

cub noun (*plural* **cubs**)
a young bear, lion, tiger, fox, or wolf

cube noun (*plural* **cubes**)
A cube is a square shape like the shape of a dice. Cubes have six square sides that are all the same size.

cuckoo noun (*plural* **cuckoos**)
a bird that lays its eggs in other birds' nests

cucumber noun (*plural* **cucumbers**)
a long, green vegetable that you eat
raw in salads

cuddle verb **cuddles, cuddling, cuddled**
When you cuddle someone, you put your
arms round them to show that you love them.

culture noun (*plural* **cultures**)
all the traditions and customs of a group of
people *We are studying Indian culture this
term.*

cunning adjective
Someone who is cunning is clever and very
good at getting what they want.
*Let's just say I've a cunning plan in my
head that could make things right for you
Jackie, and for me too with a little bit of
luck.*—Michael Morpurgo, Mr Skip

cup noun (*plural* **cups**)
1 a container with a handle, which you use for
drinking from
2 a silver cup that is given as a prize to the
winner of a competition

cupboard noun (*plural* **cupboards**)
a piece of furniture with doors on the front,
which you use for keeping things in

cure verb **cures, curing, cured**
To cure someone means to make them better
after they have been ill.

curious adjective (*say* **kure**-ee-uss)
1 If you are curious about something, you want
to know more about it.
2 Something that is curious is strange or unusual.

> **WORD FAMILY**
> • **curiosity** My curiosity got the better of me, and
> I opened the door.

curl noun (*plural* **curls**)
a piece of hair that is curved, not straight

> **WORD FAMILY**
> • **curly** She's got lovely curly hair.

currant noun (*plural* **currants**)
a small dried grape

currency noun (*plural* **currencies**)
A country's currency is the type of coins and
banknotes that it uses.

current noun (*plural* **currents**)
A current of water, air, or electricity is an
amount of it that is moving in one direction.
*The current is very strong in this part of
the river.*

curriculum noun (*plural* **curriculums** *or*
curricula)
all the subjects that you study at school

curry noun (*plural* **curries**)
meat or vegetables in a spicy sauce

curse noun (*plural* **curses**)
If someone puts a curse on a person, they
say magic words asking for the person to be
hurt or killed.

cursor noun (*plural* **cursors**)
the mark which shows your position on a
computer screen *Move the cursor to the
end of the line.*

curtain noun (*plural* **curtains**)
a piece of cloth that you can pull in front of
a window to cover it

curve noun (*plural* **curves**)
a line that is bent smoothly like the letter C

> **WORD FAMILY**
> • **curved** Draw a curved line.

cushion noun (*plural* **cushions**)
a soft object that you put on a chair to sit on
or lean against

custom noun (*plural* **customs**)
If something is a custom, you do it because
people have done it in that way for a long
time. *Each country has its own customs.*

customer noun (*plural* **customers**)
someone who buys something in a shop

cut verb **cuts, cutting, cut**
1 If you cut yourself, you
break a part of your skin
on something sharp. *He fell
over and cut his knee.*
2 When you cut something,
you use a knife or scissors
to break it into pieces.
3 (*in ICT*) When you cut
something on a computer,
you delete it.

cut noun (*plural* **cuts**)
If you have a cut on
your skin, your skin
has been broken by
something sharp.

a
b
c
d
e
f
g
h
i
j
k
l
m
n
o
p
q
r
s
t
u
v
w
x
y
z

cut and paste verb **cuts and pastes, cutting and pasting, cut and pasted**
(*in ICT*) When you cut and paste on a computer, you delete something from one file and add it to another file.

cute adjective **cuter, cutest**
If something is cute, it is pretty or nice to look at.

cutlery noun
knives, forks, and spoons

cycle verb **cycles, cycling, cycled** (*say* **sye**-kul)
When you cycle, you ride a bicycle.

> 🏠 **WORD FAMILY**
> • A **cyclist** is someone who cycles.

cylinder noun (*plural* **cylinders**)
(*say* **sil**-in-der)
a shape that looks like a tube with flat, round ends

cymbals noun (*say* **sim**-bals)
two round pieces of metal that you bang together when you are playing music

Dd

dad, daddy noun (*plural* **dads, daddies**)
Your dad is your father.

daffodil noun (*plural* **daffodils**)
a yellow flower that grows in the spring

dagger noun (*plural* **daggers**)
a short knife with two sharp edges, which people use as a weapon

daily adverb
If something happens daily, it happens every day.

dairy noun (*plural* **dairies**)
a place where people make cheese, butter, and yogurt from milk

daisy noun (*plural* **daisies**)
a small flower with white petals and a yellow centre

dam noun (*plural* **dams**)
a wall that is built across a river to hold water back

damage verb **damages, damaging, damaged**
To damage something means to break it or spoil it. *Mind you don't damage any of the paintings.*

damp adjective **damper, dampest**
Something that is damp is slightly wet. *Here he had to stay indoors except in the middle of the day, when he shivered outside in the damp playground.—Mary Hoffman, The Colour of Home*

dance verb **dances, dancing, danced**
When you dance, you move about in time to music.

> **WORD FAMILY**
> • A **dancer** is someone who dances.

dance noun (*plural* **dances**)
1 When you do a dance, you move about in time to music.
2 A dance is a party where people dance.

danger noun (*plural* **dangers**)
When there is danger, there is the chance that something horrible might happen and someone might get hurt.

dangerous adjective
Something that is dangerous might kill or hurt you. *Parachuting is quite a dangerous sport.*

dare verb **dares, daring, dared**
1 If you dare to do something, you are brave enough to do it.
2 If you dare someone to do something, you tell them to do it to show how brave they are. *I dare you to climb that tree.*

> **WORD FAMILY**
> • **daring** Sara is quite a daring girl.

dark adjective **darker, darkest**
1 If a place is dark, there is no light in it. *The streets outside were very dark.*
2 Something that is dark is nearly black in colour.

> **WORD FAMILY**
> • **darkness** I couldn't see anything in the darkness outside.

dart noun (*plural* **darts**)
a small arrow that you throw at a board in a game called **darts**

dart verb **darts, darting, darted**
To dart means to move quickly and suddenly. *He darted behind a bush.*

dash verb **dashes, dashing, dashed**
To dash means to run or move very quickly. *I dashed into the house.*

dash noun (*plural* **dashes**)
1 When you make a dash, you run or move quickly. *We made a dash for the door.*
2 a long mark like this – that you use in writing

data noun (*say* **day**-ta)
information about something

database noun (*plural* **databases**)
a store of information that is kept on a computer

date noun (*plural* **dates**)
1 If you say what the date is, you say what day of the month and what year it is. *What's the date today?*
2 If you have a date with someone, you have arranged to go out with them.
3 a sweet brown fruit that grows on a palm tree

daughter noun (*plural* **daughters**)
Someone's daughter is their female child.

dawdle verb **dawdles, dawdling, dawdled**
If you dawdle, you walk very slowly. *Stop dawdling! We're late!*

dawn noun
the time of day when the sun rises and it becomes light

day noun (*plural* **days**)
1 a period of twenty-four hours *We'll be leaving in five days.*
2 the part of the day when it is light *The days are shorter in winter, and the nights are longer.*

dazzle verb **dazzles, dazzling, dazzled**
If a bright light dazzles you, you cannot see anything because it is shining in your eyes.

dead adjective
Someone who is dead is not alive.

deaf adjective **deafer, deafest**
Someone who is deaf cannot hear.

a
b
c
d
e
f
g
h
i
j
k
l
m
n
o
p
q
r
s
t
u
v
w
x
y
z

deal verb **deals, dealing, dealt**
1 When you deal out cards, you give them to each person at the beginning of a game.
2 When you deal with something, you do the work that needs to be done on it.

dear adjective **dearer, dearest**
1 If someone is dear to you, you love them a lot.
2 Something you write before someone's name at the start of a letter.
3 Something that is dear costs a lot of money. *I couldn't have the really cool trainers because my mum said they were too dear.*

death noun (*plural* **deaths**)
Death is the time when someone dies.

debate noun (*plural* **debates**)
a discussion about something in which people put forward arguments in favour of something and against it

decay verb **decays, decaying, decayed**
When something decays, it goes bad and rots.

deceive verb **deceives, deceiving, deceived**
(*say* de-seeve)
When you deceive someone, you make them believe something that is not true.

December noun
the twelfth and last month of the year

decide verb **decides, deciding, decided**
When you decide to do something, you choose to do it.
Eddie sighed and decided to go in search of his parents. —Philip Ardagh, Dreadful Acts

decimal adjective
A decimal system counts in tens.

decimal noun (*plural* **decimals**)
(*in mathematics*) a number that has tenths shown as numbers after a dot, for example 2·5

decision noun (*plural* **decisions**)
When you make a decision, you decide what you are going to do.

deck noun (*plural* **decks**)
a floor in a ship or bus

declare verb **declares, declaring, declared**
When you declare something, you say it out loud so that everyone can hear it.

decorate verb **decorates, decorating, decorated**
1 When you decorate something, you make it look nice or pretty. *We decorated the whole house with coloured lights.*
2 When you decorate a room, you put paint or wallpaper on the walls.

WORD FAMILY
• **decorations** We put up decorations all over the house.

decrease verb **decreases, decreasing, decreased**
When something decreases, it becomes less. *The temperature decreases at night.*

deep adjective **deeper, deepest**
Something that is deep goes down a long way from the top. *Be careful, the water's quite deep.*

deer noun (*plural* **deer**)
A deer is an animal that eats grass and can run fast. Male deer have long horns called antlers.

defeat verb **defeats, defeating, defeated**
If you defeat someone, you beat them in a game or battle.

defend verb **defends, defending, defended**
To defend a place means to keep it safe and stop people from attacking it.

definite adjective
Something that is definite is certain. *Is it definite that you can come?*

WORD FAMILY
• **definitely** I'll definitely be there tomorrow.

a b c d e f g h i j k l m n o p q r s t u v w x y z

definition noun (*plural* **definitions**)
a sentence that explains what a word means

degree noun (*plural* **degrees**)
We can measure how hot or cold something is in degrees. You can write the number of degrees using the sign °. *The temperature is 22°C today.*

delay verb **delays, delaying, delayed**
1 If you are delayed, something makes you late. *The train was delayed by heavy snow.*
2 If you delay something, you put off doing it until later. *We'll delay giving the prizes until everyone is here.*

delete verb **deletes, deleting, deleted**
When you delete something that you have written, you rub it out or remove it.

deliberate adjective
If something is deliberate, someone has done it on purpose.

WORD FAMILY
• **deliberately** He pushed me over deliberately!

delicate adjective
Something that is delicate will break easily.

delicious adjective (*say* **de**-lish-uss)
Something that is delicious tastes very nice. *Next, he took them to a tea-shop, where they had some delicious cakes.*—Jean de Brunhoff, The Story of Babar

delight verb **delights, delighting, delighted**
If something delights you, it makes you feel very happy. *My mum said I could have a day off school, which delighted me.*

WORD FAMILY
• **delighted** She was delighted with her presents.

deliver verb **delivers, delivering, delivered**
When you deliver something, you take it to someone's house.

demand verb **demands, demanding, demanded**
If you demand something, you ask for it very strongly. *He demanded his money back.*

democratic adjective
In a democratic system everyone has the right to vote to choose things.

WORD FAMILY
• A **democracy** is a country that has a democratic system of government.

demonstrate verb **demonstrates, demonstrating, demonstrated**
If you demonstrate something to someone, you show them how to do it. *I will now demonstrate how the machine works.*

demonstration noun
(*plural* **demonstrations**)
1 If you give someone a demonstration of something, you show them how to do it.
2 When there is a demonstration, a lot of people march through the streets to show that they are angry about something.

den noun (*plural* **dens**)
1 a place where a wild animal lives
2 a secret place where you can hide

dense adjective **denser, densest**
Something that is dense is thick. *We couldn't see because of the dense fog.*

dent verb **dents, denting, dented**
If you dent something, you bang it and make a hollow in it.

dentist noun
(*plural* **dentists**)
someone whose job is to check and look after people's teeth

deny verb
denies, denying, denied
If you deny something, you say that it is not true. *She denied breaking the cup.*

depart verb **departs, departing, departed**
To depart means to leave a place. *The train departs from Platform 1.*

depend verb **depends, depending, depended**
If you depend on someone, you need them to help you. *The young lions depend on their mother for food.*

depress verb **depresses, depressing, depressed**
If something depresses you, it makes you feel unhappy.

WORD FAMILY
• **depressed** I was feeling rather depressed.

a b c **d** e f g h i j k l m n o p q r s t u v w x y z

depth noun (*plural* **depths**)
The depth of something is how deep it is. *We measured the depth of each hole.*

deputy noun (*plural* **deputies**)
someone who helps a person in their job and does it for them when they are not there

descend verb **descends, descending, descended** (*say* de-**send**)
To descend means to go down.

describe verb **describes, describing, described**
When you describe something, you talk about it and say what it is like.

> **WORD FAMILY**
> • **description** Can you give me a description of the thief?

descriptive adjective
Descriptive language describes what someone or something is like.

desert noun (*plural* **deserts**)
dry land where very few plants can grow

deserted adjective
A place that is deserted is empty, with no one in it.

deserve verb **deserves, deserving, deserved**
If you deserve a punishment or reward, you should get it. *He was so brave he deserves a medal.*

design verb **designs, designing, designed**
When you design something, you plan it and draw a picture of it.

> **WORD FAMILY**
> • A **designer** is someone who designs things.

desk noun (*plural* **desks**)
a table where you can read, write, and keep books

desktop noun (*plural* **desktops**)
a computer that you keep on your desk because it is too big and heavy to carry around

despair noun
If you are in despair, you are very worried about something and have almost given up hope.
'Max!' shouted Maddie in despair. 'Max, are you all right?'—Alexander McCall Smith, The Chocolate Money Mystery

desperate adjective
If you are desperate for something, you want it or need it very much. *I was tired and desperate for a drink of water.*

dessert noun (*plural* **desserts**)
sweet food that you eat at the end of a meal

destroy verb **destroys, destroying, destroyed**
To destroy something means to break it or spoil it so badly that you cannot use it again. *The earthquake destroyed several buildings.*

detail noun (*plural* **details**)
one small part of something, or one small piece of information about it *Jessica could remember every detail about the house.*

detective noun (*plural* **detectives**)
someone who looks at clues and tries to find out who committed a crime

determined adjective
If you are determined to do something, you have made up your mind that you want to do it. *We are determined to win.*

> **WORD FAMILY**
> • **determination** He carried on with great determination.

determiner noun (*plural* **determiners**)
(*in grammar*) A determiner is a word such as *a*, *the*, *some* or *many* that you use before a noun.

detest verb **detests, detesting, detested**
If you detest something, you hate it.

develop verb **develops, developing, developed**
When something develops, it changes and grows. *Acorns develop into oak trees.*

device noun (*plural* **devices**)
something that has been made to do a particular job *He had a special device for removing nails from wood.*

devour verb **devours, devouring, devoured**
To devour something means to eat it all hungrily.
Anansi set to at once and devoured the food.—Grace Hallworth, Cric Crac

dew noun
tiny drops of water that form on the ground during the night

diagonal adjective
A diagonal line goes from one corner of something to the opposite corner.

a b c **d** e f g h i j k l m n o p q r s t u v w x y z

diagram noun (*plural* **diagrams**)
a picture that shows what something is like or explains how it works

dial noun (*plural* **dials**)
a circle with numbers round it, like the one on a clock

dial verb **dials, dialling, dialled**
When you dial a number, you call that number on a telephone. *He dialled 999 and asked for an ambulance.*

dialect noun (*plural* **dialects**)
a type of language that is used by people in some parts of a country but not other parts

dialogue noun (*plural* **dialogues**)
a conversation in a book, play, or film

diameter noun (*plural* **diameters**)
The diameter of a circle is the distance across the centre of it.

diamond noun (*plural* **diamonds**)
1 a very hard jewel that looks like clear glass
2 a shape that looks like a square standing on one of its corners

diarrhoea noun (*say* **die**-a-ree-a)
an illness which makes you go to the toilet very often and gives you very watery waste

diary noun (*plural* **diaries**)
a book where you write down the things that you do each day

dice noun (*plural* **dice**)
a small cube with each side marked with a different number of dots. You use dice in various games.

dictionary noun (*plural* **dictionaries**)
a book that explains what words mean and shows you how to spell them

did verb *see* **do**

die verb **dies, dying, died**
When someone dies, they stop living.

diet noun (*plural* **diets**)
1 Your diet is the kind of food that you eat. *You should try to eat a healthy diet.*
2 If you go on a diet, you eat less food because you want to become thinner.

difference noun (*plural* **differences**)
1 A difference between things is a way in which they are different. *We had to look for five differences between the two pictures.*
2 (*in mathematics*) The difference between two numbers is the number you get when you take one away from the other. *The difference between 5 and 3 is 2.*

different adjective
If things or people are different, they are not the same. *Although we're sisters, we're very different.*

difficult adjective
Something that is difficult is not easy. *I find maths quite difficult.*

> **WORD FAMILY**
> • **difficulty** We were having a few difficulties with the boat.

dig verb **digs, digging, dug**
When you dig, you move soil away and make a hole in the ground.

digest verb **digests, digesting, digested** (*say* dye-**jest**)
When you digest food, your stomach breaks it down and changes it so that your body can use it.

digit noun (*plural* **digits**)
(*in mathematics*) one of the numbers between 0 and 9 *205 is a three-digit number.*

digital adjective
1 A digital watch or clock shows the time with numbers, rather than with hands.
2 A digital camera or television uses a special kind of electronic signal to make pictures.

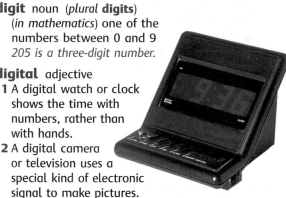

dilute verb **dilutes, diluting, diluted**
To dilute a liquid means to make it weaker by adding water.

dim adjective **dimmer, dimmest**
A dim light or a dim place is not very bright. *Violet looked around the dim and messy room.*—Lemony Snicket, The Bad Beginning

din noun
a very loud, annoying noise

a
b
c
d
e
f
g
h
i
j
k
l
m
n
o
p
q
r
s
t
u
v
w
x
y
z

dinghy noun (*plural* **dinghies**)
a small sailing boat

dining room noun (*plural* **dining rooms**)
a room where people have their meals

dinner noun (*plural* **dinners**)
the main meal of the day

dinosaur noun
(*plural* **dinosaurs**)
an animal like a huge lizard that lived millions of years ago

dip verb **dips, dipping, dipped**
When you dip something into liquid, you put it in and leave it there for only a short time. *I dipped my toe into the water.*

direct adjective
If you go somewhere in a direct way, you go straight there, without going anywhere else first. *We got on the direct train to London.*

direct verb **directs, directing, directed**
1 If you direct someone to a place, you explain to them how to get there. *Can you direct me to the station?*
2 The person who directs a play or film organizes it and tells everyone what they should do.

direction noun (*plural* **directions**)
The direction you are going in is the way you are going. *I went home, but Sam went off in the opposite direction.*

dirt noun
dust or mud

dirty adjective **dirtier, dirtiest**
Something that is dirty has mud or dirt on it.

disabled adjective
Someone who is disabled finds it hard to do some things because a part of their body does not work properly.

> **WORD FAMILY**
> • Someone who is disabled has a **disability**.

disagree verb **disagrees, disagreeing, disagreed**
If you disagree with someone, you think that they are wrong.

disappear verb **disappears, disappearing, disappeared**
When something disappears, it goes away and you cannot see it any more.

disappoint verb **disappoints, disappointing, disappointed**
If something disappoints you, you feel sad because it is not as good as you thought it would be.

> **WORD FAMILY**
> • **disappointed** I was a bit disappointed by the film.

disapprove verb **disapproves, disapproving, disapproved**
If you disapprove of something, you do not like it and do not think that it is right.

disaster noun (*plural* **disasters**)
something very bad that happens *The train crash was a terrible disaster.*

disc noun (*plural* **discs**)
1 any round, flat object
2 a round, flat piece of plastic that has music or computer information on it. This is also called a compact disc.

discipline noun (*say* **diss**-ip-lin)
When there is discipline, people behave well and do the things they are told to do.

disco noun (*plural* **discos**)
a party where you dance to pop music

discourage verb **discourages, discouraging, discouraged**
If you discourage someone from doing something, you try to stop them from doing it.

discover verb **discovers, discovering, discovered**
When you discover something, you find it, or find out about it.
I hope to discover the secret of the twelve dancing princesses, and win a wife and a kingdom. —Anne Fine, The Twelve Dancing Princesses

> **WORD FAMILY**
> • **discovery** This was an important discovery.

discuss verb **discusses, discussing, discussed**
When people discuss something, they talk about it.

> **WORD FAMILY**
> • **discussion** We had a very interesting discussion.

disease noun (*plural* **diseases**)
an illness

disgraceful adjective
If something is disgraceful, it is **very** bad and you should be ashamed of it. *That was disgraceful behaviour!*

disguise noun (*plural* **disguises**)
special clothes that you wear so that you will look different and people will not recognize you

disgust verb **disgusts, disgusting, disgusted**
If something disgusts you, it is horrible and you hate it.

> **WORD FAMILY**
> • **disgusting** What's that disgusting smell?

dish noun
(*plural* **dishes**)
1 a bowl in which food is served
2 food that has been prepared and cooked in a particular way

dishonest adjective
Someone who is dishonest is not honest and does not tell the truth.

disk noun (*plural* **disks**)
a flat piece of plastic on which computer information is stored

dislike verb **dislikes, disliking, disliked**
If you dislike something, you do not like it.

dismiss verb **dismisses, dismissing, dismissed**
To dismiss someone means to send them away. *Miss Watkins asked me a few questions, then she dismissed me.*

disobey verb **disobeys, disobeying, disobeyed**
If you disobey someone, you do not do what they have told you to do.

display noun (*plural* **displays**)
a show or exhibition *We made a display of our paintings.*

dissolve verb **dissolves, dissolving, dissolved**
When something dissolves in water, it mixes with the water so that you can no longer see it. *Sugar will dissolve in water, but sand will not.*

distance noun (*plural* **distances**)
The distance between two places is the amount of space between them. *We measured the distance between the two buildings.*

distant adjective
Something that is distant is far away.

distinct adjective
If something is distinct, you can see it or hear it quite clearly.

> **WORD FAMILY**
> • **distinctly** As I approached the cave, I could hear voices quite distinctly.

district noun (*plural* **districts**)
part of a town, city, or country

disturb verb **disturbs, disturbing, disturbed**
1 If you disturb someone, you interrupt them and stop them from doing something. *I'm working, so please don't disturb me.*
2 If something disturbs you, it makes you feel worried.

ditch noun
(*plural* **ditches**)
a long, narrow hole in the ground

dive verb **dives, diving, dived**
If you dive into water, you jump in head first.

> **WORD FAMILY**
> • A **diver** is someone who dives into water and swims around under the water, wearing special equipment.

divide verb **divides, dividing, divided**
1 When you divide things, you share them out. *Divide the sweets equally between you.*
2 When you divide something, you split it into smaller parts. *The cake was divided into eight pieces.*
3 (*in mathematics*) When you divide numbers, you find out how many times one number goes into another. Six divided by two is three, $6 \div 2 = 3$.

> **WORD FAMILY**
> • When you divide numbers, you do **division**.

a b c **d** e f g h i j k l m n o p q r s t u v w x y z

divisible adjective
(*in mathematics*) If one number is divisible by another, it can be divided by that number without leaving a remainder. *Ten is divisible by two.*

divorce noun (*plural* **divorces**)
When there is a divorce, two people end their marriage.

> **WORD FAMILY**
> • **divorced** My parents are divorced.

Diwali noun
Diwali is an important Hindu festival at which lamps are lit. It is held in October or November.

dizzy adjective **dizzier, dizziest**
If you feel dizzy, you feel as if everything is spinning round you.

do verb **does, doing, did, done**
When you do something, you carry out that action. *She did a little dance in the middle of the room.*

doctor noun (*plural* **doctors**)
someone whose job is to give people medicines and treatment when they are ill, to help them get better

document noun (*plural* **documents**)
1 an important piece of paper with official information on it *Your passport is a very important document.*
2 (*in ICT*) a piece of work that you write and store on a computer

does verb *see* **do**

dog noun
(*plural* **dogs**)
A dog is an animal people often keep as a pet. Dogs can bark, and you can train them to obey you.

doll noun (*plural* **dolls**)
a toy in the shape of a baby or person

dollar noun (*plural* **dollars**)
A dollar is a unit of money. Dollars are used in the United States of America, Australia, and some other countries.

dolphin noun (*plural* **dolphins**)
A dolphin is a large animal that swims like a fish and lives in the sea. Dolphins are mammals, and breathe air.

dome noun (*plural* **domes**)
a round roof that is shaped like the top half of a ball

donate verb **donates, donating, donated**
If you donate something, you give it to someone in order to help them.

> **WORD FAMILY**
> • **donation** Would you like to make a donation?

done verb *see* **do**

donkey noun (*plural* **donkeys**)
an animal that looks like a small horse with long ears

don't verb
do not *Don't be silly!*

door noun (*plural* **doors**)
something that you can open and go through to get into a place

dose noun (*plural* **doses**)
A dose of medicine is the amount that you have to take.

dot noun (*plural* **dots**)
a small spot that looks like a full stop

double adjective
Something that is double the size of something else is twice as big.

double verb **doubles, doubling, doubled**
If you double an amount, you make it twice as big.

doubt noun (*plural* **doubts**) (*rhymes with* out)
If you have doubts about something, you are not sure about it.

doubt verb **doubts, doubting, doubted** (*rhymes with* out)
If you doubt something, you do not believe it. *I doubt that we'll hear from him again.*

a
b
c
d
e
f
g
h
i
j
k
l
m
n
o
p
q
r
s
t
u
v
w
x
y
z

dove noun (*plural* **doves**)
a bird that looks like a small pigeon

down noun
very soft feathers

download verb **downloads, downloading, downloaded**
(*in ICT*) When you download information, you copy it from the Internet onto your computer.

downward, downwards adverb
When something goes downwards, it goes towards a lower place. *The bird glided slowly downwards.*

doze verb **dozes, dozing, dozed**
If you are dozing, you are nearly asleep. If you doze off, you fall asleep.

dozen noun (*plural* **dozens**)
a set of twelve *I bought a dozen eggs.*

draft noun (*plural* **drafts**)
a first copy of a piece of work, which you do not do very neatly

drag verb **drags, dragging, dragged**
When you drag something heavy, you pull it along the ground.

dragon noun (*plural* **dragons**)
a large monster with wings, that you read about in stories

dragonfly noun (*plural* **dragonflies**)
a large insect with a brightly coloured body that lives near water

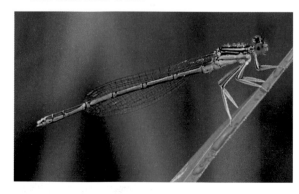

drain noun (*plural* **drains**)
a pipe that carries water away under the ground

drain verb **drains, draining, drained**
When water drains away, it flows away.

drama noun
acting in a play or story *Why don't you join a drama club?*

dramatic adjective
Something that is dramatic is very exciting.

drank verb *see* **drink**

draught noun (*plural* **draughts**) (*say* draft)
1 cold air that blows into a room
2 Draughts are round pieces of wood or plastic that you move across a board when you are playing a game called draughts.

draw verb **draws, drawing, drew, drawn**
1 When you draw a picture, you make a picture with a pen, pencil, or crayon.
2 When you draw curtains, you open them or close them.
3 When two people draw in a game, they have the same score at the end of the game. *We drew 1–1.*

drawer noun (*plural* **drawers**)
a part of a piece of furniture that you can pull out and use for keeping things in

drawing noun (*plural* **drawings**)
a picture that someone has drawn

dreadful adjective
Something that is dreadful is very bad. *It was an accident, a dreadful accident. No one's fault.*—Michael Morpurgo, Cool!

dream noun (*plural* **dreams**)
1 things that you seem to see when you are asleep
2 something that you would like very much *My dream is to become a pop singer.*

dream verb **dreams, dreaming, dreamed** *or* **dreamt**
1 When you dream, you seem to see things in your head when you are asleep.
2 If you dream about something, you think about it because you would like to do it. *He had always dreamt of being an Olympic champion.*

drench verb **drenches, drenching, drenched**
To drench something means to soak it with water.

dress noun (*plural* **dresses**)
A dress is a piece of clothing that a woman or girl wears. It has a skirt, and also covers the top half of her body.

dress verb **dresses, dressing, dressed**
When you dress, you put on clothes. You can also say that you **get dressed**.

a
b
c
d
e
f
g
h
i
j
k
l
m
n
o
p
q
r
s
t
u
v
w
x
y
z

dressing gown noun (plural **dressing gowns**)
a piece of clothing that you wear over your pyjamas or nightie to keep warm when you are walking around

drew verb see **draw**

dribble verb **dribbles, dribbling, dribbled**
1 If you dribble, water comes out of your mouth. Babies often dribble.
2 When you dribble with a ball, you kick it as you run along, so that it stays close to your feet.

drift verb **drifts, drifting, drifted**
If something drifts along, it is carried along gently by water or air. *The empty boat drifted along on the sea.*

drill noun
(plural **drills**)
a tool that you use for making holes

drink verb **drinks, drinking, drank, drunk**
When you drink, you swallow liquid.

drink noun (plural **drinks**)
a liquid that you take into your mouth and swallow

drip verb **drips, dripping, dripped**
When water drips, it falls in small drops. *The snow was melting, and water was dripping off the roof.*

drive verb **drives, driving, drove, driven**
1 When you drive, you control a car, bus, train, or lorry. *You can learn to drive when you're seventeen.*
2 When you drive animals, you make them move along. *We drove the cows into the field.*

> **WORD FAMILY**
> • A **driver** is someone who drives a car, bus, or lorry.

drizzle noun
very light rain

drop noun (plural **drops**)
A drop of water is a very small amount of it. *I felt a few drops of rain on my face.*

drop verb **drops, dropping, dropped**
If you drop something, you do not hold it tightly enough and it falls out of your hands.

drought noun (plural **droughts**) (rhymes with out)
a time when there is very little rain and the ground becomes very dry

drove verb see **drive**

drown verb **drowns, drowning, drowned**
If you drown, you die because you are under water and cannot breathe.

drug noun (plural **drugs**)
1 a medicine that can help you feel better if you are ill or in pain
2 A drug is a substance that some people take for pleasure because it changes the way they feel or behave. This type of drug is illegal and dangerous.

drum noun (plural **drums**)
a hollow musical instrument that you bang with a stick or with your hands

drunk verb see **drink**

dry adjective **drier, driest**
Something that is dry is not wet or damp.

duck noun (plural **ducks**)
a bird that lives near water and swims on the water

duck verb **ducks, ducking, ducked**
If you duck, you bend down quickly so that something will not hit you.

due adjective
The time that something is due is the time you expect it to arrive. *The train is due at two o'clock.*

duel noun (plural **duels**)
a fight between two people using swords or guns

duet noun
(plural **duets**)
(say dyoo-**ett**)
a piece of music that two people play or sing together

dug verb see **dig**

dull adjective **duller, dullest**
1 A dull colour is not very bright.
2 Something that is dull is boring and not interesting. *History of Magic was the dullest subject on their timetable.* —J. K. Rowling, Harry Potter and the Chamber of Secrets

dump noun (plural **dumps**)
a place where people leave rubbish

dump verb **dumps, dumping, dumped**
1 When you dump rubbish, you leave it somewhere because you want to get get rid of it.
2 When you dump something, you put it down carelessly. *She dumped her school bag on the floor.*

dungeon noun (plural **dungeons**)
a prison underneath a castle

during preposition
while something else is going on *I fell asleep during the film.*

dusk noun
the dim light at the end of the day, just before it gets dark

dust noun
dry dirt that is like powder *There was dust everywhere in the attic.*

WORD FAMILY
• **dusty** The room was full of dusty old furniture.

dustbin noun (plural **dustbins**)
a large container for putting rubbish in

duty noun (plural **duties**)
If it is your duty to do something, you have to do it.

duvet noun (plural **duvets**) (say **doo**-vay)
a thick, warm cover for a bed

DVD noun (plural **DVDs**)
A DVD is a round, flat disc on which music, pictures, or film can be stored. DVD is short for **digital versatile disc**.

dye verb **dyes, dyeing, dyed**
When you dye something, you change its colour by putting it in a special coloured liquid.

dying verb see **die**

dyslexic adjective (say dis-**lex**-ic)
Someone who is dyslexic finds it difficult to learn to read and write because their brain muddles up letters and words.

a b c d e f g h i j k l m n o p q r s t u v w x y z

Ee

each adjective
every *She gave each child a present.*

eager adjective
If you are eager to do something, you are very keen to do it.
He opened the door, and five dogs rushed out, cavorting in the snow, all eager for some exercise.—Alexander McCall Smith, The Chocolate Money Mystery

eagle noun (*plural* **eagles**)
An eagle is a large bird that hunts and eats small animals. Eagles live in mountain areas.

ear noun (*plural* **ears**)
Your ears are the parts of your body that you use for hearing.

early adjective **earlier, earliest**
1 If you are early, you arrive before people are expecting you. *We were ten minutes early.*
2 When it is early in the day, it is in the morning, not the afternoon or evening. *I got up very early this morning.*

earn verb **earns, earning, earned**
When you earn money, you get it by working for it.

earphone noun (*plural* **earphones**)
Earphones are small speakers that you wear in your ears so that you can listen to music from a music player.

earring noun (*plural* **earrings**)
Earrings are jewellery that you wear in your ears.

earth noun
1 the planet that we all live on
2 the soil in which plants grow

earthquake noun (*plural* **earthquakes**)
When there is an earthquake, the ground suddenly shakes. Strong earthquakes can destroy buildings.

east noun
East is the direction where the sun rises in the morning.

> **WORD FAMILY**
> • The **eastern** part of a country is the part in the east.

Easter noun
the day when Christians celebrate Jesus Christ coming back from the dead

easy adjective **easier, easiest**
If something is easy, you can do it or understand it without any trouble. *Do you find maths easy?*

> **WORD FAMILY**
> • **easily** I managed to do all my homework quite easily.

eat verb **eats, eating, ate, eaten**
When you eat, you put food in your mouth and swallow it.

echo noun (*plural* **echoes**) (*say* **ek**-oh)
When you hear an echo, you hear a sound again as it bounces back off something solid. You often hear echoes in caves and tunnels.

eclipse noun (*plural* **eclipses**)
When there is an eclipse of the sun, the moon moves in front of it and hides it for a short time. When there is an eclipse of the moon, the sun moves in front of it and hides it for a short time.

eczema noun (*say* ex-ma)
If you have eczema, your skin is dry or red and itchy.

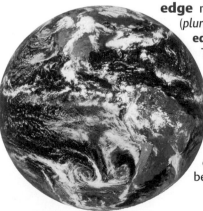

edge noun (*plural* **edges**)
The edge of something is the part along the end or side of it. *He put the book down on the edge of the table.*

edit verb **edits, editing, edited**
1 When you edit something that you have written, you check it and change some parts so that it is better.

2 When people edit a film or television programme, they choose the parts that they want to keep and take some parts out.

educate verb **educates, educating, educated**
To educate someone means to teach them things they need to know like reading and writing. *A teacher's job is to educate children.*

> **WORD FAMILY**
> • **education** Children go to school to get a good education.

effect noun (*plural* **effects**)
If something has an effect, it makes something else happen. *Some chemicals have a harmful effect on the environment.*

effort noun (*plural* **efforts**)
If you put effort into something, you work hard to do it. *You should put more effort into your work.*

egg noun (*plural* **eggs**)
An egg is an oval object with a thin shell. Eggs are laid by birds, snakes, and insects. We can cook and eat hens' eggs.

Eid noun (*say* eed)
a Muslim festival that marks the end of Ramadan

eight noun (*plural* **eights**)
the number 8

eighteen noun
the number 18

eighty noun
the number 80

either adjective
one or the other *There are two cakes. You can have either one.*

elastic noun
a strip of material that can stretch and then go back to its usual size

elbow noun (*plural* **elbows**)
Your elbow is the joint in the middle of your arm, where your arm can bend.

elect verb **elects, electing, elected**
When people elect someone, they choose them by voting for them. *Each year we elect a class representative for the school council.*

> **WORD FAMILY**
> • When there is an **election**, people vote to choose the people who will be in charge of their town or country.

electricity noun
Electricity is the power or energy that is used to give light and heat and to work machines. It comes along wires or from batteries.

> **WORD FAMILY**
> • An **electric or electrical** machine is worked by electricity.

electronic adjective
An electronic machine uses electrical signals to control the way it works. televisions, computers, and automatic washing machines have electronic devices inside them.

elegant adjective
Someone who is elegant is beautiful and graceful. Something that is elegant is smart and attractive, and looks expensive.

elephant noun (*plural* **elephants**)
a very big grey animal with tusks and a very long nose called a trunk

eleven noun
the number 11

else adverb
different *Let's do something else today.*

email noun (*plural* **emails**)
a message that you send from your computer to someone else's computer

embarrass verb **embarrasses, embarrassing, embarrassed**
If something embarrasses you, it makes you feel shy, nervous, or ashamed.

> 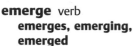 **WORD FAMILY**
> • **embarrassed** I felt really embarrassed!
> • **embarrassing** My dad is so embarrassing!
> • **embarrassment** My face was red with embarrassment.

emerald noun (*plural* **emeralds**)
a green jewel or precious stone

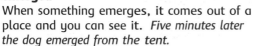

emerge verb **emerges, emerging, emerged**
When something emerges, it comes out of a place and you can see it. *Five minutes later the dog emerged from the tent.*

emergency noun (*plural* **emergencies**)
When there is an emergency, something very dangerous suddenly happens and people must act quickly so that no one gets hurt. *Call the doctor, it's an emergency.*

emotion noun (*plural* **emotions**)
Your emotions are your feelings.

employ verb **employs, employing, employed**
To employ someone means to pay them to work for you.

> 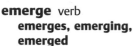 **WORD FAMILY**
> • If you are **employed**, you have a job and work for someone.

empty adjective
Something that is empty has nothing in it. *I looked in the box, but it was empty.*

empty verb **empties, emptying, emptied**
When you empty something, you take everything out of it. *He emptied his pocket.*

enchanted adjective
Something that is enchanted is under a magic spell.

encourage verb **encourages, encouraging, encouraged**
When you encourage someone, you tell them to do something and make them feel brave enough to do it. *Everyone encouraged me to try again.*

encyclopedia noun (*plural* **encyclopedias**)
(*say* en-sye-clo-**pee**-dee-a)
a book that gives you information about a lot of different things

end noun (*plural* **ends**)
The end of something is the place or time where it stops. *We walked on to the end of the lane.*

> 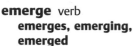 **WORD FAMILY**
> • The **ending** of a film or book is the way in which it ends.

end verb **ends, ending, ended**
When something ends, it stops.

endangered adjective
An animal or plant that is endangered may soon not exist anymore.

enemy noun (*plural* **enemies**)
1 someone who wants to hurt you
2 the people fighting against you

energy noun
1 If you have energy, you feel strong and fit.
2 Energy is the power that comes from coal, electricity, and gas. Energy makes machines work and gives us heat and light.

energetic adjective
If you are energetic, you have a lot of energy and run around a lot. *I wasn't feeling very energetic.*

engine noun (plural engines)
a machine that can make things move

engineer noun (*plural* **engineers**)
someone who makes machines, or plans the building of roads and bridges

enjoy verb **enjoys, enjoying, enjoyed**
If you enjoy something, you like doing it or watching it.
Pigs enjoy eating, and they also enjoy lying around most of the day, thinking about eating again.—Dick King-Smith, The Sheep-Pig

> 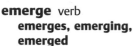 **WORD FAMILY**
> • **enjoyable** We had a very enjoyable day.
> • **enjoyment** The bad weather didn't spoil our enjoyment.

enormous adjective
Something that is enormous is very big.
One of the crocodiles was enormous. The other was not so big.—Roald Dahl, The Enormous Crocodile

enough adjective
If you have enough of something, you have as much as you need. *I haven't got enough money to buy an ice cream.*

enter verb **enters, entering, entered**
1 When you enter a place, you go into it. *I knocked on the door and entered the room.*
2 If you enter a race or competition, you take part in it.

entertain verb **entertains, entertaining, entertained**
To entertain people means to do things that they enjoy watching, or things that make them laugh. *There were singers and dancers there to entertain the guests.*

WORD FAMILY
• **entertainment** Sit down and enjoy the entertainment.

enthusiastic adjective
If you are enthusiastic about something, you are very keen on it and want to do it.

entirely adverb
completely *It wasn't entirely my fault!*

entrance noun (*plural* **entrances**)
the way into a place *He finally found the entrance to the secret cave.*

entry noun (*plural* **entries**)
a way into a place *We couldn't go in because there was a sign on the door saying 'No Entry'.*

envelope noun (*plural* **envelopes**)
a paper cover that you put a letter in before you send it

envious adjective (*say* en-vee-**uss**)
If you feel envious, you want something that someone else has. *I was so envious of Salim when he told me he'd got a ticket for the Cup Final.*

environment noun (*plural* **environments**)
the world we live in, especially the plants, animals, and things around us *Planting more trees will improve our environment.*

envy noun
the feeling you have when you would like to have something that someone else has

episode noun (*plural* **episodes**)
one programme in a radio or TV serial *Did you see last week's episode of Dr Who?*

equal adjective
If two things are equal, they are the same size or worth the same amount. *Divide the mixture into two equal amounts.*

WORD FAMILY
• **equally** We shared the money out equally between us.

equator noun
The equator is an imaginary line round the middle of the earth. Countries near the equator are very hot.

equipment noun
the things that you need for doing something *If you want to play ice hockey, you will have to buy a lot of expensive equipment.*

error noun (*plural* **errors**)
a mistake

erupt verb **erupts, erupting, erupted**
When a volcano erupts, hot, liquid rock comes up out of it.

escape verb **escapes, escaping, escaped**
If you escape, you get away from a place and become free. *How are we going to escape from here?*

especially adverb
more than anything else *I love fruit, especially apples.*

essential adjective
very important or absolutely necessary

estate noun (*plural* **estates**)
an area of land with a lot of houses on it

estimate verb **estimates, estimating, estimated**
When you estimate an amount, you guess how much it will be. *Can you estimate how long it would take to walk twenty kilometres?*

EU noun
The EU is an organization of countries in Europe that work together.

euro noun (*plural* **euros**)
A euro is a unit of money. Euros are used in several countries in Europe.

evaporate verb **evaporates, evaporating, evaporated**
When water evaporates, it changes into a gas and so disappears.

WORD FAMILY
• **evaporation** Puddles in the road dry up through evaporation.

a
b
c
d
e
f
g
h
i
j
k
l
m
n
o
p
q
r
s
t
u
v
w
x
y
z

even adjective
1 Something that is even is smooth and level. *You need an even surface to work on.*
2 Amounts that are even are equal. *The scores were even at half time.*
3 (*in mathematics*) An even number is a number that you can divide by two. 4, 6, and 8 are even numbers.

WORD FAMILY
• **evenly** We should divide the work up evenly between us.

evening noun (*plural* **evenings**)
the time at the end of the day before people go to bed

event noun (*plural* **events**)
something important that happens *Sports Day is a big event in our school.*

eventually adverb
in the end *We got home eventually.*

ever adverb
at any time *Have you ever been to America?*
for ever always

evergreen noun (*plural* **evergreens**)
a tree that keeps its green leaves all through the year

every adjective
each *I go swimming every week.*

everybody, everyone
every person *Everybody cheered when he scored the winning goal.*

everything pronoun
all things *Put everything away in the cupboard.*

everywhere adverb
in all places *I've looked everywhere but I can't find my phone.*

evidence noun
anything that proves that something is true, or that something happened *These footprints are evidence that someone was here last night.*

evil adjective
Something that is evil is wicked.

ewe noun (*plural* **ewes**) (*say* **you**)
a female sheep

exact adjective
completely right or accurate *Show me the exact spot where you were standing.*

WORD FAMILY
• **exactly** I had exactly twenty four pence.

exaggerate verb **exaggerates, exaggerating, exaggerated**
If you exaggerate, you say that something is bigger or better than it really is.

exam, examination noun (*plural* **exams, examinations**)
an important test

examine verb **examines, examining, examined**
When you examine something, you look at it very carefully.
Klaus Baudelaire, the middle child, and the only boy, liked to examine creatures in tide-pools.—Lemony Snicket, The Bad Beginning

example noun (*plural* **examples**)
1 one thing that shows what all the others are like *Can you show me an example of your handwriting?*
2 Someone who sets an example behaves well and shows other people how they should behave.

excellent adjective
Something that is excellent is very good.

except preposition
apart from *Everyone got a prize except me.*

exchange verb **exchanges, exchanging, exchanged**
If you exchange something, you give it to someone and get something else in return.

excite verb **excites, exciting, excited**
If something excites you, it makes you feel happy, interested, and keen to do something.

WORD FAMILY
• **excited** We were all really excited.
• **excitedly** 'Hurry up,' she cried excitedly.
• **exciting** It was very exciting seeing so many animals in the wild.
• **excitement** He was jumping up and down with excitement.

exclaim verb **exclaims, exclaiming, exclaimed**
When you exclaim, you shout something suddenly because you are surprised or excited.
'The jungle!' she exclaimed. What a wonderful adventure!—Alexander McCall Smith, The Bubblegum Tree

exclamation noun (*plural* **exclamations**)
An exclamation is something you say or shout which shows that you are very happy, angry, or surprised, for example *Oh, dear!*. In writing, you use an exclamation mark after an exclamation.

exclamation mark noun
(*plural* **exclamation marks**)
An exclamation mark is a mark like this ! that you use in writing. You put an exclamation mark after words to show that they have been shouted.

excuse noun (*plural* **excuses**)
(*rhymes with* goose)
a reason you give to try to explain why you have done wrong so that you will not get into trouble *So, what's your excuse for being late today?*

excuse verb **excuses, excusing, excused**
(*rhymes with* choose)
1 If you excuse someone, you forgive them. *I'm sorry for interrupting you. Please excuse me.*
2 If you are excused from doing something, you do not have to do it. *I was excused from swimming because I had a cold.*

exercise noun (*plural* **exercises**)
1 When you do exercise, you run around or move your body to make your body healthy and strong. *You should do more exercise.*
2 a piece of work that you do to make yourself better at something *We've got some some spelling exercises for homework.*

exhausted adjective
If you are exhausted, you are very tired.

exhibition noun
(*plural* **exhibitions**)
a collection of things that are put on show so that people can come to see them

exist verb **exists, existing, existed**
Things that exist are real, not imaginary. *Do you think that aliens exist?*

exit noun (*plural* **exits**)
the way out of a place

expand verb **expands, expanding, expanded**
When something expands, it gets bigger. *A balloon expands when you blow air into it.*

expect verb **expects, expecting, expected**
If you expect that something will happen, you think that it will happen. *When the door to her cell opened, the last thing Daniella expected to see was Eddie.*—Philip Ardagh, Dreadful Acts

expensive adjective
Something that is expensive costs a lot of money.

experience noun (*plural* **experiences**)
1 If you have experience of something, you have done it before and so know what it is like. *Have you had any experience of horse riding?*
2 An experience is something very good or bad that happens to you. *Going to Disneyland was a wonderful experience.*

> **WORD FAMILY**
> • **experienced** I've been swimming for five years now, so I'm quite an experienced swimmer.

experiment noun
(*plural* **experiments**)
a test that you do to find out whether an idea works *We did an experiment to see which things dissolve in water.*

expert noun
(*plural* **experts**)
someone who does something very well or knows a lot about something

explain verb **explains, explaining, explained**
When you explain something, you talk about it so that other people understand it. *Max explained to us how the machine worked.*

> **WORD FAMILY**
> • **explanation** He gave an explanation of what had happened.

explode verb **explodes, exploding, exploded**
When something explodes, it bursts or blows up with a loud bang. *Goyle's potion exploded, showering the whole class.*—J. K. Rowling, Harry Potter and the Chamber of Secrets

a b c d e f g h i j k l m n o p q r s t u v w x y z

explore verb **explores, exploring, explored**
When you explore a place, you look around it carefully to find out what it is like. *Let's explore the castle.*

explosion noun (*plural* **explosions**)
a loud bang that is made when something bursts or blows up

export verb **exports, exporting, exported**
(*say* ex-**port**)
1 When a company exports things, it sends them to another country to sell.
2 (*in ICT*) When you export information on a computer, you move it from one file to another, or from one computer to another.

express verb **expresses, expressing, expressed**
When you express your ideas or feelings, you talk about them or show them to other people.

expression noun (*plural* **expressions**)
1 Your expression is the look on your face. *He had a really sad expression on his face.*
2 An expression is a word or phrase.

extinct adjective
Animals that are extinct no longer exist because they are all dead. *Dinosaurs are extinct.*

extra adjective
Something extra is something more than you would usually have or do. *Bring some extra clothes in case it gets cold.*

extraordinary adjective
Something that is extraordinary is very unusual. *An extraordinary sight met their eyes.*

extreme adjective
1 Extreme means very great. *No plants can grow in the extreme heat of the desert.*
2 The extreme part of a place is the part that is furthest away. *These animals only live in the extreme north of the country.*

extremely adverb
very *The journey was extremely long and tiring.*

eye noun (*plural* **eyes**)
1 Your eyes are the parts of your body that you use for seeing.
2 the small hole in the top of a needle

eyesight noun
Your eyesight is your ability to see. *Owls have got very good eyesight.*

fable noun (*plural* **fables**)
A fable is a story that teaches you something, for example one that teaches you not to be selfish or greedy. Fables often have animals as their main characters.

fabulous adjective
Something that is fabulous is wonderful. *We had a fabulous time!*

face noun (*plural* **faces**)
1 Your face is the front part of your head, which has your eyes, nose, and mouth on it.
2 The face of a clock or watch is the front part of it, which shows the time.

face verb **faces, facing, faced**
The direction that you are facing is the direction in which you are looking.

fact noun (*plural* **facts**)
something that we know is true *It's a fact that the earth travels around the sun.*

factor noun (*plural* **factors**)
(*in mathematics*) a number that will divide exactly into another number without leaving a remainder *3 is a factor of 9*

factory noun (*plural* **factories**)
a large building where people make things with machines

fade verb **fades, fading, faded**
1 When a colour or light fades, it becomes less bright.
2 When a sound fades, it becomes less loud.

fail verb **fails, failing, failed**
If you fail a test, you do not pass it.

failure noun (*plural* **failures**)
1 someone who has failed a test, or has not managed to do something very well
2 something that does not work well or is not successful

faint adjective **fainter, faintest**
1 A faint sound is not very loud and you cannot hear it very well.

2 A faint colour, mark, or light is not very bright or clear.

3 If you feel faint, you feel dizzy.

faint verb **faints, fainting, fainted**
If you faint, you feel dizzy and become unconscious for a short time.

fair adjective **fairer, fairest**
1 Something that is fair treats everyone in the same way so that everyone is equal. *It's not fair if my brother gets more pocket money than me.*
2 Fair hair is light in colour.

> **WORD FAMILY**
> • **fairly** We try to treat everyone fairly.

fair noun (plural **fairs**)
a place with a lot of rides and stalls, where you can go to enjoy yourself by going on the rides and trying to win things at the stalls

fairy noun (plural **fairies**)
a small, magical person in a story

fairy tale noun (plural **fairy tales**)
a story for young children in which magic things happen

faith noun
If you have faith in something, you trust it or believe in it.

faithful adjective
If you are faithful to someone, you always help them and support them.

fake noun (plural **fakes**)
something that has been made to look like a valuable thing, but is not real *It looked like a real Roman coin, but it was a fake.*

fall verb **falls, falling, fell, fallen**
1 To fall means to drop down towards the ground. *Be careful you don't fall!*
2 When you fall asleep, you start sleeping.

false adjective
Something that is false is not true or real. *He gave a false name to the police.*

familiar adjective
If something is familiar to you, you recognize it or know about it. *His face was familiar – where had I seen him before?*

family noun (plural **families**)
1 Your family is all the people who are related to you, for example your parents, brothers and sisters, aunts and uncles.

2 A family of animals or plants is a group of them that are closely related. *Lions, tigers, and leopards all belong to the cat family.*

famine noun (plural **famines**)
If there is a famine, there is not enough food for people.

famous adjective
Someone or something famous is very well known. *A lot of people dream about being rich and famous.*

> **WORD FAMILY**
> • **fame** His fame soon spread throughout the land.

fan noun (plural **fans**)
1 a machine that blows air about to cool a place
2 something that you hold in your hand and wave in front of your face to cool your face
3 someone who supports a famous person or a sports team *Are you a Manchester United fan?*

fang noun (plural **fangs**)
Fangs are the long, sharp teeth that some animals have.

fantastic adjective
Something that is fantastic is wonderful. *The four Small Foxes scrambed up out of the tunnel and what a fantastic sight it was that now met their eyes!*—Roald Dahl, Fantastic Mr Fox

fantasy noun (plural **fantasies**)
A fantasy is something that is magical and cannot happen in real life. *I like reading fantasy stories.*

far adverb **farther, further, farthest, furthest**
Something that is far away is a long way away.

fare noun (plural **fares**)
the amount of money that you have to pay to travel on a train, bus, boat, or aeroplane

a b c d e **f** g h i j k l m n o p q r s t u v w x y z

farm noun (plural **farms**)
a piece of land where someone grows crops and keeps animals for food

> **WORD FAMILY**
> • A **farmer** is someone who has a farm.

farther, farthest adverb see **far**

fascinate verb **fascinates, fascinating, fascinated**
If something fascinates you, you are very interested in it.

> **WORD FAMILY**
> • **fascinated** I've always been fascinated by old coins.
> • **fascinating** History is a fascinating subject.

fashion noun (plural **fashions**)
A fashion is a style of clothes that is popular for a short time. Clothes that are in fashion are popular now. Clothes that are out of fashion are not popular.

fashionable adjective
Clothes that are fashionable are in fashion and popular now. *She was wearing a fashionable pair of black trousers.*

fast adjective **faster, fastest**
1 Something that is fast moves quickly.
2 If a clock or watch is fast, it shows a time that is later than the right time. *My watch is ten minutes fast.*

fast verb **fasts, fasting, fasted**
When you fast, you do not eat any food for a period of time. *During the month of Ramadan, Muslims fast every day from dawn until sunset.*

fasten verb **fastens, fastening, fastened**
1 When you fasten something, you close it or do it up. *Don't forget to fasten your seat belt.*
2 If you fasten two things together, you tie or join them together.

fat noun
1 the white, greasy part of meat
2 a substance such as butter or margarine that people use when they are cooking or preparing food *You should try not to eat too much fat.*

fat adjective **fatter, fattest**
Someone who is fat has a big, round body. *The ticket collector was a little fat man.*

father noun (plural **fathers**)
Your father is your male parent.

fault noun (plural **faults**)
1 If there is a fault in something, there is something wrong with it. *I think there is a fault in the computer program.*
2 If something is your fault, you made it happen. *It was your fault that the dog got out!*

favour noun (plural **favours**)
If you do someone a favour, you do something for them. *Please do me a favour and post those letters for me.*

favourite adjective
Your favourite thing is the one that you like the most.
'What about telly?' he asked. 'Would you let me watch all my favourite telly shows?'—Anne Fine, Care of Henry

fax noun (plural **faxes**)
a copy of a letter or a picture that you send to someone using telephone lines and a machine called a **fax machine**

fear noun (plural **fears**)
the feeling you get when you are frightened because you think something bad is going to happen

> **WORD FAMILY**
> • **fearless** He was a brave and fearless boy.

fear verb **fears, fearing, feared**
If you fear something, you are afraid of it. *Don't worry. You have nothing to fear.*

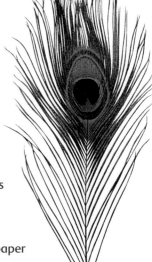

feast noun (plural **feasts**)
a special big meal for a lot of people

feather noun (plural **feathers**)
A bird's feathers are the light, soft things that it has all over its body.

feature noun (plural **features**)
an article in a newspaper or magazine

February noun
the second month of the year

fed verb see **feed**

fed up adjective
If you feel fed up, you feel tired, miserable, and bored.

feed verb **feeds, feeding, fed**
To feed a person or an animal means to give them food.

feel verb **feels, feeling, felt**
1 When you feel something, you touch it to find out what it is like.
2 When you feel an emotion such as anger, fear, or happiness, you have that emotion. *We were all feeling tired and miserable.*

feeling noun (*plural* **feelings**)
something that you feel inside yourself, like anger or love

feet noun *see* **foot**

fell verb *see* **fall**

felt verb *see* **feel**

female adjective
A female animal or person can become a mother.

feminine adjective
Something that is feminine looks as if it is suitable for girls and women, not boys and men.

fence noun (*plural* **fences**)
A fence is a kind of wall made from wood or wire. Fences are put round gardens and fields.

ferocious adjective (*say* fer-**oh**-shuss)
A ferocious animal is fierce and dangerous.

ferry noun (*plural* **ferries**)
a boat that takes people across a river or short stretch of water

fertilizer noun (*plural* **fertilizers**)
something you add to the soil to feed plants and make them grow better

festival noun (*plural* **festivals**)
a special time when people celebrate something

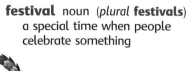

fetch verb **fetches, fetching, fetched**
When you fetch something, you go and get it. *Could you fetch my coat for me?*

fête noun (*plural* **fêtes**) (*say* fate)
an event outside with games and competitions, and a lot of stalls selling different things

fever noun (*plural* **fevers**)
If you have a fever, you have a high temperature and your body feels very hot. You sometimes have a fever when there is a germ in your body that is making you ill.

few adjective & pronoun
A few means a small number. *There were only a few people there.*

fewer adjective
not as many *We scored fewer goals than the other team, so we lost the match.*

fibre noun (*plural* **fibres**)
1 a thin thread
2 a substance in some foods which we need to help our body digest things properly

fiction noun
books and stories that are made up, not true

> **WORD FAMILY**
> • A **fictional** character is one in a story.

fiddle verb **fiddles, fiddling, fiddled**
If you fiddle with something, you keep touching it or moving it about. *Please don't fiddle with the controls.*

fidget verb **fidgets, fidgeting, fidgeted**
When you fidget, you keep moving about because you are bored or nervous. *They began to fidget and look about for an escape route.*—Dick King-Smith, The Sheep-Pig

field noun (*plural* **fields**)
1 a piece of ground with crops or grass growing on it
2 (*in ICT*) one area of a database on a computer, where one particular type of information is stored

fierce adjective **fiercer, fiercest**
A fierce animal is dangerous because it might bite you or attack you. *They were suddenly surrounded by a pack of fierce-looking dogs.*

> **WORD FAMILY**
> • **fiercely** 'Sit down!' he yelled fiercely.

fifteen noun
the number 15

fifth adjective *see* **five**

fifty noun
the number 50

fight verb **fights, fighting, fought**
When people fight, they hit each other or attack each other.

figurative adjective
When you use words in a figurative way, you do not use their proper meaning but use them to create an effect. For example, if you say that someone 'exploded with rage', you are using the word *exploded* in a figurative way.

figure noun (*plural* **figures**)
1 a number, such as 1, 2 or 3
2 Your figure is the shape of your body. *She has a very shapely figure.*

file noun (*plural* **files**)
1 a book or box that you keep pieces of paper in
2 (*in ICT*) an amount of information that is stored together on a computer
3 a tool that you rub against things to make them smooth
4 If people walk in single file, they walk in a line, with one person behind the other.

fill verb **fills, filling, filled**
1 When you fill something, you put so much in it that it is full. *We filled our bottles with water from the stream.*
2 If food fills you up, it makes you feel full.

film noun (*plural* **films**)
1 a roll of plastic you put in a camera for taking photographs
2 a moving picture that you watch on a screen at the cinema or on television

filter noun (*plural* **filters**)
You use a filter for removing substances from a liquid. You pass the liquid through the filter, and other substances which are in the liquid get caught by the filter.

filthy adjective **filthier, filthiest**
Something that is filthy is very dirty.

fin noun (*plural* **fins**)
The fins on a fish are the parts on its sides that it uses to help it swim.

final adjective
The final thing is the one that comes last. *This will be the final song in our concert.*

> **WORD FAMILY**
> • **finally** Finally I'd like to thank everyone who has helped today.

find verb **finds, finding, found**
When you find something, you see it. *I found 50 pence on the ground.*

find and replace verb
(*in ICT*) When you tell a computer to find and replace something in a computer file, it finds every example of a particular word and replaces it with a different one.

fine adjective **finer, finest**
1 Something that is fine is thin and light. *I've got very fine hair.*
2 If the weather is fine, it is sunny.
3 If you feel fine, you feel well and happy.

fine noun (*plural* **fines**)
an amount of money that you have to pay because you have done something wrong *If you don't take your library books back on time, you may have to pay a fine.*

finger noun (*plural* **fingers**)
Your fingers are the parts of your body on the ends of your hands.

> **WORD FAMILY**
> • Your **fingernails** are the nails on your fingers. Your **fingerprints** are the marks that your fingers leave on something after you have touched it.

finish verb **finishes, finishing, finished**
1 When you finish something, you come to the end of it. *Have you finished your maths yet?*
2 When something finishes, it ends. *What time does the film finish?*

fir noun (*plural* **firs**)
a tall tree that has cones, and long, thin leaves shaped like needles

fire noun (*plural* **fires**)
1 When there is a fire, something is burning.
2 A fire is a machine that gives out heat.

fire verb **fires, firing, fired**
When you fire a gun, you make it shoot.

a b c d e **f** g h i j k l m n o p q r s t u v w x y z

fire engine noun (*plural* **fire engines**)
a large truck that carries firefighters and the equipment that they need to put out fires

firefighter noun (*plural* **firefighters**)
a person whose job is to put out fires

firework noun (*plural* **fireworks**)
something that explodes with coloured lights and loud bangs

firm adjective **firmer, firmest**
1 Something that is firm is hard and does not move easily when you pull it or press on it. *I put one foot on the plank to make sure it was firm before I walked across.*
2 Someone who is firm is quite strict and will not change their mind.

first adjective
The first thing is the one that comes before all the others. *A is the first letter of the alphabet.*

first aid noun
help that you give to a person who is hurt, before a doctor comes

first person noun
(*in grammar*) When you use the first person, you use the words 'I' and 'me' to write about yourself in a story.

fish noun (*plural* **fishes** or **fish**)
A fish is an animal that swims and lives in water. Fish have fins to help them swim and scales on their bodies.

fish verb **fishes, fishing, fished**
When you fish, you try to catch fish.

fisherman noun (*plural* **fishermen**)
a person who catches fish

fist noun (*plural* **fists**)
When you make a fist, you close your hand tightly.

fit adjective **fitter, fittest**
1 If you are fit, your body is healthy and strong. *Swimming helps to keep you fit.*
2 If something is fit to use or eat, it is good enough. *This food is not fit to eat!*

fit verb **fits, fitting, fitted**
1 If something fits you, it is the right size for you to wear.
2 If something fits into a place, it is the right size to go there.

five noun (*plural* **fives**)
the number 5

WORD FAMILY
• The **fifth** thing is the one that is number 5.

fix verb **fixes, fixing, fixed**
1 When you fix one thing onto another, you join it on firmly. *My dad fixed the lamp onto my bike for me.*
2 When you fix something, you mend it. *My MP3 player's broken. Can you fix it?*

fizzy adjective **fizzier, fizziest**
A fizzy drink has a lot of tiny bubbles of gas in it.

flag noun (*plural* **flags**)
a piece of cloth with a special design on, which is fixed to a pole *Do you know the colours of the French flag?*

flake noun (*plural* **flakes**)
a small piece of something *A few flakes of snow were beginning to fall.*

flame noun (*plural* **flames**)
Flames are the orange, pointed parts that come up out of a fire.

flap noun (*plural* **flaps**)
a part of something that hangs down and can move about

a b c d e **f** g h i j k l m n o p q r s t u v w x y z

flap verb **flaps, flapping, flapped**
When something flaps, it moves up and down or from side to side. *The huge bird flapped its wings and flew off.*

flash noun (plural **flashes**)
a sudden bright light *We saw a flash of lightning.*

flash verb **flashes, flashing, flashed**
When a light flashes, it shines brightly and then stops shining again. *The lights flashed on and off.*

flashy adjective **flashier, flashiest**
Something that is flashy looks very expensive. *He was wearing a new flashy watch.*

flask noun (plural **flasks**)
a container that keeps hot drinks hot and cold drinks cold

flat adjective **flatter, flattest**
1 Something that is flat is smooth and level, and has no bumps on it. *You need a nice flat surface for rollerblading.*
2 A flat battery has no more power in it.
3 A flat tyre or ball does not have enough air in it.

flat noun (plural **flats**)
a set of rooms that you can live in inside a large building *We live in a flat on the top floor.*

flatter verb **flatters, flattering, flattered**
If you flatter someone, you praise them and say nice things to them.

flavour noun (plural **flavours**)
The flavour of something is the taste that it has when you eat it or drink it. *The ice cream had a delicious creamy flavour.*

flea noun (plural **fleas**)
a small jumping insect that lives on larger animals and sucks their blood

flee verb **flees, fleeing, fled**
When you flee, you run away.
And every single brigand leaped to his feet and fled, screaming with terror.—Philip Pullman, The Scarecrow and his Servant

fleece noun (plural **fleeces**)
1 A sheep's fleece is the wool on its body.
2 A fleece is a type of warm coat or jacket made of thick material.

flesh noun
Your flesh is the soft part of your body between your bones and your skin.

flew verb *see* **fly** verb

flexible adjective
Something that is flexible bends easily.

flick verb **flicks, flicking, flicked**
When you flick something, you knock it with your finger so that it flies through the air. *He rolled the paper into a little ball and flicked it into the air.*

flight noun (plural **flights**)
1 a journey in an aeroplane *Our flight leaves at 10 o'clock.*
2 A flight of stairs is a set of stairs.

fling verb **flings, flinging, flung**
When you fling something, you throw it as hard as you can. *He flung the book down onto the floor.*

flip verb **flips, flipping, flipped**
When you flip something over, you turn it over quickly.

flipper noun (plural **flippers**)
1 The flippers on a seal or a penguin are the parts on the sides of its body that it uses for swimming.
2 Flippers are large, flat shoes that you wear on your feet to help you swim.

flirt verb **flirts, flirting, flirted**
When you flirt with someone, you are nice to them and show them that you like them and want to go out with them.

float verb **floats, floating, floated**
When something floats, it does not sink but stays on the surface of water.

flock noun (*plural* **flocks**)
A flock of sheep or birds is a large group of them.

flood noun (*plural* **floods**)
When there is a flood, a lot of water spreads over the land.

flood verb **floods, flooding, flooded**
When a river floods, it becomes too full and spills out over the land.

floor noun (*plural* **floors**)
1 The floor in a building is the part that you walk on.
2 A floor in a tall building is one of the levels in it. *The sports department is on the third floor.*

flop verb **flops, flopping, flopped**
1 If you flop down, you sit or lie down suddenly because you are very tired.
He was so tired that he flopped down upon the nice soft sand on the floor of the rabbit-hole and shut his eyes.—Beatrix Potter, The Tale of Peter Rabbit
2 If something flops, it hangs and moves about loosely. *My hair kept flopping into my eyes.*

flour noun
Flour is a powder that is made from crushed wheat. You use flour for making bread, pastry, and cakes.

flow verb **flows, flowing, flowed**
When water flows, it moves along like a river.

flow chart noun (*plural* **flow charts**)
a diagram that shows the different stages of how something happens

flower noun (*plural* **flowers**)
the brightly-coloured part of a plant

flown verb *see* **fly** verb

flu noun
Flu is an illness that gives you a bad cold and makes you ache all over and feel very hot. Flu is short for **influenza**.

fluff noun
light, soft wool or feathers *The chicks looked like little yellow balls of fluff.*

> **WORD FAMILY**
> • **fluffy** The kittens were soft and fluffy.

fluid noun (*plural* **fluids**) (*say* **floo**-id)
a liquid

flung verb *see* **fling**

flush verb **flushes, flushing, flushed**
1 When you flush, your face goes red because you feel shy or guilty.
2 When you flush a toilet, you clean it by making water rush through it.

flute noun (*plural* **flutes**)
a musical instrument which you hold sideways across your mouth and play by blowing across a hole in it

flutter verb **flutters, fluttering, fluttered**
When something flutters, it flaps gently. *None of them noticed a large tawny owl flutter past the window.*—J. K. Rowling, Harry Potter and the Philosopher's Stone

fly noun (*plural* **flies**)
a small insect with wings

fly verb **flies, flying, flew, flown**
When something flies, it moves along through the air.

foal noun (*plural* **foals**)
a young horse

foam noun
1 a thick mass of small bubbles on the top of a liquid
2 a soft, light substance that is used inside chairs and cushions to make them soft to sit on

focus verb **focuses, focusing, focused**
When you focus a camera or telescope, you move the controls so that you get a clear picture.

fog noun
When there is fog, there is thick cloud just above the ground, which makes it difficult ⟶

a
b
c
d
e
f
g
h
i
j
k
l
m
n
o
p
q
r
s
t
u
v
w
x
y
z

to see. *The fog was so thick that we could hardly see.*

WORD FAMILY
- **foggy** It was a damp foggy day.

fold verb **folds, folding, folded**
When you fold something, you bend one part of it over another part. *She folded the letter and put it in her bag.*

folder noun (*plural* **folders**)
1 a thin cardboard case that you keep pieces of paper in
2 a place where you keep several files together on a computer

folk tale noun (*plural* **folk tales**)
a traditional story that has been passed down for many years

follow verb **follows, following, followed**
1 If you follow someone, you go after them. *I felt sure that someone was following me.*
2 If you follow a road or path, you go along it. *Follow this path until you come to a river.*
3 If you follow instructions, you do what they tell you to do.

fond adjective **fonder, fondest**
If you are fond of something, you like it a lot. If you are fond of someone, you like them a lot.

font noun (*plural* **fonts**)
a set of letters in a particular style and size that you can use on a computer

food noun (*plural* **foods**)
anything that you eat to help you grow and be healthy

food chain noun (*plural* **food chains**)
(*in science*) A food chain is a set of plants and animals that are linked because each one eats the one below it on the chain. For example, grass is eaten by a rabbit, then a rabbit is eaten by a fox.

fool noun (*plural* **fools**)
someone who is very silly

WORD FAMILY
- **foolish** Don't be so foolish!

foot noun (*plural* **feet**)
1 Your feet are the parts of your body that you stand on.

2 We can measure length in feet. One foot is about 30 centimetres.

WORD FAMILY
- A **footprint** is a mark on the ground left by someone's foot. A **footstep** is the sound of someone walking along.

football noun
1 a game in which two teams try to score goals by kicking a ball into a net
2 a ball that you use for playing football

for preposition
1 If something is for a person, you are going to give it to that person. *I've bought a present for you.*
2 If you say what something is for, you are saying how you use it. *You need a sharp knife for cutting bread.*

forbid verb **forbids, forbidding, forbade, forbidden**
To forbid someone to do something means to tell them that they must not do it. If something is forbidden, you are not allowed to do it.

force noun (*plural* **forces**)
1 If you use force to do something, you use your strength. *They had to use force to open the door.*
2 (*in science*) A force is something that pushes or pulls an object.
3 A police force is all the police who work together in one town or area.

force verb **forces, forcing, forced**
1 If you force someone to do something, you make them do it. *You can't force me to help you!*
2 If you force something open, you use your strength to open it.

force meter noun (*plural* **force meters**)
a tool or machine that you use for measuring force

forecast noun (*plural* **forecasts**)
When you give a forecast, you say what you think is going to happen.

forehead noun (*plural* **foreheads**)
Your forehead is the part of your head that is above your eyes.

foreign adjective
Things that are foreign come from other countries or are to do with other countries. *Can you speak any foreign languages?*

forest noun (*plural* **forests**)
an area of land where a lot of trees grow close together

forge verb **forges, forging, forged**
If you forge something, you copy it because you want to trick people. *Someone had forged my signature.*

forget verb **forgets, forgetting, forgot, forgotten**
If you forget something, you do not remember it. *I forgot to do my homework.*

forgive verb **forgives, forgiving, forgave, forgiven**
If you forgive someone, you stop being angry with them.

forgot, forgotten verb
see **forget**

fork noun (*plural* **forks**)
1 A fork is a tool with three sharp points called prongs. You use a fork for eating food, and you use a large fork for digging in the ground.
2 A fork in a road is a place where the road splits, and two roads go off in different directions.

form noun (*plural* **forms**)
1 a piece of paper that has writing on it and spaces where you must fill in your name and other information
2 a class in a school *Which form are you in?*
3 a type *A bicycle is a form of transport.*

form verb **forms, forming, formed**
When something forms, it is made. *These rocks formed millions of years ago.*

formal adjective
1 Formal events or clothes are very smart and not relaxed.
2 Formal language is language that you write down, not language you use when you are talking to friends.

fort noun (*plural* **forts**)
a strong building that looks like a castle

fortnight noun (*plural* **fortnights**)
A fortnight is two weeks.

fortress noun (*plural* **fortresses**)
a big fort

fortunate adjective
If you are fortunate, you are lucky. *I know I'm very fortunate to have such good friends.*

> **WORD FAMILY**
> • **fortunately** Fortunately, no one was hurt.

fortune noun (*plural* **fortunes**)
A fortune is a very large amount of money.

forty noun
the number 40

forwards, forward
1 towards the place that is in front of you *The train moved slowly forwards.*
2 If you are looking forward to something, you are excited because it is going to happen.

fossil noun (*plural* **fossils**)
part of a dead plant or animal that has been in the ground for millions of years and has gradually turned to stone

a
b
c
d
e
f
g
h
i
j
k
l
m
n
o
p
q
r
s
t
u
v
w
x
y
z

fought verb *see* **fight**

foul adjective **fouler, foulest** (*rhymes with* owl)
Something that is foul is dirty and nasty.
There was a foul smell outside.

foul noun (*plural* **fouls**) (*rhymes with* owl)
If you commit a foul in a game such as
football, you push or kick another player.

found verb *see* **find**

fountain noun (*plural* **fountains**)
a jet of water that shoots up into the air

four noun (*plural* **fours**)
the number 4

> 🏠 **WORD FAMILY**
> • The **fourth** thing is the one that is number 4.

fourteen noun
the number 14

fox noun (*plural* **foxes**)
a wild animal that looks like a dog and has
red fur and a long, furry tail

fraction noun (*plural* **fractions**)
(*in mathematics*) A fraction is a number that is
not a whole number. ⅓, ½, and ¾ are fractions

fracture noun (*plural* **fractures**)
a place where a bone is cracked or broken

fragile adjective (*say* **fraj**-ile)
Something that is fragile will break easily if
you drop it.

fragment noun (*plural* **fragments**)
a small piece that has broken off something
There were fragments of glass on the floor.

frame noun (*plural* **frames**)
1 the part round the outside of a picture or a
pair of glasses *On the wall was a picture in a
silver frame.*
2 the part that supports an object *Most tents
have a metal frame.*

freckle noun (*plural* **freckles**)
Freckles are the small brown spots that some
people have on their skin, especially when
they have been in the sun.

free adjective **freer, freest**
1 If you are free, you can go where you want
and do what you want to do.
*After five days locked in that room I was
finally free.*
2 If something is free, you do not have to pay
for it. *Entry to the museum is free.*

free verb **frees, freeing, freed**
To free someone means to let them go after
they have been locked up.

freedom noun
If you have freedom, you can go where you
want and do what you want to do.

free verse noun
poetry which does not rhyme and does not
have a regular rhythm

freeze verb **freezes, freezing, froze,
frozen**
1 When something freezes, it becomes very cold
and hard and changes into ice. *The lake froze
over last winter.*
2 If you are freezing or frozen, you are very cold.

freezer noun (*plural* **freezers**)
a large, very cold container in which you can
store frozen food for a long time

frequent adjective
Something that is frequent happens quite
often.

> 🏠 **WORD FAMILY**
> • **frequently** The old car broke down quite
> frequently.

fresh adjective **fresher, freshest**
1 Something that is fresh is clean and new. *I
went home and changed into some fresh clothes.*
2 Fresh food has been made or picked only a
short time ago.
3 Fresh air is clean and cool.

4 Fresh water is not salty.
5 If you feel fresh, you do not feel tired.

> **WORD FAMILY**
> • **freshly** I could smell freshly baked bread.

friction noun
(*in science*) the force which is produced when one thing rubs against another

Friday noun (*plural* **Fridays**)
the day after Thursday

fridge noun (*plural* **fridges**)
A fridge is a large cool container that you keep food in so that it does not go bad. Fridge is short for **refrigerator**.

friend noun (*plural* **friends**)
Your friends are the people you like and know well.

> **WORD FAMILY**
> • **friendly** Everyone here is very friendly.
> • **friendship** Her friendship means a lot to me.

fright noun (*plural* **frights**)
a sudden feeling of fear *I looked up and saw a face at the window, which gave me a bit of a fright.*

frighten verb **frightens, frightening, frightened**
If something frightens you, it makes you feel scared. *I'm sorry, I didn't mean to frighten you.*

> **WORD FAMILY**
> • **frightened** I had never been so frightened in all my life.
> • **frightening** It was quite frightening walking through the forest.

fringe noun (*plural* **fringes**)
short hair that hangs down over your forehead

frog noun (*plural* **frogs**)
A frog is a small animal with a smooth, wet skin and long back legs. Frogs live near water and can jump by using their strong back legs.

from preposition
1 When you go away from a place, you leave that place. *We flew from London to Paris.*
2 If a present is from a person, that person gave it to you. *I got a lovely present from my aunt.*

front noun (*plural* **fronts**)
The front of something is the part that faces forwards. *We sat at the front of the bus.*

frost noun (*plural* **frosts**)
ice that looks like powder and covers the ground when the weather is cold

> **WORD FAMILY**
> • **frosty** It was a cold frosty morning.

frown verb **frowns, frowning, frowned**
When you frown, you have lines on your forehead because you are angry or worried.

froze, frozen verb *see* **freeze**

frozen adjective
Something that is frozen has turned to ice. *We skated on the frozen pond.*

fruit noun (*plural* **fruits** or **fruit**)
A fruit is the part of a plant which contains seeds. A lot of fruits taste sweet and are good to eat. Apples, oranges, and bananas are all types of fruit.

fry verb **fries, frying, fried**
When you fry food, you cook it in hot fat.

fuel noun (*plural* **fuels**) (*say* **fyoo**-el)
anything that people burn to give heat or power *What type of fuel does your car use?*

full adjective **fuller, fullest**
If something is full, it has as much inside it as it can hold. *The room was full of people.*

full stop noun (*plural* **full stops**)
a dot which you put at the end of every sentence

fun noun
When you have fun, you enjoy yourself. *We had great fun on the beach.*

fund noun (*plural* **funds**)
an amount of money that people have collected so that they can use it for something special *Our school is raising funds to buy new computers.*

funeral noun (*plural* **funerals**)
the ceremony that takes place when a dead person is buried or burned

funnel noun (*plural* **funnels**)
a chimney on a ship or steam engine

funny adjective **funnier, funniest**
1 Something that is funny makes you laugh or smile.
2 Something that is funny is strange or surprising. *There was a funny smell in the classroom.*

fur noun (*plural* **furs**)
the soft hair that covers some animals

furious adjective
If you are furious, you are very angry.

> **WORD FAMILY**
> • **furiously** 'I don't care!' he shouted furiously.

furniture noun
things such as beds and tables that you need inside a house

furry adjective **furrier, furriest**
A furry animal is covered in fur.

further adverb *see* **far**

fuss verb **fusses, fussing, fussed**
If you fuss about something, you worry about it too much.

fussy adjective **fussier, fussiest**
Someone who is fussy only likes certain things and so is difficult to please. *You shouldn't be so fussy with your food.*

future noun
The future is the time that will come. *Nobody knows what will happen in the future.*

fuzzy adjective **fuzzier, fuzziest**
A picture or sound that is fuzzy is not very clear.

gain verb **gains, gaining, gained**
If you gain something, you get something good or useful. *I got the answer right and gained two points for my team.*

galaxy noun (*plural* **galaxies**)
A galaxy is a large group of stars and planets. The Milky Way is a galaxy.

gale noun (*plural* **gales**)
a very strong wind

gallery noun (*plural* **galleries**)
a building or large room where there are paintings on the walls for people to look at

gallon noun (*plural* **gallons**)
We can measure liquids in gallons. A gallon is about 4$\frac{1}{2}$ litres.

gallop verb **gallops, galloping, galloped**
When a horse gallops, it runs as fast as it can.

game noun (*plural* **games**)
something that you play for fun *Shall we have a game of tennis?*

gang noun (plural **gangs**)
a group of people who spend time together and do things together *It took a while for the other members of the gang to accept me.*

gangster noun (plural **gangsters**)
someone who belongs to a gang that robs and kills people

gaol noun (plural **gaols**) (say **jail**)
a prison

gap noun (plural **gaps**)
a hole, or an empty space between two things *We climbed through a gap in the fence.*

gape verb **gapes, gaping, gaped**
1 If you gape at something, you stand and look at it with your mouth open, because you are so surprised.
As I passed the Crazy Cossacks one by one, all they could do was gape at me in sheer disbelief.—Michael Morpurgo, Mr Skip
2 Something that is gaping is wide open. *He fell down a big gaping hole in the ground.*

garage noun (plural **garages**)
1 a building in which people keep a car or bus
2 a place that sells petrol and mends cars

garbage noun (US)
things that you have thrown away because you do not want them any more

garden noun (plural **gardens**)
a piece of ground where people grow flowers, fruit, or vegetables

garlic noun
a plant like an onion with a very strong smell and taste

gas noun (plural **gases**)
A gas is any substance that is like air, and is not a solid or a liquid. We can burn some types of gas to give heat to cook with or heat our homes. *Oxygen is a gas.*

gash noun (plural **gashes**)
a deep cut in your skin *I fell over and got a nasty gash on my forehead.*

gasp verb **gasps, gasping, gasped**
When you gasp, you breathe in quickly and noisily because you are surprised, or because you have been running. *I can't run any further, he gasped.*

gate noun (plural **gates**)
a door in a wall or fence

gather verb **gathers, gathering, gathered**
1 When people gather, they come together. *A crowd gathered to watch the fight.*
2 When you gather things, you collect them and bring them together. *I need to gather some information for my project.*

gave verb *see* **give**

gaze verb **gazes, gazing, gazed**
If you gaze at something, you look at it for a long time.
Dorothy leaned her chin upon her hand and gazed thoughtfully at the Scarecrow.—L. Frank Baum, The Wizard of Oz

gear noun (plural **gears**)
1 The gears on a bicycle or car help to control how fast you go by changing the speed at which the wheels go round.
2 Your gear is all the things that you need to play a game or do a job. *Don't forget to bring your tennis gear.*

gel noun (say **jell**)
a thick, sticky liquid that you put on your hair to hold it in place

general adjective
1 Something that is general includes most people. *There was general agreement that something had to be done.*
2 Something that is general does not go into details. *We had a general discussion about what life was like in Roman times.*

generally adverb
usually *It is generally very cold here in the winter.*

generation noun (plural **generations**)
all the people who are the same age
This film will be popular with the older and younger generations.

generous adjective
Someone who is generous is kind and always ready to give or share the things that they have.

WORD FAMILY
• **generously** Sam very generously shared his sweets with us.

---

genius noun (plural **geniuses**)
(say **jee**-nee-uss)
someone who is extremely clever

a
b
c
d
e
f
g
h
i
j
k
l
m
n
o
p
q
r
s
t
u
v
w
x
y
z

genre noun (*plural* **genres**)
A genre is one type of writing. Poetry, adventure stories, and fairy tales are examples of different genres.

gentle adjective **gentler, gentlest**
If you are gentle, you touch something in a kind, careful way and are not rough. *I gave Ali a gentle nudge.*

> **WORD FAMILY**
> • **gently** She very gently put the baby bird back in the nest.

gentleman noun (*plural* **gentlemen**)
a polite name for a man

genuine adjective (*say* **jen**-yoo-in)
Something that is genuine is real. *Do you think this is genuine gold?*

geography noun (*say* **jee**-og-ra-fee)
the subject in which you learn about the earth, with its mountains, rivers, countries, and the people who live in them

geology noun
the subject in which you learn about rocks and fossils

germ noun (*plural* **germs**)
A germ is a tiny living thing, that is too small to see. Germs sometimes make you ill if they get inside your body.

get verb **gets, getting, got**
1 When you get something, you receive it, buy it, or earn it, and it becomes yours. *What did you get for your birthday?*
2 To get means to become. *Are you getting tired yet?*

ghost noun (*plural* **ghosts**)
the shape of a dead person that some people think they can see

giant noun (*plural* **giants**)
a very big person, especially in stories

gift noun (*plural* **gifts**)
a present

gigantic adjective
Something that is gigantic is very big. *He lifted the tree with one of his gigantic arms.*

giggle verb **giggles, giggling, giggled**
If you giggle, you laugh in a silly way.

gill noun (*plural* **gills**)
The gills on a fish are the parts on its sides that it breathes through.

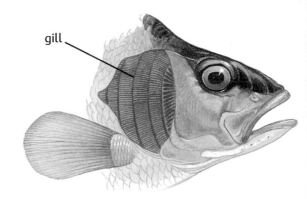

gill

ginger noun
a spice with a strong, hot taste

ginger adjective
Ginger hair is a reddish-orange colour.

giraffe noun (*plural* **giraffes**)
A giraffe is a very tall African animal with a very long neck. Giraffes are the tallest animals in the world, and they use their long necks to reach up and eat leaves off trees.

girl noun (*plural* **girls**)
a female child

girlfriend noun (*plural* **girlfriends**)
A boy's girlfriend is the girl he is going out with.

give verb **gives, giving, gave, given**
If you give something to someone, you let them have it.

glad adjective
If you are glad about something, you are happy about it.
Then the crocodile and the monkey and the parrot were very glad and began to sing because they were going back to Africa, their real home.—Hugh Lofting, The Story of Doctor Dolittle

> **WORD FAMILY**
> • **gladly** I will gladly help you.

glamorous adjective
Someone who is glamorous looks elegant, rich, and beautiful.

glance verb **glances, glancing, glanced**
If you glance at something, you look at it quickly.
I glanced at my watch. 'Let's get a move on. It's quarter past eight.'—Narinder Dhami, Bindi Babes

glare verb **glares, glaring, glared**
1 If you glare at someone, you look at them angrily. *Mr Dempster glared at the two boys.*
2 If a light glares, it shines with a very bright light that hurts your eyes.

glass noun (*plural* **glasses**)
1 the hard, clear substance that windows are made of
2 a cup made of glass, which you drink out of

glasses noun
two round pieces of glass in a frame, which some people wear over their eyes to help them to see better or to shade their eyes from the sun

gleam verb **gleams, gleaming, gleamed**
If something gleams, it shines. *The cat's eyes gleamed in the dark.*

glide verb **glides, gliding, glided**
When something glides along, it moves along very smoothly. *The skaters glided over the ice.*

glider noun (*plural* **gliders**)
a type of aeroplane without an engine

glimmer verb **glimmers, glimmering, glimmered**
If something glimmers, it shines with a faint light.

glimpse verb **glimpses, glimpsing, glimpsed**
If you glimpse something, you see it for only a few seconds. *I glimpsed an animal in the bushes.*

glint verb **glints, glinting, glinted**
If something glints, it shines or sparkles. *The water was glinting in the moonlight.*

glisten verb **glistens, glistening, glistened**
If something glistens, it shines and sparkles because it is wet. *The grass glistened with dew.*

glitter verb **glitters, glittering, glittered**
If something glitters, it shines and sparkles brightly.
Trees of diamonds under the earth! Sparkling brighter than frost. Glittering more brilliantly than sun on water.—Anne Fine, The Twelve Dancing Princesses

gloat verb **gloats, gloating, gloated**
If you gloat, you show that you are pleased because you have done well and someone else has done badly.

global warming noun
the process by which the earth is gradually getting warmer because of pollution in the atmosphere

globe noun (*plural* **globes**)
a ball with the map of the whole world on it

> **WORD FAMILY**
> • Something that is **global** happens all over the world.

gloomy adjective **gloomier, gloomiest**
1 A gloomy place is dark.
2 If you feel gloomy, you feel sad.

glorious adjective
Something that is glorious is beautiful or magnificent. *It was a glorious summer's day.*

a b c d e f **g** h i j k l m n o p q r s t u v w x y z

glory noun
If you win glory, you do very well and become famous.

glossary noun (*plural* **glossaries**)
a list at the back of a book, which explains the meanings of difficult words that are used in the book

glossy adjective **glossier, glossiest**
Something that is glossy is smooth and shiny.

glove noun (*plural* **gloves**)
A glove is something that you wear on your hands in cold weather. Gloves have separate parts for your thumb and each finger.

glow verb **glows, glowing, glowed**
1 If something glows, it shines with a warm, gentle light.
2 When your cheeks glow, they are pink because you are cold or have been running around.

glue noun (*plural* **glues**)
a sticky substance that you use for sticking things together

glum adjective
If you feel glum, you feel sad.

gnarled adjective (**gn-** in this word sounds like **n-**)
Something that is gnarled is bent and twisted because it is very old. *We sat on a gnarled old tree trunk.*

gnaw verb **gnaws, gnawing, gnawed** (**gn-** in this word sounds like **n-**)
When an animal gnaws on something, it keeps biting it. *The dog was outside, gnawing on a bone.*

gnome noun (*plural* **gnomes**) (**gn-** in this word sounds like **n-**)
a small, ugly fairy in stories

go verb **goes, going, went, gone**
1 When you go somewhere, you move or travel so that you are there. *Where are you going?*
2 If a machine is going, it is working.
3 To go means to become. *Clay goes hard when you bake it.*

goal noun (*plural* **goals**)
1 the net where you must kick or throw the ball to score a point in a game such as football or netball
2 something that you want to achieve *Her goal in life is to become a professional singer.*

goat noun (*plural* **goats**)
an animal with horns that is sometimes kept on farms for its milk

god noun (*plural* **gods**)
a person or thing that people worship

WORD FAMILY
• A **goddess** is a female god.

goggles noun
special thick glasses that you wear to protect your eyes, for example when you are swimming

go-kart noun (*plural* **go-karts**)
a type of small car that people use for racing

gold noun
a shiny, yellow metal that is very valuable

WORD FAMILY
• **golden** They drank from golden cups.

golf noun
Golf is a game that you play by hitting small, white balls with sticks called **golf clubs**. You have to hit the balls into holes in the ground.

gone verb *see* **go**

good adjective **better, best**
1 Something that is good is nice, pleasant, or enjoyable. *Have you had a good day at school?*
2 Someone who is good is kind and honest. *You have been a very good friend to me.*
3 When you are good, you behave well and do not do anything naughty. *Be good for your aunt and uncle.*
4 If you are good at something, you can do it well. *I'm not very good at swimming.*

goodbye interjection
the word you say to someone when you are leaving them

goods noun
Goods are things that people buy and sell.

goose noun (*plural* **geese**)
A goose is a large bird that is kept on farms for its meat and eggs. A male goose is called a **gander**.

gorgeous adjective
Something that is gorgeous is very nice indeed. *This chocolate ice cream is gorgeous!*

gorilla noun (*plural* **gorillas**)
A gorilla is an African animal like a very large monkey with long arms and no tail. A gorilla is a type of ape.

gossip verb **gossips, gossiping, gossiped**
If you gossip, you talk about other people, sometimes in an unkind way.

got verb *see* **get**

government noun (*plural* **governments**)
The government is the group of people who are in charge of a country.

gown noun (*plural* **gowns**) (*rhymes with* down)
a long dress

grab verb **grabs, grabbing, grabbed**
If you grab something, you take hold of it quickly or roughly. *The thief grabbed my purse and ran off.*

graceful adjective
Someone who is graceful moves in a smooth, gentle way. *She is a very graceful dancer.*

> 🏠 **WORD FAMILY**
> • **gracefully** The dancers moved gracefully across the floor.

grade noun (*plural* **grades**)
a mark that you get for a piece of work, which shows how good your work is

gradual adjective
Something that is gradual happens slowly, bit by bit, not all at once.

> 🏠 **WORD FAMILY**
> • **gradually** I was gradually beginning to feel better.

graffiti noun (*say* gra-**fee**-tee)
writing and pictures that people have scribbled or scratched onto walls

grain noun (*plural* **grains**)
1 Grain is the seeds of plants like corn and wheat.
2 A grain of salt or sand is one tiny bit of it.

gram noun (*plural* **grams**)
We can measure weight in grams. There are 1000 grams in one kilogram.

grammar noun
Grammar is all the rules of a language, which tell us how to put the words together correctly.

grand adjective **grander, grandest**
Something that is grand is very big and important.

grandchild noun (*plural* **grandchildren**)
Someone's grandchild is a child of their son or daughter. A grandchild can also be called a **granddaughter**, or a **grandson**.

grandparent noun (*plural* **grandparents**)
Your grandparents are the parents of your father or mother. You can also call your grandparents your **grandmother** and **grandfather**. A grandmother is often called **grandma** or **granny**. A grandfather is often called **grandpa** or **grandad**.

a
b
c
d
e
f
g
h
i
j
k
l
m
n
o
p
q
r
s
t
u
v
w
x
y
z

grape noun (*plural* **grapes**)
a small, soft green or purple fruit that grows in bunches

grapefruit noun (*plural* **grapefruits**)
a large, sour-tasting fruit that has thick yellow skin

graph noun
(*plural* **graphs**)
a diagram that shows information about something *We drew a graph showing how tall our plant grew.*

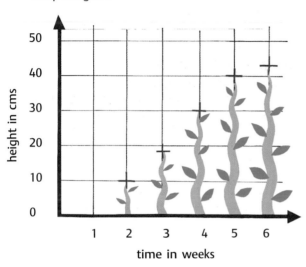

graphics noun
pictures or designs, especially pictures that are made on a computer *Some computer games have got brilliant graphics.*

grasp verb **grasps, grasping, grasped**
If you grasp something, you get hold of it and hold it tightly. *She grasped my arm to stop herself from falling.*

grass noun (*plural* **grasses**)
a green plant that covers the ground and is used for lawns and parks

grasshopper noun (*plural* **grasshoppers**)
an insect that has long back legs and can jump a long way

grate verb **grates, grating, grated**
When you grate food, you cut it into very small pieces by rubbing it against a rough tool. *Sprinkle the grated cheese over the top of the pizza.*

grateful adjective
If you are grateful for something, you are glad that you have it. *We are very grateful for all your help.*

> **WORD FAMILY**
> • **gratefully** He accepted the food gratefully.

grave noun (*plural* **graves**)
a place where a dead person is buried in the ground

grave adjective **graver, gravest**
Something that is grave is very serious and worrying.

gravel noun
tiny stones that are used to make paths *Her feet crunched over the gravel.*

gravity noun
(*in science*) the force that pulls things towards the earth

graze verb **grazes, grazing, grazed**
1 If you graze a part of your body, you hurt it by scraping it against something and making it bleed. *I fell over and grazed my knee.*
2 When animals graze, they eat grass. *The sheep were grazing in the field.*

grease noun
a thick, oily substance

great adjective **greater, greatest**
1 Something that is great is very big and impressive.
The edge of the river was lined with great trees, which seemed to get even taller further away.—Alexander McCall Smith, The Bubblegum Tree
2 A great person is very clever and important. *Van Gogh was a great artist.*
3 Something that is great is very good. *It's a great film!*

greedy adjective **greedier, greediest**
Someone who is greedy wants more food or money than they need.

green adjective
Something that is green is the colour of grass.

greengrocer noun (*plural* **greengrocers**)
someone who sells fruit and vegetables
in a shop

greenhouse noun (*plural* **greenhouses**)
a glass building that people use for growing
plants in

greet verb **greets, greeting, greeted**
When you greet someone, you welcome them
and say hello to them.

> **WORD FAMILY**
> • A **greeting** is something that you say when you
> greet someone.

grew verb *see* **grow**

grey adjective (*rhymes with* day)
Something that is grey is the colour of the
sky on a cloudy day.

grid noun (*plural* **grids**)
a pattern of straight lines that cross over each
other to make squares

grill verb **grills, grilling, grilled**
When you grill food, you cook it on metal
bars either under or over heat. *We grilled
some sausages for tea.*

grin verb **grins, grinning, grinned**
When you grin, you smile in a cheerful way.
*The Enormous Crocodile grinned, showing
hundreds of sharp white teeth.*—Roald Dahl,
The Enormous Crocodile

grind verb **grinds, grinding, ground**
When you grind something, you crush it into
tiny bits. *The wheat is taken to the mill and
ground into flour.*

grip verb **grips, gripping, gripped**
When you grip something, you hold on to
it tightly.

gripping adjective
A book or film that is gripping is very
exciting.

groan verb **groans, groaning, groaned**
When you groan, you make a low sound
because you are in pain or are disappointed
about something.

grocer noun (*plural* **grocers**)
someone who sells tea, sugar, jam, and other
kinds of food in a shop

groom noun (*plural* **grooms**)
1 a person who looks after horses
2 another word for a bridegroom

groove noun (*plural* **grooves**)
a long, narrow cut in something

grope verb **gropes, groping, groped**
If you grope around, you try to find
something by feeling for it with your hands
because you cannot see. *I groped for the door
in the dark.*

ground noun (*plural* **grounds**)
1 The ground is the earth.
2 A sports ground is a piece of land that people
play sport on.

ground verb *see* **grind**

group noun (*plural* **groups**)
1 a number of people, animals, or things that are
together or belong together *There was a group
of children standing by the ice cream stall.*
2 a number of people who play music together
What's your favourite pop group?

grow verb **grows, growing, grew, grown**
1 To grow means to become bigger.
*My aunt looked at me and said, 'My! Haven't
you grown!'*
2 When you grow plants,
you put them in the
ground and look
after them.
3 To grow means
to become.
*Everyone
was
beginning
to grow
tired.*

growl verb **growls, growling, growled**
When an animal growls, it makes a deep,
angry sound in its throat.

a
b
c
d
e
f
g
h
i
j
k
l
m
n
o
p
q
r
s
t
u
v
w
x
y
z

grown-up noun (*plural* **grown-ups**)
a man or woman who is not a child any more

growth noun
the way in which something grows and gets bigger *We measured the growth of the plants.*

grub noun (*plural* **grubs**)
1 an animal that looks like a small worm and will become an insect when it is an adult
2 (informal) food

gruff adjective **gruffer, gruffest**
A gruff voice is deep and rough.

> **WORD FAMILY**
> • **gruffly** 'What do you want?' he asked gruffly.

grumble verb **grumbles, grumbling, grumbled**
If you grumble about something, you complain about it.
His sister used to grumble about all these animals and said they made the house untidy.—Hugh Lofting, The Story of Doctor Dolittle

grumpy adjective **grumpier, grumpiest**
Someone who is grumpy is bad-tempered.

grunt verb **grunts, grunting, grunted**
When a pig grunts, it makes a rough sound.

guarantee noun (*plural* **guarantees**) (**gu-** in this word sounds like **g-**)
a promise that something you have bought will be mended or replaced free if it goes wrong

guard verb **guards, guarding, guarded**
1 When you guard a place, you watch it to keep it safe from other people. *The dog was guarding the house.*
2 When you guard a person, you watch them to keep them safe or to stop them from escaping.

guard noun (*plural* **guards**)
someone who protects a place or watches a person to keep them safe or stop them from escaping

guess verb **guesses, guessing, guessed**
When you guess, you say what you think the answer to a question is when you do not really know. *Can you guess what I've got in my pocket?*

guest noun (*plural* **guests**)
a person who is invited to a party or is invited to stay in someone else's home for a short time

guide noun (*plural* **guides**)
1 a person who shows you around a place
2 a book that gives you information about something

guide verb **guides, guiding, guided**
If you guide someone to a place, you lead them or take them there.

guilty adjective **guiltier, guiltiest**
1 If you are guilty, you have done something wrong. *The prisoner was found guilty of murder.*
2 If you feel guilty, you feel bad because you have done something wrong.

guitar noun (*plural* **guitars**)
A guitar is a musical instrument with strings across it. You hold a guitar in front of your body and play it by pulling on the strings with your fingers.

gulf noun (*plural* **gulfs**)
an area of the sea that stretches a long way into the land

gull noun (*plural* **gulls**)
A gull is a sea bird. A gull is also called a **seagull**.

gulp verb **gulps, gulping, gulped**
When you gulp food or drink, you swallow it very quickly.

gum noun (*plural* **gums**)
1 Your gums are the hard pink parts of your mouth that are around your teeth.
2 Gum is a sweet that you chew but do not swallow.

gun noun (*plural* **guns**)
a weapon that fires bullets from a metal tube

gurdwara noun (*plural* **gurdwaras**)
a Sikh temple

gurgle verb **gurgles, gurgling, gurgled**
1 When water gurgles, it makes a bubbling sound.
2 When a baby gurgles, it makes a happy, laughing sound.

guru noun (*plural* **gurus**)
a Hindu religious leader

gush verb **gushes, gushing, gushed**
When water gushes, it moves very fast.

gust noun (*plural* **gusts**)
A gust of wind is a sudden rush of wind.

gutter noun (*plural* **gutters**)
1 a place at the side of a road where water collects and flows away when it rains
2 a pipe that goes along the edge of a roof and collects water from the roof when it rains

gym noun (*plural* **gyms**) (*say* **jim**)
A gym is a large room with special equipment in for doing exercises. A gym is also called a **gymnasium**.

gymnastics
special exercises that you do to make your body strong and to show how well you can bend, stretch, and twist your body

habit noun **habits**
If something that you do is a habit, you do it without thinking, because you have done it so often before.

habitat noun (*plural* **habitats**)
The habitat of an animal or plant is the place where it usually lives or grows. *These flowers grow in a woodland habitat.*

hack verb **hacks, hacking, hacked**
1 To hack something means to cut it roughly. *They hacked their way through the jungle.*
2 (*in ICT*) To hack into a computer means to get into it and use it illegally.

had verb *see* **have**

haiku noun (*plural* **haikus** or **haiku**) (*say* **hye**-koo)
a short poem with three lines and a fixed number of syllables in each line

hail noun
small pieces of ice that fall from the sky like rain

hair noun (*plural* **hairs**)
Your hair is the long, soft stuff that grows on your head. An animal's hair is the soft stuff that grows all over its body.

hairdresser noun (*plural* **hairdressers**)
someone who cuts people's hair

hairy adjective **hairier, hairiest**
Something that is hairy is covered with hair. A person who is hairy has a lot of hair on their body.

Hajj noun
The Hajj is the journey to Mecca that all Muslims try to make at least once in their lives.

half noun (*plural* **halves**)
One half of something is one of two equal parts that the thing is divided into. It can also be written as ½. *The front half of the room was empty.*

a
b
c
d
e
f
g
h
i
j
k
l
m
n
o
p
q
r
s
t
u
v
w
x
y
z

halfway adverb
in the middle *I'll meet you halfway between my house and your house.*

hall noun (*plural* **halls**)
1 the part of a house that is just inside the front door
2 a very big room *The concert will take place in the school hall.*
3 a large, important building

hallo, hello interjection
the word you say to someone when you meet them

Hallowe'en noun
the 31st October, when some people think that witches and ghosts appear

halt verb **halts, halting, halted**
When something halts, it stops.

halve verb **halves, halving, halved**
To halve something means to cut it into two equal parts.

ham noun
meat from a pig's leg that has been salted or smoked

hamburger noun (*plural* **hamburgers**)
A hamburger is a round flat piece of minced beef. You usually eat a hamburger in a bread roll.

hammer noun (*plural* **hammers**)
a heavy tool that you use for hitting nails

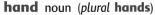

hand noun (*plural* **hands**)
Your hands are the parts of your body at the ends of your arms.

WORD FAMILY
• A **handful** of something is an amount that you can hold in your hand.

handbag noun (*plural* **handbags**)
a small bag in which women carry money and other things

handheld adjective
A handheld computer is a very small computer that you can hold in your hand and carry around with you.

handkerchief noun (*plural* **handkerchiefs**)
a piece of material you use for blowing your nose

handle noun (*plural* **handles**)
the part of something that you hold in your hand

handle verb **handles, handling, handled**
When you handle something, you pick it up and hold it in your hands. *You have to handle the young animals very gently.*

handsome adjective
A handsome man or boy is attractive to look at.

hands-on adjective
If something is hands-on, you can touch it and use it yourself, rather than just looking at it.

handstand noun
(*plural* **handstands**)
When you do a handstand, you put your hands on the ground and swing your legs up into the air.

handwriting noun
Your handwriting is the way in which you write. *Try to make your handwriting as neat as possible.*

handy adjective **handier, handiest**
Something that is handy is useful and easy to use.

hang verb **hangs, hanging, hung**
When you hang something up, you put it on a hook or nail. *You can hang your coat up in the hall.*

hanger noun (*plural* **hangers**)
a piece of wood or metal that you hang clothes on

Hanukkah noun (*say* **hah**-noo-ka)
the Jewish festival of lights, which lasts for eight days and begins in December

a b c d e f g h i j k l m n o p q r s t u v w x y z

happen verb **happens, happening, happened**
1 When something happens, it takes place. *When did the accident happen?*
2 If you happen to do something, you do it by chance, without planning to do it.

happy adjective **happier, happiest**
When you are happy, you feel pleased and you are enjoying yourself.

> **WORD FAMILY**
> • **happiness** She was crying tears of happiness.

harbour noun (*plural* **harbours**)
a place where people can tie up boats and leave them

hard adjective **harder, hardest**
1 Something that is hard is not soft. *In winter the ground is often hard and frozen.*
2 Something that is hard is difficult. *The last maths test was really hard.*

hard adverb
When you work hard, you work a lot and with a lot of effort.

hard disk noun (*plural* **hard disks**)
the part inside a computer where information is stored

hardly adverb
If you can hardly do something, you can only just do it. *I was so tired that I could hardly walk.*

hardware noun
1 tools, nails, and other things made of metal
2 (*in ICT*) A computer's hardware is the parts that you can see, and the parts inside that make it work. The **software** is the programs you put into it.

hare noun (*plural* **hares**)
A hare is an animal that looks like a big rabbit with very long ears. Hares have strong back legs and can run very fast.

> **WORD FAMILY**
> • **hare** We read a story about the hare and the tortoise.
> • **hair** I've got blonde hair.

harm verb **harms, harming, harmed**
To harm something means to damage it or spoil it in some way. To harm someone means to hurt them.

> **WORD FAMILY**
> • **harmful** Pollution from cars is harmful to the environment.
> • **harmless** Some snakes are poisonous, but others are harmless.

harmony noun (*plural* **harmonies**)
a group of musical notes that sound nice together

harness noun (*plural* **harnesses**)
1 a set of straps that you wear round your body to keep you safe *You must wear a safety harness when you are rock climbing.*
2 a set of straps that you put over a horse's head and round its neck so that you can control it

harp noun
(*plural* **harps**)
A harp is a musical instrument. It has a large frame with strings stretched across it, and you play it by pulling on the strings with your fingers.

harsh adjective **harsher, harshest**
1 Something that is harsh is not soft or gentle. *His violin made a harsh, unpleasant sound.*
2 Someone who is harsh is very strict and sometimes unkind. *The new headmistress is very harsh.*

> **WORD FAMILY**
> • **harshly** 'You're a fool!' he said harshly.

a
b
c
d
e
f
g
h
i
j
k
l
m
n
o
p
q
r
s
t
u
v
w
x
y
z

harvest noun (*plural* **harvests**)
the time when farmers gather in the crops that they have grown

hat noun (*plural* **hats**)
something that you wear on your head

hatch verb **hatches, hatching, hatched**
When a baby bird or animal hatches, it comes out of an egg and is born.

hate verb **hates, hating, hated**
If you hate something, you do not like it at all. If you hate someone, you do not like them at all.
I hate sitting still.—Jacqueline Wilson, Double Act

WORD FAMILY
• **hatred** His eyes gleamed with hatred.

haul verb **hauls, hauling, hauled** (*rhymes with* ball)
To haul something means to pull it along.
They hauled the boat out of the river.

haunted adjective
A haunted place has ghosts in it.

have verb **has, having, had**
1 If you have something, you own it. *I don't have a computer at home.*
2 If you have an illness, you are suffering from it. *I think you may have chickenpox.*
3 If you have to do something, you must do it. *We have to find the map before the pirates get back!*

hay noun
dry grass that people use to feed animals

hay fever noun
If you have hay fever, some types of flowers, trees, or grass make you sneeze in the summer.

head noun (*plural* **heads**)
1 Your head is the part at the top of your body that contains your brain, eyes, and mouth.
2 The head is the person in charge of something.

headache noun (*plural* **headaches**)
If you have a headache, your head hurts.

heading noun (*plural* **headings**)
words you write as a title at the top of a piece of writing

headlight noun (*plural* **headlights**)
The headlights on a car are the lights that you use at night so that you can see where you are going.

headline noun (*plural* **headlines**)
the words in large print at the top of a piece of writing in a newspaper

headphones noun
a set of small speakers that you wear over your ears so that you can listen to music from a music player

headquarters noun
the place where an organization is based, and where the people in charge of it work

headteacher noun (*plural* **headteachers**)
A headteacher is the person in charge of all the teachers and children in a school. A headteacher is also called a **headmaster** or **headmistress**.

heal verb **heals, healing, healed**
When a cut or broken bone heals, it gets better. *It usually takes about six weeks for a broken bone to heal.*

health noun
Your health is how well you are.

healthy adjective **healthier, healthiest**
1 When you are healthy, you are not ill.
2 Things that are healthy are good for you and keep you fit and well.

WORD FAMILY
• **healthily** You should try to eat healthily.

heap noun (*plural* **heaps**)
an untidy pile of things *There was a big heap of clothes on the floor.*

hear verb **hears, hearing, heard**
When you hear something, you notice it through your ears.

hearing noun
Your hearing is your ability to hear things.

heart noun (*plural* **hearts**)
1 Your heart is the part of your body in your chest that pumps blood all round your body.
2 A heart is a curved shape that looks like the shape of a heart and is used to represent love.

heat noun
the hot feeling you get from a fire or from the sun

heat verb **heats, heating, heated**
When you heat something, you make it warm or hot.

heaven noun
Heaven is the place where some people believe that a god lives. Some people believe that good people go to heaven when they die.

heavy adjective **heavier, heaviest**
Something that is heavy weighs a lot and is hard to lift.

hedge noun (*plural* **hedges**)
a line of bushes that are growing very close together and make a sort of wall round a garden or field

hedgehog noun (*plural* **hedgehogs**)
a small animal that is covered with spines like sharp needles

heel noun (*plural* **heels**)
Your heel is the back part of your foot.

height noun (*plural* **heights**) (*rhymes with* bite)
The height of something is how high it is. The height of a person is how tall they are. *We measured the height of the door.*

held verb *see* **hold**

helicopter noun (*plural* **helicopters**)
a flying machine with a big propeller that spins round on its roof

hell noun
a place where some people believe bad people are punished after they die

hello, hallo interjection
the word you say to someone when you meet them

helmet noun (*plural* **helmets**)
a strong hat that you wear to protect your head

help verb **helps, helping, helped**
1 When you help someone, you do something for them that makes things easier for them.
2 When you help yourself to something, you take it. *Please help yourselves to pizza.*

> 🏠 **WORD FAMILY**
> • **helper** Can you do that on your own, or do you need a helper?
> • **helpful** Thank you, you've been very helpful.

helping noun (*plural* **helpings**)
A helping of food is an amount that you give to one person. *Can I have just a small helping, please?*

helpless adjective
If you are helpless, you cannot look after yourself.

hemisphere noun (*plural* **hemispheres**) (*say* **hem**-iss-fere)
one half of the earth *Britain is in the northern hemisphere.*

a
b
c
d
e
f
g
h
i
j
k
l
m
n
o
p
q
r
s
t
u
v
w
x
y
z

hen noun (*plural* **hens**)
a bird that is kept on farms for the eggs that it lays

heptagon noun (*plural* **heptagons**)
a shape with seven straight sides

herb noun (*plural* **herbs**)
A herb is a plant that people add to food when they are cooking to make it taste nice. Parsley and mint are herbs.

herbivore noun (*plural* **herbivores**)
an animal that eats grass or plants

> **WORD FAMILY**
> • **herbivorous** Rabbits are herbivorous animals.

herd noun (*plural* **herds**)
A herd of animals is a group of animals that live and feed together.

here adverb
in this place *Please wait here until I get back.*

hero noun (*plural* **heroes**)
1 a boy or man who has done something very brave
2 The hero of a story is the man or boy who is the main character.

heroine noun (*plural* **heroines**)
1 a girl or woman who has done something very brave
2 The heroine of a story is the woman or girl who is the main character.

hesitate verb **hesitates, hesitating, hesitated**
If you hesitate, you wait for a little while before you do something because you are not sure what you should do.

> **WORD FAMILY**
> • **hesitation** Joe jumped up to help without a moment's hesitation.

hexagon noun (*plural* **hexagons**)
a shape with six straight sides

hibernate verb **hibernates, hibernating, hibernated**
When animals hibernate, they spend the winter in a special kind of deep sleep. Bats, tortoises, and hedgehogs all hibernate.

hiccup verb **hiccups, hiccuping, hiccuped**
When you hiccup, you make a sudden, sharp gulping sound which you cannot stop. You sometimes hiccup when you eat or drink too quickly.

hide verb **hides, hiding, hid, hidden**
1 When you hide, you go to a place where people cannot see you.
2 If you hide something, you put it in a secret place so that people cannot find it. *I hid the letter under my mattress.*

hideous adjective
Something that is hideous is very ugly and horrible to look at.

> **WORD FAMILY**
> • **hideously** The old woman was hideously ugly.

hieroglyphics noun (*say* hye-ro-**glif**-iks)
the type of writing that was used by the ancient Egyptians and was made up of small pictures and symbols

high adjective **higher, highest**
1 Something that is high is very tall. *There was a high wall around the garden.*
2 Something that is high up is a long way above the ground. *We could see an aeroplane high up in the sky.*
3 A high voice or sound is not deep or low.

highlight verb **highlights, highlighting, highlighted**
1 When you highlight something on paper, you draw over it using a special brightly-coloured pen so that you can see it easily.
2 (*in ICT*) When you highlight something on a computer, you move the mouse over it so that it changes colour.

hilarious adjective (*say* hil-**air**-ee-uss)
Something that is hilarious is very funny.

hill noun (*plural* **hills**)
a bit of ground that is higher than the ground around it

hind adjective
An animal's hind legs are its back legs.

Hindu noun (*plural* **Hindus**)
someone who follows the religion of **Hinduism**, which is an Indian religion with many gods

hinge noun (*plural* **hinges**)
A hinge is a piece of metal that is fixed to a door and to the wall. A hinge can move so that you can open and shut the door.

hint verb **hints, hinting, hinted**
When you hint, you suggest something without saying exactly what you mean. *Salim looked at the food and hinted that he was feeling a bit hungry.*

hip noun (*plural* **hips**)
Your hips are the parts of your body where your legs join the rest of your body.

hippopotamus noun (*plural* **hippopotamuses**)
A hippopotamus is a very large, heavy, African animal that lives near water. It is sometimes called a **hippo** for short.

hire verb **hires, hiring, hired**
When you hire something, you pay to use it for a short time. *You can hire skates at the ice rink.*

hiss verb **hisses, hissing, hissed**
When a snake hisses, it makes a long sss sound.

history noun
the subject in which you learn about things that happened in the past

> **WORD FAMILY**
> • **historical** Do you enjoy reading historical novels?

hit verb **hits, hitting, hit**
To hit something means to bang against it. To hit someone means to knock them or slap them.

hi-tech adjective
Hi-tech equipment is very modern and uses the latest computer technology.

hive noun (*plural* **hives**)
A hive is a special box that bees live in. It is designed so that people can collect the honey that the bees make.

hoarse adjective
A hoarse voice sounds rough and deep.

hobby noun (*plural* **hobbies**)
something that you do for fun in your spare time

hockey noun
a game in which two teams try to score goals by hitting a ball into a net with a special stick

hold verb **holds, holding, held**
1 When you hold something, you have it in your hands. *Please can I hold the puppy?*
2 The amount that something holds is the amount that you can put inside it. *This jug will hold one litre of water.*

hole noun (*plural* **holes**)
a gap or an empty space in something *I've got a hole in my sock.*

Holi noun (*say* **hoe**-li)
a Hindu festival that happens in the spring

holiday noun (*plural* **holidays**)
a time when you do not have to go to school or work

hollow adjective
Something that is hollow has an empty space inside it. *Owls often make their nests in hollow trees.*

holy adjective **holier, holiest**
Something that is holy is special because it has something to do with a god or religion.

home noun (*plural* **homes**)
Your home is the place where you live.

home page noun (*plural* **home pages**)
the main page on a Website, which you can look at by using the Internet

homework noun
school work that you do at home, in the evenings or at the weekend

homograph noun (*plural* **homographs**)
Homographs are words that have the same spelling but different meanings.

homonym noun (*plural* **homonyms**)
Homonyms are words that have the same spelling, or sound the same, but have different meanings. for example **read** (to read a book) and **reed** (a plant).

homophone noun (*plural* **homophones**)
Homophones are words that sound the same but have different meanings and sometimes different spellings. For example, **night** and **knight** are homophones.

honest adjective
Someone who is honest does not steal or cheat or tell lies.

> **WORD FAMILY**
> • **honesty** I admire your honesty.

honey noun
a sweet, sticky food that is made by bees

hood noun (*plural* **hoods**)
the part of a coat that you put over your head when it is cold or raining

hoof noun (*plural* **hoofs** *or* **hooves**)
An animal's hooves are the hard parts on its feet.

hook noun (*plural* **hooks**)
a curved piece of metal that you use for hanging things on or catching things with

hoop noun (*plural* **hoops**)
a big wooden or plastic ring that you use in games *If you manage to throw a hoop over a plastic duck, you win a prize.*

hoot verb **hoots, hooting, hooted**
To hoot means to make a sound like an owl or the horn of a car. *A van drove past and hooted at us.*

hop verb **hops, hopping, hopped**
1 When you hop, you jump on one foot.
2 When animals hop, they jump with two feet together. *A large bird was hopping across the grass.*

hope verb **hopes, hoping, hoped**
If you hope that something will happen, you want it to happen. *I hope I get a new phone for my birthday.*

hopeful adjective
If you are hopeful, you think that something you want to happen will happen.

> **WORD FAMILY**
> • **hopefully** Hopefully I'll be allowed to go to the cinema with you.

hopeless adjective
1 You say that something is hopeless when you think that it is never going to work. *I tried to open the door again, but it was hopeless.*
2 If you are hopeless at something, you are very bad at it. *He was hopeless at swimming.*

horizon noun
the line in the distance where the sky and the land or sea seem to meet *I can see a ship on the horizon.*

horizontal adjective
Something that is horizontal is flat and level.

horn noun (*plural* **horns**)
1 The horns on some animals are the hard, pointed parts that grow on their heads.
2 A horn is a musical instrument made of brass. You play it by blowing into it.
3 The horn on a car is the part that makes a loud noise to warn people when there is danger.

horrible adjective
Something that is horrible is very nasty or frightening. *The medicine tasted horrible.*

horrid adjective
Something that is horrid is very nasty. Someone who is horrid is very unkind. *Why is everyone being so horrid to me?*

horror noun
a feeling of very great fear

horse noun (*plural* **horses**)
a big animal that people can ride on or use to pull carts

hospital noun (*plural* **hospitals**)
a place where people who are ill or hurt are looked after until they are better

hot adjective **hotter, hottest**
1 Something that is hot is very warm. *It was a lovely hot summer's day.*
2 Hot food has a strong, spicy taste.

hotel noun (*plural* **hotels**)
a building where you can pay to stay the night and to have meals

hour noun (*plural* **hours**)
We measure time in hours. There are sixty minutes in one hour, and 24 hours in one day.

house noun (*plural* **houses**)
a building where people live

hover verb **hovers, hovering, hovered**
When something hovers in the air, it stays in one place in the air. *The helicopter hovered overhead.*

hovercraft noun the plural is the same
a type of boat that travels on a cushion of air just above the surface of the water

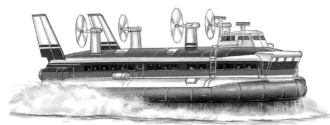

how adverb
1 a word that you use to ask questions *How old are you?*
2 a word you use to explain the way something works or happens *He explained how a camera works.*

however adverb
1 no matter how much *You'll never catch him, however fast you run.*
2 in spite of this *We were losing 3–0 at half time. However, we still kept trying.*

howl verb **howls, howling, howled**
To howl means to make a long, high sound, like the sound of an animal crying or a strong wind blowing.
It was very dark, and the wind howled horribly around her.—L. Frank Baum, The Wizard of Oz

hug verb **hugs, hugging, hugged**
When you hug someone, you hold them in your arms to show you love them.

huge adjective
Something that is huge is very big. *There was a huge spider in the bath!*

hum verb **hums, humming, hummed**
When you hum, you sing a tune with your lips closed.

human noun (*plural* **humans**)
A human is a man, woman, or child.
A human is also called a **human being**.

humour noun
1 If you have a sense of humour, you enjoy laughing at things.
2 If you are in a good humour, you are in a good mood.

> **WORD FAMILY**
> • **humorous** Some of the stories were quite humorous.

hump noun (*plural* **humps**)
a round bump on a camel's back

hundred noun (*plural* **hundreds**)
the number 100

hung verb *see* **hang**

hungry adjective **hungrier, hungriest**
If you are hungry, you feel that you need food.

> **WORD FAMILY**
> • **hunger** I felt weak with hunger.
> • **hungrily** He ate the bread and cheese hungrily.

hunt verb **hunts, hunting, hunted**
1 To hunt means to chase and kill animals for food or as a sport. *Young lions have to learn to hunt.*
2 When you hunt for something, you look for it in a lot of different places.

hurl verb **hurls, hurling, hurled**
When you hurl something, you throw it as hard as you can or as far as you can.
Mrs Mariposa hurled the mop into the corner and took Hugo on her knee.—Anne Fine, Care of Henry

a
b
c
d
e
f
g
h
i
j
k
l
m
n
o
p
q
r
s
t
u
v
w
x
y
z

hurricane noun (*plural* **hurricanes**)
a storm with a very strong wind

hurry verb **hurries, hurrying, hurried**
When you hurry, you walk or run quickly,
or try to do something quickly.

hurt verb **hurts, hurting, hurt**
1 To hurt someone means to make them feel
pain. *You shouldn't ever hurt animals.*
2 If a part of your body hurts, it feels sore.
My leg hurts.

husband noun (*plural* **husbands**)
A woman's husband is the man she is
married to.

hut noun (*plural* **huts**)
a small building made of wood

hutch noun (*plural* **hutches**)
a small box or cage that you keep a pet
rabbit in

hymn noun (*plural* **hymns**) (*sounds
like* **him**)
a Christian song that praises God

hypermarket noun (*plural*
hypermarkets)
a very big supermarket

hyphen noun (*plural* **hyphens**) (*say* **hye**-fen)
A hyphen is a mark like this - that you use in
writing to join parts of words together. The
word grown-up has a hyphen.

hypnotize verb **hypnotizes, hypnotizing,
hypnotized** (*say* **hip**-no-tize)
To hypnotize someone means to send them
into a deep sleep, so that you can control
what they do.

ice noun
water that has frozen hard

iceberg noun (*plural* **icebergs**)
a very big piece of ice floating in the sea

ice cream noun (*plural* **ice creams**)
a very cold, frozen food that is made from
milk or cream and flavoured with sugar and
fruit or chocolate

a
b
c
d
e
f
g
h
i
j
k
l
m
n
o
p
q
r
s
t
u
v
w
x
y
z

ice hockey noun
a game in which two teams skate on ice and try to score goals by hitting a flat disc into a net using special sticks

ice skate noun (*plural* **ice skates**)
Ice skates are special shoes with blades on the bottom, which you use for skating on ice.

WORD FAMILY
• **ice skating** Do you like ice skating?

icicle noun (*plural* **icicles**)
a thin, pointed piece of ice hanging down from a high place

icing noun
a sweet mixture that you spread over cakes to decorate them

ICT noun
ICT is the subject in which you study computers. It stands for information and communication technology.

icy adjective **icier, iciest**
1 Something that is icy is very cold.
2 When the road is icy, it is slippery because it is covered with ice.
3 If someone behaves or speaks in an icy way, they are very unfriendly.

idea noun (*plural* **ideas**)
1 When you have an idea, you think of something that you could do. *I've got a good idea.*
2 If you have an idea about something, you have a picture of it in your mind. *The film gave us an idea about what life was like in ancient Rome.*

ideal adjective
Something that is ideal is perfect. *It was ideal weather for going to the beach.*

identical adjective
Things that are identical are exactly the same.
We're twins. I'm Ruby. She's Garnet. We're identical.—Jacqueline Wilson, Double Act

identify verb **identifies, identifying, identified**
To identify someone means to recognize them and say who they are.

idiom noun (*plural* **idioms**)
An idiom is an expression with a special meaning that is not to do with the meaning of the words in it. For example, the idiom *over*

the moon does not have anything to do with the moon, but means 'very happy'.

idle adjective **idler, idlest**
Someone who is idle is lazy.

idol noun (*plural* **idols**)
a famous person that a lot of people love *Would you like to be a pop idol?*

igloo noun (*plural* **igloos**)
a small, round house that is made of blocks of hard snow

ignore verb **ignores, ignoring, ignored**
If you ignore someone, you refuse to speak to them or take any notice of them. *I said hello to her, but she ignored me.*

ill adjective
If you are ill, you are not very well. *I feel too ill to go to school.*

illegal adjective
Something that is illegal is against the law, and you are not allowed to do it.

illness noun (*plural* **illnesses**)
An illness is something that makes people ill. Measles, chickenpox, and colds are illnesses.

illustrate verb **illustrates, illustrating, illustrated**
To illustrate a book or story means to add pictures to it.

WORD FAMILY
• **illustrated** Is that book illustrated?
• **illustration** This book has got beautiful illustrations.

image noun (*plural* **images**)
a picture

imaginary adjective
Something that is imaginary does not really exist, but is only in your mind or in a story. *Dragons are imaginary animals.*

a
b
c
d
e
f
g
h
i
j
k
l
m
n
o
p
q
r
s
t
u
v
w
x
y
z

imagine verb **imagines, imagining, imagined**
When you imagine something, you make a picture of it in your mind. *I closed my eyes and tried to imagine I was back at home.*

> **WORD FAMILY**
> • **imagination** When you write a story, you have to use your imagination.

Imam noun (*plural* **Imams**)
a Muslim religious leader

imitate verb **imitates, imitating, imitated**
To imitate someone means to copy the way they speak or behave.

imitation noun (*plural* **imitations**)
something that has been made to look like something valuable *It's not a real diamond, it's only an imitation.*

immediate adjective
Something that is immediate happens straight away.

> **WORD FAMILY**
> • **immediately** Come here immediately!

immigrate verb **immigrates, immigrating, immigrated**
When people immigrate, they come and live in a country.

> **WORD FAMILY**
> • **Immigration** is when people come to live in a country. An **immigrant** is someone who has come to live in a country.

impatient adjective
Someone who is impatient gets bored and angry if they have to wait for something. *Don't be so impatient! It's your turn next.*

> **WORD FAMILY**
> • **impatiently** 'Don't be silly,' he said impatiently.

import verb **imports, importing, imported** (*say* im-**port**)
1 When a country imports things, it buys them from another country.
2 (*in ICT*) When you import information on a computer, you move it into your file or onto your computer from somewhere else.

important adjective
1 If something is important, you must think about it carefully and seriously. *I've got an important message for you.*

2 An important person is special and well known.

> **WORD FAMILY**
> • **importance** Do you understand the importance of this letter?

impossible adjective
If something is impossible, no one can do it. *It's impossible to undo this knot.*

impress verb **impresses, impressing, impressed**
If something impresses you, you think it is very good.

> **WORD FAMILY**
> • **impressive** He could do some very impressive jumps on his bike.

impression noun (*plural* **impressions**)
If you have an impression about something, you have a vague idea or feeling about it. *I get the impression he doesn't like me.*

improve verb **improves, improving, improved**
1 To improve something means to make it better. *You need to improve your handwriting.*
2 When something improves, it gets better. *Your maths is improving.*

> **WORD FAMILY**
> • **improvement** There has been a great improvement in your reading this year.

improvise verb **improvises, improvising, improvised**
When you improvise, you play music and make up the tune as you are playing.

in preposition
1 inside *My pencil case is in my bag.*
2 wearing *I was still in my school uniform.*

inch noun (*plural* **inches**)
We can measure length in inches. One inch is about 2½ centimetres.

incisor noun (*plural* **incisors**)
Your incisors are the flat sharp teeth at the front of your mouth.

include verb **includes, including, included**
If you include something you put it with other things and make it part of the set or group. If you include someone, you let them join a group.

incorrect adjective
Something that is incorrect is wrong and not correct. *Two of your answers were incorrect.*

increase verb **increases, increasing, increased**
When an amount increases, it gets bigger. *Our speed gradually increased to 70 miles per hour.*

incredible adjective
Something that is incredible seems too strange or amazing to believe.

> **WORD FAMILY**
> • **incredibly** He was incredibly strong.

independent adjective
Someone who is independent can do things for themselves and does not need help from other people.

index noun (*plural* **indexes**)
a list at the back of a book, which tells you what things are in the book and where to find them

indignant adjective
If you are indignant, you feel angry because someone has said or done something unfair.

individual adjective
Something that is individual is for just one person. *You can have group lessons or individual lessons.*

indoors adverb
inside a building

industry noun (*plural* **industries**)
An industry is all the factories and companies that make one particular thing. *Japan has a big car industry.*

> **WORD FAMILY**
> • An **industrial** place has a lot of factories.

infant noun
(*plural* **infants**)
a very young child

infection noun
(*plural* **infections**)
If you have an infection, you have a germ in your body which is making you ill. *I can't go swimming because I've got an ear infection.*

infinity noun
Infinity is a time, place, or amount that has no end or limit.

inflate verb **inflates, inflating, inflated**
To inflate something means to put air into it. *Use a pump to inflate the tyres.*

inflection noun (*plural* **inflections**)
(*in grammar*) a change to the ending of a word, which changes its meaning slightly, for example *walk, walks, walked*

influence verb **influences, influencing, influenced**
If you influence someone, you change the way that they think or behave.

inform verb **informs, informing, informed**
When you inform someone about something, you tell them about it. *You should inform your teacher if you feel ill.*

informal adjective
1 Informal events or clothes are relaxed and not too smart.
2 Informal language is language that you use when you are talking to friends, not language you would write down.

information noun
facts about something *We're collecting information about rainforests.*

infuriate verb **infuriates, infuriating, infuriated** (*say* in-**fyoor**-ee-ate)
If something infuriates you, it makes you very angry.

ingredient noun (*plural* **ingredients**)
Ingredients are the things that you mix together when you are cooking something. *Sugar, flour, eggs, and butter are the main ingredients of most cakes.*

inhabit verb **inhabits, inhabiting, inhabited**
To inhabit a place means to live in it.

> **WORD FAMILY**
> • The **inhabitants** of a place are the people who live in it.

initial noun (*plural* **initials**)
Your initials are the first letters of each of your names.

injection noun (*plural* **injections**)
When you have an injection, a doctor puts a needle into your arm to put medicine into your body.

injure verb **injures, injuring, injured**
To injure someone means to hurt them.

> **WORD FAMILY**
> • **injured** Are you injured
> • **injury** I don't think it's a serious injury.

ink noun (plural **inks**)
the coloured liquid inside a pen, which comes out onto the paper when you write

inn noun (plural **inns**)
a small hotel

innocent adjective
If you are innocent, you have not done anything wrong.

> **WORD FAMILY**
> • **innocently** Rachel smiled innocently.

input noun
(in ICT) The input is the information that you put into a computer. The information that you get out is the **output**.

insect noun (plural **insects**)
An insect is a small creature with six legs. Flies, ants, butterflies, and bees are all different types of insect.

insert verb **inserts, inserting, inserted**
1 When you insert something, you put it into a hole or a slot. *He inserted a coin into the slot.*
2 (in ICT) When you insert something into a computer document, you add it.

inside adverb & preposition
in something *Come inside, it's raining.*

insist verb **insists, insisting, insisted**
If you insist on something, you say very firmly that you want to do it. *He insisted on coming with us.*

inspect verb **inspects, inspecting, inspected**
When you inspect something, you look at it very carefully to check that it is all right.

> **WORD FAMILY**
> • When you do an **inspection**, you inspect something.

inspector noun (plural **inspectors**)
1 someone whose job is to check that things are done properly
2 an important policeman

instalment noun (plural **instalments**)
one part of a story that is told in parts *I can't wait for next week's instalment!*

instant adjective
1 Something that is instant happens immediately.
2 Instant food is food that you can make very quickly.

> **WORD FAMILY**
> • **instantly** I felt better instantly.

instead adverb
in place of something else *They gave us water instead of lemonade.*

instinct noun (plural **instincts**)
something that an animal or person does naturally, without thinking about it *Spiders spin webs by instinct.*

instruct verb **instructs, instructing, instructed**
1 To instruct someone means to tell them how to do something.
2 If you instruct someone to do something, you order them to do it.

> **WORD FAMILY**
> • **instructions** You must follow my instructions very carefully.

instrument noun (plural **instruments**)
1 something that you use for playing music *Violins and flutes are musical instruments.*
2 a tool or machine that you use for doing a job *A microscope is an instrument for looking at very tiny things.*

insulate verb **insulates, insulating, insulated**
(*in science*) To insulate something means to stop electricity or heat from passing in or out.

> **WORD FAMILY**
> • **insulator** Rubber is a good insulator because it doesn't conduct electricity.

insult verb **insults, insulting, insulted**
To insult someone means to upset them by saying rude or nasty things to them. *She insulted me by saying I was stupid.*

integer noun (*plural* **integers**)
(*in mathematics*) a whole number such as 1, 2, 54, or 79

intelligent adjective
Someone who is intelligent is clever and can learn things quickly.
Klaus was a little older than twelve and wore glasses, which made him look intelligent.—Lemony Snicket, The Bad Beginning

> **WORD FAMILY**
> • **intelligence** He was a man of great intelligence.

intend verb **intends, intending, intended**
If you intend to do something, you plan to do it.

intentional adjective
If something was intentional, you did it on purpose.

> **WORD FAMILY**
> • **intentionally** I didn't do it intentionally!

interactive adjective
(*in ICT*) An interactive computer program is one in which you can change and control things.

interactive whiteboard noun (*plural* **interactive whiteboards**)
An interactive whiteboard is a whiteboard that looks like a large computer screen and is connected to a computer. You can write on it using a special pen.

interdependent adjective
If people are interdependent, they depend on each other and need each other. *In a society, we are all interdependent.*

interest verb **interests, interesting, interested**
If something interests you, you think it is exciting and you want to see it or learn about it. *Ancient buildings interest me a lot.*

> **WORD FAMILY**
> • **interested** Are you interested in sport?
> • **interesting** This is a really interesting book.

interfere verb **interferes, interfering, interfered**
If you interfere, you get involved with something that has nothing to do with you.

interjection noun (*plural* **interjections**)
(*in grammar*) An interjection is a word that you say or shout on its own, not as part of a sentence. *Hello* and *hooray* are interjections.

international adjective
Something that is international involves people from different countries. *We're going to watch an international football match.*

Internet noun
a system that allows computers all over the world to get information and send messages to each other

interrupt verb **interrupts, interrupting, interrupted**
If you interrupt someone, you disturb them while they are talking or working, and make them stop.

> **WORD FAMILY**
> • **interruption** I'm going to work, and I don't want any interruptions.

interval noun (*plural* **intervals**)
a short break in the middle of a play or concert

interview verb **interviews, interviewing, interviewed**
To interview someone means to ask someone questions to find out what they are like, or what they think, or what they know.

into preposition
in *He threw a stone into the water.*

intonation noun (*plural* **intonations**)
Your intonation is the way in which you say a word, for example whether you make it sound like a question, or whether you say it in an angry way.

introduce verb **introduces, introducing, introduced**
When you introduce people, you bring them together and let them meet each other. *Suraya introduced me to the professor.*

a
b
c
d
e
f
g
h
i
j
k
l
m
n
o
p
q
r
s
t
u
v
w
x
y
z

introduction noun (*plural* **introductions**)
a short part at the beginning of a book or piece of music

invade verb **invades, invading, invaded**
When people invade a country, they attack it.

> **WORD FAMILY**
> • **invasion** We're reading about the Roman invasion of Britain.

invent verb **invents, inventing, invented**
If you invent something new, you are the first person to make it or think of it.
Do you know the name of the man who invented the computer?

> **WORD FAMILY**
> • **invention** This is a wonderful invention.

invertebrate noun (*plural* **invertebrates**)
An invertebrate is an animal with no backbone. Worms, butterflies, and spiders are all invertebrates.

inverted commas noun
the marks like this ' ' or this " " that you use in writing to show what someone has said

investigate verb **investigates, investigating, investigated**
If you investigate something, you try to find out about it.

invisible adjective
If something is invisible, no one can see it.

invite verb **invites, inviting, invited**
When you invite someone, you ask them to come to your house or to go somewhere with you.

> **WORD FAMILY**
> • **invitation** Have you had an invitation to the wedding?

involved adjective
If you are involved in something, you take part in it or help to do it.

iPod noun (*plural* **iPods**)
(*trademark*) a small music player that plays music you have downloaded onto it from the Internet

iron noun (*plural* **irons**)
1 a type of strong, heavy metal
2 An iron is an object that you use for making

clothes smooth and flat. It has a flat piece of metal with a handle, and you heat it before you use it.

irritate verb **irritates, irritating, irritated**
To irritate someone means to make them feel annoyed.

> **WORD FAMILY**
> • **irritated** I was feeling rather irritated.
> • **irritating** Sometimes my little brother can be very irritating.

Islam noun
the religion that Muslims follow

> **WORD FAMILY**
> • Things that are **Islamic** are to do with Islam.

island noun (*plural* **islands**)
a piece of land with water all round it

italics noun
sloping letters printed like this

itch verb **itches, itching, itched**
When your skin itches, it is uncomfortable and feels as if you need to scratch it.

> **WORD FAMILY**
> • **itchy** Insect bites are sometimes very itchy.

item noun (*plural* **items**)
one thing in a list or group of things
What's the first item on the list?

it's
1 it is *It's raining.*
2 it has *Look at that dog. It's only got three legs.*

Jj

jab verb **jabs, jabbing, jabbed**
When you jab something, you poke it roughly with your finger or with something sharp.

jacket noun (*plural* **jackets**)
a short coat

jagged adjective
Something that is jagged has a sharp, uneven edge. *We climbed over the jagged rocks.*

jail noun (*plural* **jails**)
a prison

jam noun (*plural* **jams**)
1 a thick, sweet, sticky food that is made by cooking fruit and sugar together *Would you like some raspberry jam on your bread?*
2 If there is a traffic jam, there are too many cars on the road and they cannot move forward. *The bus got stuck in a traffic jam.*

jam verb **jams, jamming, jammed**
When something jams, it gets stuck and you cannot move it. *The back door keeps getting jammed.*

January noun
the first month of the year

jar noun (*plural* **jars**)
a glass container that food is kept in

jargon noun
special language that is used by people who do a particular job

jaw noun (*plural* **jaws**)
Your jaws are the bones that hold your teeth in place. You move your lower jaw to open your mouth.

jealous adjective
If you are jealous of someone, you are unhappy because they have something that you would like, or they can do something better than you can. *I think Anita is jealous of me because I've got lots of friends.*

jeans noun
trousers that are made of strong cotton cloth

jelly noun (*plural* **jellies**)
a sweet food made from fruit and sugar that shakes when you move it

jellyfish noun (*plural* **jellyfish**)
A jellyfish is a sea animal that has a soft, clear body. Some types of jellyfish can sting you.

jerk verb **jerks, jerking, jerked**
When something jerks, it moves suddenly and roughly. *The bus jerked forward.*

jersey noun (*plural* **jerseys**)
a warm piece of clothing with long sleeves

jet noun (*plural* **jets**)
1 A jet of water is a thin stream that comes out of a small hole very quickly.
2 a fast aeroplane

jewel noun (*plural* **jewels**)
a beautiful and valuable stone *Diamonds and rubies are jewels.*

Jewish adjective
Someone who is Jewish follows the religion of **Judaism**.

jewellery noun
necklaces, bracelets, and rings

jigsaw puzzle noun (*plural* **jigsaw puzzles**)
a set of small pieces of cardboard or wood that fit together to make a picture

jingle verb **jingles, jingling, jingled**
When something jingles, it makes a light, ringing sound. *The keys jingled in my pocket as I walked along.*

jingle noun (*plural* **jingles**)
a short song or poem that is used to advertise something

job noun (*plural* **jobs**)
1 the work that someone does to earn money *What is your dad's job?*

a
b
c
d
e
f
g
h
i
j
k
l
m
n
o
p
q
r
s
t
u
v
w
x
y
z

2 something useful that you have to do *It's my job to wash up.*

jog verb **jogs, jogging, jogged**
1 When you jog, you run slowly.
2 If you jog something, you knock it or bump it. *He jogged my elbow and I spilled my drink.*

join verb **joins, joining, joined**
1 When you join things together, you fasten or tie them together.
2 When you join a club or group, you become a member of it. *I've joined a swimming club.*

joint noun
(*plural* **joints**)
1 Your joints are the parts of your arms and legs that you can bend and turn. Your ankles, elbows, and hips are all joints.
2 a large piece of meat

joke noun (*plural* **jokes**)
something you say or do to make people laugh

joke verb **jokes, joking, joked**
When you joke, you say things to make people laugh.

jolt verb **jolts, jolting, jolted**
1 When something jolts, it moves with sudden and rough movements. *The old bus jolted along.*
2 If you jolt something, you knock it or bump it.

journal noun (*plural* **journals**)
a diary in which someone writes about what they do each day

journalist noun (*plural* **journalists**)
someone who writes about the news in a newspaper

journey noun (*plural* **journeys**)
When you go on a journey, you travel somewhere. *By the evening we were coming to the end of our journey.*

joy noun
a feeling of great happiness
Aunt Bat rose to her feet and did a little dance of joy.—Alexander McCall Smith, The Banana Machine

WORD FAMILY
• **joyful** There were joyful celebrations in the streets.

joystick noun
(*plural* **joysticks**)
a lever that you move forwards, backwards, or sideways to control a computer game or a machine

Judaism noun
the religion that Jews follow

judge verb **judges, judging, judged**
When you judge something, you say how good or bad it is.

judo noun
a sport in which people fight with their hands and try to throw each other to the floor

jug noun (*plural* **jugs**)
a container with a handle that you use for pouring out water and other liquids

juggle verb **juggles, juggling, juggled**
When you juggle, you keep throwing several balls or other things into the air and catching them again quickly.

juice noun
(*plural* **juices**)
the liquid that is in fruit and vegetables
Would you like some orange juice?

WORD FAMILY
• **juicy** The tree was covered with juicy plums.

July noun
the seventh month of the year

jumble noun
A jumble of things is a lot of different things all mixed up together.

jumble sale noun (*plural* **jumble sales**)
a sale of old clothes and other things that people have given away

jump verb **jumps, jumping, jumped**
When you jump, you push yourself up into the air.

jumper noun (*plural* **jumpers**)
a warm piece of clothing with long sleeves which you wear on the top half of your body

junction noun (*plural* **junctions**)
a place where two roads or railway lines meet

June noun
the sixth month of the year

jungle noun (*plural* **jungles**)
a thick forest in a hot country

junior adjective
Junior means for young children. *I play football for a junior football team.*

junk noun
useless things that people do not want any more *The garage was full of old junk.*

jury noun (*plural* **juries**) (*say* **joor**-ee)
the group of people in a court who decide whether a person is guilty or innocent of a crime

just adverb
1 exactly *This game is just what I wanted.*
2 hardly *I only just caught the bus.*
3 recently *She has just left.*
4 only *I'll just brush my hair and then we can go.*

justice noun
fair treatment for everyone

kangaroo noun
(*plural* **kangaroos**)
A kangaroo is an Australian animal that jumps along on its strong back legs. Female kangaroos have pouches in which they carry their babies.

karate noun
(*say* ka-**rah**-tee)
a sport in which people fight with their hands and feet

kebab noun (*plural* **kebabs**)
pieces of meat and vegetable that you cook on a long spike called a skewer

keen adjective **keener, keenest**
1 If you are keen on something, you like it. *He's very keen on football.*
2 If you are keen to do something, you want to do it. *The children were keen to start exploring, but they knew that there would be plenty of time for that.*—Alexander McCall Smith, The Bubblegum Tree

keep verb **keeps, keeping, kept**
1 If you keep something, you have it for yourself and do not get rid of it or give it to anyone else.
2 When you keep something in a certain way, you make it stay that way. *I like to keep my hair short in the summer.*
3 If you keep doing something, you go on doing it. *Sam keeps teasing me!*
4 If you keep animals, you look after them.

a
b
c
d
e
f
g
h
i
j
k
l
m
n
o
p
q
r
s
t
u
v
w
x
y
z

kennel noun (*plural* **kennels**)
a little hut for a dog to sleep in

kenning noun (*plural* **kennings**)
A kenning is an expression that is used to describe what something is without saying its name. For example, a kenning for a cat is mouse catcher.

kept verb *see* **keep**

kerb noun (*plural* **kerbs**)
the edge of a pavement, where you step down to go onto the road

ketchup noun
a type of thick, cold tomato sauce

kettle noun (*plural* **kettles**)
a container that you boil water in

key noun (*plural* **keys**)
1 a piece of metal that is shaped so that it fits into a lock
2 The keys on a piano or computer keyboard are the parts that you press to make it work.

keyboard noun (*plural* **keyboards**)
The keyboard on a piano or computer is the set of keys that you press to make it work.

kick verb **kicks, kicking, kicked**
When you kick something, you hit it with your foot.

kid noun (*plural* **kids**)
1 a child
2 a young goat

kidnap verb **kidnaps, kidnapping, kidnapped**
To kidnap someone means to take them away and say that you will only let them go if someone pays you money.

kidney noun (*plural* **kidneys**)
Your kidneys are the parts inside your body that remove waste substances from your blood.

kill verb **kills, killing, killed**
To kill a person or animal means to make them die.

kilogram noun (*plural* **kilograms**)
We can measure weight in kilograms. There are 1000 grams in one kilogram. A kilogram is also called a **kilo**.

kilometre noun (*plural* **kilometres**)
We can measure distance in kilometres. There are 1000 metres in one kilometre.

kilt noun (*plural* **kilts**)
A kilt is a skirt with pleats at the back. In Scotland, men sometimes wear kilts as part of their traditional costume.

kind noun (*plural* **kinds**)
a type *A terrier is a kind of dog.*

kind adjective **kinder, kindest**
Someone who is kind is friendly and nice to people. *It was very kind of you to help us.*

> **WORD FAMILY**
> • **kindly** 'Don't worry,' she said kindly.
> • **kindness** Thank you for your kindness.

king noun (*plural* **kings**)
a man who rules a country

kingdom noun (*plural* **kingdoms**)
a land that is ruled by a king or queen

kiss verb **kisses, kissing, kissed**
When you kiss someone, you touch them with your lips because you like them or love them.

kit noun (*plural* **kits**)
1 the clothes and other things that you need to do a sport *I can't find my football kit.*
2 a set of parts that you fit together to make something *I got a model aeroplane kit for my birthday.*

kitchen noun (*plural* **kitchens**)
the room in a house in which people prepare and cook food

kite noun (*plural* **kites**)
A kite is a light frame covered in cloth or paper. You hold a kite at the end of a long string and make it fly in the air.

kitten noun (*plural* **kittens**)
a young cat

kiwi fruit noun
(*plural* **kiwi fruits**)
a fruit with a brown, hairy skin and green flesh

knee noun (*plural* **knees**)
Your knee is the part in the middle of your leg, where your leg can bend.

kneel verb **kneels, kneeling, kneeled**
When you kneel, you go down onto your knees.

knew verb *see* **know**

knife noun (*plural* **knives**)
a tool with a long, sharp edge that you use for cutting things

knight noun (*plural* **knights**)
a man who wore armour and rode into battle on a horse, in the past

knit verb **knits, knitting, knitted**
When you knit, you make clothes out of wool by twisting the wool over a pair of long needles or using a machine.

knob noun (*plural* **knobs**)
1 a round handle on a door or drawer
2 a round button that you turn to make a machine work

knock verb **knocks, knocking, knocked**
When you knock something, you bang it or hit it.

knot noun (*plural* **knots**)
the twisted part where pieces of string or cloth have been tied together *I can't undo the knot in my shoelaces.*

know verb **knows, knowing, knew, known** (*say* **no**)
1 If you know something, you have learnt it and have it in your mind.
2 If you know someone, you have met them before and you recognize them.

knowledge noun (*say* **noll**-idge)
all the things that you know and understand *He has a lot of knowledge about animals.*

knuckle noun (*plural* **knuckles**)
Your knuckles are the parts where your fingers bend.

koala noun (*plural* **koalas**) (*say* koh-**ah**-la)
a furry Australian animal that lives in trees and looks like a small bear

Koran noun
the holy book of the religion of Islam

a
b
c
d
e
f
g
h
i
j
k
l
m
n
o
p
q
r
s
t
u
v
w
x
y
z

Ll

label noun (*plural* **labels**)
a piece of paper or cloth that is put on something to show what it is or tell you something about it

laboratory noun (*plural* **laboratories**)
a room in which people do scientific experiments

lace noun (*plural* **laces**)
1 Lace is a type of thin, pretty material with a pattern of holes in it.
2 Laces are pieces of string that you use to tie up your shoes.

ladder noun (*plural* **ladders**)
A ladder is a tall frame that you can climb up. It has two long poles with short bars between them, which you climb up like steps.

lady noun (*plural* **ladies**)
1 a polite name for a woman
2 a title that is given to some important women

ladybird noun (*plural* **ladybirds**)
a red or yellow insect with black spots on its back

laid verb *see* **lay**

lain verb
see **lie** verb

lake noun (*plural* **lakes**)
a large area of fresh water with land all around it

lamb noun (*plural* **lambs**)
a young sheep

lame adjective
A lame animal cannot walk properly because it has hurt one of its legs.

lamp noun (*plural* **lamps**)
A lamp is a light, especially one that you can hold or move around. The big lights in a street are called **street lamps**. *She switched on a lamp in the sitting room.*

land noun (*plural* **lands**)
1 Land is the the dry part of the earth where there is no water.
2 A land is a country. *He had travelled to many foreign lands.*

land verb **lands, landing, landed**
To land means to arrive on land again after being in the air. *What time will our plane land?*

landscape noun
The landscape is everything you can see when you look out over an area of land.

lane noun (*plural* **lanes**)
1 a narrow road *We walked along a quiet country lane.*
2 a strip of road that one line of traffic can drive along *Some motorways have six lanes.*

language noun (*plural* **languages**)
Your language is the words that you use when you speak or write.

lantern noun (*plural* **lanterns**)
a candle inside a container

lap noun (*plural* **laps**)
1 Your lap is the flat part of your legs when you are sitting down. *Can I sit on your lap?*

2 A lap of a race course is once round it. *We had to do five laps of the race track.*

lap verb **laps, lapping, lapped**
1 When an animal laps, it drinks with its tongue.
2 When water laps, it moves gently backwards and forwards. *The waves lapped gently against the side of the boat.*

laptop noun (*plural* **laptops**)
a small computer that you can carry around with you and hold on your knees when you are sitting down

large adjective **larger, largest**
Something that is large is big.
On the table was a large wicker basket from which came mews and squeaks.—Jill Murphy, The Worst Witch

larva noun
an animal that looks like a small worm and will become an insect when it is an adult

laser noun (*plural* **lasers**)
A laser is a machine that makes a very narrow beam of strong light. Some lasers are used to cut metal, and some are used by doctors in medical operations.

last adjective
The last thing is the one that comes after all the others. *Z is the last letter of the alphabet.*

last verb **lasts, lasting, lasted**
If something lasts for a certain time, it goes on for that amount of time. *The film lasted two hours.*

late adjective **later, latest**
1 If you are late, you arrive after the time when people are expecting you. *The bus was ten minutes late.*
2 When it is late in the day, it is near the middle or end of the day, not the morning. *Hurry up, it's getting late.*

lately adverb
not very long ago *Have you seen Ali lately?*

laugh verb **laughs, laughing, laughed**
When you laugh, you make sounds that show that you are happy or think something is funny.

WORD FAMILY
• **laughter** I could hear the sounds of laughter coming from downstairs.

launch verb **launches, launching, launched**
1 To launch a boat means to put it into water.
2 To launch a rocket or spaceship means to send it into space.

lava noun
very hot, liquid rock that comes out of a volcano

law noun (*plural* **laws**)
The law is all the rules that everyone in a country must obey.

lawn noun (*plural* **lawns**)
a piece of ground in a garden that is covered with short grass

lawyer noun (*plural* **lawyers**)
a person who has studied the law and who helps people or talks for them in a court of law

lay verb **lays, laying, laid**
1 When you lay something somewhere, you put it there. *We laid the map out on the table.*
2 When you lay a table, you put knives, forks, and other things on it so that it is ready for a meal.
3 When a bird lays an egg, it produces one.

layer noun (*plural* **layers**)
A layer of something is a covering of it on top of something else. *There was a thick layer of dust on everything.*

layout noun (*plural* **layouts**)
The layout of text on a computer is the way it is arranged on each page.

lazy adjective **lazier, laziest**
Someone who is lazy does not want to work.

lead verb **leads, leading, led** (*rhymes with* seed)
1 If you lead people, you go in front of them and take them somewhere. *He led us to the secret cave.*

a
b
c
d
e
f
g
h
i
j
k
l
m
n
o
p
q
r
s
t
u
v
w
x
y
z

2 If you lead people, you are in charge of them and tell them what to do.

3 If you are leading in a game or competition, you are winning.

> **WORD FAMILY**
> • A **leader** is a person who leads other people.

lead noun (*plural* **leads**) (*rhymes with* seed)

1 a long strap that you fasten to a dog's collar so that you can keep hold of it and control it

2 If you are in the lead, you are winning in a race or competition.

lead noun (*rhymes with* bed)

a type of heavy, grey metal

leaf noun

(*plural* **leaves**)
The leaves on a plant are the parts that grow at the ends of the stems and branches.

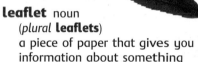

leaflet noun

(*plural* **leaflets**)
a piece of paper that gives you information about something

leak verb **leaks, leaking, leaked**

If something is leaking, it has a hole or crack in it and liquid can get through. *My water bottle's leaking.*

lean verb **leans, leaning, leaned** *or* **leant**

1 If you lean forwards or backwards, you bend your body that way.

2 When you lean against something, you rest against it.

lean adjective **leaner, leanest**

Lean meat does not have any fat on it.

leap verb **leaps, leaping, leaped** *or* **leapt**

To leap means to jump.
Achilles leapt up to welcome them when he saw them coming.—Rosemary Sutcliff, Black Ships before Troy

leap year noun (*plural* **leap years**)

A leap year is a year which has 366 days instead of 365. Every four years is a leap year.

learn verb **learns, learning, learned** *or* **learnt**

1 When you learn about something, you find out about it. *We're learning about the Vikings in history.*

2 When you learn to do something, you find out how to do it. *I learnt to swim last year.*

least adjective

less than all the others *My mum wanted me to buy the least expensive trainers.*

leather noun

Leather is a strong material that is made from the skins of animals. Shoes and bags are often made of leather.

leave verb **leaves, leaving, left**

1 When you leave a place, you go away from it. *I leave home every morning at eight o'clock.*

2 When you leave something in a place, you let it stay there and do not take it away. *I'm sorry, I've left my homework at home.*

led verb *see* **lead** verb

ledge noun (*plural* **ledges**)

a narrow shelf that sticks out from a wall

left verb *see* **leave**

left adjective & adverb

The left side of something is the side that is opposite the right side. Most people write with their right hand, not their left hand. *She had a letter in her left hand.*

leg noun (*plural* **legs**)

1 Your legs are the parts of your body between your hips and your feet. You use your legs for walking and running.

2 The legs on a table or chair are the parts that it stands on.

legend noun (*plural* **legends**) (*say* lej-**end**)

an old story that has been handed down from the past *I like reading old myths and legends.*

leisure noun

Leisure time is time when you can do what you want because you do not have to work.

lemon noun

(*plural* **lemons**)
a yellow fruit with a very sour taste

lemonade noun

a fizzy drink made from lemons, sugar, and water

lend verb **lends, lending, lent**
If you lend something to someone, you let them use it for a short time. *Can you lend me a pencil?*

length noun
The length of something is how long it is. *We measured the length of the playground.*

lens noun (*plural* **lenses**)
A lens is a curved piece of glass or plastic that makes things look bigger or smaller when you look through it. Glasses and telescopes all have lenses.

lent verb *see* **lend**

less adverb
not as much *A bike causes less pollution than a car.*

lesson noun (*plural* **lessons**)
1 a time when someone is teaching you *Maths is our first lesson this morning.*
2 something that you have to learn *Road safety is an important lesson for everyone.*

let verb **lets, letting, let**
If you let someone do something, you allow them to do it. *Sam let me use his phone.*

letter noun (*plural* **letters**)
1 Letters are the signs that we use for writing words, such as **a**, **b**, or **c**.
2 A letter is a message that you write down and send to someone.

lettuce noun (*plural* **lettuces**)
a vegetable with green leaves that you eat in salads

level adjective
1 Something that is level is flat and smooth. *You need level ground to play tennis on.*
2 If you are level with someone, you are walking or running next to them.
3 If people are level in a game or competition, they have the same number of points.

level noun (*plural* **levels**)
If something is at a different level, it is higher or lower.

lever noun (*plural* **levers**)
a bar that you pull down to make a machine work

liar noun (*plural* **liars**)
someone who tells lies

library noun (*plural* **libraries**)
a building or room where a lot of books are kept for people to use or borrow

licence noun (*plural* **licences**)
a printed piece of paper that says that you can do something or have something *You have to have a driving licence before you can drive a car.*

lick verb **licks, licking, licked**
When you lick something, you move your tongue over it.

lid noun (*plural* **lids**)
a cover on the top of a box or jar

lie verb **lies, lying, lied**
When you lie, you say something that you know is not true.

lie noun (*plural* **lies**)
something you say that you know is not true *Don't tell lies.*

lie verb **lies, lying, lay, lain**
1 When you lie down, you rest with your body spread out on the ground or on a bed.
2 When something lies somewhere, it is there. *Thick snow lay on the ground.*

life noun (*plural* **lives**)
Your life is the time when you are alive.

lifeboat noun (*plural* **lifeboats**)
a boat that goes out to sea in bad weather to rescue people

life cycle noun (*plural* **life cycles**)
(*in science*) The life cycle of an animal is the way in which it is born, grows, has babies, and dies.

lift verb **lifts, lifting, lifted**
When you lift something, you pick it up or move it upwards. *I lifted the lid of the box to see what was inside.*

lift noun (*plural* **lifts**)
1 a machine that takes people up and down inside a building
2 If someone gives you a lift, they take you somewhere in their car.

light noun (*plural* **lights**)
1 Light is brightness that comes from the sun, the stars, fires, and lamps. Light helps us to see things.
2 A light is a lamp, bulb, or torch that gives out light. *Please could you switch the light on?*

a
b
c
d
e
f
g
h
i
j
k
l
m
n
o
p
q
r
s
t
u
v
w
x
y
z

light adjective **lighter, lightest**
1 Something that is light is not heavy. *My suitcase is quite light.*
2 A place that is light is not dark, but has plenty of light in it.
3 A light colour is pale and not very bright. *She was wearing a light blue top.*

light verb **lights, lighting, lit**
1 To light something means to put light in it so that you can see. *We used our torches to light the tunnel.*
2 To light a fire means to make it burn. *We tried to light the bonfire.*

lighthouse noun (*plural* **lighthouses**)
a tower with a bright light that warns ships about rocks or other dangers

lightning noun
a bright flash of light that you see in the sky when there is a thunderstorm

like verb **likes, liking, liked**
If you like something, you think it is nice. If you like someone, you think that they are nice.

like preposition
If one thing is like another, it is similar to it. *This tastes like roast lamb.*

likely adjective **likelier, likeliest**
If something is likely to happen, it will probably happen. *Do you think it's likely to rain?*

limb noun (*plural* **limbs**)
Your limbs are your arms and legs.

limerick noun (*plural* **limericks**)
a funny poem with five lines and a strong rhythm

limit noun (*plural* **limits**)
an amount or a point which people must not go past *You must not drive faster than the speed limit.*

limp verb **limps, limping, limped**
When you limp, you walk with uneven steps because you have hurt one of your legs or feet.

line noun (*plural* **lines**)
1 a long mark like this _____
2 a row of people or things *There was a long line of people waiting to get into the cinema.*
3 A railway line is the two metal rails a train moves along.
4 A line of writing is the words that are written next to each other on a page. *I don't know the next line of the poem.*
5 A fishing line is a piece of special thin string that you use for catching fish.

line graph noun (*plural* **line graphs**)
a graph which uses lines to show information

link noun (*plural* **links**)
The links in a chain are the rings that are all joined together to make the chain.

link verb **links, linking, linked**
To link two things means to join them together. *The Channel Tunnel links Britain to France.*

lion noun (*plural* **lions**)
A lion is a big, light brown wild cat that lives in Africa and India. A female lion is called a **lioness**.

lip noun (*plural* **lips**)
Your lips are the parts round the edges of your mouth.

liquid noun (*plural* **liquids**)
any substance that is like water, and is not a solid or a gas

lisp verb **lisps, lisping, lisped**
If you lisp, you say the sound 's' as if it was 'th'.

list noun (*plural* **lists**)
a number of words or names that are written down one after the other *We made a list of all the things we needed to buy.*

listen verb **listens, listening, listened**
When you listen, you pay attention so that you can hear something.

lit verb *see* **light** verb

literacy noun
Literacy is being able to read and write.

literature noun
stories, plays, and poetry

litre noun (*plural* **litres**)
We can measure liquids in litres. There are 100 centilitres in one litre.

litter noun (*plural* **litters**)
1 Litter is rubbish that people have dropped or left lying about.
2 A litter is all the young animals that are born to the same mother at the same time.

little adjective
1 Something that is little is not very big. *We set out in our little rowing boat.*
2 If you have little of something, you do not have very much. *I've got very little money.*

live verb **lives, living, lived**
1 To live means to be alive. *Dinosaurs lived millions of years ago.*
2 If you live somewhere, that is where your home is.

live adjective (*rhymes with* dive)
1 A live animal is alive. *You can see live animals in the zoo.*
2 A live television programme is not recorded, but is broadcast as it is happening.

lively adjective **livelier, liveliest**
Someone who is lively has a lot of energy and enjoys having fun.

liver noun (*plural* **livers**)
Your liver is the part inside your body that keeps your blood clean and healthy.

living noun
When you earn a living, you earn enough money to live.

living room noun (*plural* **living rooms**)
the room in a house with comfortable chairs, where people sit and talk or watch television

lizard noun (*plural* **lizards**)
A lizard is an animal with skin like a snake and four legs. Lizards are reptiles and live in warm countries.

load noun (*plural* **loads**)
A load of things is an amount that someone is carrying. *The lorry brought another load of sand.*

load verb **loads, loading, loaded**
1 When you load things into a car or lorry, you put them in. *Load the suitcases into the car.*
2 When you load a gun, you put bullets in it.
3 When you load a program onto a computer, you put it on so that you can use it.

loaf noun
(*plural* **loaves**)
A loaf of bread is a large piece of bread that you cut into slices to eat.

local adjective
Something that is local is near where you live. *You can borrow books from your local library.*

loch noun (*plural* **lochs**)
a lake in Scotland

lock noun (*plural* **locks**)
1 The lock on a door, gate, or window is the part that you can open and shut with a key.
2 A lock of hair is a small piece of hair.

lock verb **locks, locking, locked**
When you lock something, you shut it and fasten it with a key. *Don't forget to lock the door when you go out.*

loft noun (*plural* **lofts**)
a room in the roof of a house, where you can store things

log noun (*plural* **logs**)
A log is a part of a tree that has been chopped down. You can burn logs on a fire.

log verb **logs, logging, logged**
When you log in to a computer, you switch it on so that you can use it. When you log out, you shut it down and switch it off.

logical adjective (*say* **loj**-ik-al)
Something that is logical is sensible or makes sense.

logo noun (*plural* **logos**)
a small picture that represents a company

lolly noun (*plural* **lollies**)
a sweet on the end of a stick

lonely adjective **lonelier, loneliest**
1 If you feel lonely, you feel sad because you are on your own.
2 A lonely place is far away from people and houses.

long adjective **longer, longest**
1 Something that is long measures a lot from one end to the other. *This piece of string isn't long enough.*
2 Something that is long takes a lot of time. *I was looking forward to a lovely long holiday.*

long verb **longs, longing, longed**
If you long for something, you want it a lot. *I have always longed and longed to own a sweet-shop.*—Roald Dahl, The Giraffe and the Pelly and Me

look verb **looks, looking, looked**
1 When you look at something, you point your eyes at it so that you can see it. *Hey! Look at me!*
2 The way something looks is the way it seems. *That dog doesn't look very friendly.*

3 When you look for something, you try to find it.
4 When you look after someone, you take care of them.
5 When you look forward to something, you feel excited that it is going to happen.

loop noun (*plural* **loops**)
a ring made in a piece of string or rope

loose adjective **looser, loosest**
1 Something that is loose is not fixed firmly in place. *I've got a loose tooth.*
2 Loose clothes do not fit tightly.
3 If a wild animal is loose, it has escaped and is free.

> **WORD FAMILY**
> • **loosen** We loosened the ropes.

lord noun (*plural* **lords**)
a title that is given to some important men

lorry noun (*plural* **lorries**)
a big truck that is used for carrying heavy things by road

lose verb **loses, losing, lost**
1 When you lose something, you do not have it and do not know where it is. *I've lost my coat.*
2 When you lose a game, someone else wins. *Our team lost the match.*

lost adjective
If you are lost, you do not know where you are or where you should go. *Don't get lost in the woods!*

lot noun (*plural* **lots**)
A lot means a large number or a large amount. *I've got lots of friends.*

lottery noun (*plural* **lotteries**)
a competition in which people buy tickets or choose numbers, and win a prize if their tickets or numbers are picked

loud adjective **louder, loudest**
Something that is loud makes a lot of noise. *Suddenly there was a loud bang.*

> **WORD FAMILY**
> • **loudly** I called his name as loudly as I could.

loudspeaker noun (*plural* **loudspeakers**)
the part of a TV, radio, or music system that the sound comes from

a b c d e f g h i j k l m n o p q r s t u v w x y z

---

lounge noun (*plural* **lounges**)
a room with comfortable chairs in it, where people can sit and talk or watch television

love noun
the strong feeling you have when you like someone very much

love verb **loves, loving, loved**
1 If you love someone, you like them very much.
2 If you love something, you like it a lot. *I love chocolate.*

lovely adjective **lovelier, loveliest**
Something that is lovely is beautiful or very nice. *What lovely flowers!*

low adjective **lower, lowest**
1 Something that is low is not high. *We sat down on the low bench by the swings.*
2 A low price is a small price.
3 A low voice or sound is deep.

> **WORD FAMILY**
> • **lower** We lowered the boat into the water.

lower case adjective
Lower case letters are small letters, not capital letters.

loyal adjective
If you are loyal to someone, you always help them and support them.

luck noun
Luck is when something happens by chance, without anyone planning it.

lucky adjective **luckier, luckiest**
If you are lucky, you have good luck. *We were lucky we got home before the storm started.*

> **WORD FAMILY**
> • **luckily** Luckily, nobody was hurt.

luggage noun
bags and suitcases that you take with you on a journey

lump noun (*plural* **lumps**)
1 A lump of something is a piece of it. *He took some bread and a lump of cheese.*
2 A lump is a bump on your skin that you get when you have knocked it.

> **WORD FAMILY**
> • **lumpy** The sauce was lumpy and disgusting.

lunar adjective
Lunar means to do with the moon. *Have you ever seen a lunar eclipse?*

lunch noun (*plural* **lunches**)
a meal that you eat in the middle of the day

lung noun (*plural* **lungs**)
Your lungs are the parts inside your chest that you use for breathing.

luxury noun (*plural* **luxuries**)
something expensive that you like but do not really need

lying verb *see* **lie** verb

lyrics noun
The lyrics of a song are its words.

Mm

machine noun (*plural* **machines**)
something that has an engine and moving parts, and can do a job or make things *A lot of work in factories is done by machines.*

mad adjective **madder, maddest**
1 Someone who is mad is ill in their mind.
2 If you are mad about something, you like it a lot. *Jake's mad about football.*
3 If you are mad, you are very angry. *My mum was really mad with me.*

made verb *see* **make**

magazine noun (*plural* **magazines**)
a thin book that is made and sold every week or month with different stories and pictures in it

magic noun
In stories, magic is the power that some people have to make impossible and wonderful things happen.

> **WORD FAMILY**
> • **magical** She has special magical powers.
> • **magically** She clicked her fingers and the carriage disappeared magically.

magician noun (*plural* **magicians**)
1 a person who does magic tricks to entertain people
2 a person in stories who has the power to use magic

magnet noun (*plural* **magnets**)
a piece of metal that attracts pieces of iron or steel towards it

> **WORD FAMILY**
> • **magnetic** A huge magnetic crane lifts the cars up.

horseshoe magnet

bar magnet

magnificent adjective
Something that is magnificent is very good or beautiful.
'In all my born days I have never seen such a magnificent pot!' exclaimed Anansi.—Grace Hallworth, Cric Crac

magnify verb **magnifies, magnifying, magnified**
To magnify something means to make it look bigger. *We magnified the insect under the microscope.*

mail noun
letters, cards, and parcels that are sent through the post and delivered to people's houses

main adjective
the main thing is the biggest or most important one You shouldn't cycle on the main road.

main clause noun (*plural* **main clauses**)
(*in grammar*) The main clause in a sentence is the most important clause, which could be a sentence on its own.

major adjective
A major thing is very important or serious. *There has been a major accident on the motorway.*

majority noun (*plural* **majorities**)
A majority is most of the people in a group. *The majority of our class voted for changing the school uniform.*

make verb **makes, making, made**
1 When you make something, you create it. *I've made a cake for you. Please don't make too much mess.*
2 To make something happen means to cause it to happen. *The horrible smell made me feel sick.*
3 If you make someone do something, you force them to do it.
4 If you make something up, you invent it and it is not true.

make-up noun
coloured creams and powders that people put on their faces to make themselves look nice

male adjective
A male person or animal can become a father.

mammal noun
(*plural* **mammals**)
A mammal is an animal that gives birth to live babies and feeds its young with its own milk. Cats, dogs, whales, lions, and people are all mammals.

man noun (*plural* **men**)
a grown-up male person

manage verb **manages, managing, managed**
1 If you manage to do something difficult, you do it after trying very hard. *At last I managed to get the door open.*
2 To manage a shop or business means to be in charge of it.

> **WORD FAMILY**
> • The person who manages a shop or business is a **manager**.

mane noun
(*plural* **manes**)
An animal's mane is the long hair on its neck.

mango noun
(*plural* **mangoes**)
a fruit with sweet, yellow flesh, which grows in hot countries

manner noun
The manner in which you do something is the way you do it.

manners noun
Your manners are the ways in which you behave when you are talking to people or eating your food. *It's bad manners to talk with your mouth full.*

mansion noun (*plural* **mansions**)
a very big house

many adjective & pronoun
Many means a large number. *Were there many people on the bus?*

map noun (*plural* **maps**)
a drawing of a town, a country, or the world

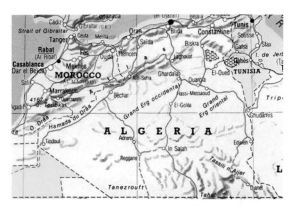

marathon noun (*plural* **marathons**)
a running race which is about 40 kilometres long

marble noun (*plural* **marbles**)
1 Marbles are small, glass balls that you use to play games with.
2 Marble is a type of smooth stone that is used for building or making statues.

March noun
the third month of the year

march verb **marches, marching, marched**
When you march, you walk with regular steps like a soldier.
A soldier came marching down the road: Left/right! Left right!—Hans Christian Andersen, The Tinderbox

mare noun (*plural* **mares**)
a female horse

margarine noun
a food that looks and tastes like butter, but is made from vegetable oils, not milk

margin noun (*plural* **margins**)
an empty space on the side of a page, where there is no writing

marine adjective
Marine animals live in the sea.

a
b
c
d
e
f
g
h
i
j
k
l
m
n
o
p
q
r
s
t
u
v
w
x
y
z

mark noun (*plural* **marks**)
1 a dirty stain or spot on something
How did you get those dirty marks on your shirt?
2 The mark that you get for a piece of work is the number or letter that shows how well you have done.

mark verb **marks, marking, marked**
To mark a piece of work means to give it a number or letter to show how good it is.

market noun (*plural* **markets**)
a group of stalls where people sell food and other things

marmalade noun
jam made from oranges or lemons

marry verb **marries, marrying, married**
When you marry someone, you become their husband or wife.

> **WORD FAMILY**
> • **married** My grandparents have been married for thirty years.

marsh noun (*plural* **marshes**)
a piece of very wet, soft ground

marsupial noun (*plural* **marsupials**) (*say* mar-**soo**-pee-al)
A marsupial is an animal that carries its young in a special pouch on the front of its body. Kangaroos are marsupials.

martial art noun (*plural* **martial arts**)
Martial arts are sports such as judo and karate, in which people fight with each other.

marvellous adjective
Something that is marvellous is wonderful.
He lived in India, in a town called Bombay, which is a marvellous, exciting place, I can tell you.—Alexander McCall Smith, The Bubblegum Tree

masculine adjective
Something that is masculine looks as if it is suitable for boys and men, not girls and women.

mash verb **mashes, mashing, mashed**
When you mash food, you crush it until it is soft and smooth. *We're having sausages and mashed potatoes for tea.*

mask noun (*plural* **masks**)
something that you wear over your face to hide it or protect it

mass noun (*plural* **masses**)
A mass is a large amount of something, or a large number of things. *We've got masses of homework!*

massive adjective
Something that is massive is very big.
I remembered a huge toyshop and a big Ferris wheel and a museum with massive dinosaurs.—Jacqueline Wilson, Best Friends

mast noun (*plural* **masts**)
a tall pole that holds up a ship's sails

master noun (*plural* **masters**)
An animal's master is the man or boy who controls it.

mat noun (*plural* **mats**)
1 a small carpet
2 something that you put under a hot plate on a table

match noun (*plural* **matches**)
1 a small, thin stick that makes a flame when you rub it against something rough
2 a game that two people or teams play against each other *Did you watch the football match on TV last night?*

match verb **matches, matching, matched**
Things that match are the same or go well together.

material noun (*plural* **materials**)
1 A material is something that you use to make things with. *Wood and stone are building materials.*
2 Material is cloth.

mathematics, maths noun
the subject in which you learn about numbers, measurement, and shapes

matter noun (*plural* **matters**)
1 something that you need to talk about or deal with *There is an important matter we have to talk about.*
2 When you ask someone what the matter is, you are asking what is wrong.

matter verb **matters, mattering, mattered**
If something matters, it is important. *It doesn't matter if you are a bit late.*

mattress noun (*plural* **mattresses**)
the soft part of a bed that you lie on

mature adjective
Someone who is mature behaves in a grown-up way.

May noun
the fifth month of the year

may verb
1 If you may do something, you are allowed to do it. *May I have a drink, please?*
2 If something may happen, it is possible that it will happen. *It may rain later.*

maybe adverb
perhaps

mayor noun (*plural* **mayors**)
A mayor is the person in charge of the council of a town or city. A woman who is a mayor can also be called a **mayoress**.

maze noun (*plural* **mazes**)
a set of lines or paths that twist and turn so much that it is very easy to lose your way

meadow noun (*plural* **meadows**)
a field of grass and flowers

meal noun (*plural* **meals**)
the food that you eat at breakfast, lunch, dinner, tea, or supper

mean verb **means, meaning, meant**
When you say what a word means, you say what it describes or shows. *What does the word 'delicious' mean?*

mean adjective **meaner, meanest**
1 Someone who is mean does not like sharing things.
2 Someone who is mean is unkind. *That was a really mean thing to do!*

meaning noun (*plural* **meanings**)
The meaning of a word is what it means. *If you don't know the meaning of a word, look it up in the dictionary.*

meanwhile adverb
during the time something else is happening *Grace went to phone the fire brigade. Meanwhile I made sure there was no one left in the building.*

measles noun
an illness that gives you red spots all over your body

measure verb **measures, measuring, measured**
When you measure something, you find out how big it is or how much there is.

measurement noun (*plural* **measurements**)
a number that you get when you measure something

meat noun
the flesh from animals that we can eat

mechanic noun (*plural* **mechanics**)
a person who repairs cars or machines

mechanical adjective
Something that is mechanical has parts that move like a machine. *They used a mechanical digger to dig a deep ditch.*

medal noun (*plural* **medals**)
a special piece of metal that is given tosomeone who has won a competition or done something very brave

medicine noun (*plural* **medicines**)
a special liquid or tablet that you take when you are ill to make you better

medium adjective
Medium means not very big and not very small, but in the middle.

meet verb **meets, meeting, met**
1 When people meet, they see each other and talk to each other. *Let's meet at two o'clock.*
2 When two roads or rivers meet, they join together.

meeting noun (*plural* **meetings**)
When people have a meeting, they meet to talk about something.

a
b
c
d
e
f
g
h
i
j
k
l
m
n
o
p
q
r
s
t
u
v
w
x
y
z

melt verb **melts, melting, melted**
When something melts, it becomes a liquid because it has become warm. *Ice melts as it warms up.*

member noun (*plural* **members**)
someone who belongs to a club or group

memory noun (*plural* **memories**)
1 Your memory is your ability to remember things. *Have you got a good memory?*
2 A memory is something that you can remember. *The old man had happy memories of when he was a boy.*
3 The memory in a computer is the part that stores information.

men noun *see* **man**

mend verb **mends, mending, mended**
When you mend something that is broken, you fix it or put it right so that you can use it again.

mental adjective
Something that is mental happens in your mind. *At school we have to do mental arithmetic.*

mention verb **mentions, mentioning, mentioned**
If you mention something, you talk about it.

menu noun (*plural* **menus**)
1 a list of the different kinds of food you can choose for your meal
2 (*in ICT*) a list that appears on a computer screen showing the different things you can ask the computer to do

mercy noun
If you show mercy to someone, you are kind and do not punish them.

mermaid noun (*plural* **mermaids**)
In stories, a mermaid is a sea creature that looks like a woman but has a fish's tail instead of legs.

merry adjective **merrier, merriest**
Someone who is merry is cheerful and laughing.

mess noun
If something is a mess, it is very untidy. *The whole house was in a terrible mess.*

WORD FAMILY
• **messy** The room was dirty and messy.

message noun (*plural* **messages**)
words that you write down or record for someone when you cannot see them or speak to them yourself

met verb *see* **meet**

metal noun (*plural* **metals**)
Metal is a hard, strong material. Gold, silver, iron, and tin are all types of metal.

meteor noun (*plural* **meteors**) (*say* **mee**-tee-or)
A meteor is a piece of rock or metal that flies through space and burns up when it gets near the earth. A piece of rock or metal that falls to earth without burning up is called a meteorite.

meter noun (*plural* **meters**)
a machine that measures how much of something has been used

method noun (*plural* **methods**)
the way in which you do something *Describe the method you used to do the experiment.*

metre noun (*plural* **metres**)
We can measure length in metres. There are 100 centimetres in a metre.

metric adjective
The metric system of measurement uses units of 10 and 100. Millimetres, centimetres, and metres are all part of the metric system.

miaow verb **miaows, miaowing, miaowed**
When a cat miaows, it makes a long, high sound.

mice noun *see* **mouse**

microchip noun (*plural* **microchips**)
one of the tiny pieces in a computer that makes it work

microphone noun (*plural* **microphones**)
something that you speak into when you want to record your voice or make it sound louder

microscope noun (*plural* **microscopes**)
an instrument that makes tiny things look bigger

microwave noun (*plural* **microwaves**)
an oven that cooks food very quickly by passing special radio waves through it

midday noun
twelve o'clock in the middle of the day

middle noun (plural **middles**)
1 the part near the centre of something, not at the edges *There was a huge puddle in the middle of the playground.*
2 the part that is not near the beginning or end of something *The phone rang in the middle of the night.*

midnight noun
twelve o'clock at night

might verb *see* **may** verb

mighty adjective **mightier, mightiest**
Something that is mighty is very big or strong.

migrate verb **migrates, migrating, migrated**
When birds or animals migrate, they travel to another place at the same time each year.

mild adjective **milder, mildest**
1 Something that is mild is not very strong. *The soup had a mild but pleasant flavour.*
2 Mild weather is quite warm.

mile noun (plural **miles**)
We can measure distance in miles. One mile is the same as about 1¹/₂ kilometres.

military adjective
Military things are used by soldiers.

moist noun
Milk is a white liquid that you can drink. All female mammals make milk to feed their babies. People can drink cows' milk.

mill noun (plural **mills**)
a place where grain is crushed to make flour

millennium noun (plural **milleniums** or **millennia**)
a period of 1000 years

millilitre noun (plural **millilitres**)
We can measure liquid in millilitres. There are 1000 millilitres in one litre.

millimetre noun (plural **millimetres**)
We can measure length in millimetres. There are 1000 millimetres in one metre.

million noun (plural **millions**)
the number 1,000,000

millionaire noun (plural **millionaires**)
a very rich person who has more than a million pounds or dollars

mime verb **mimes, miming, mimed**
When you mime, you pretend to do something using only actions, not words.

mince noun
meat that has been cut into very small pieces

mind noun (plural **minds**)
Your mind is your ability to think, and all the thoughts, ideas, and memories that you have.

mind verb **minds, minding, minded**
If you do not mind about something, it does not upset or worry you. *I don't mind if you don't buy me a present.*

mine noun (plural **mines**)
1 a place where people work to dig coal, metal, or stones out of the ground
2 A mine is a bomb that is hidden in the ground or the sea. It explodes when something touches it.

mineral noun (plural **minerals**)
Minerals are things such as salt that form naturally in the ground.

minor adjective
A minor thing is not very important or serious. *He only suffered a minor injury.*

mint noun (plural **mints**)
1 a green plant that is added to food to give it flavour
2 a sweet that tastes of mint

minus adjective & preposition
1 (*in mathematics*) take away *Six minus two is four, $6 - 2 = 4$*
2 (*in mathematics*) A minus number is less than 0. *The temperature outside was minus three.*

minute noun (plural **minutes**) (*say* **min**-it)
We measure time in minutes. There are 60 seconds in one minute, and 60 minutes in one hour.

minute adjective (*say* my-**newt**)
Something that is minute is very small.

miracle noun (*plural* **miracles**)
something wonderful that has happened, although it did not seem possible *It's a miracle no one was hurt in the train crash.*

mirror noun (*plural* **mirrors**)
a piece of glass, in which you can see yourself

misbehave verb **misbehaves, misbehaving, misbehaved**
If you misbehave, you behave in a naughty way.

mischief noun
If you get into mischief, you do silly or naughty things.

WORD FAMILY
• **mischievous** She gave a mischievous grin.

miserable adjective
If you are miserable, you are very unhappy.

misfortune noun (*plural* **misfortunes**)
bad luck

misprint noun (*plural* **misprints**)
a small mistake in something that has been printed or typed

miss verb **misses, missing, missed**
1 If you miss something, you do not catch it or hit it. *I tried to hit the ball but I missed it.*
2 If you miss someone, you feel sad because they are not with you.

missile noun (*plural* **missiles**)
a weapon which is thrown or fired through the air

motorway adjective
Something that is missing is lost. *My cat's gone missing.*

mould noun
When there is mist, there is a lot of cloud just above the ground, which makes it difficult to see.

mistake noun (*plural* **mistakes**)
If you make a mistake, you do something wrong.

mistake verb **mistakes, mistaking, mistook, mistaken**
If you mistake someone for another person, you think they are the other person.

mistress noun (*plural* **mistresses**)
An animal's mistress is the woman or girl who controls it.

mix verb **mixes, mixing, mixed**
When you mix things together, you put them together and stir them.

mixture noun (*plural* **mixtures**)
something that is made of different things mixed together

moan verb **moans, moaning, moaned**
1 When you moan, you make a low sound because you are in pain.
2 When you moan about something, you complain about it.

moat noun (*plural* **moats**)
a deep ditch filled with water round a castle

mobile adjective
Something that is mobile can be moved or carried around easily.

mobile phone noun (*plural* **mobile phones**)
A mobile phone is a telephone that you can carry around with you. It is also called a **mobile**.

model noun (*plural* **models**)
1 a small copy of something *We built a model of a spaceship.*
2 someone who shows new clothes to people by wearing them and walking around in them

modern adjective
Something that is modern uses new ideas, not old-fashioned ones. *Modern cars are much safer than old cars.*

modest adjective
1 Someone who is modest does not boast.
2 Someone who is modest is shy.

WORD FAMILY
• **modestly** 'It was nothing really,' she said modestly.

moist adjective **moister, moistest**
Something that is moist is slightly wet.

moisture noun
tiny drops of water in the air or on the surface of something

molar noun (*plural* **molars**)
Your molars are the big teeth at the back of your mouth.

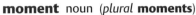

mole noun (*plural* **moles**)
1 a small, furry animal that digs holes and tunnels under the ground
2 a small brown mark on your skin

moment noun (*plural* **moments**)
a very small amount of time *Please could you wait a moment?*

Monday noun (*plural* **Mondays**)
the day after Sunday

money noun
the coins and pieces of paper that we use to buy things

mongrel noun (*plural* **mongrels**)
a dog that is not one breed, but is a mixture of more than one breed

monitor noun (*plural* **monitors**)
(*in ICT*) a computer screen

monkey noun (*plural* **monkeys**)
A monkey is a furry animal with a long tail. Monkeys are very good at climbing and swinging in trees.

monsoon noun (*plural* **monsoons**)
a time of year when it rains a lot in some hot countries

monster noun (*plural* **monsters**)
a large, fierce animal in stories

month noun (*plural* **months**)
A month is a period of 28, 30, or 31 days. There are twelve months in a year.

monument noun (*plural* **monuments**)
a statue that helps people to remember an important person or event

mood noun (*plural* **moods**)
Your mood is the the way you feel, for example whether you are happy or sad. *Anita's in a very good mood today.*

moon noun
The moon is the large, round thing that you see shining in the sky at night. The moon travels round the earth in space. *There's a full moon tonight.*

moonlight noun
light from the moon

moor noun (*plural* **moors**)
an area of high land that has bushes but no trees

mop noun (*plural* **mops**)
You use a mop for cleaning floors. It has a bundle of loose strings on the end of a long handle.

moral noun (*plural* **morals**)
a lesson that a story teaches you about what is right or wrong

more adjective & adverb
a bigger number or amount *My brother's always got more money than I have.*

morning noun (*plural* **mornings**)
the time from the beginning of the day until the middle of the day

mosaic noun (*plural* **mosaics**) (*say* **moh**-zay-ik)
a picture made from a lot of small, coloured pieces of glass or stone

mosque noun (*plural* **mosques**)
a building where Muslims pray and worship

mosquito noun (*plural* **mosquitoes**)
a small insect that bites people and animals

moss noun (*plural* **mosses**)
a plant that forms soft lumps when it grows on the ground or on old walls

most adjective & adverb
more than any other *Which story did you like the most?*

moth noun (*plural* **moths**)
an insect like a butterfly, that flies around at night

mother noun (*plural* **mothers**)
Your mother is your female parent.

motive noun (*plural* **motives**)
Your motive for doing something is your reason for doing it.

motor noun (*plural* **motors**)
an engine that makes something move

motor bike, motor cycle noun
(*plural* **motor bikes, motor cycles**)
a large, heavy bicycle with an engine

motorway noun (*plural* **motorways**)
a wide, straight road on which people can drive fast and travel a long way

mould noun (*plural* **moulds**) (*rhymes with* old)
1 the grey or green substance that grows on food that has gone bad
2 a container that you use for making liquids set into a particular shape

> **WORD FAMILY**
> • **mouldy** All we had to eat was some mouldy bread.

mound noun (*plural* **mounds**)
a pile of earth

mount verb **mounts, mounting, mounted**
When you mount a horse or a bicycle, you get onto it so that you can ride it.

mountain noun (*plural* **mountains**)
a very high hill

mouse noun (*plural* **mice**)
1 a small furry animal with a long tail
2 (*in ICT*) A computer mouse is the part that you move about on your desk to choose things on the screen.

moustache noun (*plural* **moustaches**)
hair that grows on a man's top lip

mouth noun (*plural* **mouths**)
1 Your mouth is the part of your face that you can open and use for eating and speaking.
2 The mouth of a river is the place where it flows into the sea.

move verb **moves, moving, moved**
1 When you move something, you take it from one place and put it in another place.
2 When something moves, it goes from one place to another. *The dog just sat still and didn't move.*

> **WORD FAMILY**
> • **movement** I saw a sudden movement in the bushes.

movie noun (*plural* **movies**)
a film that you watch on a screen at the cinema or on television

mow verb **mows, mowing, mowed, mown**
When you mow grass, you cut it.

MP3 player noun (*plural* **MP3 players**)
a small music player that plays music you have downloaded onto it from the Internet

much adjective
a lot *Hurry up! We haven't got much time! I don't like carrots very much.*

mud noun
wet, sticky soil *My boots were covered in mud.*

> **WORD FAMILY**
> • **muddy** Are your boots muddy?

muddle noun (*plural* **muddles**)
If something is in a muddle, it is messy or untidy.

muesli noun (*say* **mooz-li**)
a type of breakfast cereal made with nuts and dried fruit

muffled adjective
A muffled sound is not clear, and is hard to hear.

mug noun (*plural* **mugs**)
a big cup

multiple noun (*plural* **multiples**)
(*in mathematics*) The multiples of a number are the numbers that it will divide into exactly. For example, 10, 15, and 20 are multiples of 5.

multiply verb **multiplies, multiplying, multiplied**
(*in mathematics*) When you multiply a number, you make it a number of times bigger. Five multiplied by three is fifteen, $5 \times 3 = 15$.

> **WORD FAMILY**
> • When you multiply numbers you do **multiplication**.

mum, mummy noun (*plural* **mums** *or* **mummies**)
Your mum is your mother.

mumble verb **mumbles, mumbling, mumbled**
When you mumble, you speak without saying the words clearly.

mumps noun
an illness that makes the sides of your face swell up

munch verb **munches, munching, munched**
When you munch something, you chew it noisily. *We munched our way through a whole packet of biscuits.*

murder verb **murders, murdering, murdered**
To murder someone means to kill them on purpose.

murmur verb **murmurs, murmuring, murmured**
When you murmur, you speak in a very soft, low voice.

muscle noun (*plural* **muscles**)
Your muscles are the strong parts of your body that you use to make your body move.

museum noun (*plural* **museums**)
a place where things from the past are kept for people to go and see

mushroom noun (*plural* **mushrooms**)
a small plant with a stem and a grey, round top that you can eat

music noun
the nice sound that you make when you sing or play instruments

musical adjective
A musical instrument is an instrument that you use to play music.

musician noun (*plural* **musicians**)
a person who plays or composes music

Muslim noun (*plural* **Muslims**)
someone who follows the religion of Islam

must verb
If you must do something, you have to do it. *You must go to school.*

mustard noun
a cold, yellow sauce with a hot, strong taste

mutter verb **mutters, muttering, muttered**
When you mutter, you speak in a quiet voice because you do not want people to hear you. *Mildred muttered the spell under her breath – and Ethel vanished.*—Jill Murphy, The Worst Witch

mystery noun (*plural* **mysteries**) (*say* **miss**-ter-ee)
If something is a mystery, it is strange and puzzling and you do not understand it.

> **WORD FAMILY**
> • **mysterious** Who is this mysterious boy?

myth noun (*plural* **myths**)
a very old story, often one about gods and goddesses *We've been reading some Greek myths at school.*

> **WORD FAMILY**
> • **mythical** Unicorns are mythical creatures.

a
b
c
d
e
f
g
h
i
j
k
l
m
n
o
p
q
r
s
t
u
v
w
x
y
z

nail noun (plural **nails**)
1 Your nails are the hard parts at the ends of your fingers and toes.
2 A nail is a small thin piece of metal with a sharp point at the end. You bang nails into wood with a hammer to hold pieces of wood together.

nail verb **nails, nailing, nailed**
When you nail pieces of wood together, you join them together with nails.

name noun (plural **names**)
Your name is what people call you.

name verb **names, naming, named**
To name someone means to give them a name.

nanny noun (plural **nannies**)
someone whose job is to look after children while their parents are at work

narrative noun (plural **narratives**)
a story or an account of something that has happened

narrator noun (plural **narrators**)
the person who tells a story

narrow adjective **narrower, narrowest**
Something that is narrow is not very wide. *We drove along a very narrow road.*

nasty adjective **nastier, nastiest**
1 Something that is nasty is horrible. *There was a nasty smell in the classroom.*
2 Someone who is nasty is mean or unkind. *Mr Bonecrusher appeared to be nasty through and through.*—Philip Ardagh, Dreadful Acts

nation noun (plural **nations**)
a country

WORD FAMILY
• **national** He reached the national finals of the competition.

natural adjective
1 Something that is natural has been made by nature, not by people or machines.
2 Something that is natural is normal. *It is natural to feel upset sometimes.*

nature noun
1 everything in the world that was not made by people, for example mountains, rivers, animals, and plants
2 Your nature is the type of person that you are. *It's not in Salim's nature to be mean and selfish.*

naughty adjective **naughtier, naughtiest**
(say **nor**-tee)
If you are naughty, you behave badly.

navigate verb **navigates, navigating, navigated**
When you navigate, you make sure that a ship, aeroplane, or car is going in the right direction.

navy noun (plural **navies**)
an army that fights at sea, in ships

near adjective & adverb **nearer, nearest**
not far away *We live near the school.*

nearly adverb
almost *It's nearly 3 o'clock.*

neat adjective **neater, neatest**
Something that is neat is clean and tidy.

WORD FAMILY
• **neatly** He arranged the papers neatly on the desk.

necessary adjective
If something is necessary, it has to be done. *It is necessary to water plants in dry weather.*

neck noun (plural **necks**)
Your neck is the part of your body that joins your head to your shoulders.

necklace noun (plural **necklaces**)
a chain or string of beads or jewels that you wear around your neck

need verb **needs, needing, needed**
1 If you need something, you have to have it.
2 If you need to do something, you have to do it. *We need to watch him carefully to see where he puts the money.*

need noun (*plural* **needs**)
1 Your needs are the things that you need.
2 If someone is in need, they do not have enough money, food, or clothes.

needle noun (*plural* **needles**)
1 a thin, pointed piece of metal with a hole at one end that you use for sewing
2 A knitting needle is a long, thin stick that you use for knitting.
3 The needles on a pine tree are its thin, pointed leaves.

negative adjective
1 (*in grammar*) A negative sentence is one that has the word 'not' or 'no' in it. 'Rebecca is not very happy' is a negative sentence.
2 (*in mathematics*) A negative number is less than zero.

negotiate verb **negotiates, negotiating, negotiated**
When people negotiate, they try to reach an agreement about something by discussing it.

neigh verb **neighs, neighing, neighed**
(*say* **nay**)
When a horse neighs, it makes a loud, high sound.

neighbour noun (*plural* **neighbours**)
(*say* **nay**-ber)
Your neighbours are the people who live near you.

nephew noun (*plural* **nephews**)
Your nephew is the son of your brother or sister.

nerve noun (*plural* **nerves**)
The nerves in your body are the parts that carry messages to and from your brain, so that your body can feel and move.

nervous adjective
If you feel nervous, you feel slightly afraid. *To tell the truth, Jack felt a little nervous, because it isn't every day you find a Scarecrow talking to you.*—Philip Pullman, The Scarecrow and his Servant

WORD FAMILY
• **nervously** 'Do you think he's all right?' she asked nervously.

nest noun (*plural* **nests**)
a home that a bird or small animal makes for its babies

nest

net noun (*plural* **nets**)
1 A net is a piece of material with small holes in it. You use a net for catching fish.
2 (*in ICT*) The net is the Internet.

netball noun
a game in which two teams of players try to score goals by throwing a ball through a round net on a pole

nettle noun (*plural* **nettles**)
a plant with leaves that can sting you if you touch them

network noun (*plural* **networks**)
(*in ICT*) a group of computers that are connected to each other

never adverb
not ever *I will never tell a lie again!*

new adjective **newer, newest**
1 Something that is new has just been made or bought and is not old. *I got some new trainers for my birthday.*
2 Something that is new is different. *We're moving to a new house.*

news noun
The news is all the things that are happening in the world, which you can see on television or read about in newspapers.

newspaper noun (*plural* **newspapers**)
A newspaper is paper folded together so that you can turn the pages like a book. Newspapers contain articles about things that are happening in the world.

Newton noun (*plural* **Newtons**)
(*in science*) We measure force in Newtons.

next adjective
1 The next thing is the one that is nearest to you. *My friend lives in the next street.*
2 The next thing is the one that comes after this one. *We're going on holiday next week.*

nibble verb **nibbles, nibbling, nibbled**
When you nibble something, you eat it by biting off a little bit at a time.

nice adjective **nicer, nicest**
1 Something that is nice is pleasant or enjoyable.
2 Someone who is nice is kind.

WORD FAMILY
• **nicely** She said thank you very nicely.

nickname noun (*plural* **nicknames**)
a friendly name that your family or friends call you

a
b
c
d
e
f
g
h
i
j
k
l
m
n
o
p
q
r
s
t
u
v
w
x
y
z

niece noun (*plural* **nieces**)
Your niece is the daughter of your brother or sister.

night noun (*plural* **nights**)
the time when it is dark

nightmare noun (*plural* **nightmares**)
a very frightening dream

nil noun
nothing, the number 0 *The score was three nil to our team.*

nine noun (*plural* **nines**)
the number 9

nineteen noun
the number 19

ninety noun
the number 90

nobody pronoun
no person *There's nobody here.*

nocturnal adjective
Nocturnal animals move around and feed at night. *Bats are nocturnal.*

nod verb **nods, nodding, nodded**
When you nod, you move your head up and down to show that you agree with someone.

noise noun (*plural* **noises**)
a sound that you can hear, especially a loud or strange one *Did you hear a noise?*

> **WORD FAMILY**
> • **noisy** Please don't be so noisy.

none pronoun
not any *I went into the kitchen to find some food, but there was none there.*

non-fiction noun
books that have information in that is true

nonsense noun
something silly that does not mean anything

noon noun
twelve o'clock in the middle of the day

no one pronoun
nobody

normal adjective
Something that is normal is ordinary and not different or surprising.

north noun
North is one of the directions in which you can face or travel. On a map, north is the direction towards the top of the page.

> **WORD FAMILY**
> • The **northern** part of a country is the part in the north.

nose noun (*plural* **noses**)
Your nose is the part of your face that you use for breathing and smelling.

nostril noun (*plural* **nostrils**)
Your nostrils are the two holes at the end of your nose, which you breathe through.

nosy adjective **nosier, nosiest**
If you are nosy, you try to find out about things that other people are doing.

note noun (*plural* **notes**)
1 a short letter
2 A musical note is one sound in a piece of music. *I'll play the first few notes, then you join in.*
3 A note is a piece of paper money.

notebook noun (*plural* **notebooks**)
1 a small book for writing notes in
2 a small computer that you can carry around with you

nothing noun
not anything *There was nothing in the box.*

notice noun (*plural* **notices**)
1 a written message that is put up on a wall for people to see
2 If you take no notice of something, you ignore it.

notice verb **notices, noticing, noticed**
If you notice something, you see it.
At that moment I noticed a huge stack of pancakes.—Jostein Gaarder, The Frog Castle

nought noun (*plural* **noughts**)
nothing, the number 0

noun noun (*plural* **nouns**)
(*in grammar*) A noun is a word that is the name of a person, place, thing, or idea. Words like *chair*, *cat*, *London*, and *sport* are all nouns.

novel

novel noun
(*plural* **novels**)
a book that tells a long story *'Oliver Twist' is a novel by Charles Dickens.*

November noun
the eleventh month of the year

now adverb
at this time *Do you want to go now?*

nowhere adverb
not anywhere

nudge verb **nudges, nudging, nudged**
When you nudge someone, you push them with your elbow to make them notice something.

nuisance noun (*plural* **nuisances**)
(*say* new-sans)
If something is a nuisance, it is annoying.
It's a nuisance that we missed the bus.

numb adjective
If a part of your body is numb, you cannot feel anything with it. *My toes were numb with cold.*

number noun (*plural* **numbers**)
A number is a word or sign that tells you how many things there are. 1, 2, and 3 are numbers.

123

numeracy noun (*say* **new**-mer-ass-ee)
Numeracy is being able to count and work with numbers.

numerous adjective (*say* **new**-mer-uss)
If there are numerous things, there are a lot of them.

nurse noun (*plural* **nurses**)
someone who works in a hospital and looks after people who are ill or hurt

nursery noun (*plural* **nurseries**)
1 a place where very young children go to play and be looked after
2 a place where people grow plants to sell

nut noun (*plural* **nuts**)
1 A nut is a hard fruit that grows on some trees and plants. You can eat some types of nuts.
2 a piece of metal with a hole in it which you screw on the end of a long piece of metal called a **bolt** *You use nuts and bolts to fix things together.*

hazlenut

nutrition noun
all the food that you need to keep you alive and well

a
b
c
d
e
f
g
h
i
j
k
l
m
n
o
p
q
r
s
t
u
v
w
x
y
z

Oo

oak noun (*plural* **oaks**)
a large tree that produces nuts called acorns

oar noun (*plural* **oars**) (*say* **or**)
a pole with a flat part at one end, which you use for rowing a boat

oasis noun (*plural* **oases**) (*say* oh-**ay**-sis)
a place in a desert where there is water, and where trees and plants grow

obedient adjective (*say* oh-**bee**-dee-ent)
If you are obedient, you do what other people tell you to do.
It was a splendid dog, and like all Swiss dogs it was extremely obedient and well-mannered.—Alexander McCall Smith, The Chocolate Money Mystery

WORD FAMILY
• **obediently** The dog trotted towards her obediently.

obey verb **obeys, obeying, obeyed**
When you obey someone, you do what they tell you to do.

object noun (*plural* **objects**) (*say* **ob**-jikt)
1 anything that you can see, touch, or hold *There were some interesting objects in the museum.*
2 (*in grammar*) The object in a sentence is the noun that shows which person or thing receives the action of the verb. For example, in the sentence 'The cat chased the dog', dog is the object of the verb.

object verb **objects, objecting, objected**
(*say* ob-**jekt**)
If you object to something, you say that you do not like it.

oblong noun (*plural* **oblongs**)
An oblong is a shape that looks like a long square. It is also called a **rectangle**.

observe verb **observes, observing, observed**
When you observe something, you watch it carefully.

obstacle noun (*plural* **obstacles**)
something that is in your way and stops you doing what you want to do

obtain verb **obtains, obtaining, obtained**
When you obtain something, you get it.

obvious adjective
If something is obvious, it is very easy to see or understand.

WORD FAMILY
• **obviously** He was obviously very excited.

occasion noun (*plural* **occasions**)
an important event *A wedding is usually a happy occasion.*

occasionally adverb
If you do something occasionally, you do it sometimes.

occupy verb **occupies, occupying, occupied**
1 If a place is occupied, someone is using it or living in it. *Is this seat occupied?*
2 To occupy someone means to keep them busy. *My mum gave us some jobs to do to keep us occupied.*

occur verb **occurs, occurring, occurred**
1 When something occurs, it happens. *The accident occurred at six o'clock last night.*
2 When something occurs to you, you think of it.

ocean noun (*plural* **oceans**)
a big sea *They sailed across the Atlantic Ocean.*

o'clock adverb
a word you use to say what time it is
I'll meet you at one o'clock.

octagon noun (*plural* **octagons**)
a shape with eight straight sides

October noun
the tenth month of the year

octopus noun
(*plural* **octopuses**)
a sea creature
with eight
tentacles

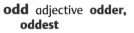
octopus

odd adjective **odder,
oddest**
1 Something that is
odd is strange.
2 (*in mathematics*) An odd number that cannot
be divided by two. *Five is an odd number.*

of preposition
1 made from *He wore a crown of solid gold.*
2 belonging to *The handle of my bag is
broken.*

off adverb & preposition
1 down from something or away from
something *He fell off the wall.*
2 not switched on *The heating's off.*

offend verb **offends, offending, offended**
To offend someone means to hurt their
feelings.

offer verb **offers, offering, offered**
1 If you offer something to someone, you ask
if they would like it. *She offered me a piece
of cake.*
2 If you offer to do something, you say that you
will do it. *I offered to lay the table.*

office noun (*plural* **offices**)
a room with desks, where people work

officer noun (*plural* **officers**)
1 a person in the army, navy, or air force who is
in charge of other people and gives them orders
2 a policeman or policewoman

official adjective
Something that is official is decided or done
by a person in charge. *I got an official letter
about my prize.*

often adverb
many times *We often go swimming on
Saturdays.*

oil noun
Oil is a thick, slippery liquid. You can use
some types of oil as fuel, or to make
machines work more smoothly. You use
other types of oil in cooking.

ointment noun (*plural* **ointments**)
a cream that you put on sore skin or cuts

OK, okay adjective
Something that is OK is all right.

old adjective **older, oldest**
1 Someone who is old has lived for a long time.
2 Something that is old was made a long time
ago. *Our car is quite old.*

old-fashioned adjective
Something that is old-fashioned looks old
and not modern. *She was wearing very
old-fashioned clothes.*

on preposition & adverb
1 on top of *Put your books on your desk.*
2 on the subject of *I've got a new book
on dinosaurs.*
3 working *Is the heating on?*

once adverb
1 one time *I only missed school once last term.*
2 at one time *Once dinosaurs roamed the
earth.*

one noun (*plural* **ones**)
the number 1

onion noun (*plural* **onions**)
a round, white vegetable that has a very
strong smell and taste

online adjective
When you work online on a computer, the
computer is connected to the Internet.

only adjective
An only child is a child who has no brothers
or sisters.

only adverb
not more than *It's only four o'clock.*

onomatopoeia noun (*say*
on-om-at-o-**pee**-a)
the use of words which sound like the thing
they describe, for example hiss and plop

onto preposition
on *I stuck a label onto the parcel.*

onwards adverb
forwards *We walked onwards until we came
to the river.*

a
b
c
d
e
f
g
h
i
j
k
l
m
n
o
p
q
r
s
t
u
v
w
x
y
z

opaque adjective (*say* oh-**pake**)
   If something is opaque, you cannot see through it. Curtains are opaque.

curtains

open adjective
   1 When a door or window is open, it is not shut.
   2 When a shop is open, you can go into it and buy things.

open verb **opens, opening, opened**
   1 When you open a door or window, you move it so that it is open.
   2 When a shop opens, you can go into it and buy things.

opening noun (*plural* **openings**)
   a space or hole in something

operation noun (*plural* **operations**)
   When you have an operation, doctors mend or take out a part of your body to make you healthy again.

opinion noun (*plural* **opinions**)
   Your opinion is what you think about something. *In your opinion, which colour looks best?*

opponent noun (*plural* **opponents**)
   Your opponent is the person that you are fighting or playing a game against. *We beat our opponents easily.*

opportunity noun (*plural* **opportunities**)
   If you have an opportunity to do something, you have the chance to do it.
   This seemed to Alice a good opportunity for making her escape.—Lewis Carroll, *Alice's Adventures in Wonderland*

opposite adjective & preposition
   1 facing something *The school is opposite the library.*
   2 Things that are opposite are completely different. *North is the opposite direction to south.*

opposite noun (*plural* **opposites**)
   The opposite of something is the thing that is completely different to it. *Big is the opposite of small.*

optician noun (*plural* **opticians**) (*say* op-**tish**-an)
   someone who tests people's eyes and sells glasses to help them see better

optimistic adjective
   If you are optimistic, you think that something good will happen.

option noun (*plural* **options**)
   something that you can choose to do *I had to go for help – there was no other option.*

orange noun (*plural* **oranges**)
   a round, juicy fruit with a thick, orange skin and sweet, juicy flesh

orange adjective
   Something that is orange is the colour that you make when you mix red and yellow together.

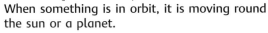

an orange

orbit noun (*plural* **orbits**)
   When something is in orbit, it is moving round the sun or a planet.

orchard noun (*plural* **orchards**)
   a field where a lot of fruit trees grow

orchestra noun (*plural* **orchestras**) (-**ch**- in this word sounds like -**k**-)
   a large group of people who play musical instruments together

order noun (*plural* **orders**)
   1 When you give someone an order, you tell them what they must do.
   2 The order that things are in is the way that they are arranged, one after the other. *The words in a dictionary are in alphabetical order.*

order verb **orders, ordering, ordered**
   1 If you order someone to do something, you tell them that they must do it. *'Come with me,' he ordered.*
   2 If you order something in a shop or restaurant, you ask for it. *We ordered pizza and chips.*
   3 When you order things in a computer file, you arrange them in a particular order, for example in alphabetical order.

a
b
c
d
e
f
g
h
i
j
k
l
m
n
o
p
q
r
s
t
u
v
w
x
y
z

ordinary adjective
Something that is ordinary is normal and not different or special.

organ noun (*plural* **organs**)
1 a musical instrument like a piano with large air pipes where the sound comes out
2 Your organs are the parts inside your body like your heart and brain, that each do a particular job.

organic adjective
Food that is organic has been grown without using strong chemicals.

organize verb **organizes, organizing, organized**
When you organize something, you plan it and arrange it. *I helped to organize the concert.*

organization noun (*plural* **organizations**)
a large number of people who work together to do a job

origin noun (*plural* **origins**)
The origin of something is the way in which it started.

original adjective
1 An original part of something was there when it was first made. *My dad's old bike still has its original tyres.*
2 Something that is original is new and has not been copied from something else. *Try to think of some original ideas.*

> **WORD FAMILY**
> • **originally** This building was originally a factory.

ornament noun (*plural* **ornaments**)
something that you put in a place to make it look pretty

orphan noun (*plural* **orphans**)
a child whose mother and father are dead

ostrich noun (*plural* **ostriches**)
An ostrich is a very large bird with long legs and a heavy body. Ostriches can run very fast, but they cannot fly.

ostrich

other adjective & pronoun
The other thing is a different thing, not this one. *I can't find my other shoe.*

otherwise adverb
or else *Hurry up otherwise we'll be late.*

ought verb (*say* **ort**)
If you ought to do something, you should do it. *You ought to spend more time on your homework.*

ounce noun (*plural* **ounces**)
We can measure weight in ounces. One ounce is about 28 grams.

out adverb
1 away from *I took the letter out of the envelope.*
2 not at home *I'm afraid Minal's out at the moment.*

outfit noun (*plural* **outfits**)
a set of clothes that you wear together *Mum bought me a new outfit to wear at the wedding.*

outing noun (*plural* **outings**)
a trip to a place

outline noun (*plural* **outlines**)
The outline of something is its shape.

output noun
(*in ICT*) The output is the information that you get out of a computer. The information that you put in is the **input**.

outside preposition & adverb
not inside *You'll need your coat on if you're going outside.*

oval noun
a shape that looks like an egg

oven noun (*plural* **ovens**)
the part of a cooker where you can bake or roast food

over adverb & preposition
1 above or on top of *He put a plaster over the cut.*
2 more than *There were over 200 people there.*
3 about *They were fighting over some sweets.*

overboard adverb
If you fall overboard, you fall from a boat into the water.

overcoat noun (*plural* **overcoats**)
a thick, warm coat

a
b
c
d
e
f
g
h
i
j
k
l
m
n
o
p
q
r
s
t
u
v
w
x
y
z

overdue adjective
If something is overdue, it is late.

overflow verb **overflows, overflowing, overflowed**
When water overflows, it comes over the sides of the container that it is in.

overgrown adjective
A place that is overgrown is covered with messy plants.

overhead adverb
above your head *We saw a plane flying overhead.*

overhear verb **overhears, overhearing, overheard**
If you overhear something, you hear what other people are saying.

overseas adverb
When you go overseas, you go to another country.

oversleep verb **oversleeps, oversleeping, overslept**
When you oversleep, you sleep for too long. *Put your alarm clock on so that you don't oversleep.*

overtake verb **overtakes, overtaking, overtook, overtaken**
To overtake someone means to catch them up and go past them. *Max overtook me just before I reached the finishing line.*

overweight adjective
Someone who is overweight is too heavy and should lose some weight.

owe verb **owes, owing, owed**
If you owe money to someone, you have to pay it to them.

owl noun
(*plural* **owls**)
a bird with large eyes that hunts at night for small animals

owl

own adjective & pronoun
1 Something that is your own belongs to you.
2 If you are on your own, no one is with you.

own verb
owns, owning, owned
If you own something, it is yours and it belongs to you.

WORD FAMILY
• **owner** Who is the owner of this dog?

oxygen noun (*say* **ox**-i-jen)
the gas in the air that everyone needs to breathe in order to stay alive

ozone noun (*say* **oh**-zone)
Ozone is a type of oxygen. The **ozone layer** is a layer of ozone high above the earth which protects us from the dangerous rays of the sun.

a b c d e f g h i j k l m n o p q r s t u v w x y z

Pp

pace noun (*plural* **paces**)
a step forwards or backwards

pack noun (*plural* **packs**)
1 A pack of things is a number of things that you buy together. *I bought a pack of three chocolate bars.*
2 A pack of cards is a set of cards that you use for playing games.
3 A pack of dogs or wolves is a large group of them.

pack verb **packs, packing, packed**
When you pack things into a box, bag, or suitcase, you put them in.

package noun (*plural* **packages**)
a parcel

packaging noun
the box or paper that something is wrapped in when you buy it

packet noun (*plural* **packets**)
a small box or bag that you buy things in *We bought a packet of biscuits.*

pad noun (*plural* **pads**)
1 A pad is a piece of thick, soft material that you use as a cushion or to protect something.
2 A helicopter pad is a place on the ground where a helicopter can land.
3 A pad of paper is a set of sheets that are joined together.

pad verb **pads, padding, padded**
If something is padded, it is thick and soft because it is filled with thick, soft material. *Goalkeepers wear special padded trousers.*

paddle verb **paddles, paddling, paddled**
1 When you paddle, you walk about in shallow water. *We went paddling in the sea.*
2 When you paddle a canoe, you make it move through water.

padlock noun (*plural* **padlocks**)
a lock that you can put on a gate or bicycle

page noun (*plural* **pages**)
a piece of paper that is part of a book

paid verb *see* **pay**

pail noun (*plural* **pails**)
a bucket

pain noun (*plural* **pains**)
the feeling that you have in your body when something hurts

> **WORD FAMILY**
> • **painful** The cut on my arm was still very painful.

paint noun (*plural* **paints**)
a coloured liquid that you use for making pictures or for putting onto walls

paint verb **paints, painting, painted**
When you paint, you use paints to make a picture or decorate a wall.

> **WORD FAMILY**
> • **painter** Who's the best painter in your class?
> • **painting** On the wall there was a painting of a ship.

pair noun (*plural* **pairs**)
two things that belong together *I need a new pair of trainers.*

palace noun (*plural* **palaces**)
a very large house where a king or queen lives

pale adjective **paler, palest**
1 If you look pale, your face looks white because you are ill.
2 A pale colour is light and not dark. *She was wearing a pale green jumper.*

palm noun (*plural* **palms**)
1 Your palm is the inside part of your hand.
2 A palm tree is a tree that grows in tropical countries.

a
b
c
d
e
f
g
h
i
j
k
l
m
n
o
p
q
r
s
t
u
v
w
x
y
z

pan noun (*plural* **pans**)
a metal pot that you use for cooking

pan

pancake noun (*plural* **pancakes**)
a flat cake that you make by mixing together flour, milk, and eggs and then frying the mixture in a pan

panda noun (*plural* **pandas**)
A panda is an animal that looks like a large black and white bear. Pandas live in China and eat bamboo.

panda

pane noun (*plural* **panes**)
A pane of glass is a piece of glass in a window.

panic verb **panics, panicking, panicked**
If you panic, you suddenly feel very frightened and cannot think what to do.
He panicked when he saw the fire.

pant verb **pants, panting, panted**
When you pant, you take short, quick breaths because you have been running.
'What do you mean, Mr Beaver?' panted Peter as they all scrambled up the steep bank of the valley together.—C. S. Lewis, The Lion, the Witch and the Wardrobe

pantomime noun (*plural* **pantomimes**)
a special play with jokes and songs, which people perform at Christmas

pants noun
a piece of clothing that you wear over your bottom, underneath your other clothes

paper noun (*plural* **papers**)
1 Paper is the thin material that you use to write and draw on.
2 A paper is a newspaper.

parable noun (*plural* **parables**)
a short story that tries to teach you something about how to behave

parachute noun
(*plural* **parachutes**)
(*say* **pa**-ra-shoot)
a large piece of cloth that opens over your head and stops you from falling too quickly when you jump out of an aeroplane

parade noun
(*plural* **parades**)
a long line of people marching along, while other people watch them

paragraph noun (*plural* **paragraphs**)
A paragraph is one section in a long piece of writing. You begin each new paragraph on a new line.

parallel adjective
Parallel lines are straight lines that go in the same direction and are always the same distance away from each other.

parallelogram noun (*plural* **parallelograms**)
a shape with four sides, in which two opposite sides are the same length and parallel to each other

parcel noun (*plural* **parcels**)
something that is wrapped up in paper

parent noun (*plural* **parents**)
Your parents are your mother and father.

park noun (*plural* **parks**)
a large space with grass and trees where people can walk or play

park verb **parks, parking, parked**
When you park a car, you leave it in a place until you need it again.

parliament noun (*plural* **parliaments**)
the people who make the laws of a country

parrot noun (*plural* **parrots**)
a bird with brightly coloured feathers that lives in tropical forests

parrot

part noun (*plural* **parts**)
One part of something is one bit of it. *I've only read the first part of the story.*

participle noun (*plural* **participles**)
(*in grammar*) a part of a verb that can be used as an adjective, for example *frightened* or *frightening*

particular adjective
1 only this one and no other *I like this particular song.*
2 Someone who is particular is fussy and will only choose certain things. *She's very particular about what she eats.*

partly adverb
not completely *The new school is only partly built.*

partner noun (*plural* **partners**)
Your partner is the person you are doing something with, for example when you are working or dancing.

part of speech noun (*plural* **parts of speech**)
(*in grammar*) A part of speech is a name that we give to different types of words. Adjectives, nouns, and verbs are different parts of speech.

party noun (*plural* **parties**)
a time when people get together to have fun and celebrate something

pass verb **passes, passing, passed**
1 When you pass something, you go past it. *I pass the swimming pool every day on my way to school.*
2 If you pass something to someone, you pick it up and give it to them. *Please could you pass me the salt?*
3 If you pass a test, you do well and are successful.

passage noun (*plural* **passages**)
a corridor *We got out through a secret underground passage.*

passenger noun (*plural* **passengers**)
a person who is travelling in a bus, train, ship, or aeroplane

Passover noun
a Jewish religious festival

passport noun (*plural* **passports**)
A passport is a special book or piece of paper with your name and photograph on it. Your passport shows who you are, and you usually have to take it with you when you go to another country.

password noun (*plural* **passwords**)
a secret word that you use to go into a place or to use a computer

past noun
the time that has already gone
In the past people used candles instead of electric lights.

past preposition
1 If you go past something, you go from one side of it to the other side. *We drove past the school.*
2 If it is past a certain time, it is after that time. *We didn't get home until past midnight.*

pasta noun
Pasta is a type of food made from flour and water. Spaghetti is a type of pasta.

pasta

a
b
c
d
e
f
g
h
i
j
k
l
m
n
o
p
q
r
s
t
u
v
w
x
y
z

139

paste noun
something that is like a very thick, sticky liquid

paste verb **pastes, pasting, pasted**
1 When you paste something, you stick it with glue.
2 (in ICT) To paste something into a computer document means to add it into that document after you have deleted it from another document.

pastime noun (plural **pastimes**)
something that you do to enjoy yourself in your free time

pastry noun
a mixture of flour, fat, and water that you roll flat and use for making pies

pat verb **pats, patting, patted**
When you pat something, you touch it gently with your hand. *Tom patted the dog gently on the head.*

patch noun (plural **patches**)
a small piece of material that you put over a hole in your clothes

path noun (plural **paths**)
a narrow road that you can walk along but not drive along

patient noun (plural **patients**) (say pay-shunt)
someone who is ill and being looked after by a doctor

patient adjective (say pay-**shunt**)
If you are patient, you can wait without getting cross or bored. *You will all have to be patient and wait your turn.*

> **WORD FAMILY**
> • **patiently** Sara was waiting outside patiently.

pattern noun (plural patterns)
a design with lines, shapes, and colours

> **WORD FAMILY**
> • **patterned** She was wearing blue and white patterned shorts.

pause noun (plural **pauses**)
a short time when you stop what you are doing

pause verb **pauses, pausing, paused**
When you pause, you stop what you are doing for a short time.
At the foot of the steps, the woman paused, looking to right and left.—Roald Dahl, Fantastic Mr Fox

pavement noun (plural **pavements**)
the path that people walk on along the side of a street

paw noun (plural **paws**)
An animal's paws are its feet.

pay verb **pays, paying, paid**
When you pay for something, you give someone money so that you can have it.

PC noun (plural **PCs**)
A PC is a small computer for one person to use. PC is short for **personal computer**.

PE noun
PE is a lesson at school in which you do sports and games. PE is short for **physical education**.

pea noun (plural **peas**)
a small, round, green vegetable

peace noun
1 When there is peace, there is no war.
2 When there is peace, there is no noise.

peaceful adjective
When a place is peaceful, there is no noise. *They looked forward to a peaceful day.*—Dick King-Smith, The Sheep-Pig

> **WORD FAMILY**
> • **peacefully** The baby was sleeping peacefully.

peach noun (plural **peaches**)
a round, soft, juicy fruit with yellow flesh and a large stone in the middle

peacock noun (plural **peacocks**)
a large bird with long, brightly coloured tail feathers

peak noun (*plural* **peaks**)
  1 A mountain peak is the top of a mountain.
  2 The peak on a cap is the part that sticks out in front.

peanut noun (*plural* **peanuts**)
  a small, round nut that grows in a pod in the ground

pear noun (*plural* **pears**)
  a sweet, juicy fruit that is narrow at the top and round at the bottom

pearl noun (*plural* **pearls**) (*rhymes with* girl)
  A pearl is a small, shiny, white ball that grows inside the shells of some oysters. People use pearls for making jewellery.

pebble noun (*plural* **pebbles**)
  a small, round stone *We collected some pebbles on the beach.*

peck verb **pecks, pecking, pecked**
  When a bird pecks something, it touches it or picks it up with its beak.

peculiar adjective
  Something that is peculiar is strange. *The ice cream had a peculiar taste.*

pedal noun (*plural* **pedals**)
  a part of a machine that you push with your foot to make it go

peel noun
  The peel on a fruit or vegetable is its skin.

apple peel

peel verb **peels, peeling, peeled**
  When you peel fruit or vegetables, you take their skin off.

peep verb **peeps, peeping, peeped**
  If you peep at something, you look at it quickly.

peer verb **peers, peering, peered**
  If you peer at something, you look at it for a long time because you cannot see it very well. *I long to explore inside it but the door is always locked, and when I peer through*

a window all I can see is darkness and dust.— Roald Dahl, The Giraffe and the Pelly and Me

peg noun (*plural* **pegs**)
  1 a small clip that you use for fixing washing onto a line
  2 a piece of metal or wood that you can hang things on *You can hang your coats on the pegs in the hall.*

pen noun (*plural* **pens**)
  something that you hold in your hand and use for writing with ink

pence noun
  pennies *The pencils cost thirty pence each.*

pencil noun (*plural* **pencils**)
  something that you hold in your hand and use for writing or drawing

pendown adjective
  (*in ICT*) In some computer programs, when you move the pen on the screen in the pendown position, the pen draws as it moves.

pendulum noun (*plural* **pendulums**)
  A pendulum is a weight that swings backwards and forwards. Some large old-fashioned clocks have pendulums to make them work.

penguin noun (*plural* **penguins**)
  A penguin is a large black and white bird that swims in the sea but cannot fly. Penguins live at the South Pole, and catch and eat fish.

penknife noun (*plural* **penknives**)
  a small knife that folds up so that you can carry it safely

penknife

penny noun (*plural* **pence**)
a coin

pentagon noun (*plural* **pentagons**)
a shape with five straight sides

penup adjective
(*in ICT*) In some computer programs, when you move the pen on the screen in the penup position, the pen does not draw as it moves.

people noun
men, women, and children

pepper noun
1 Pepper is a powder with a hot taste that you add to food.
2 A pepper is a green, yellow, orange, or red vegetable.

perch noun (*plural* **perches**)
a place where a bird rests when it is not flying

percussion noun
Percussion instruments are musical instruments that you play by banging, hitting, or shaking them. Drums, cymbals, and tambourines are percussion instruments.

perfect adjective
Something that is perfect is so good that it cannot be any better.

> **WORD FAMILY**
> • **perfectly** The food was cooked perfectly.

perform verb **performs, performing, performed**
When you perform, you do something in front of people to entertain them. *We performed the school play in front of our parents.*

> **WORD FAMILY**
> • **performance** Well done. That was a brilliant performance.

perfume noun (*plural* **perfumes**)
a liquid with a nice smell that you put on your skin

perhaps adverb
possibly *Perhaps it will rain tomorrow.*

perimeter noun
The perimeter of something is the distance right round its edge. *We measured the perimeter of the field.*

period noun (*plural* **periods**)
a length of time *We all had to leave the building for a period of two hours.*

permanent adjective
Something that is permanent will last for ever.

permit verb **permits, permitting, permitted**
If you permit someone to do something, you allow them to do it.

> **WORD FAMILY**
> • **permission** I asked for permission to leave the room.

person noun (*plural* **people** or **persons**)
a man, woman, or child

personal adjective
Your personal things are the things that are to do with just you and no one else.

personally adverb
If you do something personally, you do it yourself. *I will talk to him personally.*

personality noun (*plural* personalities)
Your personality is the type of person you are.

persuade verb **persuades, persuading, persuaded**
If you persuade someone to do something, you make them agree to do it. *I managed to persuade my mum to take us swimming.*

persuasive adjective
Persuasive writing is writing that tries to persuade people to do something.

pessimistic adjective
If you are pessimistic, you think that something bad will happen.

pest noun (*plural* **pests**)
a person, animal, or plant that causes damage to things or annoys people

pester verb **pesters, pestering, pestered**
When you pester someone, you keep annoying them until they do what you want them to do. *Stop pestering me!*

pet noun (*plural* **pets**)
an animal which you keep and look after

petal noun (*plural* **petals**)
The petals on a flower are the coloured parts.

a b c d e f g h i j k l m n o p q r s t u v w x y z

petrol noun
a liquid that you put in cars to make them go

pH noun
(*in science*) We use pH to say how acid or alkaline a substance is. Acids have a pH between 0 and 7, and alkalis have a pH between 7 and 14.

Pharaoh noun (*plural* **Pharaohs**)
(*say* **fair-oh**)
a king in ancient Egypt

Pharaoh

phone noun (*plural* **phones**)
a telephone

phone verb **phones, phoning, phoned**
When you phone someone, you use a telephone to speak to them.

phoneme noun (*plural* **phonemes**)
(*in grammar*) A phoneme is one sound in a language. Sometimes one phoneme can be written in different ways. For example, the phoneme 'n' can be written as 'n' (in the word 'new'), or it can be written as 'kn' (in the word 'knee').

phonics noun
(*in grammar*)Phonics are the different sounds that letters represent when they are written down. You can use phonics to help you learn to read by saying the sound of each letter in a word and then putting them all together to make the whole word.

photo noun (*plural* **photos**)
a photograph

photocopier noun (*plural* **photocopiers**)
a machine which can make a copy of a piece of writing or a picture

> **WORD FAMILY**
> • **photocopy** Why don't we photocopy the map?

photograph noun (*plural* **photographs**)
a picture that you take with a camera

photograph verb **photographs, photographing, photographed**
When you photograph something, you take a photograph of it.

> **WORD FAMILY**
> • **photographer** The school photographer is coming tomorrow.

phrase noun (*plural* **phrases**)
A phrase is a group of words that you use together. 'How do you do?' is a phrase.

physical adjective (*say* **fizz**-ic-al)
Physical activities are activities that you do with your body, for example running and jumping.

piano noun (*plural* **pianos**)
a large musical instrument which has white and black keys that you press with your fingers to make different musical notes

> **WORD FAMILY**
> • **pianist** Jessica is a brilliant pianist.

pick verb **picks, picking, picked**
1 When you pick something, you choose it. *Which one are you going to pick?*
2 When you pick something up, you lift it up with your hand. *He picked up the coins and put them in his pocket.*
3 When you pick a flower or fruit, you take it off a plant.

picnic noun (*plural* **picnics**)
a meal of cold food that you eat outside

pictogram noun (*plural* **pictograms**)
a small picture that you use instead of a word

a
b
c
d
e
f
g
h
i
j
k
l
m
n
o
p
q
r
s
t
u
v
w
x
y
z

143

picture noun (*plural* **pictures**)
1 a painting, drawing, or photograph
2 When you go to the pictures, you go to a cinema to watch a film.

pie noun (*plural* **pies**)
a type of food that has meat, vegetables, or fruit in the middle and pastry on the outside *Do you like apple pie?*

piece noun (*plural* **pieces**)
A piece of something is a bit of it.

pie chart noun (*plural* **pie charts**)
A pie chart is a diagram in the shape of a circle divided into slices. The different slices show how an amount is divided up.

pierce verb **pierces, piercing, pierced**
When you pierce something, you make a hole through it. *My mum says I'm too young to have my ears pierced.*

pig noun (*plural* **pigs**)
an animal with a large snout and a curly tail that is kept on farms for its meat

pigeon noun (*plural* **pigeons**)
a grey bird that often lives in towns

pile noun (*plural* **piles**)
A pile of things is a lot of things all on top of each other.
We've got piles and piles of books in every room.—Jacqueline Wilson, Double Act

pill noun (*plural* **pills**)
a small tablet with medicine in, which you swallow when you are ill

pillar noun (*plural* **pillars**)
a wooden or stone post that helps to hold up a building

pillow noun (*plural* **pillows**)
a cushion that you rest your head on in bed

pilot noun (*plural* **pilots**)
someone who flies an aeroplane

pin noun (*plural* **pins**)
A pin is a thin piece of metal with a sharp point. You use pins to hold pieces of material together when you are sewing.

pincers noun
An animal's pincers are the claws that it uses for holding or catching things. Crabs have pincers.

pinch verb **pinches, pinching, pinched**
1 If you pinch someone, you squeeze their skin between your thumb and finger so that it hurts.
2 To pinch something means to steal it. *Who's pinched my pencil?*

pine noun (*plural* **pines**)
a tree with leaves like needles that do not fall in winter

pineapple noun (*plural* **pineapples**)
a large fruit with yellow flesh that grows in hot countries

pineapple

pink adjective
Something that is pink is very pale red.

pint noun (*plural* **pints**)
We can measure liquids in pints. One pint is about half a litre.

pip noun (*plural* **pips**)
a seed of a fruit such as an apple or orange

pipe noun (*plural* **pipes**)
1 a hollow tube that gas or liquid can go along
2 A pipe is a tube with a small bowl at one end. People put tobacco in the bowl and smoke it through the tube.

pirate noun (*plural* **pirates**)
someone who sails in a ship and attacks and robs other ships at sea

pit noun (*plural* **pits**)
a deep hole in the ground

pitch noun (*plural* **pitches**)
A sports pitch is a piece of ground that is marked out so that you can play a game on it.

pity noun
1 If you feel pity for someone, you feel sorry for them.
2 If something is a pity, it is a shame. *What a pity you won't be able to come with us!*

pizza noun (*plural* **pizzas**)
a flat piece of dough with tomatoes, cheese, and other things on top

pizza

place noun (*plural* **places**)
a building or area of land *We found an ideal place to camp.*

place verb **places, placing, placed**
When you place something somewhere, you put it there. *Please place all your rubbish in the bin.*

plain adjective **plainer, plainest**
Something that is plain is ordinary, and not different or special.

plain noun (*plural* **plains**)
a large area of flat ground *You can see for miles over the plain.*

plait verb **plaits, plaiting, plaited**
(*say* **platt**)
When you plait hair, you twist three pieces together by crossing them over and under each other.

plan noun (*plural* **plans**)
1 If you have a plan, you have an idea about how to do something. *A plan was gradually forming in my mind.*
2 a map of a building or a town

plan verb **plans, planning, planned**
When you plan something, you decide what you are going to do and how you are going to do it.

plane noun (*plural* **planes**)
an aeroplane

planet noun
(*plural* **planets**)
A planet is a very large object in space that moves around a star or around our sun. The earth is a planet.

planet

plank noun (*plural* **planks**)
a long, flat piece of wood

plant noun (*plural* **plants**)
A plant is a living thing that grows in the soil. Trees, flowers, and vegetables are all plants.

plant verb **plants, planting, planted**
When you plant something, you put it in the ground to grow.

plaster noun (*plural* **plasters**)
1 a piece of sticky material that you put over a cut to keep it clean
2 Plaster is a soft mixture that goes hard when it dries. Plaster is put onto the walls of buildings. A different sort of plaster is put onto someone's arm or leg when they have broken a bone.

plastic noun
a light strong material that is made in factories and is used for making all kinds of things

plate noun (*plural* **plates**)
a flat dish that you eat food from

platform noun (*plural* **platforms**)
1 the place in a station where people wait beside the railway lines for a train to come
2 a small stage in a hall

play verb **plays, playing, played**
1 When you play, you have fun.
2 When you play an instrument, you use it to make music. *Can you play the piano?*

WORD FAMILY
• A **player** is someone who is playing a game.

play noun (*plural* **plays**)
a story which people act so that other people can watch

playground noun (*plural* **playgrounds**)
a place outside where children can play

playgroup noun (*plural* **playgroups**)
a place where young children can go to play and learn things

pleasant adjective
Something that is pleasant is nice.

a
b
c
d
e
f
g
h
i
j
k
l
m
n
o
p
q
r
s
t
u
v
w
x
y
z

145

please verb **pleases, pleasing, pleased**
1 To please someone means to make them happy.
2 use when you want to ask for something politely *Please may I have another biscuit?*

> **WORD FAMILY**
> • **pleased** I was really pleased that our team won.

pleasure noun
the feeling that you have when you are happy and enjoying yourself

plenty noun
If there is plenty of something, there is as much as you need.
There's plenty of food. —Jacqueline Wilson, Double Act

plot noun (*plural* **plots**)
1 a secret plan
2 the story of a novel, film, or play

plough noun (*plural* **ploughs**) (*rhymes with* how)
a large machine that is used on farms for digging and turning over the soil so that crops can be planted

pluck verb **plucks, plucking, plucked**
1 When you pluck something, you take it from the place where it is growing. *He plucked an apple from the tree.*
2 When you pluck a musical instrument, you play it by pulling on the strings with your fingers.

plug noun (*plural* **plugs**)
1 a round piece of plastic that you put into the hole in a bath or sink to stop the water from running out
2 the part of an electric machine or tool that you put into an electric socket to make it work

plum noun (*plural* **plums**)
a juicy fruit with a stone in the middle

plumber noun (*plural* **plumbers**)
a person whose job is to fit and mend water pipes and taps

plump adjective **plumper, plumpest**
Someone who is plump is quite fat.

plunge verb **plunges, plunging, plunged**
If you plunge into water, you jump in.

plural noun (*plural* **plurals**)
(*in grammar*) A plural is the form of a word that you use when you are talking about more than one person or thing.

plus preposition
(*in mathematics*) add *Three plus three is six, 3 + 3 = 6.*

pocket noun (*plural* **pockets**)
a part of a piece of clothing that is like a small bag that you can keep things in

pocket money noun
money which someone gives you each week to buy things that you want

pod noun (*plural* **pods**)
A pod is a long thin part of a plant that has seeds inside. Peas grow in pods.

podcast noun (*plural* **podcasts**)
a radio programme that you can download from the Internet onto a music player

poem noun (*plural* **poems**)
a piece of writing that is written in lines and uses rhythms and rhymes in a clever way

poet noun (*plural* **poets**)
someone who writes poems

poetry noun
poems *Do you like reading poetry?*

point noun (*plural* **points**)
1 a thin, sharp part on the end of something.
2 a particular place or time *At that point I realised that we were lost.*
3 a mark that you score in a game *Our team scored the most points.*

point verb **points, pointing, pointed**
1 When you point at something, you show it to someone by holding your finger out towards it.
2 When you point a weapon at something, you aim the weapon towards it.

pointed adjective
something that is pointed has a sharp point at one end

poison noun (*plural* **poisons**)
something that will kill you or make you ill if you swallow it

> **WORD FAMILY**
> • **poisonous** Be careful, some of these plants may be poisonous.

poke verb **pokes, poking, poked**
If you poke something, you push it with your finger or with a stick.
Umpin began to poke at the snow with one foot.—Jostein Gaarder, The Frog Castle

polar bear noun (*plural* **polar bears**)
a very large, white bear that lives near the North Pole

polar bear

pole noun (*plural* **poles**)
a long stick

police noun
The police are the people whose job is to catch criminals and make sure that people do not break the law.

polish verb **polishes, polishing, polished**
When you polish something, you rub it to make it shine.

polite adjective **politer, politest**
Someone who is polite has good manners and is not rude to people.
He was very polite, and insisted on carrying their suitcase for them.—Alexander McCall Smith, The Chocolate Money Mystery

WORD FAMILY
• **politely** She smiled politely.

politician noun (*plural* **politicians**) (*say* pol-i-**tish**-un)
a person who works in the government of a country

politics noun
the work that a government does

pollen noun
Pollen is a yellow powder that you find inside flowers. Pollen is carried from one flower to another by the wind or by insects so that the flowers can produce seeds.

pollute verb **pollutes, polluting, polluted**
To pollute air or water means to make it dirty. *Some factories pollute rivers by tipping chemicals into them.*

WORD FAMILY
• **pollution** Cars cause a lot of pollution.

polygon noun (*plural* **polygons**)
(*say* **pol**-ee-gon)
A polygon is a flat shape with three or more sides. Triangles, squares, and octagons are all polygons.

polythene noun (*say* **pol**-i-theen)
a type of plastic material that is used for making bags

pond noun (*plural* **ponds**)
a small lake

pony noun (*plural* **ponies**)
a small horse

ponytail noun (*plural* **ponytails**)
If you wear your hair in a ponytail, you wear it tied in a long bunch at the back of your head.

a
b
c
d
e
f
g
h
i
j
k
l
m
n
o
p
q
r
s
t
u
v
w
x
y
z

pool noun (*plural* **pools**)
a small area of water

poor adjective **poorer, poorest**
1 Someone who is poor does not have very much money.
2 Something that is poor is bad. *This is very poor work. You can do better than this!*
3 A poor person is unlucky or unhappy. *You poor child!*

pop verb **pops, popping, popped**
If something pops, it bursts with a loud bang.

pop noun
Pop is modern music that people dance to.

popcorn noun
a food that is made by heating grains of corn until they burst and become big and fluffy

popular adjective
If something is popular, a lot of people like it. *Football is the most popular sport in the world.*

population noun
The population of a place is the number of people who live there.

porch noun (*plural* **porches**)
a place in front of the door of a building where people can wait before they go in

pork noun
meat from a pig

port noun (*plural* **ports**)
a place on the coast where ships can come to the land to load or unload goods

portable adjective
If something is portable, you can carry it or move it easily.

portion noun (*plural* **portions**)
A portion of food is an amount that you give to one person. *I bought a small portion of chips.*

portrait noun (*plural* **portraits**)
a painting or drawing of a person

posh adjective **posher, poshest**
Something that is posh is very smart and expensive.

position noun (*plural* **positions**)
1 The position of something is the place where it is. *We don't know the exact position of the ship at the moment.*
2 Your position is the way that you are standing, sitting, or lying. *I had to sit in a very uncomfortable position.*

possess verb **possesses, possessing, possessed**
If you possess something, you own it.

possible adjective
If something is possible, it might happen, or it might be true. *It's possible that someone has stolen the money.*

> **WORD FAMILY**
> - **possibility** There is still a possibility that we can win.
> - **possibly** She couldn't possibly have seen me!

post noun (*plural* **posts**)
1 A post is a pole that is fixed in the ground.
2 The post is all the letters and parcels that are delivered to people's houses.

post verb **posts, posting, posted**
When you post a letter or parcel, you send it to someone.

postcard noun (*plural* **postcards**)
A postcard is a piece of card with a picture on one side. You write on the other side and send it to someone.

postcode noun (*plural* **postcodes**)
letters and numbers that you put at the end of someone's address when you are sending them a letter

poster noun (*plural* **posters**)
a large picture or notice that you put up on a wall

postman noun (*plural* **postmen**)
A postman is a man who delivers letters and parcels to people's houses. A woman who does this is a **postwoman**.

post office noun (*plural* **post offices**)
a place where you can go to buy stamps, and post letters and parcels

postpone verb **postpones, postponing, postponed**
If you postpone something, you decide to do it later.

pot noun (*plural* **pots**)
a round container that you can put or keep things in

potato noun (*plural* **potatoes**)
a round white vegetable that you dig out of the ground

pottery noun
cups, plates, and other things that are made from clay

pouch noun (*plural* **pouches**)
1 a small bag that you can keep things in
2 a pocket of skin that some animals have on their bodies for carrying their young

pounce verb **pounces, pouncing, pounced**
To pounce on something means to attack it by jumping on it suddenly.

pound noun (*plural* **pounds**)
1 We can measure weight in pounds. One pound is about half a kilogram. *We'll need two pounds of sugar.*
2 A pound is a unit of money. Pounds are used in Britain and some other countries.

pour verb **pours, pouring, poured**
1 When you pour a liquid, you tip it into a container. *Dad poured some milk into a glass.*
2 When a liquid is pouring out of something, it is coming out very quickly. *Water was pouring out of the burst pipe.*

powder noun
a substance like flour that is dry and made of lots of tiny bits

power noun (*plural* **powers**)
1 If you have power, you can do what you want, or make other people do what you want.
2 If you have special powers, you are able to do magic things.
3 Power is energy that makes machines work. *There isn't enough power in these old batteries.*

powerful adjective
1 Someone who is powerful has a lot of power over other people. *He was a rich and powerful king.*
2 Something that is powerful is very strong. *They had to use a very powerful crane to lift the lorry out of the ditch.*

practical adjective
A practical person is good at working with their hands and doing useful things.

practice noun
practice is when you do something again and again so that you will get better at it

practise verb **practises, practising, practised**
When you practise, you keep doing something over and over again so that you will get better at it. *If you keep practising you'll soon improve.*

praise verb **praises, praising, praised**
To praise someone means to tell them that they have done well.

pram noun (*plural* **prams**)
a bed on wheels in which you can push a baby along

prawn noun (*plural* **prawns**)
A prawn is a small sea creature with a shell. You can cook and eat prawns.

pray verb **prays, praying, prayed**
When people pray, they talk to a god.

> **WORD FAMILY**
> • When people pray, they say a **prayer**.

preach verb **preaches, preaching, preached**
When someone preaches, they talk to people about religion.

precious adjective (*say* **presh**-uss)
Something that is precious is worth a lot of money, or is very special to someone. *She hid the precious jewels under her bed.*

precise adjective
Something that is precise is exact and correct.

> **WORD FAMILY**
> • **precisely** We left at precisely ten o'clock.

predator noun (*plural* **predators**)
an animal that hunts and kills other animals for food

predict verb **predicts, predicting, predicted**
If you predict something, you say that it will happen in the future.

prefer verb **prefers, preferring, preferred**
If you prefer one thing to another, you like it more. *I don't like wearing skirts. I prefer to wear jeans.*

a
b
c
d
e
f
g
h
i
j
k
l
m
n
o
p
q
r
s
t
u
v
w
x
y
z

prefix noun (plural **prefixes**)
(in grammar) A prefix is a group of letters that are added to the front of a word to change its meaning. Un- and dis- are prefixes.

prehistoric adjective
Prehistoric times were times long ago.

prejudice noun (plural **prejudices**)
If you have a prejudice against someone, you do not like them but have no reason not to like them.

prepare verb **prepares, preparing, prepared**
When you prepare something, you get it ready.
Mr Bhalla had prepared a magnificent meal of coconut rice.—Alexander McCall Smith, The Bubblegum Tree

> **WORD FAMILY**
> • **preparation** We were all busy with preparations for the party.

preposition noun (plural **prepositions**)
(in grammar) a word such as in or on, that goes in front of a noun

present adjective (say **prez**-ent)
1 If you are present in a place, you are there.
2 The present time is the time that is happening now.

present noun (plural **presents**) (say **prez**-ent)
1 something that you give to someone
2 The present is the time that is happening now.

present verb **presents, presenting, presented** (say pri-**zent**)
1 If you present something to someone, you give it to them. The head presented the prizes to the winners.
2 When someone presents a show, they introduce it.

> **WORD FAMILY**
> • A **presenter** is someone who presents a show on television.

president noun (plural **presidents**)
someone who rules a country

press verb **presses, pressing, pressed**
When you press something, you push it with your finger. What will happen if I press this button?

press noun
The press is a general name for newspapers.

pressure noun (say **presh**-er)
1 Pressure is a force which pushes against something. If you cut yourself, you need to apply pressure to the cut to stop it bleeding.
2 If you put pressure on someone, you try to make them do something.

pretend verb **pretends, pretending, pretended**
When you pretend, you say things or do things that are not really true. We all thought that Ali was hurt, but he was only pretending.

pretty adjective **prettier, prettiest**
1 Something that is pretty is nice to look at. That's a very pretty dress.
2 A pretty girl or woman has a beautiful face.

prevent verb **prevents, preventing, prevented**
If you prevent something from happening, you stop it from happening. He shut the door to prevent anyone from leaving.

prey noun
An animal's prey is the animal that it hunts and kills.

price noun (plural **prices**)
The price of something is the amount of money you have to pay for it.

prick verb **pricks, pricking, pricked**
When you prick something, you make a tiny hole in it with something sharp. I pricked my finger with a needle.

prickle noun (plural **prickles**)
Prickles are sharp points on a plant.

pride noun
the feeling you have when you are proud

priest noun (plural **priests**)
a person who leads other people in religious ceremonies

prime minister noun (plural **prime ministers**)
the leader of a country's government

prime number noun (plural **prime numbers**)
(in mathematics) A prime number is a number that can only be divided by the number 1 and by itself. 3 and 7 are prime numbers.

prince noun (plural **princes**)
the son of a king or queen

princess noun (plural **princesses**)
1 the daughter of a king or queen
2 the wife of a prince

principle noun (plural **principles**)
an important rule that you follow *One of our principles is that all children must take part in sports day.*

print verb **prints, printing, printed**
1 When you print words, you write them with letters that are not joined together. *Please print your name at the top of the page.*
2 When a machine prints words or pictures, it puts them onto paper.

> **WORD FAMILY**
> • A **printer** is a machine that can print words and pictures from a computer onto paper.

print-out noun (plural **print-outs**)
a printed copy of a computer document

prison noun (plural **prisons**)
a place where people are kept as a punishment

prisoner noun (plural **prisoners**)
someone who is locked up in a place and not allowed to leave

private adjective
Something that is private is only for some people, not for everyone. *The hotel has its own private beach.*

prize noun (plural **prizes**)
something that you get if you win a game or competition

probable adjective
If it is probable that something will happen, it is very likely that it will happen.

> **WORD FAMILY**
> • **probably** We'll probably go to Spain on holiday again this year.

problem noun (plural **problems**)
something that is difficult *I would love to come to the cinema with you, but the problem is I can't get there.*

procedure noun (plural **procedures**)
a fixed way of doing something, in which you do the same things in the same order each time

process noun (plural **processes**)
a series of actions that you do one after the other, and that take a long time *Making computers is quite a complicated process.*

produce verb **produces, producing, produced**
1 To produce something means to make it. *Cows produce milk.*
2 If you produce something, you bring it out of a box or bag. *The woman produced a camera from her bag.*

product noun (plural **products**)
1 something that has been made so that it can be sold to people in shops
2 (*in mathematics*) the number you get when you multiply two numbers together *The product of 2 and 3 is 6.*

professional adjective
Someone who is professional does something as their job, not just for fun. *It's very difficult to become a professional dancer.*

professor noun (plural **professors**)
someone who teaches in a university

profit noun (plural **profits**)
If you make a profit, you make money by selling something for more than you paid to buy it or make it.

program noun (plural **programs**)
A computer program is a list of instructions that the computer follows.

programme noun (plural **programmes**)
1 a show on the radio or television
2 a small book that tells you what will happen at an event

progress noun
When you make progress, you get better at doing something. *You have made a lot of progress with your maths this term.*

project noun (plural **projects**)
a piece of work where you find out as much as you can about something interesting and write about it *We're doing a project on India.*

projector noun (plural **projectors**)
a machine that shows pictures or films on a screen

promise verb **promises, promising, promised**
If you promise to do something, you say that you will definitely do it. *Don't forget – you promised to help me wash the car.*

pronoun noun (plural **pronouns**)
(*in grammar*) A pronoun is a word that you use instead of a noun. *He, she,* and *it* are all pronouns.

a b c d e f g h i j k l m n o **p** q r s t u v w x y z

pronounce verb **pronounces, pronouncing, pronounced**
The way you pronounce a word is the way you say it. *How do you pronounce your name?*

> **WORD FAMILY**
> • **pronunciation** Sometimes the pronunciation of a word isn't the same as the spelling.

proof noun
If there is proof that something happened, there is something that shows that it definitely happened. *We think we know who stole the books, but we have no proof.*

prop verb **props, propping, propped**
If you prop something somewhere, you lean it there so that it does not fall over. *He propped his bicycle against the wall.*

propeller noun (*plural* **propellers**)
a set of blades that spin round to make something move

proper adjective
The proper thing is the correct or right one. *Put the books back in their proper places.*

> **WORD FAMILY**
> • **properly** Make sure you clean your teeth properly.

proper noun noun (*plural* **proper nouns**)
(*in grammar*) A proper noun is a noun that is the name of a person or place. For example, *London* and *Tom* are proper nouns.

property noun (*plural* **properties**)
If something is your property, it belongs to you.

prophet noun (*plural* **prophets**)
(**ph-** in this word sounds like **f-**)
1 someone who says what will happen in the future
2 a great religious teacher

propose verb **proposes, proposing, proposed**
If you propose something, you suggest it as an idea. *I propose that we leave now.*

prose noun
writing which is not poetry or a play

protect verb **protects, protecting, protected**
To protect someone means to keep them safe and stop them being hurt. *A mother cat will always protect her young.*

> **WORD FAMILY**
> • **protection** The trees gave us some protection from the rain.

protein noun
Protein is a substance found in some types of food, for example meat, eggs, and cheese. Your body needs protein to help you grow.

protest verb **protests, protesting, protested**
If you protest about something, you say that you do not like it or do not agree with it. *'No, no! Don't do that!' protested the Scarecrow.*—Philip Pullman, The Scarecrow and his Servant

proud adjective **prouder, proudest**
If you are proud of something, you are pleased with it and think that it is very good. *I'm very proud of this painting.*

> **WORD FAMILY**
> • **proudly** 'I did it myself,' he said proudly.
> • **pride** Her mother smiled with pride.

prove verb **proves, proving, proved**
(*say* **proov**)
To prove that something is true means to show that it is definitely true. *These footprints prove that someone has been in the garden.*

proverb noun (*plural* **proverbs**)
a short, well-known saying which gives you advice about something

provide verb **provides, providing, provided**
If you provide something for people, you give it to them. *The school provides us with books and pencils.*

prowl verb **prowls, prowling, prowled**
To prowl means to walk around very quietly and secretly.

pry verb **pries, prying, pried**
If you pry, you try to find out about something that has nothing to do with you. *You shouldn't pry into other people's business.*

pub noun (*plural* **pubs**)
a place where people can go to have a drink and meet friends

public adjective
Something that is public can be used by everyone. *Is there a public swimming pool in your town?*

publish verb **publishes, publishing, published**
To publish a book means to print it and sell it.

pudding noun (*plural* **puddings**)
any sweet food which you eat after the main part of a meal *What are we having for pudding?*

puddle noun (*plural* **puddles**)
a small pool of water

puff verb **puffs, puffing, puffed**
1 When a train puffs, it blows out smoke as it goes along.
2 If you are puffing, you are out of breath because you have been running.

pull verb **pulls, pulling, pulled**
When you pull something, you get hold of it and move it towards you.

pullover noun (*plural* **pullovers**)
a jumper

pump noun (*plural* **pumps**)
a machine that pushes air or water into something or out of something *You use a bicycle pump to put air into tyres.*

pump verb **pumps, pumping, pumped**
When you pump water or air, you force it into something or out of something. *The firemen pumped all the water out of the flooded house.*

pumpkin noun (*plural* **pumpkins**)
a very large, round orange vegetable

pun noun (*plural* **puns**)
A pun is a joke that is funny because it uses words that sound the same, or words that have two different meanings. For example, *eggs are very eggs-pensive* is a pun.

punch verb **punches, punching, punched**
If you punch someone, you hit them with your fist.

punctuation noun
all the marks such as commas and full stops that you put into a piece of writing to make it easier to read

puncture noun (*plural* **punctures**)
a small hole in a tyre

punish verb **punishes, punishing, punished**
To punish someone means to make them suffer because they have done something wrong. *The teacher punished us by keeping us inside at lunch time.*

WORD FAMILY
• **punishment** I wondered what punishment he would give us.

pupil noun (*plural* **pupils**)
1 A pupil is a child who goes to school. *This school has 500 pupils.*
2 Your pupils are the black circles in the middle of your eyes.

puppet noun (*plural* **puppets**)
a small doll that you can move by pulling on strings, or by putting it over your hand like a glove and then moving your hand

puppy noun (*plural* **puppies**)
a young dog

pure adjective **purer, purest**
Something that is pure is one thing only, with nothing else mixed in. *She was wearing a necklace made of pure gold.*

purple adjective
Something that is purple is the colour that you make by mixing red and blue together.

purpose noun (*plural* **purposes**)
The purpose of something is the reason why you are doing it. **on purpose** If you do something on purpose, you do it deliberately. *I'm sorry, I didn't do it on purpose.*

purr verb **purrs, purring, purred**
When a cat purrs, it makes a low, rumbling sound because it is happy.

purse noun (*plural* **purses**)
a small bag that you carry money in

push verb **pushes, pushing, pushed**
When you push something, you use your hands to move it away from you.

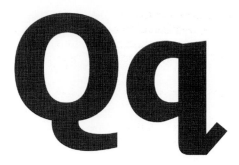

put verb **puts, putting, put**
1 When you put something in a place, you move it so that it is there. *Please put the books back on the shelf.*
2 If you put something off, you decide to do it later instead of now.

puzzle noun (*plural* **puzzles**)
1 a game in which you have to do something difficult or find the answer to a difficult question
2 If something is a puzzle, no one can explain it or understand it. *The disappearance of the jewels is still a puzzle.*

puzzle verb **puzzles, puzzling, puzzled**
If something puzzles you, it seems strange and you do not understand it.

WORD FAMILY
• **puzzled** Sam looked puzzled.

pyjamas noun
loose trousers and a top that you wear in bed

pyramid noun (*plural* **pyramids**)
1 a large, stone building that was made by the ancient Egyptians to bury a dead king or queen
2 a solid shape with a square base and four triangular sides that come together in a point at the top

python noun (*plural* **pythons**)
a large snake that kills animals by wrapping its body around them and crushing them

quack verb **quacks, quacking, quacked**
When a duck quacks, it makes a loud sound.

quadrilateral noun (*plural* **quadrilaterals**)
A quadrilateral is any shape that has four straight sides. A square is a type of quadrilateral.

quaint adjective **quainter, quaintest**
Something that is quaint is pretty and old-fashioned. *What a quaint little cottage!*

qualify verb **qualifies, qualifying, qualified**
1 When you qualify, you pass a test or exam so that you are allowed to do a job. *My mum has just qualified as a doctor.*
2 When you qualify in a competition, you get enough points to go on to the next part of the competition. *England managed to qualify for the World Cup.*

quality noun (*plural* **qualities**)
The quality of something is how good or bad it is. *You need good quality paper for model-making.*

quantity noun (*plural* **quantities**)
A quantity is an amount. *We measured the quantity of water in the jug.*

quarrel verb **quarrels, quarrelling, quarrelled**
When people quarrel, they argue with each other in an angry way.

quarry noun (*plural* **quarries**)
a place where people cut stone out of the ground so that it can be used for building

quarter noun (*plural* **quarters**)
One quarter of something is one of four equal parts that the thing is divided into. It can also be written as $1/4$.

quay noun (*plural* **quays**) (*say* **key**)
a place where ships can be loaded and unloaded

queen noun (*plural* **queens**)
A queen is a woman who rules a country. A woman becomes queen because she is born into a royal family, or because she marries a king.

query noun (*plural* **queries**) (*say* **queer**-ee)
a question

quest noun (*plural* **quests**)
a long journey in which you are searching for something

question noun (*plural* **questions**)
When you ask a question, you ask someone something because you want to know the answer.

question mark noun (*plural* **question marks**)
A question mark is a mark like this ? that you use in writing. You put a question mark at the end of a sentence to show that it is a question.

questionnaire noun (*plural* **questionnaires**)
a sheet of paper with a lot of questions on it to collect information from people

queue verb **queues, queueing, queued**
When people queue, they wait in a line.

quiche noun (*plural* **quiches**) (*say* keesh)
a type of food with pastry on the bottom and sides and a filling made from eggs, cheese, and other things

quick adjective **quicker, quickest**
Something that is quick does not take very long. *We had a quick lunch and then set out.*

> **WORD FAMILY**
> • **quickly** I quickly got dressed and ran out of the house.

quiet adjective **quieter, quietest**
1 If a place is quiet, there is no noise there. *The school was deserted and all the classrooms were quiet.*
2 Something that is quiet is not very loud. *He spoke in a very quiet voice.*

> **WORD FAMILY**
> • **quietly** 'I want to go home,' he said very quietly.

quilt noun (*plural* **quilts**)
a thick, warm cover for a bed

quit verb **quits, quitting, quitted**
1 If you quit doing something, you stop doing it.
2 When you quit a file or program on a computer, you close it.

quite adverb
1 slightly, but not very *The film was quite good.*
2 completely *We haven't quite finished.*

quiz noun (*plural* **quizzes**)
a game in which people try to answer a lot of questions

quote verb **quotes, quoting, quoted**
When you quote words from a book or poem, you repeat them. *He quoted some lines from an old poem.*

quotation marks noun
Quotation marks are marks like this ' ' or this " " that you use in writing. You put these marks round words to show that someone has spoken them.

quotient noun (*plural* **quotients**)
(*in mathematics*) the number that you get when you divide one number by another *If you divide 12 by 3, the quotient is 4.*

a
b
c
d
e
f
g
h
i
j
k
l
m
n
o
p
q
r
s
t
u
v
w
x
y
z

Rr

rabbi noun (*plural* **rabbis**) (*say* **ra**-bye)
a Jewish religious leader

rabbit noun (*plural* **rabbits**)
A rabbit is a small furry animal with long ears. Rabbits live in holes in the ground and use their strong back legs to hop about.

race verb **races, racing, raced**
When people race, they run or swim against each other to find out who is the fastest.

race noun (*plural* **races**)
1 a competition in which people run or swim against each other to find out who is the fastest
2 a group of people who come from the same part of the world and look the same because they have the same colour skin, the same type of hair, and so on

racist noun (*plural* **racists**)
someone who treats other people unfairly because they have different colour skin or come from a different country

rack noun (*plural* **racks**)
a shelf made of bars that you can put things on

racket noun (*plural* **rackets**)
1 A racket is a bat that you use for hitting a ball in a game of tennis or badminton. It has a round frame with strings stretched across it.
2 If someone is making a racket, they are making a lot of loud noise.

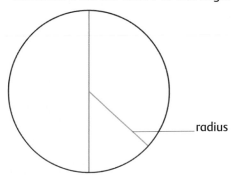

tennis racket

radar noun
a way of finding where a ship or aeroplane is when you cannot see it by using radio waves

radiator noun (*plural* **radiators**)
a metal heater which hot water flows through to keep a room warm

radio noun (*plural* **radios**)
a machine that picks up signals that are sent through the air and changes them into music or talking that you can listen to

radius noun (*plural* **radii**)
The radius of a circle is how much it measures from the centre to the edge.

radius

raffle noun (*plural* **raffles**)
A raffle is a competition in which people buy tickets with numbers on them. If their tickets are chosen, they win a prize.

raft noun (*plural* **rafts**)
a flat boat made of logs joined together

rag noun (*plural* **rags**)
A rag is a torn piece of cloth.

WORD FAMILY
• **ragged** His clothes were all ragged and torn.

rage noun (*plural* **rages**)
a feeling of very strong anger *His face was scarlet with rage.*

rail noun (*plural* **rails**)
1 A rail is a metal or wooden bar that is part of a fence.
2 Rails are the long metal bars that trains travel on.
3 When you travel by rail, you travel in a train.

railings noun
a fence made of a row of metal bars that stand upright next to each other

railway noun (*plural* **railways**)
1 A railway line is the long metal bars that trains travel on.

2 When you travel on the railway, you travel by train.

rain noun
drops of water that fall from the sky

rain verb **rains, raining, rained**
When it rains, drops of water fall from the sky. *We'll go out when it stops raining.*

rainbow noun (*plural* **rainbows**)
a curved band of different colours you see in the sky when the sun shines through rain

rainforest noun (*plural* **rainforests**)
a large forest in a tropical part of the world, where there is a lot of rain

raise verb **raises, raising, raised**
1 When you raise something, you lift it up so that it is higher.
2 When you raise money, you collect it so that you can give it to a school or charity.

raisin noun (*plural* **raisins**)
a dried grape that you use to make fruit cakes

rake noun (*plural* **rakes**)
a tool that you use in the garden for making the soil smooth

rake verb **rakes, raking, raked**
When you rake the ground, you pull a rake over it to make it smooth. *We raked up the dead leaves.*

RAM noun
RAM is one of the types of memory on a computer. RAM stands for **random-access memory**.

ram noun (*plural* **rams**)
a male sheep

Ramadan noun
Ramadan is the ninth month of the Muslim year. During Ramadan, Muslims do not eat or drink anything during the day, from the time the sun comes up each morning until it sets in the evening.

ramp noun (*plural* **ramps**)
a slope that you can walk or drive up to go from one level to another level

ran verb *see* **run**

ranch noun (*plural* **ranches**)
a large farm in America where a lot of cows or horses are kept

rang verb *see* **ring** verb

range noun (*plural* **ranges**)
1 A range of mountains or hills is a line of them.
2 A range of things is a collection of different things. *The shop sells a wide range of sports equipment.*

rank noun (*plural* **ranks**)
Someone's rank is the title that they have, which shows how important they are. *He joined the navy and rose to the rank of captain.*

rap verb **raps, rapping, rapped**
When you rap on a door, you knock on it. *He rapped sharply with the knocker.—* Catherine Storr, Little Polly Riding Hood

rap noun (*plural* **raps**)
1 A rap on a door is a knock on a door.
2 Rap is a type of poetry that you speak aloud with a strong rhythm.

rapid adjective
Something that is rapid happens very quickly.

> **WORD FAMILY**
> • **rapidly** The storm was approaching rapidly.

rare adjective **rarer, rarest**
If something is rare, you do not see it or find it very often. *Pandas are very rare animals.*

rash noun (*plural* **rashes**)
If you have a rash, you have red spots on your skin.

raspberry noun (*plural* **raspberries**)
a soft, sweet, red berry

raspberries

a b c d e f g h i j k l m n o p q **r** s t u v w x y z

rat noun (plural **rats**)
an animal that looks like a large mouse

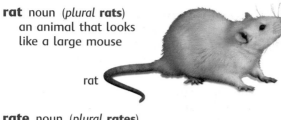

rat

rate noun (plural **rates**)
The rate at which something happens is how quickly it happens. *The tide was coming in at an alarming rate.*

rather adverb
1 quite *I was rather annoyed.*
2 If you would rather do something, you would prefer to do it. *I don't like shopping – I'd rather stay at home.*

ration noun (plural **rations**)
an amount of food that one person is allowed to have when there is not very much

rattle verb **rattles, rattling, rattled**
When something rattles, it makes a loud noise because it is being shaken.

rattle noun (plural **rattles**)
a toy for a baby which makes a noise when you shake it

rave verb **raves, raving, raved**
If you rave about something, you talk about it in a very excited way, and say how good it is.

raw adjective
Food that is raw has not been cooked. *Do you like raw carrots?*

ray noun
(plural **rays**)
A ray of light or heat is a beam of it that shines onto something. *A ray of light shone through the roof of the cave.*

razor noun
(plural **razors**)
a very sharp blade that people use for shaving hair off their body

reach verb **reaches, reaching, reached**
1 When you reach a place, you get there. *We reached home by 6 o'clock.*
2 When you reach for something, you put out your hand to touch it or pick it up. *He reached across for a cake.*

react verb **reacts, reacting, reacted**
The way that you react to something is the way that you behave when it happens. *How did Ali react when you told him about the fire?*

WORD FAMILY
• Your **reaction** to something is the way in which you react.

read verb **reads, reading, read**
When you read words that are written down, you look at them and understand them. *My little brother is just learning to read.*

ready adjective
1 If you are ready, you are prepared so that you can do something straight away. *Are you ready to leave?*
2 If something is ready, it is finished and you can have it or use it straight away. *Is dinner ready?*

real adjective
1 Something that is real is true, and not made-up or imaginary. *There are no unicorns in real life.*
2 Something that is real is genuine, and not a copy. *Is this a real diamond?*

realistic adjective
Something that is realistic looks real. *We used tomato sauce for blood, and it was quite realistic.*

realize verb **realizes, realizing, realized**
When you realize something, you suddenly notice it or know that it is true. *I suddenly realized that everyone was looking at me.*

really adverb
1 very *The water's really cold!*
2 If something is really true, it is true in real life. *Are you really moving to Spain?*

rear noun
The rear of something is the part at the back of it.

reason noun (plural **reasons**)
The reason for something is why it happens. *She was very upset, but I didn't know the reason why.*

a b c d e f g h i j k l m n o p q r s t u v w x y z

reasonable adjective
Something that is reasonable is fair and right.

receipt noun (*plural* **receipts**) (*say* re-**seet**)
a piece of paper which proves that you have paid for something

receive verb **receives, receiving, received**
When you receive something, someone gives it to you or sends it to you. *I haven't received your letter yet.*

recent adjective (*say* **ree**-sent)
Something that is recent happened only a short time ago. *They are still celebrating their recent victory.*

> **WORD FAMILY**
> • **recently** We moved here quite recently.

reception noun (*plural* **receptions**)
1 When you give someone a reception, you welcome them to a place. *We gave the visitors a warm reception.*
2 The reception in a large building is the place where people go when they first arrive. There is someone there to help people and answer their questions.

recipe noun (*plural* **recipes**) (*say* **ress**-ip-ee)
a list of the things you need to cook something, and instructions that tell you how to cook it

recite verb **recites, reciting, recited**
When you recite something, you say it out loud from memory. *I've got to recite a poem in the school concert.*

recognize verb **recognizes, recognizing, recognized**
If you recognize someone, you know who they are because you have seen them before.

recommend verb **recommends, recommending, recommended**
1 When you recommend something, you tell people that it is good. *I would recommend this book to anyone who loves adventure stories.*
2 When you recommend something, you tell someone that they should do it. *I recommend that you see a doctor.*

record noun (*plural* **records**) (*say* **rek**-ord)
1 The record for something is the best that anyone has ever done. *She has set a new world record for the women's high jump.*

2 If you keep a record of something, you write it down. *We keep a record of all the birds we see.*
3 A record in a computer database is one of the individual pieces of information that is stored in it.

record verb **records, recording, recorded** (*say* ree-**kord**)
1 When you record music or pictures, you store them on a tape or CD. *We can record the film and watch it later.*
2 When you record information, you write it down.

recorder noun (*plural* **recorders**)
a musical instrument that you play by blowing into one end and covering holes with your fingers to make different notes

recorder

recover verb **recovers, recovering, recovered**
1 When you recover, you get better after you have been ill. *Have you recovered from your cold?*
2 When you recover something that you have lost, you get it back. *The police recovered the stolen car.*

rectangle noun (*plural* **rectangles**)
A rectangle is a shape with four straight sides and four right angles. A rectangle looks like a long square and is also called an **oblong**.

recycle verb **recycles, recycling, recycled** (*say* ree-**sye**-kal)
To recycle things means to use them again instead of throwing them away. Glass and paper can be recycled.

red adjective
Something that is red is the colour of blood.

reduce verb **reduces, reducing, reduced**
When you reduce something, you make it smaller or less. *Reduce speed when you approach a bend.*

reed noun (*plural* **reeds**)
a plant that looks like tall grass and grows near water

refer verb **refers, referring, referred**
When you refer to something, you talk about it. *She had never referred to her uncle before.*

a
b
c
d
e
f
g
h
i
j
k
l
m
n
o
p
q
r
s
t
u
v
w
x
y
z

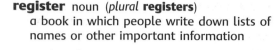

referee noun (*plural* **referees**)
someone who is in charge of a game and makes sure that all the players keep to the rules

reference book noun (*plural* **reference books**)
A reference book is a book that gives you information. Dictionaries are reference books.

reflect verb **reflects, reflecting, reflected**
1 If something reflects light, it makes the light shine back off it.
2 When something is reflected in glass or water, you can see a picture of it there. *The trees were reflected in the still water.*

> **WORD FAMILY**
> • **reflection** I could see my reflection in the window.

reflex noun (*plural* **reflexes**)
a way in which your body moves without you thinking about it or controlling it

refresh verb **refreshes, refreshing, refreshed**
If something refreshes you, it makes you feel fresh and less tired.

> **WORD FAMILY**
> • **refreshing** The water was cool and refreshing.

refreshments noun
drinks and snacks

refrigerator noun (*plural* **refrigerators**)
a fridge

refugee noun (*plural* **refugees**)
someone who has had to leave their own country because of a war

refuse verb **refuses, refusing, refused** (*say* ri-**fewz**)
If you refuse to do something, you say that you will not do it. *He refused to go home.*

region noun (*plural* **regions**)
one part of a country *These snakes live in the desert regions of Africa.*

refrigerator

register noun (*plural* **registers**)
a book in which people write down lists of names or other important information

regret verb **regrets, regretting, regretted**
If you regret doing something, you are sorry that you did it.

regular adjective
1 Something that is regular happens at the same time every day or every week. *There is a regular bus service into the city centre.*
2 A regular pattern stays the same and does not change.
3 A regular shape has sides and angles that are all equal.

> **WORD FAMILY**
> • **regularly** We go swimming quite regularly.

rehearse verb **rehearses, rehearsing, rehearsed**
When you rehearse, you practise something before you do it in front of an audience.

> **WORD FAMILY**
> • **rehearsal** We're having a rehearsal for the play on Sunday.

reign verb **reigns, reigning, reigned** (*say* **rain**)
When a king or queen reigns, they rule over a country.

reign noun (*plural* **reigns**) (*say* **rain**)
The reign of a king or queen is the time when they are ruling a country.

reindeer noun (*plural* **reindeer**) (*say* **rain**-deer)
a deer with large antlers that lives in very cold countries

reindeer

reins noun
the two long straps that you hold when you are riding a horse and use for guiding the horse

reject verb **rejects, rejecting, rejected**
If you reject something, you do not accept it. *Marcus rejected our ideas.*

relate verb **relates, relating, related**
When you relate a story, you tell it.

related adjective
People who are related belong to the same family.

relation noun (*plural* **relations**)
Your relations are all the people who belong to your family.

relative noun (*plural* **relatives**)
Your relatives are all the people who belong to your family.

relax verb **relaxes, relaxing, relaxed**
1 When you relax, you do things that make you calm and happy. *Sometimes I just want to sit down and relax in front of the TV.*
2 When a muscle relaxes, it becomes looser and softer.

> **WORD FAMILY**
> • **relaxed** Everyone was very happy and relaxed.
> • **relaxing** Listening to music is very relaxing.

relay noun (*plural* **relays**)
a race for teams of people, in which each person in the team runs or swims one part of the race

release verb **releases, releasing, released**
To release someone means to set them free.

reliable adjective
If someone is reliable, you can trust them.

relief noun
the feeling you have when you are no longer worried about something *It was such a relief when we got home safely!*

relieved adjective
If you feel relieved, you feel happy because you are no longer worried about something.

religion noun (*plural* **religions**)
A religion is a set of ideas that people have about a god or gods. Different religions worship different gods, and have different festivals and traditions.

> **WORD FAMILY**
> • Something that is **religious** is to do with religion.

rely verb **relies, relying, relied**
If you rely on something, you need it. If you rely on someone, you need them to do something for you. *The young birds rely on their mother for food.*

remain verb **remains, remaining, remained**
To remain means to stay. *Please remain in your seats.*

remainder noun
(*in mathematics*) an amount that is left over after you have worked out a sum

remains noun
The remains of a building are the parts that are left after it has fallen down. *We visited the remains of a Roman fort.*

remark verb **remarks, remarking, remarked**
To remark means to say something. *'I shall sit here,' the Footman remarked, 'till tomorrow.'*—Lewis Carroll, Alice's Adventures in Wonderland

remark noun (*plural* **remarks**)
something that you say *He made some rude remarks about my clothes.*

remember verb **remembers, remembering, remembered**
If you can remember something, you can think of it and have not forgotten it. *Can you remember his name?*

remind verb **reminds, reminding, reminded**
If you remind someone about something, you tell them about it again so that they do not forget it. *My mum reminded me that I needed to take my PE kit to school.*

remote adjective **remoter, remotest**
A place that is remote is far away from towns and cities.

remote control noun (*plural* **remote controls**)
something that you hold in your hand and use to switch a television on and off from a distance

remove verb **removes, removing, removed**
When you remove something, you take it off or take it away. *Please remove your muddy boots.*

rent noun
an amount of money that you pay each week to live in a house that belongs to another person

repair verb **repairs, repairing, repaired**
When you repair something, you mend it. *Can you repair my bike?*

a
b
c
d
e
f
g
h
i
j
k
l
m
n
o
p
q
r
s
t
u
v
w
x
y
z

repeat verb **repeats, repeating, repeated**
When you repeat something, you say it or do it again.

> **WORD FAMILY**
> • **repeatedly** Our old car broke down repeatedly.

repel verb **repels, repelling, repelled**
(*in science*) To repel something means to force it to move away. *One magnet sometimes repels another magnet.*

> **WORD FAMILY**
> • **repulsion** With magnets you can see the forces of attraction and repulsion.

replace verb **replaces, replacing, replaced**
1 When you replace something, you put it back in the place where it was before. *He replaced the book on the shelf.*
2 When you replace something, you change it for something else. *This computer is getting quite old now, so we will have to replace it soon.*

reply noun (*plural* **replies**)
an answer *I knocked on the door, but there was no reply.*

reply verb **replies, replying, replied**
When you reply to someone, you answer them. *I asked him his name, but he didn't reply.*

report verb **reports, reporting, reported**
to tell someone about something that has happened *We reported the accident to the police.*

> **WORD FAMILY**
> • A **reporter** is someone who writes reports about things that have happened.

report noun (*plural* **reports**)
1 an account of something that has happened, for example in a newspaper *We had to write a report on the burglary.*
2 A school report is something that teachers write about each child, to say how well they have been working.

represent verb **represents, representing, represented**
If a drawing or picture represents something, it is meant to be that thing. *These red lines on the map represent roads.*

reptile noun (*plural* **reptiles**)
A reptile is an animal that is cold-blooded, has a dry, smooth skin, and lays eggs. Snakes and crocodiles are reptiles.

request verb **requests, requesting, requested**
When you request something, you ask for it politely.

require verb **requires, requiring, required**
If you require something, you need it.

re-scale verb **re-scales, re-scaling, re-scaled**
(*in ICT*) If you re-scale a picture in a computer document, you change its size.

rescue verb **rescues, rescuing, rescued**
If you rescue someone, you save them from danger. *We managed to rescue all the animals from the fire.*

research noun
When you do research, you find out about something so that you can learn about it.

resent verb **resents, resenting, resented**
If you resent something, you feel angry about it. *I resent having to tidy up other people's mess!*

reserve verb **reserves, reserving, reserved**
If you reserve something, you ask someone to keep it for you.

> **WORD FAMILY**
> • **reserved** Are these seats reserved?

reservoir noun (*plural* **reservoirs**)
a big lake that has been built to store water in

resident noun (*plural* **residents**)
The residents of a place are the people who live in that place.

resign verb **resigns, resigning, resigned**
When someone resigns, they give up their job.

resist verb **resists, resisting, resisted**
When you resist something, you fight against it.

resistance noun
the ability of a material to stop the flow of electricity

re-size verb **re-sizes, re-sizing, re-sized**
(*in ICT*) If you re-size a picture in a computer document, you change its size.

resolution noun (*plural* **resolutions**)
When you make a resolution, you decide that you are definitely going to do something. *I made a resolution to stop eating chocolate.*

resource noun (*plural* **resources**)
something that is useful to people *Oil is an important natural resource.*

respect noun
If you have respect for someone, you admire them and think that their ideas and opinions are important.

respect verb **respects, respecting, respected**
If you respect someone, you admire them and think that their ideas and opinions are important.

WORD FAMILY
• **respectful** She was always polite and respectful.

respond verb **responds, responding, responded**
When you respond, you answer someone. *I called his name, but he didn't respond.*

responsible adjective
1 If you are responsible for doing something, it is your job to do it. *You are responsible for feeding the fish.*
2 If you are responsible for something, you did it or made it happen. *Who is responsible for all this mess?*
3 Someone who is responsible behaves in a sensible way.

responsibility noun (*plural* **responsibilities**)
something that you have to do because it is your job or duty to do it *It was my responsibility to feed the animals every day.*

rest noun (*plural* **rests**)
1 When you have a rest, you sleep or sit still for a while.
2 The rest means all the others. *Only half the children are here, so where are the rest?*

rest verb **rests, resting, rested**
When you rest, you sit or lie still for a while. *We sat down to rest.*

restaurant noun (*plural* **restaurants**)
a place where you can buy a meal and eat it

restore verb **restores, restoring, restored**
When you restore something, you mend it and make it as good as it was before. *The old theatre has now been restored.*

result noun (*plural* **results**)
1 If something happens as a result of something else, it happens because of it. *Some buildings were damaged as a result of the explosion.*
2 The result at the end of a game is the score.

retire verb **retires, retiring, retired**
When someone retires, they stop working because they are too old or ill.

retreat verb **retreats, retreating, retreated**
If you retreat, you go back because it is too dangerous to go forwards.

return verb **returns, returning, returned**
1 If you return to a place, you go back there. *We returned home at tea time.*
2 If you return something to someone, you give it back to them. *You must return all your books to the library by next week.*

reveal verb **reveals, revealing, revealed**
To reveal something means to uncover it so that people can see it.

revenge noun
If you take revenge on someone, you do something nasty to them because they have hurt you or one of your friends.

reverse verb **reverses, reversing, reversed**
When you reverse, you go backwards in a car.

review noun (*plural* **reviews**)
a piece of writing that describes what a book or film is about, and says whether it is good or not

revise verb **revises, revising, revised**
When you revise, you learn something again so that you are ready for a test.

revolting adjective
Something that is revolting is horrible and disgusting.

revolve verb **revolves, revolving, revolved**
When something revolves, it turns round and round like a wheel.

a
b
c
d
e
f
g
h
i
j
k
l
m
n
o
p
q
r
s
t
u
v
w
x
y
z

reward noun (*plural* **rewards**)
something that is given to someone because they have done something good, or done something to help someone *We offered a reward of £20 to anyone who could find our kitten.*

rhinoceros noun (*plural* **rhinoceroses**)
(*say* rye-**noss**-er-us)
A rhinoceros is a very big, wild animal that lives in Africa and Asia and has one or two large horns on its nose. It is also called a **rhino**.

rhino

rhombus noun (*plural* **rhombuses**)
a shape that has four sides of the same length but no right angles, for example a diamond shape

rhyme noun (*plural* **rhymes**) (*say* **rime**)
A rhyme is a word that has the same sound as another word. *Can you think of a rhyme for 'hat'?*

rhyme verb **rhymes, rhyming, rhymed**
If two words rhyme, they sound the same. *Fish rhymes with dish.*

rhythm noun (*plural* **rhythms**) (*say* **rith**-um)
The rhythm in a piece of music is its regular beat. The rhythm in a poem is the regular pattern that the words make as you read them.

rib noun (*plural* **ribs**)
Your ribs are the curved bones in your chest that protect your heart and lungs.

ribbon noun (*plural* **ribbons**)
a strip of coloured material that you tie round a parcel or in your hair

rice noun
white or brown grains that you cook and eat

rich adjective **richer, richest**
Someone who is rich has a lot of money.

rid verb
When you get rid of something, you throw it away or give it to someone else so that you no longer have it.

riddle noun (*plural* **riddles**)
a clever question or puzzle that is difficult to answer because it is a trick or joke

ride verb **rides, riding, rode, ridden**
1 When you ride on a horse or bicycle, you sit on it while it moves along.
2 When you ride in a car, bus, or train, you sit in it while it moves along.

ride noun (*plural* **rides**)
When you go for a ride, you ride on a horse or bicycle, or in a bus, train, or car.

ridiculous adjective
Something that is ridiculous is very silly and makes people laugh.
St Geobad seems a ridiculous name for a waterfall to me, boy.—Philip Ardagh, Dreadful Acts

rifle noun (*plural* **rifles**)
a long gun that you hold with both hands and put up against your shoulder when you want to fire it

right adjective
1 The right side of something is the side that is opposite the left side. Most people write with their right hand, not their left hand. *She was holding a torch in her right hand.*
2 Something that is right is correct. *Yes, that's the right answer.*
3 Something that is right is fair and honest. *It is not right to cheat.*

right angle noun (*plural* **right angles**)
A right angle is an angle that measures 90 degrees. A square has four right angles.

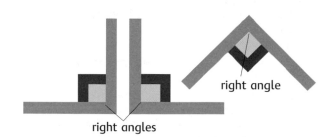
right angles
right angle

rim noun (*plural* **rims**)
1 The rim of a cup or jug is the edge around the top of it.
2 The rim of a wheel is the edge around the outside of it.

ring noun (*plural* **rings**)
1 a circle *The dogs formed a ring around us.*
2 a circle of gold or silver that you wear on your finger

ring verb **rings, ringing, rang, rung**
1 When something rings, it makes a sound like a bell. *The doorbell rang.*
2 When you ring someone, you phone them.

rinse verb **rinses, rinsing, rinsed**
When you rinse something, you wash it in clean water after you have washed it using soap.

rip verb **rips, ripping, ripped**
If you rip something, you tear it.

ripe adjective **riper, ripest**
Fruit that is ripe is soft and ready to eat.

ripple noun (*plural* **ripples**)
a tiny wave on the surface of water
The rain was making ripples on the surface of the pond.

rise verb **rises, rising, rose, risen**
1 When something rises, it moves upwards.
2 When you rise, you stand up.
3 When the sun or moon rises, it moves up into the sky.

risk noun (*plural* **risks**)
If there is a risk, there is a danger that something bad or dangerous might happen. *When you go parachuting, there is always a risk that your parachute will not open.*

rival noun (*plural* **rivals**)
someone who is trying to beat you in a competition or game

river noun (*plural* **rivers**)
a large stream of water that flows into the sea

road noun (*plural* **roads**)
a wide path that cars, buses, and lorries go along

roam verb **roams, roaming, roamed**
When you roam, you travel around without going in any particular direction. *The animals are free to roam wherever they want.*

roar verb **roars, roaring, roared**
When an animal like a lion roars, it makes a loud, fierce sound.

roast verb **roasts, roasting, roasted**
When you roast meat or vegetables, you cook them in the oven. *We'll roast the chicken in the oven.*

rob verb **robs, robbing, robbed**
To rob someone means to steal something from them. *A band of thieves attacked him and robbed him.*

WORD FAMILY
• A **robber** is someone who robs people. A **robbery** is a crime in which someone is robbed.

robin noun (*plural* **robins**)
a small, brown bird with a red patch on its chest

robot noun (*plural* **robots**)
a machine that can do some of the jobs that a person can do *In some factories cars are made by robots.*

rock noun (*plural* **rocks**)
1 A rock is a very big stone. *They hurled huge rocks into the sea.*
2 Rock is the hard, stony substance that mountains, hills, and the ground are made of.

rock verb **rocks, rocking, rocked**
When something rocks, it moves gently backwards and forwards or from side to side.

rocket noun (*plural* **rockets**)
1 a firework that shoots high into the air and then explodes with bright lights and a loud bang
2 A rocket is something that can travel very fast through the air or into space. Some rockets are used as weapons, and some are used to take people up into space.

a b c d e f g h i j k l m n o p q r s t u v w x y z

rod noun (*plural* **rods**)
A fishing rod is a long, thin piece of wood or metal. You attach a piece of thin fishing line to it and use it for catching fish.

rode verb *see* **ride** verb

rodent noun (*plural* **rodents**)
A rodent is an animal that has big front teeth, which it uses for biting and chewing things. Rats and mice are rodents.

role noun (*plural* **roles**)
Your role in a play or film is the character that you play.

roll verb **rolls, rolling, rolled**
When something rolls, it moves along on wheels or by turning over and over like a ball. *The barrel rolled down the hill.*

roll noun (*plural* **rolls**)
1 A roll of cloth or paper is a piece that has been rolled up into the shape of a tube.
2 A roll is a very small loaf of bread for one person. *We had warm rolls for breakfast.*

Rollerblade noun (*plural* **Rollerblades**)
(*trademark*) Rollerblades are boots with wheels on the bottom.

rollerblade

roller skate noun (*plural* **roller skates**)
Roller skates are special shoes with wheels on the bottom.

ROM noun
ROM is one of the types of memory on a computer. ROM stands for **read-only memory**.

roof noun (*plural* **roofs**)
the sloping part on the top of a building

room noun (*plural* **rooms**)
1 The rooms in a building are the different parts inside it.
2 If there is room for something, there is enough space for it.

root noun (*plural* **roots**)
the part of a plant that grows under the ground

root word noun (*plural* **root words**)
(*in grammar*) A root word is a word to which a prefix or suffix can be added to make a new word *In the word unhappy, 'un' is a prefix and 'happy' is the root word.*

rope noun (*plural* **ropes**)
a long piece of thick, strong material which you use for tying things together

rose noun (*plural* **roses**)
a flower which has a sweet smell and sharp thorns on its stem

rose verb *see* **rise**

rot verb **rots, rotting, rotted**
When something rots, it goes bad and soft and sometimes smells nasty.

rotate verb **rotates, rotating, rotated**
When something rotates, it turns round in a circle, like a wheel.

rotten adjective
1 Something that is rotten is not fresh, but has gone bad and soft.
2 Something that is rotten is bad or nasty. *That was a rotten thing to do!*

rough adjective **rougher, roughest** (*say* ruff)
1 Something that is rough is not smooth or flat. *With this bike, you can ride over rough ground.*
2 Someone who is rough is not gentle.
3 Something that is rough is more or less right, but not exactly right. *He looks about fifteen, but that's only a rough guess.*

roughly adverb
1 If you touch or hold something roughly, you do it in a way that is not gentle.
2 about, but not exactly *There will be roughly twenty people at my party.*

round adjective
Something that is round is shaped like a circle or ball.

round adverb & preposition
1 turning in a circle *The wheels spun round and round.*
2 on all sides of something *There was a high wall round the garden.*

round verb **rounds, rounding, rounded**
(*in mathematics*) When you round a number up or down, you raise it or lower it to the nearest 10, 100, or 1000. *If you round 18 to the nearest ten, the answer is 20.*

roundabout noun (*plural* **roundabouts**)
1 a circle in the middle of the road which cars must drive round
2 a big machine that you can ride on at a fair

rounders noun
a game in which two teams try to hit a ball with a special bat and score points by running round a square

route noun (*plural* **routes**) (*say* root)
The route that you follow is the way you go to get to a place.

routine noun (*plural* **routines**) (*say* roo-**teen**)
Your routine is the way in which you usually do things at the same time and in the same way. *My routine in the morningis to get up, get dressed, then have my breakfast.*

row noun (*plural* **rows**) (*rhymes with* toe)
A row of people or things is a long, straight line of them.

row verb **rows, rowing, rowed** (*rhymes with* toe)
When you row a boat, you push oars through the water to make it move along.

row noun (*plural* **rows**) (*rhymes with* how)
1 When you make a row, you make a lot of loud noise.
2 When people have a row, they have an angry, noisy argument.

royal adjective
Royal things belong to a king or queen.

rub verb **rubs, rubbing, rubbed**
1 When you rub something, you move your hands backwards and forwards over it. *She woke up and rubbed her eyes.*
2 When you rub out something that you have written, you make it disappear by rubbing it.

rubber noun (*plural* **rubbers**)
1 Rubber is a type of soft material that stretches, bends, and bounces. Rubber is used for making car tyres.
2 A rubber is a small piece of rubber that you use for rubbing out pencil marks.

rubber tyre

rubbish noun
1 things that you have thrown away because you do not want them any more *The garden was full of rubbish.*
2 If something that you say is rubbish, it is silly and not true.
To Fly, sheep-talk was just so much rubbish, to which she had never paid any attention.—Dick King-Smith, The Sheep-Pig

rucksack noun (*plural* **rucksacks**)
a bag that you carry on your back

rude adjective **ruder, rudest**
Someone who is rude says or does things that are not polite.

rug noun (*plural* **rugs**)
1 a small carpet
2 a thick blanket

rugby noun
a game in which two teams throw, kick, and carry a ball, and try to score points by taking it over a line at one end of the pitch

ruin noun (*plural* **ruins**)
a building that has fallen down *We visited the ruins of a Roman fort.*

ruin verb **ruins, ruining, ruined**
To ruin something means to spoil it completely. *You've ruined my picture!*

rule noun (*plural* **rules**)
something that tells you what you must and must not do *In netball you are not allowed to run with the ball – it's against the rules.*

rule verb **rules, ruling, ruled**
The person who rules a country is in charge of it.

a b c d e f g h i j k l m n o p q r s t u v w x y z

ruler noun (*plural* **rulers**)
1 someone who rules a country
2 a flat, straight piece of wood, metal, or plastic that you use for measuring things and drawing lines

rumour noun (*plural* **rumours**) (*say* **room**-er)
something that a lot of people are saying, although it might not be true *There's a rumour that our teacher might be leaving at the end of this term.*

run verb **runs, running, ran, run**
1 When you run, you move along quickly by taking very quick steps.
2 When you run something, you control it and are in charge of it. *Who runs the school shop?*

> **WORD FAMILY**
> • **runner** Are you a fast runner?

rung noun (*plural* **rungs**)
The rungs on a ladder are the bars that you step on.

rung verb *see* **ring** verb

runny adjective **runnier, runniest**
Something that is runny is like a liquid.

runway noun (*plural* **runways**)
a strip of land where an aeroplane can take off and land

rush verb **rushes, rushing, rushed**
When you rush, you run or do something very quickly.
'I'm come, your Majesty,' said Edmund, rushing eagerly forward.—C. S. Lewis, The Lion, the Witch and the Wardrobe

rust noun
a rough, red stuff that you see on metal that is old and has got wet *The old car was covered in rust.*

> **WORD FAMILY**
> • **rusty** Why do you want to keep that rusty old bike?

rustle verb **rustles, rustling, rustled**
When something rustles, it makes a soft sound like the sound of dry leaves or paper being squashed.

sack noun (*plural* **sacks**)
a large, strong bag

sacred adjective
Something that is sacred is special because it is to do with religion.

sad adjective **sadder, saddest**
If you feel sad, you feel unhappy.

> **WORD FAMILY**
> • **sadly** 'I never win,' he said sadly.
> • **sadness** Her eyes were full of sadness.

saddle noun (*plural* **saddles**)
the seat that you sit on when you are riding a bicycle or a horse

safari noun (*plural* **safaris**)
a trip to see lions and other large animals in the wild

safe adjective **safer, safest**
1 If you are safe, you are not in any danger.
2 If something is safe, you will not get hurt if you go on it or use it. *The bridge didn't look very safe.*

> **WORD FAMILY**
> • **safely** It's important to use tools safely.

safe noun (*plural* **safes**)
a strong metal box with a lock where you can keep money and jewellery

safety noun
Safety is being safe and not in danger. *After crossing the river we finally reached safety.*

said verb *see* **say**

sail noun (*plural* **sails**)
A sail is a large piece of strong cloth which is attached to a boat. The wind blows into the sail and makes the boat move along.

sail verb **sails, sailing, sailed**
When you sail, you go somewhere in a boat. *We sailed across the lake to the island.*

sailing boat

sailor noun (*plural* **sailors**)
someone who works on a ship

salad noun (*plural* **salads**)
a mixture of vegetables that you eat raw or cold

sale noun (*plural* **sales**)
1 If something is for sale, people can buy it.
2 When a shop has a sale, it sells things at lower prices than usual.

saliva noun
the liquid in your mouth

salmon noun (*plural* **salmon**)
a large fish that you can eat

salt noun
a white powder that people often add to food for its flavour

> **WORD FAMILY**
> • **salty** Crisps have a salty taste.

salute verb **salutes, saluting, saluted**
When you salute, you touch your forehead with your fingers to show that you respect someone. Soldiers often salute each other.

same adjective
1 Things that are the same are like each other. *Your jeans are the same as mine.*
2 If two people share the same thing, they share one thing and do not have two different ones. *We both go to the same school.*

sample noun (*plural* **samples**)
a small amount of something that you can try to see what it is like

sand noun (*plural* **sands**)
Sand is a powder made from tiny bits of crushed rock. You find sand in a desert or on a beach.

sandal noun (*plural* **sandals**)
Sandals are shoes with straps that you wear in warm weather.

sandwich noun (*plural* **sandwiches**) two slices of bread and butter with a layer of a different food in between them

sandwich

sang verb *see* **sing**

sank verb *see* **sink** verb

sap noun
Sap is the sticky liquid inside a plant. Sap carries water and food to all parts of the plant.

sardine noun (*plural* **sardines**)
a small sea fish you can eat

sari noun (*plural* **saris**)
A sari is a type of dress that women and girls from India and other countries in Asia wear. It is a long piece of cloth that you wrap round your body.

sat verb *see* **sit**

satellite noun (*plural* **satellites**)
A satellite is a machine that is sent into space to collect information and send signals back to Earth. Satellites travel in orbit round the Earth. Some satellites collect information about the weather, and some receive radio and television signals and send them back to Earth.

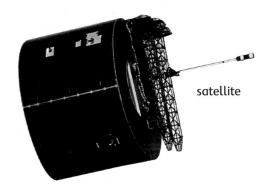
satellite

satellite dish noun (*plural* **satellite dishes**)
an aerial shaped like a large dish which can receive television signals sent by satellite

satisfactory adjective
Something that is satisfactory is not very good, but is good enough.

satisfy verb **satisfies, satisfying, satisfied**
If something satisfies you, it is good enough to make you feel pleased or happy.

Saturday noun (*plural* **Saturdays**)
the day after Friday

sauce noun (*plural* **sauces**)
a thick liquid that you put over food
Do you like tomato sauce?

saucepan noun (*plural* **saucepans**)
a metal pan that you use for cooking

saucer noun (*plural* **saucers**)
a small plate that you put a cup on

sausage noun (*plural* **sausages**)
minced meat that has been made into a long, thin shape and cooked

savage adjective
A savage animal is wild and fierce.

save verb **saves, saving, saved**
1 If you save someone, you take them away from danger and make them safe.
2 When you save money, you keep it so that you can use it later.
3 (*in ICT*) When you save a computer file, you instruct the computer to keep a copy of it on its hard disk.

savings noun
Your savings are money that you have saved to use later.

saw noun (*plural* **saws**)
A saw is a tool that you use to cut wood. It has a row of sharp teeth which you push backwards and forwards over the wood to cut it.

saw verb **saws, sawing, sawed, sawn**
When you saw wood, you cut it with a saw.

saw verb *see* **see**

say verb **says, saying, said**
When you say something, you speak.
'Hello,' he said.

saying noun (*plural* **sayings**)
a well-known sentence that people often say because it tells you something that is true or gives you advice about something

scab noun (*plural* **scabs**)
a piece of hard skin that grows over a cut or graze while it is getting better

scald verb **scalds, scalding, scalded**
If you scald yourself, you burn yourself with very hot liquid.

scale noun (*plural* **scales**)
1 A scale is a line of numbers that you use for measuring something.
2 The scale of a map is how big things on the map are compared to how big they are in real life.
3 The scales on a fish are the small, round pieces of hard skin all over its body.

scales noun
something that you use for weighing things

scales

scamper verb **scampers, scampering, scampered**
To scamper around means to run around quickly.

scan verb **scans, scanning, scanned**
1 When a machine scans something, it moves a beam of light over it to make a picture of it.
2 When you scan a piece of writing, you read it quickly.

scanner noun (*plural* **scanners**)
a machine that copies a picture or piece of writing from paper onto a computer

scar noun (*plural* **scars**)
a mark that is left on your skin after a cut or burn has healed

scarce adjective **scarcer, scarcest**
If something is scarce, there is not very much of it. *Water is scarce in the desert.*

scare verb **scares, scaring, scared**
If something scares you, it makes you feel frightened.

> **WORD FAMILY**
> • **scared** Are you scared of spiders?
> • **scary** We watched a really scary film.

scarecrow noun (*plural* **scarecrows**)
something that looks like a person and is put in a field to frighten away birds

scarf noun (*plural* **scarves**)
a piece of material that you wear round your neck to keep you warm

scarlet adjective
Something that is scarlet is bright red.

scatter verb **scatters, scattering, scattered**
1 When you scatter things, you throw them all around you. *She scattered some crumbs for the birds.*
2 When people scatter, they all run away in different directions.

scene noun (*plural* **scenes**) (*say* seen)
1 The scene of something is the place where it happens. *Police are still examining the scene of the crime.*
2 A scene in a play is one part of the play.

scenery noun (*say* **seen**-er-ee)
1 things that you can see around you when you are out in the country *The scenery in the mountains was beautiful.*
2 things that you put on the stage of a theatre to make it look like a real place

scent noun (*plural* **scents**) (*say* **sent**)
1 perfume that you put on your skin so that you will smell nice
2 a pleasant smell *The garden was full of the scent of roses.*
3 An animal's scent is its smell.

scheme noun (*plural* **schemes**) (*say* **skeme**)
a clever plan

school noun (*plural* **schools**)
1 a place where children go to learn things
2 A school of fish is a large group of them swimming together.

science noun (*plural* **sciences**)
the subject in which you study the things in the world around you, for example plants and animals, wood and metal, light, and electricity

> **WORD FAMILY**
> • Someone who studies science is a **scientist**.

science fiction noun
stories about things that happen in the future or on other planets

scissors noun
a tool that you use for cutting paper or cloth

scoop noun (*plural* **scoops**)
a deep spoon that you use for serving ice cream

scoop verb **scoops, scooping, scooped**
If you scoop something up, you pick it up with both hands.

scooter noun (*plural* **scooters**)
1 a motorbike with a small engine
2 a toy with two wheels that you ride by standing on it with one foot and pushing the ground with the other foot

scooter

scorch verb **scorches, scorching, scorched**
To scorch something means to burn it and make it go brown. *The hot sun had scorched the grass.*

a b c d e f g h i j k l m n o p q r s t u v w x y z

171

score noun (*plural* **scores**)
The score in a game is the number of points that each player or team has.

score verb **scores, scoring, scored**
When you score in a game, you get a point or a goal.

scowl verb **scowls, scowling, scowled**
(*rhymes with* owl)
When you scowl, you look cross.
Gran scowled and sucked her teeth. — Jacqueline Wilson, Double Act

scramble verb **scrambles, scrambling, scrambled**
If you scramble over things, you climb over them using your hands and feet.

scrap noun (*plural* **scraps**)
1 A scrap of paper or cloth is a small piece.
2 Scrap is anything that you do not want anymore.

scrape verb **scrapes, scraping, scraped**
1 If you scrape something off, you get it off by pushing it with something sharp. *Scrape the mud off your shoes.*
2 If you scrape a part of your body, you cut it by rubbing it against something. *I fell over and scraped my knee.*

scratch verb **scratches, scratching, scratched**
1 To scratch something means to cut it or make a mark on it with something sharp. *Mind you don't scratch the paint on the new car.*
2 When you scratch, you rub your skin because it is itching.

scream verb **screams, screaming, screamed**
When you scream, you shout or cry loudly because you are frightened or hurt.

screech verb **screeches, screeching, screeched**
When you screech, you shout or cry in a loud, high voice. *'Go away!' she screeched.*

screen noun (*plural* **screens**)
1 the part of a television or computer where the words and pictures appear
2 the large, flat surface at a cinema, on which films are shown

screw noun (*plural* **screws**)
A screw is a pointed piece of metal that you use for fixing pieces of wood together. You fix a screw into wood by turning it round with a screwdriver.

screw

screw verb **screws, screwing, screwed**
1 When you screw things together, you fix them together using screws.
2 When you screw a lid on or off, you put it on or take it off by turning it round and round.

screwdriver noun (*plural* **screwdrivers**)
a tool that you use for fixing screws into wood

scribble verb **scribbles, scribbling, scribbled**
When you scribble, you write or draw something quickly, in an untidy way.

script noun (*plural* **scripts**)
The script of a play is all the words that the characters say.

scroll verb **scrolls, scrolling, scrolled**
(*in ICT*) When you scroll up or down on a computer screen, you move up or down on the screen to see what comes before or after.

scrub verb **scrubs, scrubbing, scrubbed**
When you scrub something, you rub it hard to clean it.

sculpture noun (*plural* **sculptures**)
a statue made out of stone or wood

sea noun (*plural* **seas**)
The sea is the salty water that covers large parts of the earth.

> **WORD FAMILY**
> • The **seabed** is the bottom of the sea. A **seagull** is a bird that lives near the sea.

a
b
c
d
e
f
g
h
i
j
k
l
m
n
o
p
q
r
s
t
u
v
w
x
y
z

seal noun (*plural* **seals**)
A seal is an animal that
has flippers and lives in the sea.
Seals have thick fur
to keep them warm
in cold water.

seal

seam noun (*plural* **seams**)
a line of sewing that joins two pieces of
material together

search verb **searches, searching, searched**
When you search for something, you look for
it very carefully.

search engine noun (*plural* **search engines**)
a computer program that helps you find
information on the Internet

seaside noun
a place by the sea where people go on
holiday to enjoy themselves

season noun (*plural* **seasons**)
1 The four seasons are the four parts of the year,
which are spring, summer, autumn, and winter.
2 The season for a sport is the time of year
when it is played. *When does the cricket
season start?*

seat noun (*plural* **seats**)
anything that you can sit on

seat belt noun (*plural* **seat belts**)
a strap that you wear round your body to
keep you safe in a car

seaweed noun
a plant that grows in the sea

second adjective
The second thing is the one that comes after
the first.

second noun (*plural* **seconds**)
We measure time in seconds. There are sixty
seconds in one minute.

second person noun
(*in grammar*) When you use the second
person, you use the word 'you' to write about
someone in a story.

secret adjective
A secret thing is one that not very many
people know about. *There is a secret passage
leading into the castle.*

secret noun (*plural* **secrets**)
If something is a secret, not many
people know about it and you must not
tell anyone.

secretary noun (*plural* **secretaries**)
someone whose job is to type letters and
answer the telephone in an office

section noun (*plural* **sections**)
one part of something *The front section of
the aeroplane broke off.*

secure adjective **securer, securest**
1 Something that is secure is safe and firm.
*Make sure the ladder is secure before you
climb it.*
2 If you feel secure, you feel safe.

see verb **sees, seeing, saw, seen**
1 When you see something, you notice it with
your eyes.
2 When you can see something, you can
understand it. *Do you see what I mean?*

seed noun (*plural* **seeds**)
a small thing that a new plant grows
from

seem verb **seems, seeming, seemed**
To seem means to look, sound, or appear.
Everyone seemed very happy and relaxed.

see-saw noun (*plural* **see-saws**)
A see-saw is a toy that children can play on.
It is made of a long piece of wood that is
balanced on something in the middle so that
someone can sit on each end and make it go
up and down.

segment noun (*plural* **segments**)
one small part of something *Would you like
a segment of orange?*

seize verb **seizes, seizing, seized**
(*rhymes with* sneeze)
When you seize something, you grab it
roughly. *The thief seized the bag and
ran away.*

a
b
c
d
e
f
g
h
i
j
k
l
m
n
o
p
q
r
s
t
u
v
w
x
y
z

select verb **selects, selecting, selected**
When you select something, you choose it. *She opened the box and selected a chocolate.*

> **WORD FAMILY**
> • **selection** There was a selection of shoes to choose from.

selfish adjective
If you are selfish you only think about yourself and do not care what other people want.

> **WORD FAMILY**
> • **selfishly** Someone had selfishly finished all the cake.

sell verb **sells, selling, sold**
When you sell something, you give it to someone and they give you money for it. *I'm going to sell my old bike.*

Sellotape noun
(*trademark*) a type of sticky tape that you use for sticking pieces of paper together

semicircle noun (*plural* **semicircles**)
half of a circle

semi-colon noun (*plural* **semi-colons**)
a mark like this ; that you use in writing

send verb **sends, sending, sent**
1 When you send something somewhere, you arrange for someone to take it there. *My grandma sent me a birthday card.*
2 When you send someone somewhere, you tell them to go there. *He was sent to the headteacher for behaving badly.*

senior adjective
Someone who is senior is older or more important than other people.

sensation noun (*plural* **sensations**)
If you have a sensation in your body, you have a feeling.

sense noun
(*plural* **senses**)
1 Your senses are your ability to see, hear, smell, feel, and taste. *Dogs have a good sense of smell.*

hearing
sight
smell
taste
touch

2 If you have good sense, you know what is the right thing to do. *She had the sense to call an ambulance.*

sensible adjective
If you are sensible, you think carefully and you do the right thing.

> **WORD FAMILY**
> • **sensibly** Make sure you behave sensibly.

sensitive adjective
1 Someone who is sensitive is easily upset by other people.
2 Something that is sensitive reacts to things around it. *Some people have very sensitive skin.*

sent verb *see* **send**

sentence noun (*plural* **sentences**)
1 (*in grammar*) A sentence is a group of words that mean something together. It begins with a capital letter and ends with a full stop.
2 a punishment given to someone by a judge

separate adjective
Things that are separate are not joined together or not next to each other.

> **WORD FAMILY**
> • **separately** Wash each brush separately.

separate verb **separates, separating, separated**
When you separate people or things, you take them away from each other so that they are no longer together.

September noun
the ninth month of the year

sequence noun (*plural* **sequences**)
A sequence is a series of numbers that come after each other in a regular order. For example, 2, 4, 6, 8 is a sequence.

series noun (*plural* **series**)
1 a number of things that come one after another *We have had a series of accidents in the playground.*
2 a television show that is on regularly and is about the same thing each week *There's a new TV series on rainforests starting next week.*

serious adjective
1 Something that is serious is very important. *This is a very serious matter.*
2 Someone who is serious does not smile or joke, but thinks carefully about things.

3 Something that is serious is very bad. *There has been a serious accident on the motorway.*

> **WORD FAMILY**
> • **seriously** You could be seriously hurt if you fall off there.

servant noun (*plural* **servants**)
someone who works at another person's home, doing jobs such as cleaning and cooking

serve verb **serves, serving, served**
1 To serve someone in a shop means to help them find and buy the things that they want.
2 To serve food means to put it on people's plates.
3 When you serve in a game of tennis, you start the game by hitting the ball to the other player.

service noun (*plural* **services**)
something that is done to help people or give them something that they need *Letters are delivered by the postal service.*

set verb **sets, setting, set**
1 When you set a machine, you change the controls to a particular position. *We set the alarm clock for six o'clock.*
2 When something sets, it goes hard. *Has the glue set yet?*
3 When the sun sets, it goes down at the end of the day.
4 To set off means to leave.

set noun (*plural* **sets**)
a group of people or things that belong together *I'm trying to collect the whole set of these cards.*

settle verb **settles, settling, settled**
1 When you settle an argument, you agree and decide what to do about it.
2 When you settle down somewhere, you sit or lie down comfortably.
Fly settled comfortably back in the straw.—Dick King-Smith, The Sheep-Pig

seven noun (*plural* **sevens**)
the number 7

seventeen noun
the number 17

seventy noun
the number 70

several adjective
Several things means quite a lot of them.
The teacher told him several times to be quiet.

severe adjective **severer, severest**
Something that is severe is very bad. *We are expecting some severe weather later today.*

sew verb **sews, sewing, sewed, sewn** (*say* **so**)
When you sew, you use a needle and thread to join pieces of cloth together.

sex noun (*plural* **sexes**)
The sex of a person or an animal is whether they are male or female.

shade noun (*plural* **shades**)
1 If a place is in the shade, it is quite dark because the light of the sun cannot get to it.
2 The shade of a colour is how light or dark it is. *Do you like this shade of pink?*

shade verb **shades, shading, shaded**
When you shade something, you stop the sun from shining onto it.

shadow noun (*plural* **shadows**)
the dark shape that forms on the ground when something is blocking out the light

shadow

shake verb **shakes, shaking, shook, shaken**
1 When you shake something, you move it about quickly.
2 When something shakes, it moves about. *The ground shook as the giant came nearer.*
3 When you shake, you cannot keep your body still because you are very cold or frightened.

shall verb
I shall do something means that I will do it.

shallow adjective
Something that is shallow is not very deep. *The water is quite shallow here.*

shame noun
the feeling you have when you are unhappy because you have done wrong

a
b
c
d
e
f
g
h
i
j
k
l
m
n
o
p
q
r
s
t
u
v
w
x
y
z

shampoo noun (*plural* **shampoos**)
liquid soap that you use to wash your hair

shape noun (*plural* **shapes**)
The shape of something is what its outline looks like, for example whether it is square, round, or oval. *What shape is this room?*

> **WORD FAMILY**
> • You can say what shape something is by saying how it is **shaped**. *He was wearing slippers shaped like huge feet.*

share verb **shares, sharing, shared**
1 When you share something, you give some of it to other people. *I hope you're going to share your food with us!*
2 When people share something, they both use it. *I share a bedroom with my sister.*

shark noun (*plural* **sharks**)
a big, fierce sea fish that has sharp teeth and hunts and kills other fish to eat

sharp adjective **sharper, sharpest**
1 Something that is sharp can cut things because it is thin or pointed. *Be careful, those scissors are quite sharp.*
2 If you have sharp eyes or ears, you see or hear things easily.
3 If someone speaks in a sharp voice, they say something angrily.
4 A sharp turn is very sudden. *There was a sharp bend in the road.*

> **WORD FAMILY**
> • **sharpen** He sharpened his sword ready for the battle.
> • **sharply** 'Be quiet!' he said sharply.

shatter verb **shatters, shattering, shattered**
When something shatters, it breaks into tiny pieces. *A stone hit the window and the glass shattered.*

shave verb **shaves, shaving, shaved**
If you shave a part of your body, you cut all the hair off it to make it smooth.

shears noun
Shears look like very large scissors. You use shears for cutting hedges or for clipping wool from sheep.

shed noun (*plural* **sheds**)
a small wooden building

shed verb **sheds, shedding, shed**
To shed something means to let it fall off. *Trees shed their leaves in winter.*

sheep noun (*plural* **sheep**)
an animal that is kept on farms for its wool and meat

sheet noun (*plural* **sheets**)
1 a large piece of cloth that you put on a bed to sleep on
2 A sheet of something is a thin, flat piece of it. *I need another sheet of paper.*

shelf noun (*plural* **shelves**)
a piece of wood that is fastened to a wall so that you can put things on it *Please put the books back on the shelf.*

shell noun (*plural* **shells**)
1 A shell is a hard part on the outside of something. Eggs and nuts have shells, and some animals such as snails and tortoises have a shell on their back.
2 a large bullet that explodes when it hits something

shell

shelter noun (*plural* **shelters**)
a place that protects people from bad weather or from danger *We'll wait in the bus shelter.*

shelter verb **shelters, sheltering, sheltered**
1 To shelter someone means to keep them safe from bad weather or danger.

2 When you shelter, you stay in a place that is safe from bad weather or danger. *We sheltered from the storm in an old barn.*

shepherd noun (*plural* **shepherds**)
someone whose job is to look after sheep

sheriff noun (*plural* **sheriffs**)
In America, a sheriff is a person who makes sure that people do not break the law in their part of the country.

shield noun (*plural* **shields**)
something that soldiers or the police hold in front of their bodies to protect themselves during a battle

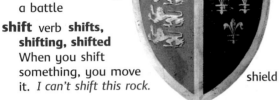
shield

shift verb **shifts, shifting, shifted**
When you shift something, you move it. *I can't shift this rock.*

shin noun (*plural* **shins**)
Your shins are the front parts of your legs below your knees.

shine verb **shines, shining, shone**
When something shines, it gives out light or looks very bright. *The sun shone all day.*

> **WORD FAMILY**
> • **shiny** Lying in the dust was a shiny piece of metal.

ship noun (*plural* **ships**)
a very large boat

shirt noun (*plural* **shirts**)
A shirt is a piece of clothing that you wear on the top half of your body. It has buttons down the front, sleeves, and a collar.

shiver verb **shivers, shivering, shivered**
When you shiver, you shake because you are cold or frightened.

shoal noun (*plural* **shoals**)
A shoal of fish is a big group of fish all swimming together.

shock noun (*plural* **shocks**)
1 If something is a shock, you were not expecting it and it upsets you when it happens. *It was a terrible shock when my grandmother died.*

2 If you get an electric shock, electricity gets into your body and hurts you.

shock verb **shocks, shocking, shocked**
If something shocks you, it gives you a nasty surprise and upsets you. *The terrible news shocked us all.*

shoe noun (*plural* **shoes**)
something that you wear on your feet to keep them warm and dry when you go outside

shone verb *see* **shine**

shook verb *see* **shake**

shoot noun (*plural* **shoots**)
a new part of a plant that has just grown

shoot verb **shoots, shooting, shot**
1 When you shoot with a gun or other weapon, you fire it.
2 When you shoot in a game such as football, you try to score a goal.

shop noun (*plural* **shops**)
a place where you can go to buy things

shop verb **shops, shopping, shopped**
When you shop, you go into a shop to buy something.

> **WORD FAMILY**
> • **shopping** I hate going shopping!

shore noun (*plural* **shores**)
the land by the edge of the sea *We swam towards the shore.*

short adjective **shorter, shortest**
1 Someone who is short is not very tall.
2 Something that is short is not very long. *The rope is too short.*
3 Something that is short does not last very long. *We only get a short holiday for half term.*

> **WORD FAMILY**
> • **shorten** We need to shorten the rope.

shorts noun
short trousers that only cover the top part of your legs

shot noun (*plural* **shots**)
1 the sound of someone firing a gun. *Suddenly, we heard a shot.*
2 a photograph *There are some lovely shots of you.*
3 one kick or hit of the ball in a game such as football or tennis *That was a brilliant shot!*

a
b
c
d
e
f
g
h
i
j
k
l
m
n
o
p
q
r
s
t
u
v
w
x
y
z

shot verb *see* **shoot** verb

should verb
If you should do something, you ought to do it. *I should go home now.*

shoulder noun (*plural* **shoulders**)
Your shoulders are the parts of the body between your neck and your arms.

shout verb **shouts, shouting, shouted**
When you shout, you speak in a very loud voice.

show noun (*plural* **shows**)
something that people perform for other people to watch at the theatre or on television

show verb **shows, showing, showed, shown**
1 When you show something to someone, you let them see it.
2 If you show someone how to do something, you do it so that they can watch you and learn how to do it. *Can you show me how to print this out from the computer?*
3 If something shows, people can see it.

shower noun (*plural* **showers**)
1 When there is a shower, it rains or snows for a short time.
2 When you have a shower, you stand under a stream of water to wash yourself.

shrank verb *see* **shrink**

shriek verb **shrieks, shrieking, shrieked**
If you shriek, you shout or scream in a high voice. *The girls were shrieking with laughter.*

shrill adjective **shriller, shrillest**
A shrill sound is high and loud.

shrimp noun (*plural* **shrimps**)
a small sea animal that you can eat

shrine noun (*plural* **shrines**)
a place that is special and holy because it is connected with a god or an important religious person

shrink verb **shrinks, shrinking, shrank, shrunk**
When something shrinks, it gets smaller. *The old woman was almost like a child herself because of this knack she had of suddenly shrinking to the size of a pepperpot.*—Alf Proysen, Mrs. Pepperpot and the Mechanical Doll

shrub noun (*plural* **shrubs**)
a bush in someone's garden

shrug verb **shrugs, shrugging, shrugged**
When you shrug your shoulders, you lift them up to show that you do not know something or do not care about it.

shrunk verb *see* **shrink**

shuffle verb **shuffles, shuffling, shuffled**
1 When you shuffle, you walk slowly, without lifting your feet off the ground. *He shuffled round the room in his slippers.*
2 When you shuffle cards, you mix them up so that they are ready for a game.

shut verb **shuts, shutting, shut**
1 When you shut something, you close it. *Don't forget to shut the door when you go out.*
2 When a shop shuts, it closes and people cannot use it.
3 When you shut down a computer, you close all the programs and switch it off.

shuttle noun (*plural* **shuttles**)
1 a train, bus, or plane which goes backwards and forwards between two places
2 A space shuttle is something that can carry people into space and back.

shy adjective **shyer, shyest**
If you are shy, you feel frightened and nervous when you meet people you do not know.

sick adjective **sicker, sickest**
1 If you are sick, you are ill.
2 If you are sick, food comes back up out of your mouth after you have eaten it.

side noun (*plural* **sides**)
1 The sides of something are the parts on the left and right of it, not at the back or the front. *There were some people standing at one side of the field.*
2 Your sides are the parts of your body on your left and right. *He had a big bruise on his right side.*
3 The sides of something are its edges. *A triangle has three sides.*
4 The two sides of a piece of paper or cloth are its front and back. *You can write on both sides of the paper.*
5 One side in a game or fight is one group that is playing or fighting against another group. *Whose side are you on?*

sideways adverb
If you move sideways, you move towards the side rather than forwards or backwards.

sieve noun (*plural* **sieves**) (*rhymes with* give)
A sieve is a dish with a lot of very small holes in. You use a sieve for separating something liquid from something solid, or for removing lumps from a powder.

sigh verb **sighs, sighing, sighed** (*rhymes with* by)
When you sigh, you breathe out heavily because you are sad or tired.

sight noun
1 Your sight is how well you can see things. *You are lucky to have good sight.*
2 A sight is something that you see. *I've never seen such a funny sight in all my life!*

sign noun (*plural* **signs**) (*rhymes with* mine)
1 a picture or mark that means something *The sign for a dollar is $.*
2 a notice that tells you something *The sign said 'Keep off the grass'.*
3 If you give someone a sign, you move your body to tell them something. *He raised his arm as a sign that the race was about to start.*

sign verb **signs, signing, signed**
When you sign something, you write your name on it.

signal noun (*plural* **signals**)
a light, sound, or movement that tells people what they should do, or tells them that something is going to happen *A red light is a signal for cars to stop.*

signature noun (*plural* **signatures**)
Your signature is your own special way of writing your name.

sign language noun
a way of communicating by using your hands to make words

Sikh noun (*plural* **Sikhs**)
a person who follows the Indian religion of Sikhism

silent adjective
1 Something that is silent does not make any noise. Someone who is silent does not speak or make a noise. *For a few moments everyone was silent.*
2 If a place is silent, there is no noise in it.

> **WORD FAMILY**
> • **silently** I crept silently downstairs.
> • **silence** There was silence in the classroom.

silk noun
a type of smooth cloth that is made from threads spun by insects called silkworms

silly adjective **sillier, silliest**
Something that is silly is stupid, not clever or sensible. Someone who is silly behaves in a silly way.
'What a silly place to dig a hole!' he thought. 'Anyone might fall in!'—Philip Ardagh, Dreadful Acts

a
b
c
d
e
f
g
h
i
j
k
l
m
n
o
p
q
r
s
t
u
v
w
x
y
z

179

silver noun
a shiny, white metal that is very valuable

similar adjective
Things that are similar are the same in some ways, but not exactly the same. *Your dress is quite similar to mine.*

silver

simile noun (*plural* **similes**) (*say* **sim**-i-li)
A simile is an expression in which you describe something by comparing it to something else. For example, the expression *as brave as a lion* is a simile.

simple adjective **simpler, simplest**
1 Something that is simple is very easy. *That's a really simple question.*
2 Something that is simple is plain and not fancy. *I did quite a simple design for my poster.*

since adverb & conjunction & preposition
1 from that time *We have been friends since last summer.*
2 because *We couldn't play outside since it was raining.*

sincere adjective
If you are sincere, you really mean what you say. *I could tell he was being sincere when he wished me good luck.*

sing verb **sings, singing, sang, sung**
When you sing, you use your voice to make music.

WORD FAMILY
• **singer** Are you a good singer?

single adjective
1 only one *The tree had a single apple on it.*
2 Someone who is single is not married.

singular noun
(*in grammar*) The singular is the form of a word you use when you are talking about only one person or thing. *Children* is a plural, and the singular is *child*.

sink noun (*plural* **sinks**)
a large bowl with taps where you can wash things

sink verb **sinks, sinking, sank, sunk**
1 When something sinks, it goes under water.
2 When something sinks, it goes downwards. *The sun sank behind the mountains.*

sip verb **sips, sipping, sipped**
When you sip a drink, you drink it slowly, a little bit at a time.

sir noun
a word you use when you are speaking politely to a man *Excuse me, sir, is this your hat?*

siren noun (*plural* **sirens**)
a machine that makes a loud sound to warn people about something

sister noun (*plural* **sisters**)
Your sister is a girl who has the same parents as you.

sit verb **sits, sitting, sat**
1 When you sit you rest on your bottom.
2 If something is sitting somewhere, it is there. *My school bag was sitting by the back door, where I had left it.*

site noun (*plural* **sites**)
A site is a piece of ground that is used for something. For example, a campsite is a place where people can camp.

sitting room noun (*plural* **sitting rooms**)
the room in a house with comfortable chairs, where people sit and talk or watch television

situation noun (*plural* **situations**)
all the things that are happening to you and to the people around you *We are now in a very difficult situation.*

six noun (*plural* **sixes**)
the number 6

sixteen noun
the number 16

sixty noun
the number 60

size noun (*plural* **sizes**)
The size of something is how big or small it is. *These trousers are the wrong size for me.*

skate noun (*plural* **skates**)
1 a boot with a special blade on the bottom, which you use for skating on ice
2 a special shoe or boot with wheels on the bottom

a b c d e f g h i j k l m n o p q r s t u v w x y z

skate verb **skates, skating, skated**
When you skate, you move smoothly over ice or over the ground wearing ice skates or roller skates.

> **WORD FAMILY**
> • **skating** Shall we go skating at the weekend?

skateboard noun (*plural* **skateboards**)
a small board on wheels that you can stand on and ride

> **WORD FAMILY**
> • **skateboarding** Skateboarding isn't allowed in the playground.

skeleton noun (*plural* **skeletons**)
Your skeleton is all the bones that are in your body.

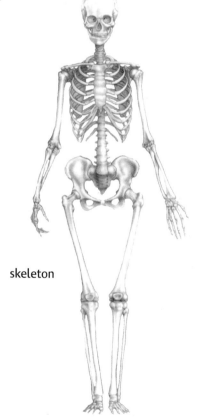

skeleton

sketch verb **sketches, sketching, sketched**
When you sketch something, you draw it quickly and roughly.

ski noun (*plural* **skis**) (*say* skee)
Skis are long, flat sticks that you strap to your feet and use for moving over snow.

ski verb **skis, skiing, skied**
When you ski, you move over snow on skis.

skier

skid verb **skids, skidding, skidded**
If a car skids, it slides out of control because the road is wet or slippery.

skill noun (*plural* **skills**)
If you have skill, you can do something well. *You need a lot of skill to do gymnastics.*

> **WORD FAMILY**
> • **skilful** He's a very skilful footballer.

skin noun (*plural* **skins**)
1 Your skin is the part of you that covers all of your body.
2 The skin on a fruit or vegetable is the tough part on the outside of it.

skinny adjective **skinnier, skinniest**
Someone who is skinny is very thin.

skip verb **skips, skipping, skipped**
1 When you skip, you run along lightly taking a little jump with each step.
2 When you skip, you turn a rope over your head and under your feet and jump over it each time it goes under your feet.

skirt noun (*plural* **skirts**)
A skirt is a piece of clothing that a woman or girl wears. It fastens around her waist and hangs down over her legs.

sky noun (*plural* **skies**)
The sky is the space above the earth where you can see the sun, moon, and stars.

skyscraper noun (*plural* **skyscrapers**)
a very tall building

slab noun (*plural* **slabs**)
A slab of something is a flat, thick piece of it. *The old well was covered with a slab of concrete.*

slack adjective **slacker, slackest**
If something is slack, it is not pulled tight. *Some of the ropes round the tent were too slack.*

a
b
c
d
e
f
g
h
i
j
k
l
m
n
o
p
q
r
s
t
u
v
w
x
y
z

slam verb **slams, slamming, slammed**
If you slam a door, you push it shut so that it makes a loud bang.
He stormed off out of the house, slamming the door.—Jacqueline Wilson, Double Act

slang noun
words that you use when you are talking to your friends, but not when you are writing or talking politely to people

slant verb **slants, slanting, slanted**
If something slants, it slopes and is not straight.

slap verb **slaps, slapping, slapped**
To slap someone means to hit them with the front of your hand.

slate noun (*plural* **slates**)
Slate is a type of smooth, grey rock. Pieces of slate are sometimes used to cover the roofs of houses.

sledge noun (*plural* **sledges**)
a piece of wood or plastic, which you sit on to slide along on snow or ice

sleek adjective **sleeker, sleekest**
Sleek hair or fur is smooth and shiny.

sleep verb **sleeps, sleeping, slept**
When you sleep, you close your eyes and rest your body and your mind.

> **WORD FAMILY**
> • **sleepy** The movement of the boat made me feel sleepy.

sleet noun
a mixture of rain and snow

sleeve noun (*plural* **sleeves**)
The sleeves on a shirt, jumper, or coat are the parts that cover your arms.

sleigh noun (*plural* **sleighs**) (*say* **slay**)
a large sledge that is pulled along by animals

slept verb *see* **sleep**

slice noun (*plural* **slices**)
A slice of something is a thin piece that has been cut off. *Would you like a slice of meat?*

slide verb **slides, sliding, slid**
When something slides, it moves along smoothly. *My skis slid across the snow.*

slide noun (*plural* **slides**)
1 A slide is a toy that children can play on. It is made of steps that you climb up, and a long sloping part that you can slide down.
2 a clip that girls sometimes wear in their hair to keep it tidy

slight adjective **slighter, slightest**
Something that is slight is small and not very important or not very bad. *I've got a slight headache.*

> **WORD FAMILY**
> • **slightly** She seemed slightly upset.

slim adjective **slimmer, slimmest**
Someone who is slim is thin.

slime noun
nasty wet, slippery stuff

> **WORD FAMILY**
> • **slimy** They had made a horrible slimy mixture.

sling noun (*plural* **slings**)
A sling is a piece of cloth that goes round your arm and is tied round your neck. You wear a sling to support your arm if you have hurt it.

slip verb **slips, slipping, slipped**
1 If you slip, your foot accidentally slides on the ground. *I slipped and fell over.*
2 When you slip somewhere, you go there quickly and quietly. *We slipped out of the room while no one was looking.*

slipper noun (*plural* **slippers**)
Slippers are soft shoes that you wear indoors.

slippery adjective
If something is slippery, it is smooth or wet and difficult to get hold of or walk on. *We had to drive slowly because the road was slippery.*

slit noun (*plural* **slits**)
a long, narrow cut in something

slither verb **slithers, slithering, slithered**
To slither along means to move along the ground. *The snake slithered into the bushes.*

slogan noun (*plural* **slogans**)
a short phrase that is used to advertise something

slope verb **slopes, sloping, sloped**
Something that slopes is not flat but goes up or down at one end. *The field slopes slightly down towards the river.*

> **WORD FAMILY**
> • **sloping** You can't play football on a sloping pitch.

slope noun (*plural* **slopes**)
a piece of ground that goes up or down like the side of a hill

slot noun (*plural* **slots**)
a narrow opening that you can put a coin into *Put a coin in the slot and you'll get a ticket.*

slow adjective **slower, slowest**
1 Something that is slow does not move very quickly. Someone who is slow does not do things quickly.
2 If a clock or watch is slow, it shows a time that is earlier than the right time. *I'm sorry I'm late, but my watch is slow.*

> **WORD FAMILY**
> • **slowly** She walked slowly to the front door.

slug noun
(*plural* **slugs**)
a small, soft animal that looks like a snail but has no shell

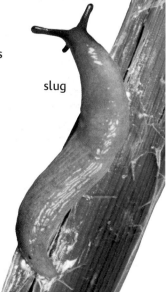

slug

slush noun
melting snow

sly adjective
slyer, slyest
Someone who is sly is clever at tricking people secretly to get what they want.

smack verb **smacks, smacking, smacked**
To smack someone means to hit them with the front of your hand.

small adjective **smaller, smallest**
Something that is small is not very big. *We live in quite a small house.*

smart adjective **smarter, smartest**
1 If you look smart, you look clean and neat and have nice clothes on.
2 Someone who is smart is clever.

smash verb **smashes, smashing, smashed**
When something smashes, it breaks into a lot of pieces with a loud noise. *I dropped a glass and it smashed.*

smear verb **smears, smearing, smeared**
To smear something means to spread it in a messy way. *The baby had smeared jam all over his face.*

smell verb **smells, smelling, smelled** or **smelt**
1 When you smell something, you notice it through your nose. *I can smell something burning.*
2 If something smells, you can notice it through your nose. *Your feet smell!*

> **WORD FAMILY**
> • **smelly** Take your smelly socks away from me!

smell noun (*plural* **smells**)
1 A smell is something that you can notice with your nose. *There was a strange smell in the kitchen.*
2 Your sense of smell is how well you can smell things. *Dogs have a very good sense of smell.*

smile verb **smiles, smiling, smiled**
When you smile, you move your mouth to show that you are happy.

smog noun
dirty air that is caused by pollution in a town or city

smoke noun
grey or black gas from a fire

smoke verb **smokes, smoking, smoked**
1 When something smokes, smoke comes off it. *The bonfire was still smoking the next morning.*
2 If someone smokes a cigarette they put it in their mouth and breathe in the smoke from it.

smooth adjective **smoother, smoothest**
Something that is smooth is flat and level, with no bumps or rough parts. *Babies have lovely smooth skin.*

a
b
c
d
e
f
g
h
i
j
k
l
m
n
o
p
q
r
s
t
u
v
w
x
y
z

SMS noun
SMS is a system for sending text messages to mobile phones. SMS stands for short message service.

smudge noun (*plural* **smudges**)
a dirty mark on something

smudge verb **smudges, smudging, smudged**
If you smudge paint or ink, you touch it while it is still wet and make it messy.

smuggle verb **smuggles, smuggling, smuggled**
To smuggle something into a place or out of a place means to take it there secretly.

> **WORD FAMILY**
> • **smuggler** These caves used to be used by smugglers.

snack noun (*plural* **snacks**)
something you can eat quickly instead of a meal

snail noun
(*plural* **snails**)
a small animal with a soft body, no legs, and a hard shell on its back

snail

snake noun (*plural* **snakes**)
an animal with a long, thin body and no legs

snap verb **snaps, snapping, snapped**
1 If something snaps, it breaks suddenly.
The rope snapped.
2 If an animal snaps at you, it tries to bite you.
3 To snap at someone means to shout at them angrily.
'Sit down,' snapped Aunt Bat.—Alexander McCall Smith, The Banana Machine

snarl verb **snarls, snarling, snarled**
When an animal snarls, it makes a fierce sound and shows its teeth.

snatch verb **snatches, snatching, snatched**
If you snatch something, you grab it quickly.

sneak verb **sneaks, sneaking, sneaked**
When you sneak somewhere, you go there quietly so that people do not see you or hear you.
I sneaked round to the back of the school, while the dinner ladies weren't looking.—Narinder Dhami, Bindi Babes

sneeze verb **sneezes, sneezing, sneezed**
When you sneeze, air suddenly comes out of your nose with a loud noise. *The dust made me sneeze.*

sniff verb **sniffs, sniffing, sniffed**
When you sniff, you breathe in noisily through your nose.

snip verb **snips, snipping, snipped**
When you snip a piece off something, you cut it off.

snooze verb **snoozes, snoozing, snoozed**
When you snooze, you have a short sleep.

snore verb **snores, snoring, snored**
If you snore, you breathe very noisily while you are asleep.

snort verb **snorts, snorting, snorted**
To snort means to make a loud noise by pushing air out through your nose. *The horse snorted and stamped its feet.*

snout noun (*plural* **snouts**)
A snout is an animal's long nose, or nose and jaws

snout

snow noun
small, light flakes of frozen water that fall from the sky when it is very cold

snowball noun
(*plural* **snowballs**)
a ball of snow that you throw at someone

snowboard noun
(*plural* **snowboards**)
a narrow board that you stand on to slide down a slope over snow

> **WORD FAMILY**
> • **snowboarding** Have you ever tried snowboarding?

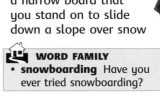

snowflake noun (*plural* **snowflakes**)
Snowflakes are small light pieces of snow that fall from the sky.

snug adjective **snugger, snuggest**
If you feel snug, you feel warm, cosy, and comfortable.

snuggle verb **snuggles, snuggling, snuggled**
When you snuggle somewhere, you curl up there so that you are warm and comfortable.

soak verb **soaks, soaking, soaked**
1 To soak something means to make it very wet. *The rain got in and soaked the carpet.*
2 If something soaks up water, the water goes into it.

soap noun (*plural* **soaps**)
1 Soap is something that you use with water for washing yourself.
2 A soap is a regular television series about the lives of ordinary people. A soap is also called a **soap opera**.

soar verb **soars, soaring, soared**
When something soars, it goes high up into the air.

sob verb **sobs, sobbing, sobbed**
If you sob, you cry in a noisy way.

soccer noun
the game of football

society noun (*plural* **societies**)
(*say* so-sye-et-ee)
1 A society is all the people who live together in the same country.
2 A society is a club. *If you like acting, you should join your local drama society.*

sock noun (*plural* **socks**)
a piece of clothing that you wear over your feet

socket noun (*plural* **sockets**)
a place on a wall that an electric plug fits into

sofa noun (*plural* **sofas**)
a long, comfortable seat for more than one person

soft adjective **softer, softest**
1 Something that is soft is not hard or stiff. *I slept on a lovely soft bed.*

2 A soft sound is not very loud. *There was soft music playing in the background.*

WORD FAMILY
• **softly** 'Don't worry,' she said softly.

software noun
(*in ICT*) the programs that you put into a computer to make it work

soggy adjective **soggier, soggiest**
Something that is soggy is wet and soft. *The cardboard box had gone all soggy in the rain.*

soil noun
the brown earth that plants grow in

solar adjective
Solar means to do with the sun. *Some houses now use solar energy.*

sold verb *see* **sell**

soldier noun (*plural* **soldiers**)
someone who is a member of an army

sole noun (*plural* **soles**)
The sole of your foot or shoe is the part underneath it.

solid adjective
1 Something that is solid is not hollow in the middle. *Tennis balls are hollow but cricket balls are solid.*
2 Something that is solid is hard and firm. *Water becomes solid when it freezes.*

solid

solid noun (*plural* **solids**)
A solid is any substance that is hard and is not a liquid or a gas. Wood, rock, and plastic are all solids.

a
b
c
d
e
f
g
h
i
j
k
l
m
n
o
p
q
r
s
t
u
v
w
x
y
z

185

solidify verb **solidifies, solidifying, solidified**
When something solidifies, it becomes hard and firm. *When water freezes, it solidifies.*

solo noun (*plural* **solos**)
a piece of music or a dance that one person performs on their own

solution noun (*plural* **solutions**)
1 The solution to a puzzle or problem is the answer.
2 (*in science*) A solution is a liquid in which something has been dissolved. *In the beaker we had a solution of sugar and water.*

solve verb **solves, solving, solved**
When you solve a puzzle or problem, you find the answer to it.

some adjective & pronoun
1 a few *Some of us can swim, but the others can't.*
2 an amount of something *Do have some cake?*

somebody, someone pronoun
a person *Somebody's taken my pencil!*

somehow adverb
in some way *We must get away somehow.*

somersault noun (*plural* **somersaults**)
When you do a somersault, you roll over forwards or backwards.

something pronoun
a thing *I'm sure I've forgotten something.*

sometimes adverb
at some times *Sometimes I cycle to school, sometimes I walk.*

somewhere adverb
in some place *I put the book somewhere but I've forgotten where.*

son noun (*plural* **sons**)
Someone's son is their male child.

song noun (*plural* **songs**)
a piece of music with words that you sing

soon adverb
in a very short time *We must go home soon.*

soot noun
black powder that is left behind after coal or wood has been burnt

sore adjective **sorer, sorest**
If a part of your body is sore, it hurts. *I've got a sore throat.*

sorry adjective **sorrier, sorriest**
1 If you are sorry that you did something, you are sad about it and wish that you had not done it. *I'm very sorry that I broke your window.*
2 If you feel sorry for someone, you feel sad because something nasty has happened to them.

sort noun (*plural* **sorts**)
a kind *Which sort of ice cream do you like?*

sort verb **sorts, sorting, sorted**
When you sort things, you put them into different groups. *We sorted the books into different piles.*

soul noun (*plural* **souls**) (*say* sole)
the part of a person that some people believe goes on living after the person has died

sound noun (*plural* **sounds**)
anything that you can hear *I thought I heard a strange sound.*

sound verb **sounds, sounding, sounded**
If a bell or alarm sounds, it makes a noise.

soup noun (*plural* **soups**)
a hot liquid made from meat or vegetables

sour adjective **sourer, sourest**
Something that is sour has a nasty bitter taste, like a lemon.

source noun (*plural* **sources**)
The source of something is the place where it comes from, or the place where it starts. *The source of the river is up in the hills.*

south noun
South is one of the directions in which you can face or travel. On a map, south is the direction towards the bottom of the page.

WORD FAMILY
• The **southern** part of a country is the part in the south.

souvenir noun (*plural* **souvenirs**)
something that you keep because it reminds you of a person or place *We brought back some shells as a souvenir.*

sow verb **sows, sowing, sowed, sown** (*rhymes with* low)
When you sow seeds, you put them into the ground so that they will grow.

a
b
c
d
e
f
g
h
i
j
k
l
m
n
o
p
q
r
s
t
u
v
w
x
y
z

space noun (plural **spaces**)

1 Space is the place around the Earth and far beyond the Earth, where the stars and planets are. *Would you like to go up into space?*

2 A space is a place with nothing in it. *There is a space here for you to write your name.*

> **WORD FAMILY**
> • A **spacecraft** or a **spaceship** is a machine like a large aeroplane that can travel through space.

spade noun (plural **spades**)

a tool with a long handle and a wide blade that you use for digging

spaghetti noun

a type of pasta that is made in long, thin pieces

spanner noun (plural **spanners**)

a tool that you use for tightening and undoing nuts

spare verb **spares, sparing, spared**

If you can spare something, you have some extra that you can give to someone else. *Can you spare a bit of money for our collection?*

spare adjective

If something is spare, you are not using it at the moment but you can use it if you need it. *I always have a spare pencil in my pencil case.*

spark noun (plural **sparks**)

1 a tiny flash of electricity *There was a spark as the wires touched.*

2 a tiny piece of something burning that shoots out from a fire *I was worried that a spark from the fire might set fire to the rug.*

sparkle verb **sparkles, sparkling, sparkled**

When something sparkles, it shines brightly. *The sea sparkled in the sunlight.*

sparrow noun (plural **sparrows**)

a small, brown bird that you often see in people's gardens

spat verb *see* **spit**

spawn noun

Frog spawn is eggs that are laid by frogs in water. The eggs are surrounded and held together by something that looks like clear jelly.

spawn

speak verb **speaks, speaking, spoke, spoken**

When you speak, you say something. *I spoke to my grandmother on the phone.*

speaker noun (plural **speakers**)

the part of a radio, television, or music player that the sound comes out of

spear noun (plural **spears**)

a long stick with a sharp point that is used as a weapon

special adjective

1 Something that is special is different and more important than other things. *Your birthday is a very special day.*

2 A special thing is for one particular person or job. *You use a special tool to tune the strings on a piano.*

> **WORD FAMILY**
> • **specially** I've bought some chocolate biscuits specially for you.

species noun (plural **species**)

a type of animal or plant *The giant panda is now an endangered species.*

spectacular adjective

Something that is spectacular is very exciting or impressive. *We watched a spectacular fireworks display.*

spectator noun (plural **spectators**)

Spectators are people who watch a sporting event or game.

speech noun (plural **speeches**)
1 Speech is the ability to speak. *People use speech to communicate with each other.*
2 A speech is a talk that someone gives to a group of people.

speech bubble noun (plural **speech bubbles**)
A speech bubble is a circle containing words, which you draw next to a person in a drawing to show what that person is saying.

speechless adjective
If you are speechless, you cannot say anything because you are so surprised, angry, or afraid.

speech marks noun
Speech marks are marks like this ' ' or this " " that you use in writing. You put these marks round words to show that someone has spoken them.

speed noun
The speed of something is how fast it moves or how quickly it happens. *We were driving along at a speed of 100 kilometres an hour.*

speed verb **speeds, speeding, sped**
To speed means to run or go along very fast. *He sped past me on his bike.*

spell verb **spells, spelling, spelled** or **spelt**
The way in which you spell a word is the letters that you use when you write it. *I can't spell your name.*

> **WORD FAMILY**
> • **spelling** We've got a list of spellings to learn.

spell noun (plural **spells**)
A spell is a set of words that people say in stories when they want something magic to happen.

spellcheck noun (plural **spellchecks**)
When you do a spellcheck on a computer, you tell the computer to check the spellings of all the words you have typed.

spend verb **spends, spending, spent**
1 When you spend money, you use it to pay for things. *I've already spent all my pocket money.*
2 When you spend time doing something, you use the time to do that thing. *We spent all day trying to mend the boat.*

sphere noun (plural **spheres**) (say **sfeer**)
the shape of a ball

spice noun (plural **spices**)
A spice is a powder or seed which is added to food to give it a strong flavour. Pepper is a spice.

> **WORD FAMILY**
> • **spicy** She cooked a dish of spicy vegetables.

spider noun
(plural **spiders**)
a small animal with eight legs that spins sticky webs to catch insects for food

spider

spike noun
(plural **spikes**)
a thin piece of metal with a sharp point

spill verb **spills, spilling, spilled** or **spilt**
If you spill something, you let some of it fall out onto the floor. *Mind you don't spill your drink.*

spin verb **spins, spinning, spun**
1 Something that spins turns round and round.
2 To spin thread from wool or cotton means to make it.
3 To spin a web means to make it. *The spider spun a web.*

spindly adjective
Something that is spindly is long and thin and not very strong.

spine noun (plural **spines**)
1 Your spine is the long line of bones down the middle of your back.
2 The spines on a plant or animal are sharp points on it.

spiral noun (plural **spirals**)
a line that keeps going round and round in circles, with each circle getting slightly bigger

spire noun (plural **spires**)
a tall, pointed part on the top of a tower on a building

spirit noun (plural **spirits**)
1 the part of a person that some people believe goes on living after the person has died
2 a ghost
3 If you have a lot of spirit, you are brave and determined.

spit verb **spits, spitting, spat**
If you spit, you push water or food out of your mouth.

spite noun
If you do something out of spite, you do it to hurt or upset someone.

spiteful adjective
Someone who is spiteful does nasty things to hurt or upset other people.

> **WORD FAMILY**
> • **spitefully** 'You won't be able to come with us,' she said spitefully.

splash verb **splashes, splashing, splashed**
If you splash water, you hit it so that it makes a noise and flies up into the air.

splinter noun (plural **splinters**)
a small, sharp bit of wood or glass

split verb **splits, splitting, split**
1 When something splits, it breaks or tears. *The bag split open and all the shopping fell out.*
2 When you split something, you break it into pieces. *He split the log with an axe.*

spoil verb **spoils, spoiling, spoiled's** or **poilt**
1 To spoil something means to damage it so that it is not as good or as nice as it was before. *You'll spoil your new trainers if you get them all muddy.*
2 To spoil a child means to give them everything that they want so that they always expect to get their own way and behave badly if they do not.

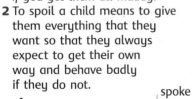
spoke

spoke noun (plural **spokes**)
The spokes on a wheel are the pieces of metal that go from the centre of the wheel to the edge.

spoke, spoken verb
see **speak**

sponge noun (plural **sponges**)
1 A sponge is a thick, soft thing with a lot of small holes in. A sponge soaks up water easily, and you use it for washing things.
2 a type of cake

sponsor verb **sponsors, sponsoring, sponsored**
If you sponsor someone, you promise to give them money if they do something difficult.

spoon noun (plural **spoons**)
a thing that you use for eating soft or liquid foods such as soup and ice cream

sport noun (plural **sports**)
A sport is a game that you play or something difficult that you do to exercise your body. Football and tennis are sports.

> **WORD FAMILY**
> • Someone who likes sport and is good at it is **sporty**. A **sportsman** is a man who does a sport. A **sportswoman** is a woman who does a sport.

spot noun (plural **spots**)
1 a small round mark on something *Leopards have spots all over their bodies.*
2 a small, sore, red lump on your skin *Teenagers often get spots on their faces.*

spot verb **spots, spotting, spotted**
If you spot something, you see it. *Out of the corner of his eye, he's spotted trouble of another sort.* —Anne Fine, The Diary of a Killer Cat

spotless adjective
Something that is spotless is perfectly clean.

spout noun (plural **spouts**)
The spout of a jug or teapot is the part that you pour liquid out of.

sprain verb **sprains, spraining, sprained**
If you sprain your wrist or ankle, you hurt it quite badly.

sprang verb *see* **spring** verb

spray verb **sprays, spraying, sprayed**
When you spray water on something, you cover it with tiny drops of water.

spread verb **spreads, spreading, spread**
1 To spread something means to open it out to its full size. *The huge bird spread its wings and flew away.*
2 When you spread butter or jam, you put a thin layer of it onto bread.

spring verb **springs, springing, sprang, sprung**
To spring means to jump.
Just inside the gate, with the moonlight shining on it, stood an enormous lion crouched as if it was ready to spring.—C. S. Lewis, The Lion, the Witch and the Wardrobe

spring noun (*plural* **springs**)
1 a piece of metal that is wound into rings so that it jumps back into shape after it has been pressed down
2 the time of the year when plants start to grow and the days get lighter and warmer

sprinkle verb **sprinkles, sprinkling, sprinkled**
When you sprinkle something, you shake a few drops or small pieces of it over something else. *She sprinkled some sugar on top of the cake.*

sprint verb **sprints, sprinting, sprinted**
When you sprint, you run as fast as you can over a short distance.

sprout verb **sprouts, sprouting, sprouted**
When a plant sprouts, it starts to grow new parts.

sprung verb *see* **spring** verb

spun verb *see* **spin**

spy noun (*plural* **spies**)
someone who works secretly to find out information about another person or country

spy verb **spies, spying, spied**
1 When you spy on someone, you watch them secretly.
2 When you spy something, you see it.

square noun (*plural* **squares**)
1 A square is a shape with four straight sides and four right angles. The sides of a square are all the same length.

2 (*in mathematics*) The square of a number is the number you get when you multiply it by itself. *The square of 4 is 16.*
3 an open space in a town with buildings all round it *We sat in the square to eat our lunch.*

square number noun (*plural* **square numbers**)
(*in mathematics*) a number that you get when you multiply another number by itself *9 and 16 are both square numbers.*

squash verb **squashes, squashing, squashed**
When you squash something, you press it hard so that it becomes flat. *My sandwiches got squashed at the bottom of my bag.*

squash noun
a sweet drink made from fruit juice and sugar *Would you like some orange squash?*

squat verb **squats, squatting, squatted**
When you squat, you bend your knees under you so that your bottom is almost touching the ground.

squawk verb **squawks, squawking, squawked**
When a bird squawks, it makes a loud, rough sound in its throat.

squeak verb **squeaks, squeaking, squeaked**
To squeak means to make a very high sound. *The door squeaked as I opened it.*

squeal verb **squeals, squealing, squealed**
When you squeal, you shout or cry in a high voice. *The two girls were squealing with delight.*

squeeze verb **squeezes, squeezing, squeezed**
1 When you squeeze something, you press it hard with your hands. *Squeeze the tube to get some toothpaste out.*
2 If you squeeze something into a place, you push it in even though there is not very much room. *Can we squeeze another person in the car?*

squirrel noun (*plural* **squirrels**)
A squirrel is a small animal with a thick, bushy tail. Squirrels live in trees and eat nuts and seeds.

squirrel

squirt verb **squirts, squirting, squirted**
When water squirts out of something, it shoots out quickly.

stable noun (*plural* **stables**)
a building in which horses are kept

stack noun (*plural* **stacks**)
A stack of things is a neat pile of them.

stadium noun (*plural* **stadiums**)
a large building where people can watch sports and games

staff noun
The staff in a school, shop, or office are all the people who work there.

stag noun (*plural* **stags**)
a male deer

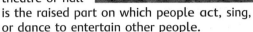
stag

stage noun
(*plural* **stages**)
The stage in a theatre or hall
is the raised part on which people act, sing, or dance to entertain other people.

stagger verb **staggers, staggering, staggered**
1 When you stagger, you walk with unsteady legs, almost falling over with each step.
2 If something staggers you, it surprises you a lot.

stain noun (*plural* **stains**)
a dirty mark on something that does not come out when you wash it or rub it

> **WORD FAMILY**
> • **stained** His clothes were old and stained.

stair noun (*plural* **stairs**)
Stairs are steps inside a building.

staircase noun (*plural* **staircases**)
a set of stairs inside a building

stale adjective **staler, stalest**
Something that is stale is not fresh. *We had nothing to eat except stale bread.*

stalk noun (*plural* **stalks**)
The stalk of a flower, leaf, or fruit, is the part that joins it to the plant.

stall noun (*plural* **stalls**)
1 a table that things are arranged on so that they can be sold, for example in a market
2 a place for one animal in a stable

stallion noun (*plural* **stallions**)
a male horse

stammer verb **stammers, stammering, stammered**
If you stammer, you keep repeating the sounds at the beginning of words when you speak.

stamp noun (*plural* **stamps**)
A stamp is a small piece of sticky paper with a picture on it. You stick a stamp on a letter or parcel to show that you have paid to post it.

stamp verb **stamps, stamping, stamped**
When you stamp your feet, you bang them heavily on the ground.

stand verb **stands, standing, stood**
1 When you stand, you are on your feet, not sitting or lying down. *The teacher asked us all to stand up.*
2 If you cannot stand something, you do not like it at all.

stand noun (*plural* **stands**)
something that you can put things on
Put your music on the music stand.

standard noun (*plural* **standards**)
The standard of something is how good or bad it is. *The standard of your work has really improved this term.*

standard adjective
Something that is standard is ordinary and not special. *This software will run on any standard computer.*

stank verb *see* **stink**

stanza noun (*plural* **stanzas**)
one verse of a poem

star noun
(*plural* **stars**)
1 Stars are the tiny, bright lights you see in the sky at night.
2 A star is a shape that has five or more points sticking out all round it.
3 A star is a famous person.

star verb **stars, starring, starred**
If someone stars in a film or show, they have an important part in it.

starch noun (plural **starches**)
Starch is a substance in food that gives you energy. There is starch in bread and potatoes.

stare verb **stares, staring, stared**
If you stare at something, you keep looking at it for a long time, without moving your eyes.

start verb **starts, starting, started**
1 When you start to do something, you begin to do it. *Georgina started to cry.*
2 When something starts, it begins. *What time does the concert start?*

start noun (plural **starts**)
The start of something is when it begins.

startle verb **startles, startling, startled**
If something startles you, it gives you a sudden shock. *The sudden noise startled me.*

starve verb **starves, starving, starved**
To starve means to be ill or to die because you have not got enough food.

state noun (plural states)
1 The state that something is in is the condition it is in, for example clean, tidy, or broken. *The house was in a terrible state.*
2 A state is a country or one part of a country that has its own laws and government.

statement noun (plural **statements**)
a sentence that is not a question or an exclamation

station noun (plural **stations**)
1 a place where trains and buses stop so that people can get on and off
2 a building where the police or firefighters work

stationary adjective
If a car is stationary, it is not moving.

stationery noun
paper, pens, and other things that you use for writing and drawing

statue noun (plural **statues**)
a model of a person made from stone, wood, or metal

stay verb **stays, staying, stayed**
1 If you stay somewhere, you remain there and do not go away. *Please stay in your seats.*
2 If you stay in a place, you live there for a while. *I'm going to stay with my grandma for the summer holidays.*
3 To stay means to remain. *I hope it stays dry for sports day.*

steady adjective **steadier, steadiest**
1 Something that is steady is firm and does not shake or move about.
2 If something moves in a steady way, it moves along at the same speed all the time.

> **WORD FAMILY**
> **steadily** We drove along steadily at forty miles per hour.

steak noun (plural **steaks**)
a thick slice of meat or fish

steal verb **steals, stealing, stole, stolen**
To steal something means to take something that belongs to someone else. *Someone's stolen my phone!*

steam noun
the hot gas that comes off water when it boils

steel noun
a type of strong, shiny metal

steep adjective **steeper, steepest**
Something that is steep slopes sharply up or down.
We had to clamber down a steep hillside.—Jostein Gaarder, The Frog Castle

steer verb **steers, steering, steered**
When you steer a car or bicycle, you make it go in the direction you want.

stem noun (*plural* **stems**)
the long, thin part of a plant that grows up out of the ground

step noun (*plural* **steps**)
1 When you take a step, you move one foot forwards or backwards.
2 Steps are stairs. *We walked down the steps to the beach.*

stepbrother noun (*plural* **stepbrothers**)
A stepbrother is a boy whose father or mother has married your father or mother.

stepfather noun (*plural* **stepfathers**)
Your stepfather is a man who has got married to your mother but is not your real father.

stepmother noun (*plural* **stepmothers**)
Your stepmother is a woman who has got married to your father but is not your real mother.

stepsister noun (*plural* **stepsisters**)
A stepsister is a girl whose father or mother has married your father or mother.

stereo noun (*plural* **stereos**)
a machine that plays music from tapes or CDs through two speakers

stern adjective **sterner, sternest**
Someone who is stern is serious and strict.
Mr Robinson had a very stern expression on his face.

WORD FAMILY
• **sternly** Mr Potts looked at me sternly.

stew noun (*plural* **stews**)
a mixture of meat or vegetables cooked in a sauce

stick noun (*plural* **sticks**)
a long, thin piece of wood

stick verb **sticks, sticking, stuck**
1 If you stick a pin or nail into something, you push it in.
2 When you stick things together, you fix them together using glue. *I stuck the pictures into my book.*
3 If something sticks, it gets jammed and you cannot move it. *Sometimes the door sticks a bit.*

sticker noun (*plural* **stickers**)
a small piece of paper with a picture or writing on one side and glue on the other side

sticky adjective **stickier, stickiest**
Something that is sticky will stick to things when it touches them.

stiff adjective **stiffer, stiffest**
Something that is stiff is hard and does not bend easily. *Use a piece of stiff cardboard for the base of your model.*

still adjective **stiller, stillest**
1 Something that is still is not moving. *The water in the lake was still and calm.*
2 A still drink is not fizzy.

still adverb
1 When you stand, sit, or lie still, you do not move.
2 even now *He's still asleep.*

sting verb **stings, stinging, stung**
If an insect stings you, it jabs you with a sharp part of its body and hurts you.

stink verb **stinks, stinking, stank** or **stunk**
If something stinks, it smells nasty.

stir verb **stirs, stirring, stirred**
1 When you stir something, you move it about with a spoon.
2 When someone stirs, they move after they have been asleep.

stitch noun (*plural* **stitches**)
1 Stitches are the loops of thread that you make when you are sewing or knitting.
2 A stitch is a sudden pain in your side that you sometimes get when you have been running.

a
b
c
d
e
f
g
h
i
j
k
l
m
n
o
p
q
r
s
t
u
v
w
x
y
z

stocking noun (*plural* **stockings**)
a piece of clothing that a woman wears over her legs and feet

stole, stolen verb
see **steal**

stomach noun
(*plural* **stomachs**)
Your stomach is the part inside your body where your food goes after you have eaten it.

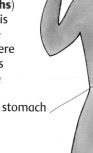

stomach

stone noun
(*plural* **stones**)
1 Stone is rock. *The castle is built of solid stone.*
2 A stone is a small piece of rock. *He threw a stone into the water.*
3 A stone is the hard seed in the middle of some fruits such as a cherry or peach.
4 We can measure weight in stones. One stone is just under 6¹/₂ kilograms.

stood verb *see* **stand** verb

stool noun (*plural* **stools**)
a small seat without a back

stoop verb **stoops, stooping, stooped**
When you stoop, you bend your body forwards. *The giraffe stooped low and went out through the tall door.*—Roald Dahl, The Giraffe and the Pelly and Me

stop verb **stops, stopping, stopped**
1 When you stop something, you make it stand still. *The policeman stopped the traffic.*
2 When something stops, it stands still. *The bus stopped outside the school.*
3 When you stop doing something, you no longer do it. *The baby finally stopped crying.*

store verb **stores, storing, stored**
When you store things, you keep them until you need them.

store noun (*plural* **stores**)
a large shop

storey noun (*plural* **storeys**)
One storey of a tall building is one floor.

storm noun (*plural* **storms**)
When there is a storm, there is a strong wind and a lot of rain or snow.

> **WORD FAMILY**
> • **stormy** It was a dark and stormy night.

story noun (*plural* **stories**)
something in a book that tells you about things that have happened

straight adjective **straighter, straightest**
Something that is straight does not bend or curl. *Have you got straight hair or curly hair?*

> **WORD FAMILY**
> • **straighten** I want to have my hair straightened.

strain verb **strains, straining, strained**
1 If you strain a muscle, you hurt it by stretching it too much.
2 If you strain to do something, you try very hard to do it by pushing or stretching with your body. *I had to strain to reach the top cupboard.*
3 When you strain a liquid, you pour it through a sieve to take out lumps.

stranded adjective
If you are stranded in a place, you are stuck there and cannot get away.

strange adjective **stranger, strangest**
1 Something that is strange is unusual and surprising. *What a strange animal!*
2 A strange place is one that you have not seen before. *She was very frightened to find herself alone in a strange place.*

> **WORD FAMILY**
> • **strangely** Lucy was behaving rather strangely.

stranger noun (*plural* **strangers**)
A stranger is someone you do not know. *You shouldn't talk to strangers.*

strap noun (*plural* **straps**)
a strip of leather or cloth that you hold when you are carrying something or use for fastening things *My watch strap has broken.*

straw noun (*plural* **straws**)
1 Straw is dry stalks of corn or wheat that you put on the ground for animals to lie on.
2 A straw is a thin tube that you sometimes put into a drink and use to drink through.

strawberry noun
(plural **strawberries**)
a small, red,
juicy fruit

stray adjective
A stray dog or cat does not
have a home but lives outside.

streak noun (plural **streaks**)
A streak of something is a long, thin line of
it. *He had a few streaks of mud on his face.*

stream noun (plural **streams**)
1 a small river
2 A stream of things is a moving line of
them. *There was a stream of cars coming
out of the car park.*

street noun (plural **streets**)
a road in a town or city with houses along
each side

strength noun
The strength of something is how strong it
is. *We need to test the strength of the rope.*

strengthen verb **strengthens, strengthening,
strengthened**
To strengthen something means to make
it stronger.

stress noun
If you are suffering from stress, you are very
worried or upset about something.

stretch verb **stretches, stretching, stretched**
1 When you stretch something, you pull it so
that it becomes longer or bigger. *He had to
stretch the trousers a bit to get them on.*
2 When you stretch, you move your arms or
legs as far as you can. *I stretched over to reach
the telephone.*

strict adjective **stricter, strictest**
Someone who is strict does not allow people
to behave badly. *My parents are very strict.*

stride verb **strides, striding, strode**
When you stride along, you walk with
long steps.

stride noun (plural **strides**)
a long step *He took three strides forward.*

strike verb **strikes, striking, struck**
1 To strike something means to hit it. To strike
someone means to hit or slap them. *His father
had never once struck him.*
2 When you strike a match, you
rub it so that it makes a flame.

3 When a clock strikes, it makes
a sound. *The old clock
struckmidnight, and I sat
up with a sudden start. My
nutcracker!*—Berlie Doherty,
The Nutcracker

string noun (plural **strings**)
1 String is thin rope. *We tied
the parcel up with string.*
2 The strings on a guitar
or violin are the parts
that you touch to
make music.

string

strip verb **strips,
stripping, stripped**
When you strip, you
take off all your clothes.

strip noun (plural **strips**)
A strip of something
is a long, narrow
piece of it.

stripe noun (plural **stripes**)
A stripe is a band of colour on something.
He was wearing a blue shirt with white stripes.

WORD FAMILY
• **striped** or **stripy** He was wearing a pair of stripy
pyjamas.

strode verb *see* **stride** verb

a
b
c
d
e
f
g
h
i
j
k
l
m
n
o
p
q
r
s
t
u
v
w
x
y
z

195

stroke verb **strokes, stroking, stroked**
When you stroke something, you move your hand over it gently. *Would you like to stroke the kitten?*

stroll verb **strolls, strolling, strolled**
When you stroll, you walk along slowly.

strong adjective **stronger, strongest**
1 If you are strong, you can lift and move heavy things.
2 Something that is strong will not break easily. *Is this rope strong enough to hold my weight?*
3 A strong taste is not mild or weak.

struck verb *see* **strike**

structure noun (*plural* **structures**)
A structure is anything that has been built. *Next to the house is a small wooden structure.*

struggle verb **struggles, struggling, struggled**
1 When you struggle, you fight with your arms and legs to try to get free.
2 If you struggle to do something, you work hard to do it because it is difficult. *I struggled a bit with some of the maths questions.*

stubborn adjective
Someone who is stubborn will not change their mind even though they might be wrong.

stuck verb *see* **stick** verb

student noun (*plural* **students**)
someone who is studying at college or university

studio noun (*plural* **studios**) (*say* **stew**-dee-oh)
1 a place where people make films or radio or television programmes
2 a room where an artist or photographer works

study verb **studies, studying, studied**
1 When you study a subject, you learn about it. *We are studying rivers in geography.*
2 When you study something, you look at it very carefully. *He studied the map, looking for the farmhouse.*

study noun (*plural* **studies**)
a room in a house where someone works or studies

stuff noun
anything that you can see and touch
There was some nasty slimy stuff on the floor. We cleared all the old stuff out of the cupboards.

stuff verb **stuffs, stuffing, stuffed**
1 When you stuff something, you fill it with things.
2 When you stuff something somewhere, you push it there roughly. *She stuffed the sweets into her pocket.*

stuffy adjective **stuffier, stuffiest**
A room that is stuffy smells nasty because there is no fresh air in it. *The attic was small and stuffy.*

stumble verb **stumbles, stumbling, stumbled**
If you stumble, you trip and fall over.

stump noun (*plural* **stumps**)
1 A stump is the part of something that is left after the main part has been broken off. *We sat down on an old tree stump.*
2 The stumps in a game of cricket are the three sticks that you put at each end of the pitch.

stun verb **stuns, stunning, stunned**
If something stuns you, it hits you on the head and makes you feel dizzy or weak.

stung verb *see* **sting** verb

stunk verb *see* **stink**

stunt noun (*plural* **stunts**)
something clever and dangerous that someone does in a film or to entertain people

stupid adjective
1 Something that is stupid is very silly. *That was a really stupid thing to do.*
2 Someone who is stupid is not very clever.

> **WORD FAMILY**
> • **stupidly** I had stupidly left my money at home.

stutter verb **stutters, stuttering, stuttered**
If you stutter, you keep repeating the sounds at the beginning of words when you speak.

sty noun (*plural* **sties**)
a building where a pig is kept

style noun (*plural* **styles**)
The style of something is its shape and design. *I like the colour of this sweatshirt, but I don't like the style.*

subject noun (*plural* **subjects**)
1 A subject is something that you learn about at school. Maths, English, and art are all subjects.

a b c d e f g h i j k l m n o p q r **s** t u v w x y z

2 (*in grammar*) The subject of a sentence is the person or thing that does the action of the verb. In the sentence 'William ate an apple', William is the subject of the sentence.

3 The subjects of a king or queen are the people they rule over.

submarine noun (*plural* **submarines**)
a ship that can go under the water

subordinate clause noun
(*plural* **subordinate clauses**)
(*in grammar*) an extra clause in a sentence, which adds more information but could not be a sentence on its own

substance noun (*plural* **substances**)
anything that is a liquid, solid, or gas
Glue is a sticky substance.

subtract verb **subtracts, subtracting, subtracted**
(*in mathematics*) When you subtract one number from another, you take it away to make a smaller number. *If you subtract 6 from 9, you get 3.*

> **WORD FAMILY**
> • When you subtract numbers, you do **subtraction**.

suburb noun (*plural* **suburbs**)
a part of a city that is a long way from the city centre *A lot of people live in the suburbs of London.*

succeed verb **succeeds, succeeding, succeeded**
(*say* suk-**seed**)
If you succeed, you manage to do something. *I finally succeeded in getting the door open.*

success noun (*plural* **successes**) (*say* suk-**sess**)
If something is a success, it works well and people like it. *The concert was a great success.*

successful adjective
1 If you are successful, you manage to do something.
2 If something is successful, it works well and people like it. *Our trip to France was very successful.*

such adjective
so much *That was such fun!*

suck verb **sucks, sucking, sucked**
1 When you suck something into your mouth, you pull it in. *I sucked some milk up through the straw.*

2 When you suck on something, you keep moving it about in your mouth without chewing it or swallowing it. *Tina was sucking on a sweet.*

sudden adjective
Something that is sudden happens quickly without any warning. *There was a sudden change in the weather.*

> **WORD FAMILY**
> • **suddenly** Suddenly I wasn't hungry any more.

suffer verb **suffers, suffering, suffered**
When you suffer, something hurts you or upsets you.

suffix noun (*plural* **suffixes**)
(*in grammar*) A suffix is a group of letters that are added to the end of a word to change its meaning or make it into a different word class. The suffix *-ly* changes an adjective into an adverb.

sugar noun
a sweet powder that you add to drinks and other foods to make them taste sweet

suggest verb **suggests, suggesting, suggested**
If you suggest something, you say that it would be a good idea.
'Maybe we can stop Auntie from coming,' Jazz suggested, as we clattered downstairs.—Narinder Dhami, Bindi Babes

> **WORD FAMILY**
> • **suggestion** Can I make a suggestion?

suit noun (*plural* **suits**)
a jacket and a pair of trousers or a skirt that are made of the same material and meant to be worn together

suit verb **suits, suiting, suited**
If something suits you, it looks nice on you. *Blue really suits you.*

suitable adjective
Something that is suitable is the right type of thing. *Are these shoes suitable for wearing in wet weather?*

suitcase noun
(*plural* **suitcases**)
a bag with stiff sides that you use for carrying clothes and other things on journeys

a
b
c
d
e
f
g
h
i
j
k
l
m
n
o
p
q
r
s
t
u
v
w
x
y
z

sulk verb **sulks, sulking, sulked**
When you sulk, you are bad-tempered and do not speak to people because you are cross about something.

> **WORD FAMILY**
> • **sulky** Rosie was sulky all morning.
> • **sulkily** 'I don't want anything to eat,' she said sulkily.

sum noun (*plural* **sums**)
1 The sum of two numbers is the number that you get when you add them together. *The sum of 7 and 3 is 10.*
2 When you do a sum, you find an answer to a question in arithmetic by working with numbers. *Have you done all your sums yet?*
3 A sum of money is an amount of money.

summarize verb **summarizes, summarizing, summarized**
To summarize something means to give a summary of it.

summary noun (*plural* **summaries**)
When you give a summary of something, you describe the important parts of it and leave out the parts that are not so important.

summer noun (*plural* **summers**)
the time of the year when the weather is hot and it stays light for longer in the evenings

summit noun (*plural* **summits**)
The summit of a mountain is the top of it.

sun noun
1 The sun is the star that we see shining in the sky during the day. The sun gives the earth heat and light.
2 If you are in the sun, the sun is shining on you. *You shouldn't stay out in the sun for too long otherwise you will burn.*

sunbathe verb **sunbathes, sunbathing, sunbathed**
to lie or sit in the sun so that your skin becomes darker in colour

sunburn noun
If you have sunburn, your skin becomes red and painful because you have spent a long time in the sun.

Sunday noun (*plural* **Sundays**)
the day of the week after Saturday

sunflower noun
(*plural* **sunflowers**)
a big yellow flower that grows very tall and always turns to face the sun

sung verb *see* **sing**

sunglasses noun
dark glasses that you wear to protect your eyes from the bright sun

sunk verb *see* **sink** verb

sunlight noun
light from the sun

sunny adjective **sunnier, sunniest**
When the weather is sunny, the sun is shining.

sunrise noun
the time in the morning when the sun comes up and it becomes light

sunscreen noun
a liquid that you put on your skin to protect it from the sun

sunset noun
the time in the evening when the sun goes down and it becomes dark

sunshine noun
the light and heat that come from the sun

super adjective
Something that is super is very good. *That's a super drawing!*

superlative adjective
(*in grammar*) The superlative form of an adjective is the part that means 'most,' for example 'biggest' is the superlative form of 'big'.

supermarket noun (*plural* **supermarkets**)
a large shop where you can buy food and other things

superstitious adjective
Someone who is superstitious believes that some things will bring you good luck or bad luck.

> **WORD FAMILY**
> • **superstition** I don't believe in those old superstitions.

supper noun (*plural* **suppers**)
a meal or snack that you eat in the evening

supple adjective
Someone who is supple can bend their body very easily.

supply verb **supplies, supplying, supplied**
If someone supplies you with something, they give it or sell it to you.

supply noun (*plural* **supplies**)
If you have a supply of things, you have some things that you are keeping ready to be used when you need them. *We keep a supply of paper in the cupboard.*

support verb **supports, supporting, supported**
1 To support something means to hold it up and stop it from falling down. *These pieces of wood support the roof.*
2 If you support someone, you help them and encourage them to do well. *Which football team do you support?*

suppose verb **supposes, supposing, supposed**
If you suppose that something is true, you think that it is true although you do not know for sure.

sure adjective
1 If you are sure about something, you know that it is definitely true. *I'm sure she lives in this street.*
2 If something is sure to happen, it will definitely happen. *Are you sure you locked the door?*

surf verb **surfs, surfing, surfed**
1 When you surf, you stand on a special board called a **surfboard** and ride in towards the shore on big waves.
2 (*in ICT*) When you surf the Internet, you look at different websites to find information.

surface noun (*plural* **surfaces**)
The surface of something is the top or outside part, not the middle. *We polished the tables to give them a shiny surface.*

surgery noun (*plural* **surgeries**)
the room where you go to see a doctor or dentist

surname noun (*plural* **surnames**)
Your surname is your last name, which is the name you share with other members of your family.

surprise noun (*plural* **surprises**)
1 If something is a surprise, you were not expecting it to happen. *It was a complete surprise when my name was called out.*
2 Surprise is the feeling you have when something happens that you were not expecting. *She looked at me in surprise.*

surprise verb **surprises, surprising, surprised**
If something surprises you, you were not expecting it to happen. *It surprised everyone when Tom won the race.*

> **WORD FAMILY**
> • **surprised** I was really surprised when I came top in the months test.
> • **surprising** It's surprising how many people have asthma.

surrender verb **surrenders, surrendering, surrendered**
When people surrender, they stop fighting or hiding and give themselves up.

surround verb **surrounds, surrounding, surrounded**
To surround a place means to form a circle all around it.

survey noun (*plural* **surveys**)
a set of questions that you ask people to find out information about something

survive verb **survives, surviving, survived**
1 If you survive, you do not die but carry on living. *A few people survived the plane crash.*
2 If something survives, it is not destroyed. *I walked all around the island. Hardly a house had survived intact.*—Michael Morpurgo, The Wreck of the Zanzibar

suspect verb **suspects, suspecting, suspected**
If you suspect that something is true, you have a feeling that it might be true.

a
b
c
d
e
f
g
h
i
j
k
l
m
n
o
p
q
r
s
t
u
v
w
x
y
z

suspense noun
excitement that you feel because you do not know what is going to happen next

suspicious adjective (*say* sus-**pish**-uss)
1 If someone behaves in a suspicious way, they behave in a strange, secret way which makes you think they are doing something wrong.
2 If you are suspicious of someone, you have a feeling that they have done something wrong and you do not trust them.

swallow verb **swallows, swallowing, swallowed**
When you swallow something, you make it go down your throat.

swam verb *see* **swim**

swan noun (*plural* **swans**)
a big white bird with a long neck that lives near water and often swims on the water

swap verb **swaps, swapping, swapped**
When you swap something, you give it to someone and get something else in return.

swarm noun (*plural* **swarms**)
A swarm of insects is a lot of them all flying together.

sway verb **sways, swaying, swayed**
To sway means to move gently from side to side. *The tall trees swayed in the wind.*

sweat verb **sweats, sweating, sweated**
When you sweat, salty liquid comes out from your skin when you are very hot.

sweater noun (*plural* **sweaters**)
a warm jumper

sweatshirt noun (*plural* **sweatshirts**)
a jumper made of thick cotton cloth

sweep verb **sweeps, sweeping, swept**
When you sweep a floor, you clean it by pushing a brush over it.

sweet adjective **sweeter, sweetest**
1 Something that is sweet tastes of sugar.
2 Something that is sweet is very nice. *What a sweet little girl!*

sweet noun (*plural* **sweets**)
1 something small and sweet which you eat as a snack *You shouldn't eat too many sweets.*
2 a pudding

sweetcorn noun
the yellow seeds of a corn plant, which you cook and eat as a vegetable

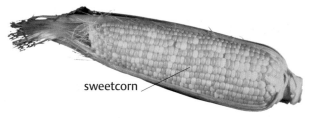

sweetcorn

swell verb **swells, swelling, swelled, swollen**
When something swells, it gets bigger.

WORD FAMILY
• **swollen** My wrist is still very swollen where I bumped it.

swept verb *see* **sweep**

swerve verb **swerves, swerving, swerved**
If a car swerves, it suddenly moves to the side so that it does not hit something. *The bus swerved sharply to avoid a dog in the road.*

swift adjective **swifter, swiftest**
Something that is swift moves very quickly. *The boy grew tall and strong and beautiful, the swiftest runner and the best archer in all the country around.*—Rosemary Sutcliff, Black Ships before Troy

swim verb **swims, swimming, swam, swum**
When you swim, you move through water by floating and moving your arms and legs.

> 🏠 **WORD FAMILY**
> • **swimmer** Are you a good swimmer?

swimming costume noun (*plural* **swimming costumes**)
a piece of clothing that a woman or girl wears when she goes swimming

swimming pool noun (*plural* **swimming pools**)
a large pool that has been built for people to swim in

swimming trunks noun
a piece of clothing that a man or boy wears when he goes swimming

swing verb **swings, swinging, swung**
When something swings, it moves backwards and forwards in the air. *There were monkeys swinging in the trees above us.*

swing noun (*plural* **swings**)
A swing is a seat that hangs down from a frame. You can sit on it and move backwards and forwards.

switch noun (*plural* **switches**)
something that you turn or press to make a machine work or a light come on *Where's the light switch?*

switch verb **switches, switching, switched**
When you switch something on, you turn or press a control so that it starts working. When you switch something off, you turn or press a control so that it stops working.

swollen verb
see **swell**

swoop verb **swoops, swooping, swooped**
When a bird swoops down, it flies downwards quickly. *The owl swooped down on its prey.*

swop verb **swops, swopping, swopped**
Swop is another spelling of **swap**.

sword noun (*plural* **swords**)
a weapon that has a handle and a long, thin, sharp blade

sword

swum verb *see* **swim**

swung verb *see* **swing** verb

syllable noun (*plural* **syllables**) (*say* **sil**-a-bal)
A syllable is one of the sounds or beats in a word. The word chim-pan-zee has three syllables.

symbol noun (*plural* **symbols**)
A symbol is a sign which stands for something or means something. The + symbol means that you add numbers together.

symmetrical adjective
A shape that is symmetrical has two halves that are exactly alike.

symmetry noun
If a shape or object has symmetry, its two halves are exactly alike. The **line of symmetry** in a shape is the line through the middle, which divides the two symmetrical halves.

a b c d e f g h i j k l m n o p q r s t u v w x y z

sympathy noun

If you have sympathy for someone, you feel sorry for them.

> **WORD FAMILY**
> • **sympathetic** Everyone was very sympathetic when I broke my arm.

synagogue noun (*plural* **synagogues**)

(*say* **sin**-a-gog)

a building where Jews pray and worship

synonym noun (*plural* **synonyms**)

(*say* **sin**-a-nim)

a word that means the same as another word *'Courageous' is a synonym of 'brave.'*

syrup noun (*plural* **syrups**)

a very sweet, sticky, liquid

system noun (*plural* **systems**)

1 If you have a system for doing something, you do it in a particular order or way every time.
2 A system is a set of machines that work together. *Our school now has a brand new heating system.*

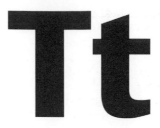

Tt

table noun (*plural* **tables**)

1 a piece of furniture with a flat top that you can put things on
2 a list of numbers or words arranged in rows or columns

tablet noun (*plural* **tablets**)

a small pill with medicine in, which you swallow when you are ill

table tennis noun

a game in which players use a bat to hit a small ball over a table that has a net across the middle

tackle verb **tackles, tackling, tackled**

1 When you tackle a difficult job, you start doing it.
2 If you tackle someone in a game such as football or rugby, you try to get the ball from them.

tactful adjective

If you are tactful, you are careful not to upset someone by saying something unkind. *Mum and Dad and Callum and Jack were very tactful and didn't ask any awkward questions.*—Jacqueline Wilson, Best Friends

tadpole noun (*plural* **tadpoles**)

A tadpole is a tiny animal that lives in water and will turn into a frog, toad, or newt. Tadpoles have long tails and no legs.

tail noun (*plural* **tails**)

1 An animal's tail is the long part at the end of its body.
2 The tail of something is the part at the back of it. *There was smoke coming out from the tail of the aeroplane.*

tail

take verb **takes, taking, took, taken**
1 When you take something, you get hold of it. *I offered him a sweet, and he took one.*
2 If you take something to a place, you have it with you when you go there. *Remember to take your PE kit to school.*
3 If someone takes something, they steal it.
4 If someone takes you to a place, you go there with them. *Dad promised to take us to the cinema.*
5 (*in mathematics*) If you take one number away from another, you subtract it.
6 When a rocket takes off, it goes up into space.

talc *or* **talcum powder** noun
a fine powder you put on your skin to make it feel smooth and smell nice

tale noun (*plural* **tales**)
a story

talent noun (*plural* **talents**)
If you have a talent for something, you can do it very well. *Aneeta has a talent for singing.*

> **WORD FAMILY**
> • **talented** She's a very talented artist.

talk verb **talks, talking, talked**
When you talk, you speak to someone.

tall adjective **taller, tallest**
1 Someone who is tall measures a lot from their head to their feet. *I'm quite tall for my age.*
2 A tall tree or building is very high.

Talmud noun
The Talmud is a book of writings about the Jewish religion.

tame adjective **tamer, tamest**
An animal or bird that is tame is not wild or fierce, and is not afraid of people.

tan noun
When you have a tan, your skin is darker than usual because you have been in the hot sun.

tangle noun (*plural* **tangles**)
If things are in a tangle, they are all twisted or knotted together and it is difficult to separate them.

> **WORD FAMILY**
> • **tangled** My hair was all tangled and untidy.

tank noun (*plural* **tanks**)
1 a very large container that you keep liquid in *There was a leak in the water tank.*

2 a very strong, heavy truck that is used in war and moves on metal tracks, not wheels

tanka noun (*plural* **tankas**)
a short poem with five lines and a fixed number of syllables in each line

tanker noun (*plural* **tankers**)
1 a large ship that carries oil
2 a large lorry that carries milk or petrol

tap noun (*plural* **taps**)
a handle which you turn to start or stop water flowing through a pipe

tap verb **taps, tapping, tapped**
When you tap something, you hit it gently. *I tapped on the window.*

tape noun (*plural* **tapes**)
1 Sticky tape is a strip of sticky paper that you use for sticking things together.
2 Tape is a special magnetic strip that you can record sound and picture on.

tape verb **tapes, taping, taped**
To tape sound or pictures means to record them.

tape measure noun
(*plural* **tape measures**)
a long strip of cloth or plastic with measurements marked on it, which you use for measuring things

tape measure

a b c d e f g h i j k l m n o p q r s t u v w x y z

203

tape recorder noun (*plural* **tape recorders**)
a machine that you use for recording music on tape and playing it back

target noun (*plural* **targets**)
something that you aim at and try to hit when you are shooting or throwing something

tart noun (*plural* **tarts**) a type of food that has pastry on the bottom and fruit, meat, or vegetables on top

fruit tart

tartan noun
a type of woollen material from Scotland with a special pattern of coloured squares on it

task noun (*plural* **tasks**)
a job that you have to do *I was given the task of washing-up.*

taste verb **tastes, tasting, tasted**
1 When you taste food, you eat a small amount to see what it is like.
2 The way something tastes is the flavour that it has. *The food tasted horrible.*

taste noun
1 The taste of something is what it is like when you eat it. *I don't like the taste of bananas.*
2 Your sense of taste is how well you can recognize things when you eat them.

> **WORD FAMILY**
> • **tasty** We had a very tasty meal.

taught verb *see* **teach**

tax noun (*plural* **taxes**)
money that people have to pay to the government

taxi noun (*plural* **taxis**)
a car that you can travel in if you pay the driver

tea noun
1 a hot drink that you make by pouring boiling water over the dried leaves of the tea plant
2 a meal that you eat in the afternoon or early evening

teach verb **teaches, teaching, taught**
When you teach someone something, you tell them about it or show them how to do it. *Miss Cummings teaches us maths.*

> **WORD FAMILY**
> • A **teacher** is someone who teaches people.

team noun (*plural* **teams**)
a group of people who work together or play together on the same side in a game

teapot noun (*plural* **teapots**)
a container with a spout that you use for making and pouring tea

tear verb **tears, tearing, tore, torn** (*rhymes with* fair)
When you tear something, you pull it apart so that it splits or makes a hole. *Mind you don't tear your dress.*

tear noun (*plural* **tears**) (*rhymes with* fear)
Tears are drops of salty water that come from your eyes when you cry.

tease verb **teases, teasing, teased**
To tease someone means to make fun of them. *People often tease me because I'm short.*

technology noun
Technology is using science and machines to help people in their lives.

teddy bear noun (*plural* **teddy bears**)
a stuffed toy bear

teenager noun (*plural* **teenagers**)
someone who is between thirteen and nineteen years old

teeth noun *see* **tooth**

telephone noun (*plural* **telephones**)
A telephone is a machine that you use to speak to someone who is far away from you. It is also called a **phone**.

teenager

telephone verb **telephones, telephoning, telephoned**
When you telephone someone, you use a telephone to speak to them.

telescope noun
(*plural* **telescopes**)
A telescope is a tube with special lenses in. When you look through a telescope, things that are far away look bigger and closer.

television noun
(*plural* **televisions**)
a machine that picks up signals that are sent through the air and changes them into pictures and sound so that people can watch them

telescope

tell verb **tells, telling, told**
1 When you tell someone something, you speak to them about it. *Uncle Jack told us all about his life at sea.*
2 If you can tell the time, you can look at a clock and say what time it is.
3 To tell someone off means to speak to them angrily because they have done something wrong.

temper noun
1 Your temper is how you are feeling. If you are in a good temper, you are happy and cheerful. If you are in a bad temper, you are cross and grumpy.
2 If you are in a temper, you are very angry. If you lose your temper, you suddenly become very angry.

temperature noun
1 The temperature of something is how hot or cold it is. *The temperature today is 22 degrees.*
2 If you have a temperature, your body is hotter than usual because you are ill.

temple noun (*plural* **temples**)
a place where people go to pray and worship a god

temporary adjective
Something that is temporary only lasts for a short time. *We're having our lessons in a temporary classroom until the new classroom is ready.*

tempt verb **tempts, tempting, tempted**
If something tempts you, it seems nice and you want it, but you think it would be wrong or dangerous.

ten noun (*plural* **tens**)
the number 10

tender adjective **tenderer, tenderest**
1 Someone who is tender is kind and loving.
2 Food that is tender is soft and easy to eat. *The meat was lovely and tender.*

tennis noun
a game in which players use a special racket to hit a ball backwards and forwards over a net

tennis racket

tense noun (*plural* **tenses**)
The different tenses of a verb are the different forms that you use to show whether you are talking about the past, present, or future. *The past tense of come is came.*

tent noun (*plural* **tents**)
A tent is a shelter made of cloth that is stretched over poles. You sleep in a tent when you go camping.

tentacle noun (*plural* **tentacles**)
The tentacles of a sea animal such as an octopus are the long parts that it can move about.

term noun (*plural* **terms**)
A school term is a time when you go to school and are not on holiday.

terrace noun (*plural* **terraces**)
a row of houses that are all joined together

terrible adjective
Something that is terrible is very bad.
The two brothers were overcome with jealousy, and they hatched a terrible plan.—Pomme Clayton, The Orchard Book of Stories from the Seven Seas

terrify verb **terrifies, terrifying, terrified**
If something terrifies you, it makes you feel very frightened.

WORD FAMILY
• **terrified** I was absolutely terrified!
• **terrifying** It was a terrifying experience.

a
b
c
d
e
f
g
h
i
j
k
l
m
n
o
p
q
r
s
t
u
v
w
x
y
z

territory noun (plural **territories**)
Someone's territory is the land that they own or use.

terror noun
a feeling of very great fear
Violet gave a little cry of terror, but flicked the switch on.—Lemony Snicket, The Bad Beginning

terrorist noun (plural **terrorists**)
someone who hurts or kills people to try to make a government do what he or she wants

test noun (plural **tests**)
a set of questions that you have to answer to show what you have learned *I got all the words right in my spelling test.*

test verb **tests, testing, tested**
1 To test someone means to give them questions to answer to show what they have learned.
2 To test something means to use it so that you can find out whether it works. *Now it is time to test our new invention.*

tetrahedron noun (plural **tetrahedrons**)
a solid shape that has four triangular sides

text noun (plural **texts**)
a piece of writing

text verb **texts, texting, texted**
When you text someone, you send them a text message.

textbook noun (plural **textbooks**)
a book which gives you information about a subject

text message noun (plural **text messages**)
a written message that you send to someone on a mobile phone

texture noun (plural **textures**)
The texture of something is what it feels like when you touch it. Lamb's wool has a lovely soft texture.

than conjunction & pronoun
compared with another person or thing
My brother is smaller than me.

thank verb **thanks, thanking, thanked**
When you thank someone, you tell them that you are grateful for something they have given you or done for you. *I thanked my uncle and aunt for their present.*

that, those adjective
the one there *That book is mine.*

thatched adjective
A thatched house has a roof made of reeds or straw.

thatched roof

thaw verb **thaws, thawing, thawed**
When something thaws, it melts and is no longer frozen. *The sun came out and the snow began to thaw.*

theatre noun (plural **theatres**)
a place where plays and shows are performed and people can go to watch them

theme noun (plural **themes**)
The theme of a book or film is the main idea that it is about.

theme park noun (plural **theme parks**)
a place where you can go on rides and take part in fun activities

then adverb
1 after that *I had breakfast and then I went to school.*
2 at that time *I was only five years old then.*

theory noun (plural **theories**)
an idea that someone suggests as a way of explaining how something works

there adverb
in that place *You can sit there.*

therefore adverb
so *We haven't got very much money and therefore we can't go on holiday.*

thermometer noun (plural **thermometers**)
something that you use for measuring temperature

thermometer

thesaurus noun
(*plural* **thesauruses**)
a book which gives
you lists of words
that have similar
meanings

these adjective *see*
this

thick adjective
thicker, thickest
1 Something that is thick is wide
and not thin. *He cut himself a thick
slice of chocolate cake.*
2 Thick clothes are made of heavy material.
3 A thick liquid is not very runny.

thief noun (*plural* **thieves**)
someone who steals things

thigh noun (*plural* **thighs**)
Your thighs are the top parts of your legs.

thin adjective **thinner, thinnest**
1 Something that is thin is not very thick or
wide. *Cut the bread into thin slices.*
2 Someone who is thin is not very fat.
3 A thin liquid is runny.

thing noun (*plural* **things**)
an object, or anything that is not a person,
animal, or plant *A pen is a thing you use to
write with.*

think verb **thinks, thinking, thought**
1 When you think, you have thoughts and ideas
in your mind. *Think carefully before you answer
the question.*
2 If you think that something is true, you believe
that it is true, but you do not know for sure.
I think we break up next Friday.

third adjective
The third thing is the one that comes after
the second.

third noun
One third of something is one of three equal
parts that the thing is divided into. It can also
be written as ⅓.

third person noun
(*in grammar*) When you use the third person,
you use the words 'he' or 'she' to write about
someone in a story.

thirsty adjective **thirstier, thirstiest**
If you are thirsty, you feel that you want to
drink something.

thirteen noun
the number 13

thirty noun
the number 30

this, these adjective
the one here *This pencil is mine. These books
are all very interesting.*

thistle noun (*plural* **thistles**)
a wild plant that has prickly leaves and
purple flowers

thorn noun (*plural* **thorns**)
a sharp, prickly point that grows on some
plants

thoroughly adverb
1 If you do a job thoroughly, you do it carefully
and properly.
2 completely *I was thoroughly exhausted.*

those adjective *see* **that**

though adverb (*rhymes with* go)
although *It was very cold though it didn't
snow.*

thought verb *see* **think**

thought noun (*plural* **thoughts**)
an idea you think of

thoughtful adjective
1 If you look thoughtful, you look quiet, as if
you are thinking about something.
2 If you are thoughtful, you are kind and think
about what other people want.

thousand noun (*plural* **thousands**)
the number 1000

thread noun (*plural* **threads**)
a long, thin piece of cotton that you use
for sewing

thread verb **threads, threading, threaded**
When you thread a needle, you put a thread
through it so that you can use it for sewing.

threaten verb **threatens, threatening,
threatened**
To threaten someone means to say that you
will do something nasty to them.

a
b
c
d
e
f
g
h
i
j
k
l
m
n
o
p
q
r
s
t
u
v
w
x
y
z

three noun (plural **threes**)
the number 3

three-dimensional
adjective
A three-dimensional object
is solid rather than flat. A
cube is a three-dimensional
shape or 3D.

threw verb *see* throw

thrill noun (plural **thrills**)
If something gives you a thrill,
it is very exciting and enjoyable.

> **WORD FAMILY**
> • **thrilling** It was a thrilling adventure.

throat noun (plural **throats**)
Your throat is the part at the back of your
mouth where you swallow food and drink.

throb verb **throbs, throbbing, throbbed**
If a part of your body throbs, it hurts
a lot. *My knee was throbbing and I could
hardly walk.*

throne noun (plural **thrones**)
a special chair that a king or queen sits on

through preposition (*rhymes with* threw)
from one side of something to the other
He climbed through the window.

throw verb **throws, throwing, threw, thrown**
1 When you throw something, you hold it in
your hand and then push it away so that it
flies through the air. *Throw the ball to me.*
2 When you throw something away, you get rid
of it because you do not want it any more.

thud noun (plural **thuds**)
a dull banging sound *The book fell to the
ground with a thud.*

thumb noun (plural **thumbs**)
Your thumb is the short, thick finger at the
side of your hand.

thump verb **thumps, thumping, thumped**
To thump someone means to hit them hard.

thunder noun
the loud, rumbling noise that you hear after
a flash of lightning in a storm

Thursday noun (plural **Thursdays**)
the day after Wednesday

3D object

tick noun (plural **ticks**)
a small mark like this ✓ that shows
that something is right

tick verb **ticks, ticking, ticked**
1 When you tick something, you
put a tick next to it. *I ticked all the
right answers.*
2 When a clock ticks, it makes
a regular clicking sound.

ticket noun (plural **tickets**)
a piece of paper that you buy so that you
can travel on a bus or train or get into a
place such as a cinema or theatre

tickle verb **tickles, tickling, tickled**
When you tickle someone, you touch
them lightly with your fingers to make
them laugh.

tide noun (plural **tides**)
The tide is the regular movement of the
sea towards the land and then away from
the land.

tidy adjective **tidier, tidiest**
If a place is tidy, everything is in the
right place and there is no mess.
Is your room tidy?

tie verb **ties, tying, tied**
To tie something means to fasten it with
a knot or a bow. *I tied my shoelaces.*

tie noun (plural **ties**)
1 a strip of material that you wear round
your neck, under the collar of a shirt
2 If there is a tie in a game,
two people or teams
have the same
number of points.
*The match ended
in a tie.*

tiger noun
(plural **tigers**)
A tiger is
a large wild
cat that lives
in Asia. It
has orange
fur with black
stripes. A
female tiger
is called
a **tigress**.

tiger

tight adjective **tighter, tightest**
1 Tight clothes fit your body closely and are not loose or baggy. *Those trousers look a bit tight.*
2 A tight knot is tied very firmly and is difficult to undo.

> **WORD FAMILY**
> • **tightly** The shoes fitted me quite tightly.
> • **tighten** Why don't you tighten your belt?

tights noun
a piece of clothing that women and girls wear over their feet, legs, and bottom

tile noun (*plural* **tiles**)
Tiles are thin pieces of baked clay that people use to cover walls or floors.

till conjunction & preposition
until *Wait till I'm ready!*

till noun (*plural* **tills**)
a machine that people use in a shop to keep money in and add up how much customers have to pay

tilt verb **tilts, tilting, tilted**
To tilt something means to tip it up so that it slopes.

timber noun
wood that people use for making things

time noun (*plural* **times**)
1 Time is the thing that we measure in seconds, minutes, hours, days, weeks, months, and years. *What time is it?*
2 If it is time to do something, it should be done now. *It's time to leave.*
3 If you do something one or two times, you do it once or twice. *I've already called you three times!*

times preposition
(*in mathematics*) One number times another number is one number multiplied by another number. *Two times four equals eight.*

timetable noun (*plural* **timetables**)
a list of times when things will happen or buses or trains will leave

timid adjective
Someone who is timid is shy and not very brave.
'Who's there?' he said in a timid voice. —James Riordan, retelling of Pinocchio

tin noun (*plural* **tins**)
1 a round metal container that food is sold in *I'll open a tin of beans for tea.*
2 a metal container for putting things in

tiny adjective **tinier, tiniest**
Something that is tiny is very small.
Ron pressed a tiny silver button on the dashboard. —J. K. Rowling, Harry Potter and the Chamber of Secrets

tip noun (*plural* **tips**)
1 The tip of something long and thin is the part right at the end of it.
2 If you give someone a tip, you give them a small amount of money to thank them for helping you.
3 A tip is a rubbish dump.

tip verb **tips, tipping, tipped**
When you tip something, you move it so that it is no longer straight. *Don't tip your chair back.*

tiptoe verb **tiptoes, tiptoeing, tiptoed**
When you tiptoe, you walk quietly on your toes.
We tiptoed past all the old clocks and rushed up the stairs to the rusty iron door. —Jostein Gaarder, The Frog Castle

tired adjective
1 If you are tired, you feel as if you need to sleep.
2 If you are tired of something, you are bored or fed up with it.

tissue noun (*plural* **tissues**)
1 Tissue paper is very thin, soft paper that you use for wrapping up things made of glass or china to stop them breaking.
2 A tissue is a paper handkerchief.

title noun (*plural* **titles**)
1 The title of a book, film, picture, or piece of music is its name.
2 Someone's title is the word like Dr, Mr, and Mrs that is put in front of their name.

to preposition
When you go to a place, you go there. *We're going to Spain next week.*

toad noun (*plural* **toads**)
A toad is an animal that looks like a big frog. It has rough, dry skin and lives on land.

toad

toadstool noun
(plural **toadstools**)
a plant that looks like a mushroom but is poisonous to eat

toadstool

toast noun
a slice of bread that has been cooked until it is crisp and brown

today noun & adverb
this day *I'm not very well today.*

toddler noun (plural **toddlers**)
a young child who is just beginning to walk

toe noun (plural **toes**)
Your toes are the parts of your body on the ends of your feet.

together adverb
1 When you join or put things together, you put them with each other. *I stuck two pieces of paper together.*
2 When people do something together, they do it at the same time as each other. *They all sang together.*

toilet noun (plural **toilets**)
a large bowl with a seat that you use when you need to empty waste from your body

told verb *see* **tell**

tolerant adjective
If you are tolerant, you accept other people and respect their opinions.

tomato noun
(plural **tomatoes**)
a soft, round, red fruit that you can eat raw in a salad or cook as a vegetable

tomato

tomorrow noun & adverb
the day after today *I'll see you tomorrow.*

ton noun (plural **tons**)
We can measure weight in tons. One ton is about 1,016 kilograms.

tone noun (plural **tones**)
The tone of your voice is how it sounds when you speak, for example whether it sounds happy or angry. *He spoke in an angry tone of voice.*

tongue noun (plural **tongues**)
(*rhymes with* sung)
Your tongue is the part inside your mouth that you can move about and use for speaking.

tonight noun & adverb
this evening or night *I'll phone you tonight.*

tonne noun (plural **tonnes**)
We can measure weight in tons. One tonne is 1,000 kilograms.

too adverb
1 also *Can I come too?*
2 more than you need *Don't use too much salt.*

took verb *see* **take**

tool noun (plural **tools**)
A tool is something that you use to help you to do a job. Hammers and saws are tools.

saw

tooth noun (plural **teeth**)
1 Your teeth are the hard, white parts inside your mouth which you use for biting and chewing.
2 The teeth on a comb or saw are the sharp, pointed parts.

> **WORD FAMILY**
> • **Toothache** is a pain in one of your teeth. A **toothbrush** is a small brush that you use for cleaning your teeth. **toothpaste** is a special thick cream that you use for cleaning your teeth.

top noun (plural **tops**)
1 The top of something is the highest part of it. *We climbed right to the top of the hill.*
2 The top on a bottle or jar is the lid.
3 A top is a piece of clothing that you wear on the top part of your body, over your chest and arms. *She was wearing black trousers and a red top.*

topic noun (plural **topics**)
a subject that you are writing or talking about

torch noun (*plural* **torches**)
an electric light that you can carry about with you

torch

tore, torn verb
see **tear** verb

tornado noun
(*plural* **tornadoes**)
(*say* tor-**nay**-doh)
a very strong wind

tortoise noun (*plural* **tortoises**)
A tortoise is an animal that has four legs and a hard shell over its body. Tortoises move slowly and hide their head and legs inside their shell when they are in danger.

toss verb **tosses, tossing, tossed**
1 When you toss something, you throw it through the air. *She tossed her apple core into the bin.*
2 When you toss a coin, you throw it into the air to see which way it lands.

total noun
The total is the amount that you get when you have added everything up.

total adjective
complete *There was total silence in the hall.*

> **WORD FAMILY**
> • **totally** That idea is totally ridiculous!

touch verb **touches, touching, touched**
1 When you touch something, you feel it with your hand.
2 When two things are touching, they are right next to each other, with no space between them.

tough adjective **tougher, toughest** (*say* tuff)
1 Something that is tough is very strong. *The ropes are made of tough nylon.*
2 Someone who is tough is brave and strong.

tour noun (*plural* **tours**)
When you go on a tour, you visit a lot of different places.

tourist noun (*plural* **tourists**)
someone who is visiting a place on holiday

tournament noun (*plural* **tournaments**)
a competition in which a lot of different people or teams play matches against each other until a winner is found

tow verb **tows, towing, towed**
(*rhymes with* low)
To tow something means to pull it along. *The car was towing a caravan.*

towards preposition
in the direction of *He walked towards the school.*

towel noun (*plural* **towels**)
a piece of cloth that you use for drying things that are wet

tower noun (*plural* **towers**)
a tall, narrow part of a building

town noun (*plural* **towns**)
A town is a place where a lot of people live close to each other. A town is smaller than a city.

toy noun
(*plural* **toys**)
something that children can play with

slinky toy

trace verb **traces, tracing, traced**
1 When you trace a picture, you copy it using thin paper that you can see through.
2 To trace something means to find it by getting information and following clues.

track noun (*plural* **tracks**)
1 The tracks that a person or animal leaves are the marks that they leave on the ground as they walk.
2 a path *We walked along a narrow track by the river.*
3 A railway track is a railway line.
4 A racing track is a piece of ground with lines marked on it so that people can use it for racing.

tractor noun (*plural* **tractors**)
a strong, heavy truck with large wheels that people drive on a farm and use for pulling farm machines

tractor

a
b
c
d
e
f
g
h
i
j
k
l
m
n
o
p
q
r
s
t
u
v
w
x
y
z

trade noun
When people do trade, they buy and sell things. *The shops do a lot of trade at Christmas.*

trademark noun (*plural* **trademarks**)
a picture or name that a company always puts on the things that it makes

tradition noun (*plural* **traditions**)
If something is a tradition, people have done it in the same way for a very long time. *Dressing up at Hallowe'en is a tradition.*

> **WORD FAMILY**
> • **traditional** It's traditional to throw flowers at a wedding.

traffic noun
cars, buses, bicycles, lorries, and other things that travel on roads *Its dangerous to play on the road because of the traffic.*

tragedy noun (*plural* **tragedies**)
something very sad that happens, especially something in which people are hurt or killed

trail noun (*plural* **trails**)
1 a rough path across fields or through woods
2 the smells or marks that an animal leaves behind as it goes along *We were able to follow the animal's trail.*

trailer noun (*plural* **trailers**)
1 a truck that is pulled along behind a car or lorry and used for carrying things
2 a short part of a film or television programme that is shown to people to encourage them to watch it

train noun (*plural* **trains**)
something that carries passengers or goods on a railway

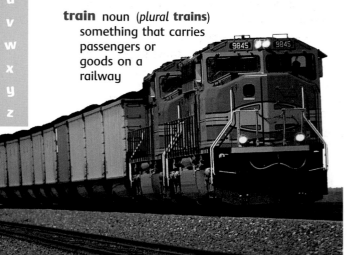

train verb **trains, training, trained**
1 To train a person or animal means to teach them how to do something. *The dog had been trained to sit up and beg for bits of food.*
2 When you train, you practise the skills you need to do a sport.

trainer noun (*plural* **trainers**)
1 A trainer is someone who trains people or animals.
2 Trainers are shoes that you wear for running or doing sport.

tram noun (*plural* **trams**)
a type of bus which runs along rails in the road

trampoline noun (*plural* **trampolines**)
a large piece of thick cloth that is joined to a metal frame and is used for jumping up and down on

transfer verb **transfers, transferring, transferred**
1 If you transfer something from one place to another, you move it. *I transferred some pencils from the tin into my pencil case.*
2 When you transfer to a new school, you start going there.

translate verb **translates, translating, translated**
If you translate something, you change it from one language into another.

transparent adjective
If something is transparent, you can see through it. *Glass is a transparent material.*

transport noun
anything that is used to take people, animals, or things from one place to another *Buses, trains, and lorries are all forms of transport.*

trap noun (*plural* **traps**)
something that is used to catch a person or an animal *The police laid a trap to catch the robbers.*

trapdoor noun (*plural* **trapdoors**)
a door in the floor or ceiling which you can open to make people fall through

trapezium noun (*plural* **trapeziums**)
A trapezium is a shape with four sides. Two of the sides are parallel, but they are not the same length.

trapped adjective
If you are trapped in a place, you are stuck there and cannot get out.

travel verb **travels, travelling, travelled**
When you travel, you go from one place to another. *They travelled right across America.*

trawler noun
(*plural* **trawlers**)
a big fishing boat that pulls a large net along the sea bottom to catch a lot of fish

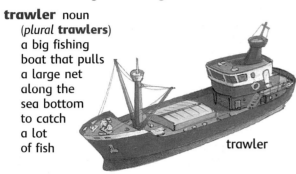
trawler

tray noun (*plural* **trays**)
a flat piece of wood, metal, or plastic that you use for carrying cups, plates, and other things

treacherous adjective
1 If someone is treacherous, you cannot trust them.
2 Something that is treacherous is very dangerous. *The pavement was treacherous because it was so icy.*

tread verb **treads, treading, trod, trodden**
If you tread on something, you walk on it. *Mind you don't tread on that spider.*

treasure noun
gold, silver, jewels, and other valuable things *I'm sure there must be buried treasure on the island!*

treat verb **treats, treating, treated**
1 The way in which you treat someone is the way you behave towards them. *Some people don't treat their animals very well.*
2 When doctors treat someone, they give them medicine or do things to them to make them better when they are ill.

> **WORD FAMILY**
> • **treatment** Some animals suffer cruel treatment from their owners.

treat noun (*plural* **treats**)
something special that you enjoy *We went to the cinema as a birthday treat.*

tree noun (*plural* **trees**)
a tall plant that has a thick trunk, branches, and leaves

monkey puzzle tree

tremble verb **trembles, trembling, trembled**
When you tremble, your body shakes because you are cold or frightened. *Then the king began to tremble and was very much afraid.*—Hugh Lofting, The Story of Doctor Dolittle

tremendous adjective
Something that is tremendous is huge or very good. *The play was a tremendous success.*

trespass verb **trespasses, trespassing, trespassed**
To trespass means to go onto someone else's land, without asking them if you can.

trial noun (*plural* **trials**)
1 When you give something a trial, you try it to see how well it works.
2 When there is a trial, a prisoner and witnesses are questioned in a court to decide whether the prisoner has done something wrong.

triangle noun (*plural* **triangles**)
a shape with three straight edges and three angles

tribe noun (*plural* **tribes**)
a group of people who live together and are ruled by a chief

trick noun (*plural* **tricks**)
1 something that you do to cheat someone or make them look silly *I thought my friends were planning to play a trick on me.*
2 something clever that you have learned to do *Can you do any card tricks?*

trick verb **tricks, tricking, tricked**
To trick someone means to make them believe something that is not true.

trickle verb **trickles, trickling, trickled**
When water trickles, it moves very slowly. *Water was trickling down the necks of the three men and into their shoes.*—Roald Dahl, Fantastic Mr Fox

a b c d e f g h i j k l m n o p q r s **t** u v w x y z

213

tricycle noun
(plural **tricycles**)
a bicycle with
three wheels

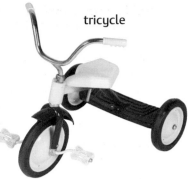
tricycle

tried verb see **try**

trigger noun
(plural **triggers**)
the part of a
gun that you
pull with your
finger to fire it

trim verb **trims,
trimming, trimmed**
To trim something means to cut it so that it
looks neat and tidy. *I had my hair trimmed.*

trip verb **trips, tripping, tripped**
If you trip, you catch your foot on something
and nearly fall over.

trip noun (plural **trips**)
a short journey *We went on a school trip
to France.*

triumph noun (plural **triumphs**)
If something is a triumph, it is a great success.

📖 **WORD FAMILY**
• **triumphant** 'I was right,' he said in a triumphant
voice.
• **triumphantly** Ruby looked at me triumphantly.

trod verb see **tread**

troll noun (plural **trolls**)
a fierce giant in stories

trolley noun
(plural **trolleys**)
a large container
on wheels that you
can put things in
and push along

troops noun
soldiers

trophy noun
(plural **trophies**)
a cup that you
can win

trophy

tropical adjective
A tropical place has
a very hot, wet climate.
*A lot of endangered
animals live in
tropical rainforests.*

trot verb **trots, trotting, trotted**
When a horse trots, it runs but does not
gallop. When a person trots, they run quite
slowly.

trouble noun (plural **troubles**)
1 If something causes trouble for you, it causes
problems for you or upsets you.
2 If you are in trouble, you have a problem or
someone is cross with you. *You'll be in trouble
when dad sees this mess!*

trough noun (plural **troughs**) (say **troff**)
a long, narrow container that holds food or
water for farm animals

trousers noun
a piece of clothing that you wear over your
legs and bottom

trout noun (plural **trout**)
a fish that lives in rivers and lakes and can be
cooked and eaten

truant noun (plural **truants**) (say **troo**-ant)
To play truant means to stay away from
school without permission.

truce noun (plural **truces**)
an agreement between two people to stop
fighting or arguing for a while

truck noun (plural **trucks**)
a small lorry

trudge verb **trudges, trudging, trudged**
When you trudge along, you walk along
slowly, with heavy steps.
*He trudged home soaking wet, hardly able to
drag one foot after another.*—James Riordan,
retelling of Pinocchio

true adjective **truer, truest**
Something that is true is
real and not made-up or
pretended. *Is this
really a true story?*

trumpet noun
(plural **trumpets**)
A trumpet is a musical
instrument made of
brass. You blow into it
and press down
buttons to make
different notes.

trumpet
player

a b c d e f g h i j k l m n o p q r s t u v w x y z

trunk noun
(*plural* **trunks**)
1 The trunk on a tree is the thick stem that grows up out of the ground.
2 An elephant's trunk is its long nose.
3 A trunk is a large box that you use for carrying things on a journey.

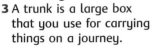
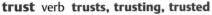
travel trunk

trust verb **trusts, trusting, trusted**
If you trust someone, you believe that they are good and honest and will not hurt you or tell you lies.

truth noun
The truth is something that is true. *Is he telling the truth?*

truthful adjective
Someone who is truthful tells the truth.

try verb **tries, trying, tried**
1 If you try to do something, you make an effort to do it. *I tried to climb that tree, but I couldn't.*
2 If you try something, you do it or use it to see what it is like. *Have you ever tried ice skating?*

T-shirt noun (*plural* **T-shirts**)
A T-shirt is a piece of clothing that you wear on the top half of your body. It has a round neck and short sleeves.

tub noun (*plural* **tubs**)
a container *We bought a tub of chocolate ice cream.*

tube noun (*plural* **tubes**)
1 a long, thin container that you can squeeze a thick liquid out of *We need a new tube of toothpaste.*
2 a long, round, hollow thing *The picture was rolled up in a tube.*

tuck verb **tucks, tucking, tucked**
If you tuck a piece of clothing in, you push the ends of it into another piece of clothing. *He tucked his shirt into his trousers.*

Tuesday noun (*plural* **Tuesdays**)
the day after Monday

tug verb **tugs, tugging, tugged**
When you tug something, you pull it hard. *I tugged the door, but it wouldn't open.*

tumble verb **tumbles, tumbling, tumbled**
To tumble means to fall. *He tumbled off the wall.*

tumble-drier noun (*plural* **tumble-driers**)
a machine that dries clothes by turning them over and over in warm air

tummy noun (*plural* **tummies**)
Your tummy is your stomach.

tuna noun (*plural* **tuna**)
a large sea fish that you can eat

tune noun (*plural* **tunes**)
a group of musical notes which make a nice sound when they are played in order

tunnel noun (*plural* **tunnels**)
a long hole under the ground that you can walk or drive through

turban noun (*plural* **turbans**)
a long piece of material that you wear wrapped round your head

turkey noun (*plural* **turkeys**)
a large bird that is kept on farms for its meat

turn verb **turns, turning, turned**
1 When you turn round, you move round. *I turned round to see who was behind me.*
2 When you turn something, you move it round. *He turned the key in the lock.*
3 To turn means to become. *A lot of leaves turn red and orange in the autumn.*
4 To turn into something means to change and become that thing. *Tadpoles turn into frogs.*

turn noun (*plural* **turns**)
If it is your turn to do something, you are the person who should do it next.

turtle noun (*plural* **turtles**)
a sea animal that looks like a tortoise

a b c d e f g h i j k l m n o p q r s t u v w x y z

tusk noun (*plural* **tusks**)
An elephant's tusks are its two very long, pointed teeth.

TV noun (*plural* **TVs**)
a television

twelve noun
the number 12

twenty noun
the number 20

twice adverb
If something happens twice, it happens two times.

twig noun (*plural* **twigs**)
a very small, thin branch on a tree

twin noun (*plural* **twins**)
Twins are two children who are born to the same mother at the same time.

twinkle verb **twinkles, twinkling, twinkled**
If something twinkles, it shines with little flashes of light. *We could see the stars twinkling in the sky above us.*

twirl verb **twirls, twirling, twirled**
To twirl means to spin round and round.

twist verb **twists, twisting, twisted**
1 When you twist something, you turn it round. *She twisted the lid off the jar.*
2 When you twist things together, you turn them round each other so that they become fixed together.

two noun (*plural* **twos**)
the number 2

two-dimensional adjective
A two-dimensional shape is flat rather than solid. A square is a two-dimensional shape.

type noun (*plural* **types**)
A type is a kind or sort. *What type of car have your parents got?*

type verb **types, typing, typed**
When you type, you write with a typewriter or computer keyboard.

typical adjective
Something that is typical is normal and usual.

tyre verb (*plural* **tyres**)
a circle of rubber that goes round the outside of a wheel

Uu

ugly adjective **uglier, ugliest**
Something that is ugly is horrible to look at.

umbrella noun
(*plural* **umbrellas**)
a round cover that you hold over your head to keep the rain off you

umberella

unable adjective
If you are unable to do something, you cannot do it. *The rocks were heavy and we were unable to move them.*

unbelievable adjective
If something is unbelievable, it is so strange that you cannot believe it.

uncertain adjective
If you are uncertain about something, you are not sure about it. *She was uncertain what to do next.*

uncle noun (*plural* **uncles**)
Your uncle is the brother of your mother or father, or your aunt's husband.

uncomfortable adjective
1 If you are uncomfortable, part of your body hurts or is not relaxed.
Edmund was already feeling uncomfortable from having eaten too many sweets, and when he heard that the Lady he had made friends with was a dangerous witch he felt even more uncomfortable. —C. S. Lewis, The Lion, the Witch and the Wardrobe
2 If a chair or bed is uncomfortable, it does not feel nice when you sit on it or lie on it.

> **WORD FAMILY**
> • **uncomfortably** The bed was uncomfortably hard.

unconscious adjective (*say* un-**kon**-shuss)
When you are unconscious, you are in a very deep sleep and cannot understand what is happening around you. *If you bang your head, sometimes you might be unconscious for a few minutes.*

under preposition
1 below *The cat is under the table.*
2 less than *If you are under 17 you are not allowed to drive a car.*

underground adjective
Something that is underground is under the ground. *They escaped and hid in an underground cave.*

underground noun
An underground is a railway that runs through tunnels under the ground. *You can travel around London by bus or on the Underground.*

undergrowth noun
bushes and plants that grow thickly together under trees

underline verb **underlines, underlining, underlined**
When you underline a word, you draw a straight line underneath it.

underneath preposition
under *The cat was sitting underneath the table.*

understand verb **understands, understanding, understood**
If you can understand something, you know what it means or how it works. *I don't understand what you're saying.*

underwater adjective
Something that is underwater is under the water. *They use special underwater cameras to film sea creatures.*

undo verb **undoes, undoing, undid, undone**
1 When you undo something, you open it so that it is no longer tied or fastened. *I can't undo my shoelaces.*
2 When you undo a change you have made on a computer, you change it back.

undress verb **undresses, undressing, undressed**
When you undress, you take your clothes off.

unemployed adjective
Someone who is unemployed does not have a job.

uneven adjective
Something that is uneven is not smooth or flat. *The road was quite uneven and bumpy.*

unexpected adjective
If something is unexpected, it is surprising because you did not expect it to happen. *We had an unexpected visitor.*

unfair adjective
If something is unfair, it is not fair or right because it treats some people badly.

unfit adjective
If you are unfit, you are not very fit so you cannot run around very well.

unfortunate adjective
If something is unfortunate, it happens because of bad luck.

> **WORD FAMILY**
> • **unfortunately** Unfortunately, the other team scored right at the end of the game.

ungrateful adjective
If you are ungrateful, you do not thank someone when they have helped you or given you something.

unhappy adjective **unhappier, unhappiest**
If you are unhappy, you are sad and not happy.

unhealthy adjective
1 If you are unhealthy, you are not strong and healthy.
2 Things that are unhealthy are not good for you and can make you ill.

unicorn noun (*plural* **unicorns**) (*say* **yoo**-ni-corn)
an animal in stories that has one long, straight horn growing from the front of its head

uniform noun (*plural* **uniforms**)
a special set of clothes that everyone in the same school, job, or club wears

a b c d e f g h i j k l m n o p q r s t u v w x y z

217

unique adjective (*say* yoo-neek)
If something is unique, there is nothing else like it. *This picture is unique.*

unit noun (*plural* **units**)
1 (*in mathematics*) Units are ones. When you add or subtract big numbers, you work with hundreds, tens, and units.
2 A unit is something that you use for measuring or counting things. Centimetres and metres are units of length.

unite verb **unites, uniting, united**
When people unite, they join together and work together.

universe noun
everything in space, including the earth, the sun, and all the stars and planets

university noun (*plural* **universities**)
a place where you can go to study after you have left school

unkind adjective **unkinder, unkindest**
Someone who is unkind is nasty or cruel to another person.

unknown adjective
If something is unknown, no one knows about it.

unleaded adjective
Unleaded petrol does not have any lead in it.

unless conjunction
if something does not happen *I won't go unless you come with me.*

unlock verb **unlocks, unlocking, unlocked**
When you unlock something, you open its lock with a key. *We need a key to unlock the door.*

unlucky adjective **unluckier, unluckiest**
If you are unlucky, you have bad luck. *We were very unlucky to lose that game.*

unnecessary adjective
If something is unnecessary, you do not need it.

unpack verb **unpacks, unpacking, unpacked**
When you unpack things, you take them out of a bag, box, or suitcase.

unpleasant adjective
Something that is unpleasant is nasty or horrible. *The meat had a rather unpleasant taste.*

unpopular adjective
If something is unpopular, not many people like it. If someone is unpopular, not many people like them.

unsafe adjective
Something that is unsafe is dangerous and not safe.

unselfish adjective
If you are unselfish, you think about other people and are not selfish.

untidy adjective **untidier, untidiest**
A place that is untidy is messy and not tidy.

untie verb **unties, untying, untied**
When you untie a piece of rope or string, you undo a knot in it. *I can't untie this knot.*

until conjunction & preposition
up to a certain time *I stayed up until midnight.*

untrue adjective
Something that is untrue is not true or correct.

unusual adjective
Something that is unusual is strange and not normal or usual.

> **WORD FAMILY**
> • **unusually** It was unusually cold that day.

unwrap verb **unwraps, unwrapping, unwrapped**
When you unwrap something, you take off the paper that is wrapped round it.

up adverb & preposition
towards a higher place *She ran up the hill.*

upon preposition
on *There was a strange expression upon his face.*

upper adjective
The upper part of something is the part that is nearest the top. *The upper half of the building was destroyed by the fire.*

upper case adjective
Upper case letters are capital letters.

upright adjective
Something that is upright is standing up straight.

uproar noun
If there is an uproar, a lot of people shout and make a noise.

upset adjective
If you are upset, you are sad or crying.

upset verb **upsets, upsetting, upset**
1 To upset someone means to make them feel sad and disappointed.
2 To upset something means to knock it over. *Someone had upset a bottle of water.*

upside-down adjective
If something is upside-down, it is turned over so that the bottom is at the top.

upwards adverb
When something goes upwards, it goes towards a higher place. *The rocket zoomed upwards.*

urgent adjective
If something is urgent, you have to do it immediately. *Please get here quickly – it's urgent.*

> **WORD FAMILY**
> • **urgently** We must get him to a hospital urgently.

use verb **uses, using, used**
1 When you use something, you do a job with it. *We used a bucket to carry water in.*
2 If you used to do something, you did it in the past but you do not do it now. *I used to go to swimming lessons.*

use noun (*plural* **uses**)
If something has a use, you can use it to make something or do a job. *I'm sure we can find a use for these old wheels.*

useful adjective
Something that is useful is good and helpful. *Mobile phones are very useful.*

useless adjective
If something is useless, you cannot use it. *This old TV is useless!*

user-friendly adjective
A machine that is user-friendly is easy to understand and use. *Modern computers are very user-friendly.*

usual adjective
Something that is usual is normal and happens quite often. *I got up at my usual time of eight o'clock.*

> **WORD FAMILY**
> • **usually** I usually catch the school bus in the mornings.

vacant adjective
A place that is vacant has no one in it.

vaccination noun (*plural* **vaccinations**)
(*say* vak-si-**nay**-shun)
an injection that stops you getting an illness

> **WORD FAMILY**
> • **vaccinate** Have you been vaccinated against measles?

vacuum cleaner noun (*plural* **vacuum cleaners**)
a machine that cleans floors by sucking up dust and dirt

vague adjective **vaguer, vaguest**
Something that is vague is not clear or certain.

vain adjective **vainer, vainest**
1 If you are vain, you think too much about how nice you look and how clever you are.
2 If you try in vain to do something, you try to do it but do not manage it.

valley noun (*plural* **valleys**)
low land between two hills

valuable adjective
Something that is valuable is worth a lot of money, or is very useful. *Some of my grandmother's jewellery is valuable.*

value noun
The value of something is how much money it is worth, or how important or useful it is.

van noun (*plural* **vans**)
a type of car with a large, covered part at the back for carrying things in

vandal noun (*plural* **vandals**)
someone who deliberately breaks things that belong to other people

> **WORD FAMILY**
> • **vandalize** Someone has vandalized the swings in the park.
> • **vandalism** There has been some vandalism in the school.

vanilla noun
something that is added to ice cream and other sweet food to make it taste nice

vanish verb **vanishes, vanishing, vanished**
If something vanishes, it disappears.

vapour noun (*plural* **vapours**)
A vapour is a mass of tiny drops of liquid in the air. Steam is a vapour.

variety noun (*plural* **varieties**)
1 A variety of things is a lot of different things. *We have a variety of colours to choose from.*
2 One variety of something is one type. *They sell over twenty varieties of ice cream.*

various adjective
Various things means a lot of different things. *There were various things to eat.*

vase noun
(*plural* **vases**)
a pot that you put flowers in

vase of flowers

vast adjective
Something that is vast is very big. *Australia is a vast country.*

vegetable noun (*plural* **vegetables**)
A vegetable is a part of a plant that we can eat. Potatoes, carrots, and beans are vegetables.

vegetarian noun (*plural* **vegetarians**)
a person who does not eat meat

vegetation noun
plants and trees

vehicle noun (*plural* **vehicles**) (*say* **vee**-ik-al)
A vehicle is anything that can travel on land and take people or things from one place to another. Cars, vans, buses, trains, and lorries are vehicles.

veil noun (*plural* **veils**)
a piece of thin material that some women or girls wear over their face or head

vein noun (*plural* **veins**) (*say* **vain**)
Your veins are the narrow tubes inside your body that carry blood to your heart.

velvet noun
a type of thick, soft cloth *The room had red velvet curtains.*

verb noun (*plural* **verbs**)
(*in grammar*) A verb is a word that describes what someone or something is doing. Words like *eat* and *bring* are verbs.

verdict noun (*plural* **verdicts**)
When the jury in a court of law reach a verdict, they decide whether someone is guilty or not guilty.

verse noun (*plural* **verses**)
1 One verse of a song or poem is one part of it that is not the chorus.
2 Verse is poetry.

version noun (*plural* **versions**)
One version of something is one form of it, which is slightly different from all the other forms. *The latest version of this game is even better than the old one.*

vertebrate noun (*plural* **vertebrates**)
A vertebrate is an animal that has a backbone. Fish, birds, dogs, and humans are all vertebrates.

vertex noun (*plural* **vertexes** or **vertices**)
The vertex of something is its highest point. The vertices of a shape are the points where different sides meet. A square has four vertices and a cube has eight.

vertical adjective
Something that is vertical is standing or pointing straight up.

a b c d e f g h i j k l m n o p q r s t u v w x y z

very adverb
extremely *That was a very silly thing to do!*

vessel noun (*plural* **vessels**)
a ship or boat

vest noun (*plural* **vests**)
a piece of clothing that you wear on the top half of the body under your other clothes

vet noun (*plural* **vets**)
a doctor for animals

via preposition
When you go via a place, you go through that place to get somewhere else.

vibrate verb **vibrates, vibrating, vibrated**
When something vibrates, it shakes. *The whole house vibrates when a lorry goes past.*

vicious adjective (*say* **vish**-uss)
Someone who is vicious is violent and cruel.

> **WORD FAMILY**
> • **viciously** The dog snarled viciously.

victim noun (*plural* **victims**)
someone who has been hurt, robbed, or killed *We must help the victims of this terrible earthquake.*

victory noun (*plural* **victories**)
A victory is when you win a game or battle.

video noun (*plural* **videos**)
1 a tape with a film or television programme recorded on it *Shall we watch a video?*
2 a machine that records and plays back television programmes on a special magnetic tape

video verb **videos, videoing, videoed**
When you video a television programme, you record it on a video so that you can watch it later.

view noun (*plural* **views**)
The view from a place is everything that you can see from that place. *We had a beautiful view of the sea from our window.*

village noun (*plural* **villages**)
A village is a small group of houses and other buildings in the country. A village is smaller than a town.

vinegar noun
a sour liquid which you use in cooking to give a sharp, sour taste to food

violent adjective
1 Someone who is violent hits or kicks other people.
2 Something that is violent is sudden and very powerful. *We were caught in the middle of a violent storm.*

> **WORD FAMILY**
> • **violence** It's wrong to react with violence even if someone is teasing you.

violin noun (*plural* **violins**)
A violin is a musical instrument made of wood with strings across it. You hold a violin under your chin and play it by pulling a bow across the strings.

violin

virtual adjective
A virtual place is one that you can look at on a computer screen. You feel as if you are really in the place because you can use the controls to move around inside it.

virus noun (*plural* **viruses**)
a tiny living thing that can make you ill if it gets into your body

visible adjective
If something is visible, you can see it. *Stars are only visible at night.*

a
b
c
d
e
f
g
h
i
j
k
l
m
n
o
p
q
r
s
t
u
v
w
x
y
z

vision noun
Your vision is how well you can see things. *Glasses will improve your vision.*

visit verb **visits, visiting, visited**
When you visit a person, you go to see them. When you visit a place, you go there to see what it is like.

> **WORD FAMILY**
> • **visitor** We're having visitors this weekend.

visual adjective
Visual things are things that you can see.

vital adjective
Something that is vital is very important.

vitamin noun (*plural* **vitamins**)
A vitamin is something that is found in your food. Your body needs vitamins to stay strong and healthy. *Oranges are full of vitamin C.*

vivid adjective
1 Vivid colours are very bright.
2 A vivid dream or memory is so clear that it seems real.

vocabulary noun
all the words that someone knows and uses *You must try to improve your vocabulary as you get older.*

voice noun (*plural* **voices**)
Your voice is the sound you make with your mouth when you are speaking or singing. *He spoke in a deep, gruff voice.*

voicemail noun (*plural* **voicemails**)
a spoken message that you can leave for someone on their mobile phone

volcano noun (*plural* **volcanoes**)
a mountain or other place on the earth's surface from which hot, liquid rock sometimes bursts from inside the earth

volleyball noun
a game in which players hit a ball over a high net with their hands

volume noun (*plural* **volumes**)
1 The volume of something is how much space it takes up. *We measured the volume of liquid in the bottle.*
2 The volume of a sound is how loud it is. *Please could you turn down the volume on your radio?*
3 one book that is part of a set of books *I have read all three volumes of this story.*

voluntary adjective
If something is voluntary, you can choose to do it if you want, but you do not have to do it.

volunteer verb **volunteers, volunteering, volunteered**
If you volunteer to do a job, you offer to do it.

volunteer noun (*plural* **volunteers**)
someone who offers to do a job

vomit verb **vomits, vomiting, vomited**
When you vomit, you are sick and food comes back up out of your stomach.

vote verb **votes, voting, voted**
When you vote, you say which person or thing you choose.

voucher noun (*plural* **vouchers**)
a piece of printed paper you can use instead of money to pay for something

vowel noun (*plural* **vowels**)
Vowels are the letters, **a**, **e**, **i**, **o**, **u**, and sometimes **y**. All the other letters of the alphabet are **consonants**.

voyage noun (*plural* **voyages**)
a long journey in a boat or spacecraft

vulture noun (*plural* **vultures**)
a large bird that eats dead animals

a b c d e f g h i j k l m n o p q r s t u v w x y z

Ww

wade verb **wades, wading, waded**
When you wade through water, you walk through it.

wag verb **wags, wagging, wagged**
When a dog wags its tail, it moves it quickly from side to side because it is happy or excited.

wagon noun (plural **wagons**)
a cart with four wheels that is pulled by horses

wail verb **wails, wailing, wailed**
If you wail, you give a long, sad cry.
'Oh, Mum, what am I going to do now?' she wailed.—Philip Pullman, Mossycoat

waist noun (plural **waists**)
Your waist is the narrow part in the middle of your body.

wait verb **waits, waiting, waited**
If you wait, you stay in a place until someone comes or until something happens.

waiter noun
(plural **waiters**)
a man who brings food to people in a restaurant

waiter

waitress noun (plural **waitresses**)
a woman who brings food to people in a restaurant

wake verb **wakes, waking, woke, woken**
When you wake up, you stop sleeping.
I woke up at six o'clock.

walk verb **walks, walking, walked**
When you walk, you move along on your feet. *I walked down the road to my friend's house.*

walk noun (plural **walks**)
When you go for a walk, you walk somewhere.

wall noun (plural **walls**)
1 The walls of a building are the parts that hold up the roof and separate the building into different rooms.
2 A wall is something built from bricks or stone around a garden or field.

wallet noun (plural **wallets**)
a small, flat, case that you carry money in

wallpaper noun
colourful paper that you stick onto the walls of a room to make it look nice

wand noun (plural **wands**)
a stick that you use for casting magic spells or doing magic tricks

wander verb **wanders, wandering, wandered**
When you wander about, you walk about in no particular direction.

want verb **wants, wanting, wanted**
If you want something, you would like to have it or do it. *Do you want a drink?*

war noun (plural **wars**)
When there is a war, two countries fight against each other.

wardrobe noun (plural **wardrobes**)
a cupboard where you hang clothes

warm adjective **warmer, warmest**
Something that is warm is quite hot. *It was a warm, sunny day.*

warn verb **warns, warning, warned**
If you warn someone about a danger, you tell them about it.
'Don't get too excited or you'll fall out of the tree,' I warned.—Jeremy Strong, The Hundred-Mile-An-Hour Dog

WORD FAMILY
• **warning** Let this be a warning to you.

warrior noun (plural **warriors**)
someone who fights in battles

wary adjective **warier, wariest**
If you are wary of something, you are slightly nervous or frightened of it.

wash verb **washes, washing, washed**
1 When you wash something, you clean it with water.
2 When you wash up, you wash the plates, knives, and forks at the end of a meal.

a b c d e f g h i j k l m n o p q r s t u v w x y z

washing noun
clothes that need to be washed or are being washed

washing machine noun (*plural* **washing machines**) a machine for washing clothes

wasp noun (*plural* **wasps**) (*say* **wosp**) A wasp is an insect with black and yellow stripes on its body. Wasps can sting you.

wasp

waste noun
something that is left over and cannot be used *The factory used to pour all the waste chemicals into the river.*

waste verb **wastes, wasting, wasted** If you waste something, you use more of it than you really need to.

watch verb **watches, watching, watched** When you watch something, you look at it. *Mum, watch me!*

watch noun (*plural* **watches**) a small clock that you wear on your wrist

water noun
Water is the clear liquid that is in rivers and seas. All living things need water to live.

water verb **waters, watering, watered**
1 When you water a plant, you pour water onto it to help it to grow.
2 When your eyes water, tears come into them. *The smoke made my eyes water.*

waterfall noun (*plural* **waterfalls**) part of a river where the water falls down over rocks

waterproof adjective
Something that is waterproof is made of material that does not let water through. *Bring a waterproof coat in case it rains.*

water-ski verb **water-skis, water-skiing, water-skied**
When you water-ski, you have special skis on your feet and you are pulled over the surface of water by a boat.

watertight adjective
Something that is watertight is closed so tightly that no water can get through. *Is this lid watertight?*

wave verb **waves, waving, waved**
1 When you wave, you lift up your hand and move it from side to side.
2 When something waves, it moves backwards and forwards or from side to side. *The flags were waving in the breeze.*

wave noun (*plural* **waves**)
1 Waves in the sea are the parts that move up and down across the top of it.
2 (*in science*) A wave is an up-and-down movement. Light, heat, and sound all move in waves.

wax noun
the substance that candles are made from

way noun (*plural* **ways**)
1 The way to a place is the roads or paths you follow to get there. *Please could you tell me the way to the station.*
2 The way you do something is how you do it. *What's the best way to cook potatoes?*

weak adjective **weaker, weakest**
1 Someone who is weak is not very strong.
2 Something that is weak will break easily. *Some of the wood was very old and weak.*
3 A weak drink has a lot of water in it and so does not have a very strong taste.

wealthy adjective **wealthier, wealthiest** Someone who is wealthy is rich.

weapon noun (*plural* **weapons**)
A weapon is something that a person can use to hurt or kill someone. Knives and guns are weapons.

wear verb **wears, wearing, wore, worn**
(*rhymes with* air)
1 When you wear clothes, you have them on your body.
2 When something wears out, it becomes so old that you cannot use it any more.

weary adjective (*say* **weer**-ee) **wearier, weariest**
If you feel weary, you feel very tired.

weather noun
The weather is what it is like outside, for example whether the sun is shining, or it is rainy, or windy.

weave verb **weaves, weaving, wove, woven**
To weave cloth means to make it from threads.

web noun (*plural* **webs**)
1 A web is a thin net that a spider spins to trap insects.
2 (*in ICT*) The web is the World Wide Web, where information is kept on computers all over the world and people can use it by using the Internet.

spider's web

webbed adjective
Animals with webbed feet have skin between the toes of their feet. Ducks have webbed feet.

webcam noun (*plural* **webcams**)
a camera that films things that are happening and broadcasts them live over the Internet

website noun (*plural* **websites**)
a place on the Internet where you can find information about something *Visit our website to find out more about all our MP3 players.*

wedding noun (*plural* **weddings**)
the time when a man and woman get married

Wednesday noun (*plural* **Wednesdays**)
the day after Tuesday

weed noun (*plural* **weeds**)
Weeds are wild plants that grow in a garden or field when you do not want them to.

week noun (*plural* **weeks**)
a period of seven days *I'll see you next week.*

weekend noun (*plural* **weekends**)
The weekend is Saturday and Sunday.

weep verb **weeps, weeping, wept**
When you weep, you cry.
Lila was nearly weeping with fear and impatience.—Philip Pullman, The Firework-Maker's Daughter

weigh verb **weighs, weighing, weighed**
(*say* **way**)
1 When you weigh something, you use a machine to find out how heavy it is. *The shop assistant weighed the apples.*
2 The amount that something weighs is how heavy it is. *How much do you weigh?*

weight noun (*plural* **weights**)
(*say* **wait**)
1 The weight of something is how heavy it is. *We measured the height and weight of each child in the class.*
2 Weights are pieces of metal that you use for weighing things.
3 Weights are heavy pieces of metal that people lift to make their bodies stronger.

weird adjective **weirder, weirdest** (*say* weerd)
Something that is weird is very strange.

welcome verb **welcomes, welcoming, welcomed**
If you welcome someone, you show that you are pleased when they arrive.

welfare noun
Someone's welfare is how healthy and happy they are. *Everyone was concerned about the children's welfare.*

well noun (*plural* **wells**)
a deep hole in the ground from which you can get water or oil

a
b
c
d
e
f
g
h
i
j
k
l
m
n
o
p
q
r
s
t
u
v
w
x
y
z

well adverb **better, best**
1 If you do something well, you do it in a good or successful way. *I can play the piano quite well now.*
2 If you do something well, you do it a lot. *Shake the bottle well before you open it.*
as well also *Can I come as well?*

well adjective
If you are well, you are healthy and not ill. *I hope you are well.*

went verb *see* **go**

wept verb *see* **weep**

west noun
West is the direction where the sun sets in the evening.

> **WORD FAMILY**
> • The **western** part of a country is the part in the west.

western noun (*plural* **westerns**)
a film about cowboys

wet adjective **wetter, wettest**
1 Something that is wet is covered or soaked in water. *My shoes are all wet!*
2 When the weather is wet, it rains. *We had to stay in because it was wet outside.*

whale noun (*plural* **whales**)
A whale is a very large sea animal. Whales are mammals and breathe air, but they live in the sea like fish.

what adjective & pronoun
Use this word when you are asking about something. *What is your name?*

wheat noun
Wheat is a plant that farmers grow. It is used to make flour.

wheel noun (*plural* **wheels**)
Wheels are the round objects that cars, buses, bicycles, and trains go along on.

wheelbarrow noun (*plural* **wheelbarrows**)
a small cart that you push along and use for carrying things

wheelchair noun
(*plural* **wheelchairs**)
a chair on wheels for a person who cannot walk very well

when adverb & conjunction
Use this word when you are talking about the time that something happens. *When will the others be here?*

where adverb & conjunction
Use this word when you are talking about the place that something happens. *Where do you live?*

whether conjunction
if *The teacher asked whether I had finished my work.*

which adjective & pronoun
Use this word when you are choosing one thing or talking about one particular thing. *Which dress do you like best?*

> **WORD FAMILY**
> • **which** Which way shall we go?
> • **witch** In the castle lived a wicked witch.

while conjunction
during the time that something else is happening *I'll lay the table while you make the tea.*

whimper verb **whimpers, whimpering, whimpered**
> To whimper means to cry softly because you are frightened or hurt.

whine verb **whines, whining, whined**
> **1** To whine means to make a long, high, sad sound. *The dog was whining to go outside.*
> **2** If you whine about something, you complain about it.

whinge verb **whinges, whingeing, whinged**
> If you whinge about something, you keep complaining about it.

whip noun (*plural* **whips**)
> a long piece of rope or leather that is used for hitting people or animals

whip verb **whips, whipping, whipped**
> **1** To whip a person or animal means to hit them with a whip.
> **2** When you whip cream, you stir it quickly until it goes thick.

whirl verb **whirls, whirling, whirled**
> To whirl round means to turn round and round very fast.

whirlpool noun (*plural* **whirlpools**)
> a place in a river or sea where the water spins round and round very quickly and pulls things down with it

whirlwind noun (*plural* **whirlwinds**)
> a strong wind that spins round and round very quickly as it moves along

whirr verb **whirrs, whirring, whirred**
> When a machine whirrs, it makes a gentle humming sound.

whisk verb **whisks, whisking, whisked**
> When you whisk eggs or cream, you stir them round round and round very fast.

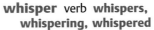

whisk

whisker noun (*plural* **whiskers**)
> **1** An animal's whiskers are the long, stiff hairs near its mouth.
> **2** If a man has whiskers, he has a beard or hair on the sides of his face.

whisper verb **whispers, whispering, whispered**
> When you whisper, you speak very quietly. *'Now listen, Maddy,' he whispered. 'Here's the plan.'*—Alexander McCall Smith, The Chocolate Money Mystery

whistle verb **whistles, whistling, whistled**
> When you whistle, you make a high sound by blowing air through your lips.

whistle noun (*plural* **whistles**)
> something that you can blow into to make a loud, high sound

white adjective **whiter, whitest**
> **1** Something that is white is the colour of snow.
> **2** Someone who is white has a skin that is naturally pale in colour.
> **3** White bread is made with just the white part of the wheat grain, not the whole grain.

whiteboard noun (*plural* **whiteboards**)
> a large board with a smooth white surface that you can write on with special pens

whizz verb **whizzes, whizzing, whizzed**
> If something whizzes along, it moves along very quickly. *He whizzed far into space. He whizzed past the moon. He whizzed past stars and planets.*—Roald Dahl, The Enormous Crocodile

who pronoun
> which person *Who broke my mug?*

a
b
c
d
e
f
g
h
i
j
k
l
m
n
o
p
q
r
s
t
u
v
w
x
y
z

whole adjective
1 A whole thing is all of it, with nothing left out. *Between us we ate the whole cake.*
2 in one piece *The bird swallowed the fish whole.*

> 🏠 **WORD FAMILY**
> • **whole** We searched the whole house.
> • **hole** We climbed through a hole in the fence.

wholemeal adjective
Wholemeal bread is brown bread.

whose adjective & pronoun
belonging to which person *Whose coat is this?*

why adverb
Use this word when you are talking about the reason that something happens. *Why are you late?*

wicked adjective
Someone who is wicked is very bad or cruel.

wide adjective **wider, widest**
Something that is wide measures a lot from one side to the other. *We had to cross a wide river.*

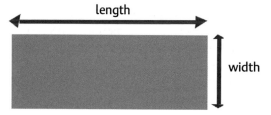
length
width

widow noun (*plural* **widows**)
a woman whose husband has died

widower noun (*plural* **widowers**)
a man whose wife has died

width noun (*plural* **widths**)
The width of something is how wide it is. *We measured the width of the room.*

wife noun (*plural* **wives**)
A man's wife is the woman he is married to.

wig noun (*plural* **wigs**)
false hair that some people wear on their head

wiggle verb **wiggles, wiggling, wiggled**
To wiggle something means to move it about. *She wiggled her finger at me.*

wild adjective **wilder, wildest**
1 Wild animals and plants live or grow in a natural way and are not looked after by people.

2 Wild behaviour is rough and not calm.

> 🏠 **WORD FAMILY**
> • **wildly** He was shouting and waving his arms about wildly.

wildlife noun
wild animals *I watched a TV programme about African wildlife.*

will verb **would**
If you will do something, you are going to do it in the future. *I will be there at ten o'clock.*

will noun (*plural* **wills**)
something that a person writes down to tell other people what they want to happen to their money and other things after they have died

willing adjective
If you are willing to do something, you are happy to do it. *We are all willing to help.*

wilt verb **wilts, wilting, wilted**
If a plant wilts, it begins to droop because it does not have enough water.

win verb **wins, winning, won**
When you win a game, competition, or battle, you beat the other people or teams. *Who won the race?*

> 🏠 **WORD FAMILY**
> • The **winner** is the person or team that wins a game or competition.

wind noun (*plural* **winds**) (*rhymes with* tinned)
Wind is air that moves over the earth. *Everything was blowing about in the wind.*

wind verb **winds, winding, wound** (*rhymes with* find)
1 To wind something round means to twist or turn it round. *She wound her scarf round her neck.*
2 If a road or river winds, it has a lot of bends in it. *The road wound up the side of the mountain.*
3 When you wind up a clock or clockwork toy, you turn a key so that it will work.

windmill noun (*plural* **windmills**)
a building with large sails that move in the wind and use the power of the wind to make a machine work

window noun (*plural* **windows**)
  1 an opening in a wall that is filled with glass to let the light in *We had to climb in through the window.*
  2 (*in ICT*) one area of a computer screen where you can see information or a document

windscreen noun (*plural* **windscreens**)
  the big window at the front of a car

windsurfing noun
  When you go windsurfing, you stand on a special board on water and hold onto a large sail. You turn the sail so that the wind blows into it and you move along.

windy adjective **windier, windiest**
  When the weather is windy, there is a strong wind.

wine noun (*plural* **wines**)
  an alcoholic drink that is made from grapes

wing noun
  (*plural* **wings**)
  1 A bird's wings are the parts that it moves up and down when it is flying.
  2 The wings on an aeroplane are the parts that stick out on each side and help the aeroplane to fly smoothly.

wings

wink verb **winks, winking, winked**
  When you wink, you close one eye.

winner noun (*plural* **winners**)
  The winner of a game or competition is the person or team that wins.

winter noun (*plural* **winters**)
  the time of the year when the weather is cold and it gets dark early in the evenings

wipe verb **wipes, wiping, wiped**
  When you wipe something, you rub it gently to clean it.

wire noun (*plural* **wires**)
  A wire is a long, thin strip of metal. Electricity goes along wires, and wires are also used to hold things in place.

wire

wireless adjective
  Something that is wireless can send and receive signals without using wires. *You can get a wireless internet connection for your computer.*

wise adjective **wiser, wisest**
  Someone who is wise understands a lot of things and knows the most sensible thing to do.

wish verb **wishes, wishing, wished**
  If you wish that something would happen, you say that you would really like it to happen. *I wish I had lots of money.*

wish noun (*plural* **wishes**)
  When you make a wish, you say what you would like to happen.

witch noun (*plural* **witches**)
  a woman in stories who uses magic

with preposition
  1 If one thing is with another thing, the two things are together. *We had apple pie with custard. I went to town with my mum.*
  2 using *You can cut paper with scissors.*

wither verb **withers, withering, withered**
  If a plant withers, it becomes dry and dies.

within preposition
  inside *You must stay within the school grounds.*

without preposition
  not having *The family was left without any money.*

witness noun (*plural* **witnesses**)
  someone who sees a crime or an accident happen *There were two witnesses to the accident.*

wizard noun (*plural* **wizards**)
  a man in stories who uses magic

wobble verb **wobbles, wobbling, wobbled**
  To wobble means to move and shake about. *The ladder began to wobble.*

woke, woken verb
  see **wake**

wolf noun (*plural* **wolves**)
  a wild animal that is like a large, grey dog

a
b
c
d
e
f
g
h
i
j
k
l
m
n
o
p
q
r
s
t
u
v
w
x
y
z

woman noun (*plural* **women**)
a grown-up female person

won verb *see* **win**

wonder noun
When you have a feeling of wonder, you feel amazed and very glad. *They stared at the gold in wonder.*

wonder verb **wonders, wondering, wondered**
If you wonder about something, you ask yourself about it. *I wonder who wrote that letter?*

wonderful adjective
Something that is wonderful is amazing and fantastic.
That ride was perhaps the most wonderful thing that happened to them in Narnia.—C. S. Lewis, The Lion, the Witch and the Wardrobe

won't verb
will not *I won't put up with this bad behaviour!*

wood noun (*plural* **woods**)
1 Wood is the hard material that trees are made of. You can burn wood as fuel or use it for making things.
2 A wood is an area of land where a lot of trees grow. *Don't go into the woods on your own.*

> **WORD FAMILY**
> • **wooden** We sat down on the wooden bench.

wool noun
the thick, soft hair that sheep have on their bodies

> **WORD FAMILY**
> • **woollen** He was wearing a thick woollen jumper.
> • **woolly** Sheep have woolly coats.

word noun (*plural* **words**)
1 a group of sounds or letters that mean something
2 If you give your word, you promise.

word class noun (*plural* **word classes**)
(*in grammar*) A word class is a name that we give to different types of words. Adjectives, nouns, and verbs are different word classes.

word processor noun (*plural* **word processors**)
A word processor is a computer program that you use to write something. You can store your writing and make changes to it

wore verb *see* **wear**

work noun
a job that you have to do *Please get on with your work quietly.*

work verb **works, working, worked**
1 When you work, you do a job or do something useful. *We worked hard at school today.*
2 If a machine works, it does what it is meant to do. *This light doesn't work.*
3 When you work out the answer to a question, you find the answer.

world noun
The world is all the countries and people on the earth.

World Wide Web noun
The World Wide Web is the system for keeping information on computers all over the world so that people can use it by using the Internet.

worm noun (*plural* **worms**)
a long, thin animal with no legs that lives in the soil

worn verb *see* **wear**

worry verb **worries, worrying, worried**
When you worry, you feel upset and nervous because you think something bad might happen. *My mum always worries about me.*

> **WORD FAMILY**
> • **worried** I was beginning to feel a bit worried.

worse adjective
1 If one thing is worse than another, it is less good. *My first painting was bad, and my second one was even worse!*
2 When you feel worse, you feel more ill than before.

worship verb **worships, worshipping, worshipped**
To worship a god means to show your love and respect.

worst adjective
The worst person or thing is the one that is worse than any other. *I'm the worst swimmer in my class.*

worth adjective
1 If something is worth an amount of money, you could sell it for that amount of money. *How much are these old coins worth?*
2 If something is worth doing or having, it is good or useful. *This film is well worth seeing.*

a
b
c
d
e
f
g
h
i
j
k
l
m
n
o
p
q
r
s
t
u
v
w
x
y
z

would verb *see* **will** verb

wound noun (*plural* **wounds**) (*rhymes with* spooned)
a cut on your body

wound verb **wounds, wounding, wounded** (*rhymes with* spooned)
To wound someone means to hurt them.

wound verb (*rhymes with* round) *see* **wind** verb

woven verb *see* **weave**

wrap verb **wraps, wrapping, wrapped**
When you wrap something, you put cloth or paper around it. *I forgot to wrap your present.*

WORD FAMILY
• A **wrapper** is a piece of paper that a sweet is

wreath noun
(*plural* **wreaths**)
a circle of
flowers or
leaves twisted
together

wreck verb
**wrecks,
wrecking,
wrecked**
To wreck
something means to break
it or destroy it completely.
The ship was wrecked on the rocks.

wreath

wreck noun (*plural* **wrecks**)
a car, ship, or aeroplane that has been damaged in an accident

wrestle verb **wrestles, wrestling, wrestled**
When people wrestle, they fight with each other by holding each other and trying to force each other to the ground.

wriggle verb **wriggles, wriggling, wriggled**
When you wriggle, you twist and turn with your body.

wrinkle noun (*plural* **wrinkles**)
Wrinkles are small lines in your skin that often appear as you get older.

wrist noun (*plural* **wrists**)
Your wrist is the thin part of your arm where it is joined to your hand.

write verb **writes, writing, wrote, written**
When you write, you put letters and words onto paper so that people can read them.

WORD FAMILY
• A **writer** is someone who writes stories.

writing noun
1 A piece of writing is something that you have written.
2 Your writing is the way you write. *Try to make your writing a bit neater.*

wrong adjective
1 Something that is wrong is not right or correct. *He gave the wrong answer.*
2 Something that is wrong is bad. *Stealing is wrong.*

wrote verb *see* **write**

a
b
c
d
e
f
g
h
i
j
k
l
m
n
o
p
q
r
s
t
u
v
w
x
y
z

Xx

X-ray noun (*plural* **X-rays**)
a photograph that shows
the bones and other
things inside your body
so that doctors can see if
there is anything wrong

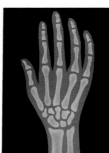

X-ray

xylophone noun
(*plural* **xylophones**)
(*say* **zye**-lo-fone)
a musical instrument
with a row of wooden
or metal bars that you
hit with small
hammers

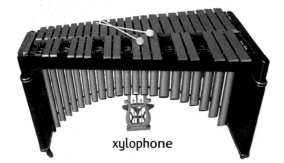

xylophone

Yy

yacht noun
(*plural* **yachts**)
(*say* **yot**)
a boat with
sails that
people use for
racing or for
pleasure

yacht

yam noun
(*plural* **yams**)
a vegetable
that grows in
tropical
countries

yard noun
(*plural* **yards**)
1 We can measure length in yards.
One yard is just under one metre.
2 a piece of ground that is next to a building and
has a wall round it

yawn verb **yawns, yawning, yawned**
When you yawn, you open your mouth and
breathe in deeply because you are tired.

year noun (*plural* **years**)
a period of twelve months, or three hundred
and sixty-five days

yell verb **yells, yelling, yelled**
If you yell, you shout very loudly.
*She couldn't walk from one end of a corridor
to the other without someone yelling at
her.*—Jill Murphy, The Worst Witch

yellow adjective
Something that
is yellow is the
colour of a
lemon.

lemons

a
b
c
d
e
f
g
h
i
j
k
l
m
n
o
p
q
r
s
t
u
v
w
x
y
z

232

yelp verb **yelps, yelping, yelped**
If an animal yelps, it gives a cry because it is in pain.

yesterday noun & adverb
the day before today *I went to the cinema yesterday.*

yet adverb & preposition
1 until now *He hasn't arrived yet.*
2 If you do not want to do something yet, you do not want to do it until later. *I don't want anything to eat yet.*
3 but *It was the middle of winter, yet it was quite warm.*

yoghurt noun
a thick liquid that is made from milk and has a slightly sour taste

yolk noun
(*plural* **yolks**)
(*rhymes with* joke)
The yolk of an egg is the yellow art inside It.

young adjective **younger, youngest**
Someone who is young is not very old. *My mum lived in London when she was young.*

🏠 **WORD FAMILY**
• A **youngster** is someone who is young.

youth noun (*plural* **youths**)
1 a youth is a boy or young man
2 Your youth is the time in your life when you are young.

yo-yo noun (*plural* **yo-yos**)
a toy that spins round as you bounce it up and down on a piece of string

Zz

zap verb **zaps, zapping, zapped**
1 To zap someone in a computer game means to shoot them.
2 When you zap between channels on the television, you keep changing channels.

zebra noun (*plural* **zebras**)
an animal that looks like a horse and has black and white stripes on its body

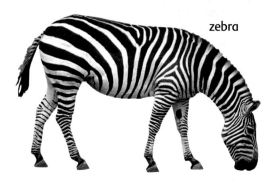

zebra

zebra crossing noun (*plural* **zebra crossings**)
a place where there are black and white stripes across a road to show that cars must stop to let people cross the road

zero noun (*plural* **zeros**)
the number 0

zigzag noun (*plural* **zigzags**)
a line with a lot of sudden, sharp turns in it like this

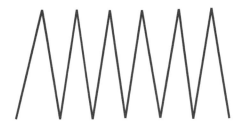

a
b
c
d
e
f
g
h
i
j
k
l
m
n
o
p
q
r
s
t
u
v
w
x
y
z

233

zip, zipper noun (*plural* **zips, zippers**)
A zip is a fastener for joining two pieces of cloth. It has two lines of teeth that come together and grip each other when you close it.

zone noun (*plural* **zones**)
an area of land that has a special use *The town centre is now a pedestrian zone.*

zoo noun (*plural* **zoos**)
a place where different kinds of wild animals are kept so that people can go and see them

zoom verb **zooms, zooming, zoomed**
To zoom means to move along very quickly. *Harry put on a burst of speed and zoomed towards the other end of the pitch.—J. K. Rowling, Harry Potter and the Chamber of Secrets*

a
b
c
d
e
f
g
h
i
j
k
l
m
n
o
p
q
r
s
t
u
v
w
x
y
z

Become a Word Explorer

You don't need a map and a compass to be an explorer: you can explore the world of words equipped with your dictionary.

For example, you can
- discover the secret to spelling success and writing with style
- work out where in the world words have come from
- explore new ways to build words

Have fun being a Word Explorer!

Explore: Spelling

Most of the long vowel phonemes can be shown in different ways.

Here are common spellings of these phonemes:

skate	tray	train	great	they	eight
sheep	please	me	field	key	these
kite	night	fly	tie	mind	
boat	snow	bone	go	toe	
moon	blue	flute	grew	shoe	move
cube	you	news	cue	unique	
car	father	are			
bird	fern	purple	earth	worm	were
horn	door	score	four	oar	straw
	ball	astronaut	drawer	caught	
boy	coin				
beard	deer	here	pier		
chair	square	bear	there	their	
cow	house				
hour	flower				

Explore: Punctuation

Use this guide to help check your punctuation

punctuation mark		when it's used	example
full stop	.	at the end of a statement	It's raining today.
question mark	?	at the end of a question	What's your favourite colour?
exclamation mark	!	at the end of an exclamation	I don't believe it!
comma	,	to separate items in a list or events in a sentence	Yesterday, when I went shopping, I bought flour, eggs, butter and sugar.
apostrophe	'	to show that some letters are missing	I can't. He won't. She couldn't. They'll be here. It's time.
		to show ownership of something.	John's coat. Anya's watch. The boy's books. The girl's pens.
speech marks	' ' or " "	to show the words someone says	'I wonder what time it is' said Raj. Tara replied, 'It's almost time to go home.' "Thank you for inviting me today," said Raj. Tara replied, "You are welcome."

Its or it's? (also see **apostrophe** in the above table)

It's is short for **it is**.
Its means '**belonging to it**'.

To decide which you need, think about the question: can I turn it into **it is**?
If you can, you need to write **it's**.
If you can't, you should write **its**.

For example:
It's (**it is**) raining today.
The cat was eating **its** food.

Explore: Grammar
Word classes

All the words in a sentence tell you different information. The kinds of words are grouped together into word classes. Common words classes are:

word class	what the word does in a sentence	example
noun	names things	The cat sat on the mat.
verb	tells you what is happening. Verbs tell you about *doing*, *being* and *having*.	The cat sat on the mat and licked its face.
adjective	gives you more information about the noun which is often descriptive	The fluffy, grey cat sat on the ragged, dirty mat and licked its furry paws.
adverb	gives you more information about the verb. It tells you *how*, *when* and *where* events are happening.	Meanwhile, the fluffy, grey cat sat quietly on the ragged, dirty mat and solemnly licked its furry paws.
preposition	tells you where things are	Meanwhile, the fluffy, grey cat sat quietly on the ragged, dirty mat and solemnly licked its furry paws with its pink tongue.

Explore: Prefixes

prefix	meaning	examples
anti-	against or opposite	anticlockwise, antibiotic (a medicine that works against an infection in your body)
co-	together with someone else	co-pilot, co-author
de-	to take something away	debug, de-ice, defrost
dis-	opposite	dislike, disagree, disobey
ex-	in the past, but not now	ex-policeman, ex-wife
in- (also **im-**)	opposite	incorrect, insane, impossible, impolite
micro-	very small	microchip, micro-computer
mid-	in the middle	midday, midnight, midsummer
mini-	very small	minibus, miniskirt
mis-	badly or wrongly	misbehave, misspell
non-	opposite	non-fiction, non-smoker, non-stop
over-	too much	oversleep, overweight
pre-	before	prehistoric (before the beginning of history), pre-school (before a child is old enough to go to school)
re-	again, for a second time	rebuild, reheat, re-open
semi-	half	semicircle, semi-final, semi-detached
sub-	under	submarine (a ship that goes under the sea), subway (a path that goes under a road)
super-	more than or bigger than	super-hero, superhuman, superstar
un-	opposite	unable, uncomfortable, undress
under	not enough	under-fed, underweight

Explore: Suffixes

for making nouns

-hood	child childhood, father fatherhood
-ity	stupid stupidity, able ability, pure purity
-ness	happy happiness, kind kindness, lazy laziness
-ment	enjoy enjoyment, move movement, replace replacement
-ship	friend friendship, champion championship, partner partnership
-sion	divide division, persuade persuasion
-tion	subtract subtraction, react reaction

for making nouns that mean a person who does something

-er, -or	paint painter, write writer, act actor
-ist	science scientist, art artist, violin violinist

for making feminine nouns

-ess	actor actress, lion lioness

for making adjectives

-able	enjoy enjoyable, break breakable, forgive forgivable
-ful	hope hopeful, colour colourful, care careful, pain painful
-ible	eat edible, reverse reversible
-ic	science scientific, photograph photographic, allergy allergic
-ish	child childish
-ive	attract attractive, compete competitive, explode explosive
-less	care careless, fear fearless, hope hopeless
-like	child childlike, life lifelike
-y	hunger hungry, thirst thirsty, anger angry, hair hairy

for making adverbs

-ly	quick quickly, slow slowly, careful carefully, normal normally

for making verbs

-ate	active activate, pollen pollinate
-en	damp dampen, short shorten, length lengthen
-ify	solid solidify, pure purify
-ize, -ise	apology apologize, fossil fossilize

Explore: Words we use too much

When you read your writing, look out for words that you use over and over again. Try to think of alternatives. This list will give you some ideas, but you may want to look at the *Oxford Junior Illustrated Thesaurus* for more. Before you choose a different word, check that it has the right meaning for your sentence.

word	other words you could try	
and	also, as well, of course, furthermore, moreover	
angry	furious, cross, bad tempered, annoyed, mad	
bad	bad person	wicked, evil
	bad food	rotten, mouldy, terrible
	bad dog	naughty, disobedient
	bad at tennis	hopeless, useless, terrible
	bad knee	injured, sore
because	so, therefore, since, consequently, hence, if... then	
but	however, in contrast, although, and yet, on the other hand, whereas	
good	good work	thorough, neat, accurate, careful, excellent
	good art	impressive, brilliant, excellent, wonderful
	good day	nice, pleasant, enjoyable
	good children	well-behaved, polite, quiet, happy
lovely	lovely clothing	pretty, beautiful, unique, gorgeous
	lovely food	delicious, tasty, wonderful
	lovely person	kind, pleasant, charming, polite
nice	nice picture	pretty, beautiful, lovely, stylish, gorgeous
	nice person	friendly, kind, thoughtful, sympathetic, pleasant, polite
	nice weather	lovely, pleasant, beautiful, warm, sunny, glorious, wonderful
said	bellowed, called, complained, cried, declared, groaned, moaned, mumbled, screamed, snarled, whispered, yelled	
then	next, later, after that, soon, meanwhile, secondly, before	
went	walked, ran, fled, crept, marched, scuttled, strolled, tiptoed, scuttled	

Explore: Words we easily confuse

word	meaning	example
to	when you go to a place, you go there	We're going to Spain this year.
too	also or more than you need	He is coming too. Don't eat too much.
two	the number 2	There will be two of us.
its	belonging to it	The cat was eating its food.
it's	short for *it is*	It's raining today.

Explorer tip: To decide which you need, think about the question: can I turn it into *it is*? If you can, you need to write it's, if you can't, you should write its.

there	in that place	Go over there.
their	belonging to them	They have lost their homework.
they're	short for *they are*	They're going home now.
loose	not tight	My tooth is loose.
lose	If you lose something, you can't find it.	Where did you lose your jumper?
than	compared with another person	I am shorter than you.
then	or thing after that	We'll do some work and then we'll have a story.
whose	belonging to which person	Whose jumper is this?
who's	short for *who is*	Who's reading next?
your	belonging to you	Have you got your coat?
you're	short for *you are*	You're looking well today.

Explore: Collective nouns

Collective nouns are words that are used to talk about
a large group of things, usually animals. There is often
more than one way to refer to the groups, but some
common examples include:

- an **army** of … caterpillars, frogs

- a **band** of … gorillas

▲ • a **brood** of … chickens

- a **colony** of …. rabbits, ants, beavers ▶

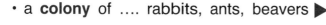

- a **flock** of …. sheep, birds

◀ • a **gaggle** of …. geese

- a **herd** of …. horses, cows, goats, yaks,
  llamas, hippopotamuses

- a **litter** of …. pigs, kittens,
  puppies, cubs ▶

• a **murder** of .... crows

• a **nest** of ... snakes ▶

◀ • a **pack** of .... wolves, polar bears

• a **pod** of ... walruses, seals, dolphins, whales

• a **pride** of ... lions ▶

• a **school** of ... sharks, salmon, whales

▼ • a **shoal** of .... fish

• a **troop** of ... monkeys, kangaroos

• a **swarm** of ... insects, bees

• an **unkindness** of ... ravens

More than one

chick	chicks	volcano	volcanoes
dog	dogs	tornado	tornadoes
giraffe	giraffes	church	churches
shark	sharks	woman	women
mouse	mice	man	men
goose	geese	person	people
sheep	sheep	child	children
fish	fish	penny	pennies
alkali	alkalis	story	stories
appendix	appendices or appendix		

Explore: Place and position

in	out
high	low
on	off
in front	behind
far	near
above	below
between	through
under	on top of/ next to
left	right
inside	outside

Explore: Word Origins

The words that we use today have come into the English language in a lot of different ways. Some have been part of our language since the times of the Angles and Saxons, around 1500 years ago. Others have been borrowed from different languages, for example Latin, French, and Italian. The word origins on these pages will help you to understand where some of the words in our language come from, and how they have changed their meaning over time to become the words that we use today.

Days of the week

Monday is the 'moon's day', and is named after the moon.
Tuesday is 'Tiu's day', and is named after Tiu, the ancient Germanic god of war.
Wednesday is 'Woden's day', and is named after Woden, or Odin, a god in Norse mythology.
Thursday is 'Thor's day', and is named after Thor, the god of thunder in Norse mythology.
Friday is 'Frigga's day', and is named after Frigga, the wife of Odin in Norse mythology.
Saturday is 'Saturn's day', and is named after Saturn, an ancient Roman god.
Sunday is the day of the sun.

Months of the year

January is named after Janus, an ancient Roman god.
February gets its name from the Latin word, 'februm', which means 'purification', because a Roman festival of purification was held at this time of year.
March is the month of Mars, the ancient Roman god of war.
April gets its name from the Latin word 'aperio', which means 'to open', because flowers open in the spring.
May is the month of Maia, an ancient Roman goddess.
June is the month of Juno, an ancient Roman goddess.
July is the month in which Julius Caesar was born, and it was named after him by the ancient Romans.
August gets its name from the name of the first Roman emperor, Augustus Caesar.
September gets its name from the Latin word 'septem', meaning 'seven', because September was the seventh month of the ancient Roman year.
October gets its name from the Latin word 'octo', meaning 'eight', because October was the eighth month of the ancient Roman year.
November gets its name from the Latin word 'novem', meaning 'nine', because November was the ninth month of the ancient Roman year.
December gets its name from the Latin word 'decem', meaning 'ten', because December was the tenth month of the ancient Roman year.

Explore: Word Origins
Words to do with food and drink

barbecue	This word comes from a word in a Carribean language meaning 'a wooden frame'.
biscuit	This word comes from the Old French word 'bescoit', which means 'twice baked', because biscuits were often baked twice to make them hard and crisp.
breakfast	This word comes from the words 'break' and 'fast'. A 'fast' is a time when you do not eat anything, so in the morning you 'break' your 'fast' and eat something.
champagne	This word has come into English from French. Champagne is an area in France where this type of wine is made.
chocolate	This word comes from an Aztec word 'chocolatl'.
curry	This word comes from the word 'kari', which is a Tamil word from southern India and means 'a spicy sauce'.
hamburger	The hamburger is named after the city of Hamburg in Germany.
jelly	This word comes from the Latin word 'gelare', which means 'to freeze'.
kebab	This word has come into English from Arabic.
ketchup	This word has come into English from the Cantonese words 'k'e chap', which mean 'tomato juice'.
lasagne	This word has come into English from Italian.
macaroni	This word has come into English from Italian.
mango	This word comes from the Tamil word 'mankay', which means 'a mango'.
muesli	This word has come into English from Swiss German.
noodles	This word has come into English from German.
pasta	This word has come into English from Italian.
pepperoni	This word comes from the Italian word 'peperone', which means 'chilli' (a spice with a hot flavour).
pizza	This word has come into English from Italian.
potato	This word has come into English from Taino, a South American language.
sandwich	This word is named after the Earl of Sandwich, who invented sandwiches so that he could eat a meal quickly, while he was doing other things.
satsuma	This word is named after Satsuma, an area in Japan where satsumas are grown.
spaghetti	This word comes from an Italian word which means 'little pieces of string'.
tangerine	This word comes from the name of the city of Tangier, on the northern coast of Morocco, where these oranges come from.
tomato	This word has come into English from a Mexican language.
whisky	This word comes from a Scottish Gaelic phrase which means 'the water of life'.

Explore: Word origins
Words to do with animals

alligator	This word comes from the Spanish words 'el lagarto', which mean 'the lizard'. why they are called canaries.
caterpillar	This word comes from the Latin words 'catta pilosa', which mean 'a hairy cat'.
chimpanzee	This word has come into English from an African language.
cobra	This word comes from the Portuguese words 'cobra de capello', which mean 'a snake with a hood'.
cobweb	'Coppe' was an Old English word for a spider, so a 'cobweb' is a 'spider's web'.
crocodile	This word comes from the Greek word 'krokodilos', which means 'worm of the stones'.
cuckoo	The cuckoo gets its name from the call that it gives, which sounds like 'cuck-oo'.
dinosaur	This word comes from the Greek words 'deinos sauros', which mean 'terrible lizard'.
dragon	This word comes from the Greek word 'drakon', which means 'a snake'.
elephant	This word comes from the Greek word 'elephas', which means 'ivory' (which elephants' tusks are made of).
herbivore	This word comes from the Latin word 'herba', meaning 'grass'.
hippopotamus	This word comes from the Greek words 'hippo ho potamius', which mean 'horse of the river'.
insect	This word comes from the Latin word 'insectum', meaning 'cut up', because an insect's body is divided into several different parts.
koala	This word has come into English from an Australian Aboriginal language.
mosquito	This word comes from a Spanish word which means 'a little fly'.
reptile	This word comes from the Latin word 'reptilis', which means 'crawling'.
rhinoceros	This word comes from the Greek words 'rhinos keras', which mean 'nose horn'.
spider	This word comes from the Old English word 'spithra', which means 'a spinner'.
turtle	This word comes from the French word 'tortue', which means 'a tortoise'.

Word origins
Words to do with clothes

anorak   This word has come into English from an Eskimo language.

cardigan   The cardigan is named after James Thomas Brudenel,
                the Earl of Cardigan, who first made cardigans popular.

jeans   Jeans get their name from the city of Genoa in Italy,
                where the cloth used for making jeans was once made.

jodhpurs   Jodhpurs are named after the city of Jodhpur in India,
                where trousers like these are worn.

leotard   This word comes from the name of the French man,
                Jules Leotard, who invented it.

pyjamas   This word comes from the Urdu word 'paejama',
                which means 'trousers'.

sandal   This word comes from the Greek word 'sandalon',
                which means 'a wooden shoe'.

sari   This word has come into English from Hindi.

turban   This word has come into English from a Persian word.

vest   This word comes from the Latin word 'vestis',
                which means 'a piece of clothing'.

wellington Wellington boots were named after the Duke of Wellington,
                who wore long leather boots.

Word origins
Words to do with sport and hobbies

acrobat
This word comes from a Greek word meaning 'to walk on tiptoe'.

badminton
The game of badminton was named after the place, Badminton House, where people first played it.

ballet
This is a French word. It comes originally from an Italian word 'balletto', which means 'a little dance'.

boomerang
This word has come into English from an Australian Aboriginal language.

judo
This word comes from the Japanese words 'ju do', which mean 'the gentle way'.

karaoke
This word has come into English from Japanese.

karate
This word comes from the Japanese words 'kara te', which mean 'empty hands'.

marathon
This word is named after the town of Marathon in Greece. In ancient times, a messenger ran from Marathon to Athens (which is about 40 kilometres) to announce that the Greek army had defeated its enemies.

martial art
The word martial comes from a Latin word which means 'belonging to Mars, the god of war'.

rugby
The game of rugby was named after Rugby School, where the game was first played.

ski
This word has come into English from Norwegian.

soccer
This word is short for the word 'Association', because football was originally called 'Association football'.

toboggan
This word has come into English from a Native American language.

Word origins
Words to do with buildings

bungalow   This word comes from the Gujarati word 'bangalo', which means 'a house built in the style of Bengal'.

cafe   This is a French word and means 'coffee' or 'a coffee shop'.

factory   This word comes from the Latin word 'factorium', which means 'a place where things are made'.

fort   This word comes from the Latin word 'fortis', which means 'strong'.

gym   This word comes from the Greek word 'gymnos', meaning 'naked', because in ancient Greece men used to do exercises and sports with no clothes on.

hospital   This word comes from the Latin word 'hospitalis', meaning 'receiving guests', because a hospital used to be a place where guests could stay.

igloo   This word comes from the Inuit word 'iglu', meaning 'a house'.

laboratory   This word comes from the Latin word 'laboratorium', which means 'a place where people work'.

palace   This word comes from the Latin word 'Palatium', the name of a hill in ancient Rome where the house of the emperor Augustus was.

pavilion   This word comes from the French word 'pavillon', which means 'a tent'.

temple   This word comes from the Latin word 'templum', which means 'a holy place'.

theatre   This word comes from the Greek word 'theatron', which means 'a place for seeing things'.

turret   This word comes from the old French word 'tourete', which means 'a little tower'.

Explore: Word origins
Words to do with technology

camcorder This word was first formed by joining together the words 'camera' and 'recorder'.

computer This word comes from the Latin word 'computare', which means 'to work things out together', because the first computers were used for doing mathematical calculations.

email The word email is short for 'electronic mail', which means mail sent using electrical signals.

helicopter This word comes from the Greek words 'helix' and 'pteron', which mean 'spiral wings'.

motor This word comes from a Latin word which means 'a mover'.

movie The word movie is short for 'moving picture'.

photograph This word comes from the Greek word 'photo' (meaning 'light') and 'graphos' (meaning 'writing'), because a camera uses light to make a picture.

submarine This word comes from the Latin words 'sub', which means 'under', and 'mare', which means 'the sea'.

tele- The Greek word 'tele' means 'far off', and many words in English that begin with tele- have meanings to do with things that happen at a distance. Telecommunications are ways of communicating with people who are a long way away. You use a telephone for talking to people at a distance. You use a telescope to look at things that are far away. A television allows you to see pictures that are sent over a distance.

video This word comes from the Latin word 'video', which means 'I see'.

Explore: Word origins
Words to do with nature

aqua- The Latin word 'aqua' means 'water', and a lot of words in English that begin with aqua- are to do with water. Aquatic animals live in water. You keep fish in a container called an aquarium. Sub-aqua diving is diving under the water.

comet This word comes from the Greek words 'aster kometes', which mean 'long-haired star', because the tail of a comet looks like long hair.

constellation This word comes from the Latin word 'stella', which means 'a star'.

daisy This word comes from the words 'day's eye', because daisies close their petals at night and open them again in the morning.

fossil This word comes from the latin word 'fossilis', which means 'dug up', because fossils are dug up out of the ground.

jungle This word comes from the Hindi word 'jangal', which means 'an area of wasteland'.

ocean This word comes from the word 'Oceanus', the name of the river which the ancient Greeks thought surrounded the world.

orbit This word comes from the Latin word 'orbis', which means 'a circle'.

planet This word comes from the Greek word 'planetes', which means 'a wanderer', because planets seem to wander about rather than staying in the same place in the sky.

tornado This word comes from the Spanish word 'tronada', which means 'a thunderstorm'.

volcano A volano gets its name from Vulcan, the ancient Roman god of fire.

Numbers

1	one	first
2	two	second
3	three	third
4	four	fourth
5	five	fifth
6	six	sixth
7	seven	seventh
8	eight	eighth
9	nine	ninth
10	ten	tenth
11	eleven	eleventh
12	twelve	twelfth
13	thirteen	thirteenth
14	fourteen	fourteenth
15	fifteen	fifteenth
16	sixteen	sixteenth
17	seventeen	seventeenth
18	eighteen	eighteenth
19	nineteen	nineteenth
20	twenty	twentieth
21	twenty-one	twenty-first
22	twenty-two	twenty-second
30	thirty	thirtieth
40	forty	fortieth
50	fifty	fiftieth
60	sixty	sixtieth
70	seventy	seventieth
80	eighty	eightieth
90	ninety	ninetieth
100	a hundred	hundredth
101	a hundred and one	hundred and first
200	two hundred	two hundredth

Shapes

2D SHAPES

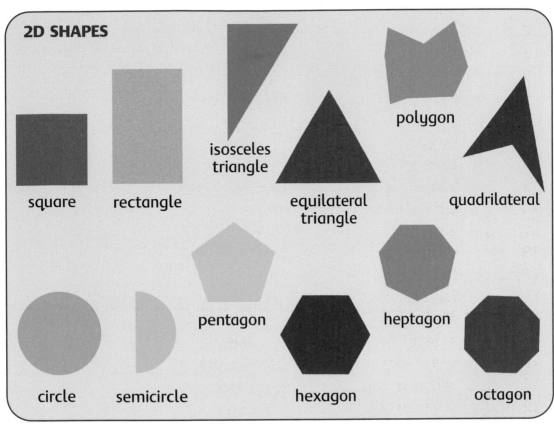

square

rectangle

isosceles triangle

equilateral triangle

polygon

quadrilateral

pentagon

heptagon

circle

semicircle

hexagon

octagon

3D SHAPES

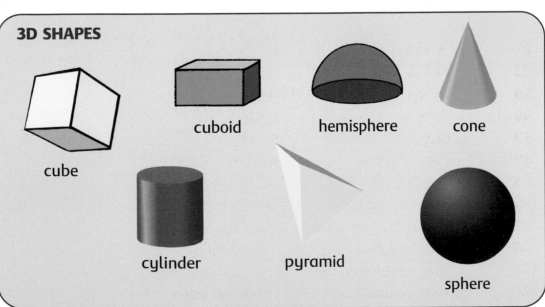

cube

cuboid

hemisphere

cone

cylinder

pyramid

sphere

Measuring

length

You can use a tape measure, a metre stick,
or a tachometer in a car to measure length.

There are 10 millimetres in a centimetre.   10mm = 1cm

There are 100 centimetres in a metre.   100cm = 1m

There are 1000 metres in a kilometre.   1000m = 1km

capacity

You can use a teaspoon, a tablespoon, a cup,
or a measuring jug to measure capacity.

There are 10 millilitres in a centilitre.   10ml = 1cl

There are 100 centilitres in a litre.   100cl = 1l

There are 1000 millilitres in a litre.   1000ml = 1l

mass

You can use balancing scales, cooking scales,
or standing scales to measure mass.

There are 1000 grams in a kilogram.   1000g = 1kg

There are 1000 kilograms in a tonne.   1000kg = 1t

Explore: Opposites

top .... bottom

long .... short

heavy .... light

come .... go

full .... empty

loud .... quiet

clean .... dirty

fast .... slow

most .... fewest

high .... low

light .... dark

dry .... wet

hot .... cold

big .... small

fat .... thin

pretty .... ugly

happy .... sad

smooth .... rough

hard .... soft

wide .... narrow

bad .... good

easy .... hard

new .... old

up .... down

open .... closed

Time

morning The time before midday is called morning.
The letters a.m. stand for *'ante meridien'* which is Latin for 'before noon'.

midday or noon The time of day when the Sun is at its highest in the sky is 12 midday or noon.

afternoon The time of day after midday is called afternoon.
The letters p.m. stand for *'post meridien'* which is Latin for 'after noon'.

9:00

nine o'clock

9:05

five past nine

9:10

ten past nine

9:15

nine fifteen
quarter past nine

9:20

twenty past nine

9:25

twenty-five past nine

9:30

nine thirty
half past nine

9:35

nine thirty-five
twenty-five to ten

9:40

nine forty-five
twenty to ten

9:45

nine forty-five
quarter to ten

9:50

nine fifty
ten to ten

9.55

nine fifty-five
five to ten

Units of time

second		
minute	=	60 seconds or 1 minute
hour	=	60 minutes or 1 hour
day	=	24 hours or 1 day
week	=	7 days or 1 week
fortnight	=	14 days or 2 weeks
month	=	30 or 31 days, except for February which is 28 or 29 days
year	=	12 months or 365 days
leap year	=	366 days
decade	=	10 years
century	=	100 years

12:00

midday (noon)

12:00

midnight

Days, months, seasons

Days of the week

Sunday	Thursday
Monday	Friday
Tuesday	Saturday
Wednesday	

Months of the year

January = 31 days	July = 31 days
February = 28 or 29 days	August = 31 days
March = 31 days	September = 30 days
April = 30 days	October = 31 days
May = 31 days	November = 30 days
June = 30 days	December = 31 days

Seasons

spring   summer   autumn   winter

Fruit and vegetables

lemon

gooseberry

melon

orange

apple

raspberry

strawberry

blackberry

pineapple

grape

peach

nectarine

grapefruit

mango

tangerine

apricot

rhubarb

pear

kiwi fruit

plum

cherry

banana

peas

spinach

cabbage

parsnip

cauliflower

garlic

onion

chilli

brussel sprout

lettuce

potato

cucumber

carrots

beetroot

tomato

avocado

radish

turnip

swede

broccoli

celery

leek

sweetcorn

beans

pumpkin

Parts of the body

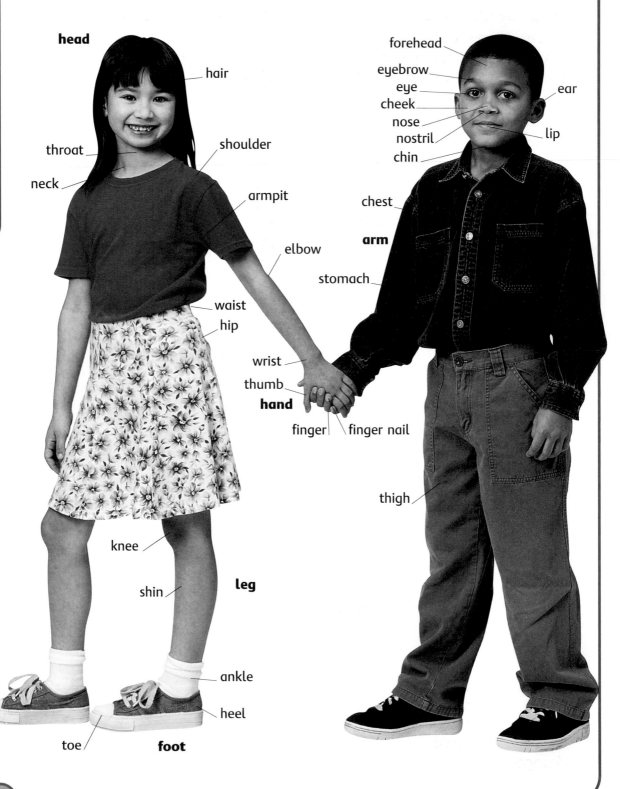

head

hair

throat

neck

shoulder

armpit

elbow

waist

hip

wrist

thumb

hand

finger · finger nail

knee

shin

leg

ankle

heel

toe

foot

forehead

eyebrow

eye

cheek

nose

nostril

chin

ear

lip

chest

arm

stomach

thigh

Words we use a lot

These words are words we use often. Some of them have unusual spellings. It is useful to spot them here so that you can recognise them when you are reading a new piece of text. You can check their spelling when you are using them in writing.

a

a	an
about	and
above	another
across	any
after	anyone
again	are
all	aren't
almost	around
along	as
also	ask
always	at
am	away

b

back	better
be	between
because	big
been	both
before	brother
began	brought
begin	but
below	by

c

call	children
called	come
came	comes
can	coming
can't	could
change	

d

dad	doesn't
day	doing
did	done
didn't	don't
different	down
do	during
does	

e

earth	everyone
every	eyes

f

father	found
first	friends
following	from
for	

g

get	gone
getting	good
go	got
goes	great
going	

h

had	help
hadn't	her
half	hers
has	here
have	he's
haven't	high
having	him
he	his
head	how
heard	

i

I	is
if	isn't
I'm	it
in	its
inside	it's (it is)
into	

j

just

k

knew	know

l

last	live
leave	lived
light	look
like	lost
little	

m

made	morning
make	mother
many	much
may	mum
me	must
might	my
mine	myself
more	

n

name	night
near	no
never	not
new	now
next	number

o

of	or
off	other
often	our
on	ours
once	out
one	outside
only	over
opened	own

p

pray	put

r

ran	round
right	

s

said	some
saw	something
second	sometimes
she	sound
should	started
show	still
see	stopped
seen	such
sister	suddenly
small	sure
so	

t

take care	those
taken	thought
than	three
that	through
the	to
their	today
theirs	together
them	told
then	too
there	took
these	tries
they	turn
think	turned
this	

u

under	upon
until	us
up	used

v

very

w

walk	while
walked	white
walking	who
was	whole
wasn't	why
want	will
watch	window
way	with
we	without
went	woke
were	woken
what	won't
when	work
where	would
which	write

y

year	you
yes	your

Age 4+

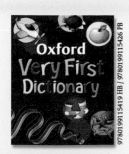

Oxford Very First Dictionary
9780199115419 HB / 9780199115426 PB

Age 5+

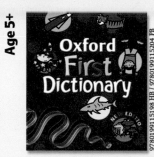

Oxford First Dictionary
9780199115198 HB / 9780199115204 PB

Oxford First Thesaurus
9780199115433 HB / 9780199115457 PB

Age 7+

Oxford Junior Illustrated Dictionary
9780199115211 HB / 9780199115228 PB

Oxford Junior Illustrated Thesaurus
9780199113194 HB / 9780199113200 PB

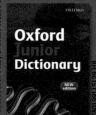

Oxford Junior Dictionary
9780199115129 HB

Oxford Junior Thesaurus
9780199115136 HB

Age 8+

Oxford Primary Dictionary
9780199115334 HB

Oxford Primary Thesaurus
9780199115167 HB

Oxford Primary French Dictionary
9780199114931 HB / 9780199113088 PB

Oxford Primary Spanish Dictionary
9780199115242 PB

Age 10+

Oxford School Dictionary
9780199115341 HB

Oxford School Thesaurus
9780199115358 HB

Oxford Dictionary & Thesaurus
9780199115365 HB / 9780199115372 PB

Oxford Pocket School Dictionary
9780199115389 PB

Oxford Pocket School Thesaurus
9780199115396 PB

Oxford Mini School Dictionary
9780199115174 PB

Oxford Mini School Thesaurus
9780199115181 PB

Oxford Mini School Dictionary & Thesaurus
9780199113736 PB

Oxford School French Dictionary
9780199115280 PB

Oxford School Spanish Dictionary
9780199115297 PB

Oxford School German Dictionary
9780199115303 PB

Oxford Mini School Dictionary
9780199115273 PB

Oxford Mini School Spanish Dictionary
9780199115259 PB

Oxford Mini School German Dictionary
9780199115266 PB

Age 14+

Oxford Student's Dictionary
9780199115327 HB / 9780199115310 PB

Oxford Student's Thesaurus
9780199116522 PB

Oxford Children's Dictionaries
Think Dictionaries. Think Oxford.
www.oup.com